VIETNAM AT THE MOVIES

VIETNAM
AT THE
MOVIES

MICHAEL LEE LANNING

FAWCETT COLUMBINE

NEW YORK

A Fawcett Columbine Book
Published by Ballantine Books
Copyright © 1994 by Michael Lee Lanning

LIBRARY OF CONGRESS CATALOG CARD NUMBER: 94-94062

ISBN: 0-449-90891-7

Cover design by Andy Baris

Cover photos from Apocalypse Now, Full Metal Jacket, Born on the Fourth of July, and Platoon courtesy of The Kobal Collection

Manufactured in the United States of America
First Edition: July 1994
10 9 8 7 6 5 4 3 2 1

To
Eunice Lanning Andrus
and
H. McKee Andrus

CONTENTS

Introduction   ix

PART ONE

1. Hollywood: The Myth Makers   3
2. The Great War: World War I   6
3. The Good War: World War II   17
4. The Not-So-Unknown War: Korea   29
5. Viet What?: Prewar Movies   38
6. Vietnam: Where Have All the Movies Gone?   45
7. Hell No! We Won't Go: The Protest Films   53
8. Coming Home: The Not-So-Welcome Back   65
9. Killers and Crazies: The Supervillains   74
10. Real-to-Reel War: Screen Combat   88
11. Ramboesque Films: The Superheroes   107
12. Stripes and Bars: The POWs   119
13. Sympathetic Veterans: The Only Good Vet
       Is a Disabled Vet   127
14. Suspicious Allies, Unusual Enemies: The Vietnamese 134
15. Strangers Seldom Seen: Comedies, Musicals,
       Horror, and More   145
16. War on the Small Screen: TV Movies and Series   150
17. The Only War We Had: Conclusions   155

PART TWO

Explanatory Notes   161
Movie Reviews   162

INTRODUCTION

Do you have flashbacks?
Can you sleep at night or do bad dreams keep you awake?
Are all of you Vietnam veterans crazy?
Have you ever thought of killing yourself?
Is what I see in the movies about Vietnam what it was
really like?

These are but a few of the questions I have been asked as a Vietnam veteran who speaks to college and high school classes and as one who has written a number of books about the individual soldiers of both sides of the war. In attempting to respond, I have asked a few questions of my own about where young people, and many older ones, have acquired their knowledge and understanding of America's longest and most unpopular war. Responses occasionally allude to a relative who served in Southeast Asia, school classes, and books, but the overwhelming majority of those to whom I've spoken admit that the major influence on their perceptions of the Vietnam War has been Hollywood's motion pictures.

The Vietnam War was a turning point in thought, culture, and values in every aspect of American life. Its influence on politics and U.S. world policy is obvious on the front pages of newspapers even today. Many of those who lived through the Vietnam Era are still confused about what really happened and why. For those who have come to maturity since the fall of Saigon, accuracy and facts untainted by propaganda or falsehood have been difficult to come by.

This book began with a simple idea—to review movies about the Vietnam War and its veterans in order to provide a brief, traditional analysis of the acting, plot, and production quality of each. Another part of the individual review would note the film's value as a means of learning about and understanding the war and its warriors. The scope of the project grew over the period of research and writing. I quickly learned that there were far more movies that touch upon the subject of Vietnam than I had anticipated. However, the more films I watched, the more I realized that, in part, Vietnam War films are an insult to veterans and moviegoers; as a whole, they represent the first group of American movies to systematically vilify the warrior as well as the war. In fact, if any group of films about a racial, religious, political, or sexual faction had delivered the same lies, exaggerations, and stereotypes, the streets would have been filled with protesters and the theaters picketed across the nation.

Despite these factors, I have made a sincere effort to present in this book the content of Vietnam at the movies as accurately and with as little bias as possible and to allow readers to make their own evaluations and form their own conclusions. I am sure I have failed at times, allowing my emotions and personal opinions to obtrude. For that, as with my participation in the Vietnam War itself, I make no apologies.

PART
ONE

1. HOLLYWOOD: THE MYTH MAKERS

THE VIETNAM WAR divided the nation, alienated the country's youth, stood the Establishment's complacency on end, and killed more than fifty-eight thousand of our finest. No system or group escaped the catalytic influence of the controversy—least of all the moviemakers, creators of magic and monsters, heroes and villains. Hollywood, too, succumbed to the changing mores, magnifying ripples into waves of change.

Until the 1960s, movies about warfare were good box office. Audiences were generally eager to experience the drama of combat vicariously on the silver screen, and nothing seems to have aroused emotion or cemented patriotism as well as the long list of motion pictures about the two world wars. Moviegoers came to define their expectations of combat and soldiers by the heroics and victories of countless war movies that glorified daring and dashing leading men. Audiences rarely questioned the accuracy of setting, dialogue, or action, preferring instead to give Hollywood free rein in the imagination department. The farther removed the viewers were from the place and time of battle, the less they wondered and the more they believed.

War and movies have proved to be a successful partnership not only for American audiences but for the world's filmgoing public as well. Since the early years of the twentieth century, when the United States movie industry became the international leader in film production, American movies have delivered not only entertainment but also information about a life style to viewers of all cultures and from all levels. The global popularity of American commercial products from cigarettes to blue jeans and from fast food to rock and roll can be directly attributed to messages and images projected on theater screens around the world. A great portion of the impressions formed about America and all things American throughout the planet have been molded not by politicians, envoys, or diplomats but by directors, actors, and Hollywood.

On the surface, in films destined for U.S. and world movie audiences, it would seem that the Vietnam War, too, should have provided the same kind of dramatic backdrop for stirring stories of combat and bravery. That, however, was not to be. Because the war lacked clear objectives and easily identified enemies, the moviemakers, like the majority of Americans, chose to ignore the conflict while it was in progress. Instead they rewrote and recast World War II epics and continued to exploit the popularity of cowboys and Indians, preferring known money-makers to the potential pitfalls of a divided audience.

A few early attempts were made to bring the war to the screen. *The Green Berets*, released in 1968, followed the World War II format—superpatriots fighting for a just cause. It was panned by critics and the public alike. Only with the military did it find a positive reception. Other ideas surfaced for Vietnam War films, but studios were unwilling to gamble on them. The occasional script that did seem promising was immediately shelved when Pentagon officials refused to provide support for production.

Only after the war did Hollywood finally turn its cameras to Vietnam. But when it did, because the war itself was so confusing and unpopular, directors generally focused not on the political aspects of the conflict but on the veterans who fought the war. If the war was unpopular and the military was considered a loathsome institution, then surely the uniformed warrior was equally unsympathetic. From low-budget motorcycle films depicting Vietnam veterans as killers and drug dealers to megabudget "epics" claiming a documentary-level approach to the war, Hollywood has turned out a barrage of movies portraying troubled veterans who neither fit in with society nor care to do so. Film companies have converted "loser" veterans into box-office winners. For the first time in American film history, movies have focused not on the accomplishments of its wartime soldiers but on their perceived failures.

While Hollywood may have known what it was doing in producing the misfit money-makers, what about the audiences? Conditioned by their own past placid acceptance of movies about previous wars as being "the way it was," moviegoers have been led astray. Where World War II movies embellished the truth for the sake of propaganda and drama, Vietnam films are more likely to use reality only as an insignificant prop.

Regardless of the intent of Hollywood moviemakers, Vietnam was not a popular war, and no one can take the film producers completely to task for presenting it in any other manner. Unfortunately, to the moviegoer seeking information about the conflict, the offerings of Hollywood are largely limited to stereotyping the veteran in a manner that makes the warrior seem as evil as the war in which he fought.

Written, produced, and directed almost exclusively by nonveterans and those actively opposed to the war during the conflict, the Vietnam movie has taken a narrow view of the war's combatants—and that portrayal seems to be concentrated on, at its best, an unemployed, maladjusted veteran who cannot cope and, at its worst, a crazed killer still wearing his U.S. Army field jacket. Mixed in are the Ramboesque characters who still want a chance to win the war. The "real" war on the screen offers a mixture of action and fighting that rarely resembles anything the combat soldier saw or recalls.

As a result, millions of Americans and citizens of the world sit in theaters and in front of VCRs without a way to discriminate between reality and artistic license, legitimate plot and propaganda, or real events and cheap-thrill action. After more than twenty years of discomfort and confusion about the war, however, it is time that film audiences be given the opportunity to understand just what they are watching when they see Vietnam at the movies.

2. THE GREAT WAR:
WORLD WAR I

EARLY IN 1898, a young British photographer working in New York, J. Stuart Blackton, hefted a primitive movie camera to a building roof and filmed a uniformed man lowering a Spanish flag from a tall pole. This few minutes of film, titled "Tearing Down the Spanish Flag," was copied and released to the country's newly established movie houses as actual footage of the Spanish-American War in Cuba. America had its first war movie, but, as with legions of films to follow, the truth was not exactly what it appeared.

A few months later, Blackton and a fellow Englishman, Albert E. Smith, set off for the Caribbean to record the real war for their newly founded company, Vitagraph. Sailing with Colonel Theodore Roosevelt and his soon-to-be-famous Rough Riders, Blackton and Smith filmed the soldiers landing at Siboney on June 17, 1898. During the next weeks they added footage of the Americans living in camp and preparing for combat. On July 1, the two Englishmen obtained the first actual film footage of Americans in combat when they filmed the Rough Riders charging up Kettle Hill on the flank of what would become famous as the Battle of San Juan Hill.

Pictures of the actual fight were limited by more than the primitive movie technology of the time. Early in the battle, two rifle rounds penetrated the filmmakers' camera, and they speedily retreated, catching the first boat to Florida.

Upon arrival back on the mainland, Blackton and Smith learned they had missed by a matter of days the war's largest naval battle. Undaunted by not having observed the actual event, the two cameramen immediately re-created the clash between the American and Spanish fleets in their New York office using a water tank, model ships, and gunpowder charges. Combining the fake sea-battle footage with the actual shots of the Rough Riders in Cuba, Vitagraph Pictures released "The Battle of Santiago Bay" as a genuine newsreel.

Blackton and Smith were the first to provide America with warfare on film, but worldwide they were outclassed by British pioneer moviemaker and war correspondent Frederick Villiers. Villiers gained the honor of being first to film combat by recording portions of the Battle of Volo in Thessaly, Greece, in April 1897 during the Greco-Turkish War, a year before Blackton and Smith went to the Caribbean. From the balcony of his residence in the British consulate in Volo, Villiers could observe the battle lines. Each morning he bicycled to the "front," where he exposed a few reels before returning to a civilized dinner at the consulate.

Thinking he had produced a highly marketable product, Villiers returned to London. He was soon disappointed to learn that in his absence while filming the actual war, Star Films of Paris had saturated the English market with fake reels of the conflict. The British citizens were already tired of the subject and had little interest in more war pictures. Villiers may have been first to film actual combat,* but he also learned that the paying movie public could find reconstruction and fakery more interesting than the real thing.

The fledgling movie industry entered the twentieth century mostly as a novelty whose welcome as a means of entertainment was wearing thin. Movies were offered as "flickers"—so named because of the flickering effect of their projection—on wall-hung bed sheets for one cent a showing and in five-cent individual peep shows. Most performances were of simple everyday actions, such as a running horse or an exercising man. If moviemakers were to stay in business, they were going to have to become more innovative—and they soon proved they were more than up to the challenge. Films quickly became longer and began to re-

---

*Unfortunately no prints of the films of either Villiers or Blackton and Smith have survived to modern times. The earliest existing film of warfare still available was made by John Bennett Stanford on November 12, 1899, of the Northumberland Fusiliers at Orange River, South Africa, during the Boer War.

late complete stories. In 1902, Georges Meliès established himself as the first great artist of the cinema with his release of *A Trip to the Moon*, which was based on the book by Jules Verne. One of the first feature films to tell an entire story, *A Trip to the Moon* was also the first science-fiction film. Meliès did most of his work in Paris, but his films were viewed worldwide; in the days of silent films, language was no barrier to movie entertainment.

In 1903, the first great American action film, *The Great Train Robbery*, was made by Edwin S. Porter and the Thomas Edison Company studios. Appropriately, this epic was also a part of another important American film genre that would thrill audiences of future generations—the western.

During the early years of the 1900s and the rise of "feature length" films, warfare and the military received little attention from moviemakers. Beyond a few attempts to film actual battles around the world, combat was considered too difficult and costly to adapt to the new, long-running format.

One of the more interesting aspects of this developmental period for motion pictures was the recognition by military leaders of the power of movies. On January 3, 1914, Mexican bandit-general Pancho Villa signed an agreement with the Mutual Film Corporation giving it the film rights to all battles his army might fight during the Mexican Revolution. The contract included provisions that, whenever possible, battles would be fought during hours of daylight and that complete access and protection would be provided the Mutual cameramen. Villa took the contract seriously and enjoyed the publicity that the resulting films provided. Once, he even postponed an attack on the town of Ojinaja so that the filmmakers would have time to arrive from another location.

It was not until 1915 that the first epic war film was produced, but it was well worth the wait. D. W. Griffith's *The Birth of a Nation* set the standard for future war films all the way into the 1960s, when Vietnam forever changed the genre. Focusing on the American Civil War and its aftermath, the film included battle scenes, soldier homecomings, and adjustments by combatant and noncombatant to the postwar period. Only one battle scene is included, but it is classic in every aspect. Griffith referred to still photographs from the Civil War by Mathew Brady and he sought advice and assistance from the faculty of the U.S. Military Academy at West Point to properly re-create troop movements, artillery barrages, and cavalry charges. In one shot a soldier risks death as he rushes forward to retrieve his country's colors from a wounded comrade. In another, a dying soldier is confronted by his enemy, and in still another a mortally wounded soldier clutches to his breast a picture of a young woman. The reunion of the film's hero with his family at war's end is as moving as any ever recorded. Despite its racist overtones, which include glorification of the Ku Klux Klan, *The Birth of a Nation* is as entertaining today as when it first reached the screen more than three-quarters of a century ago.

As the brilliant images of *The Birth of a Nation* were lighting the movie screens of America, the threatening clouds of massive war were darkening the skies of Europe. From the Great War's beginning in 1914 until the United States' entry in 1917, American films were deeply involved in the controversy of whether the country should remain neutral or join in the affray.

While praising the values and advantages of peace, the "pacifist films" of those supporting neutrality were blatant portrayals of the evils and destructiveness of war. Thomas H. Ince, one of D. W. Griffith's few rivals, directed what is considered to be the best of the pacifist films. Ince's *Civilization* (1916) has an allegorical plot about a disastrous war between two fictional countries. The film concludes with Jesus Christ descending from heaven to plead for peace on earth. Other films also delivered similar poignant antiwar messages as they encouraged peace in Europe and discouraged United States involvement in the conflict.

Other moviemakers of the period were as direct in their support of the war and in touting preparedness on the part of America. J. Stuart Blackton was still a leader in the film business, and in 1915 he released his prowar movie *The Battle Cry of Peace*. Barley Cushing's *The Fall of a Nation* (1916) also beat the drums of war.

America's leading female star, Mary Pickford, was a leader in the pro-involvement, be-prepared films that predated the United States' entry into the Great War. In *The Little American* (1917), produced shortly after the torpedoing of the luxury liner *Lusitania* by a German submarine, Pickford plays a survivor of the sinking who battles the Huns and encourages the United States to enter the war. In her role, Pickford says in an inspiring subtitle speech to a German officer, "I was neutral until I saw your men attack innocent women and murder old men. Then I stopped being neutral and became human."

The pacifist and prowar factions waged their battles on movie screens across the country until a single event united the two in support of the war. That event was the U.S. declaration of war against Germany on April 16, 1917. From that day until the armistice was signed, the American film industry worked hard to sell the war to the public, to assist in maintaining the nation's high morale, and, of course, to make a tidy profit in the process.

For the next few years, films focused on two primary aspects of the war—its effect on the people at home and the nature of the conflict itself. Movies about the war at home were of two basic varieties. First were the films illustrating extraordinary efforts to support the war by women and men not in uniform. In what would become an even more popular theme in the next "great" war (World War II), Mary Miles Minter stars as a young woman who proves she can replace male workers at shipyards and war materiel factories in *Her Country's Call* (1917). Another film with a similar patriotic title, *Her Country First* (1918), has Vivian Martin organizing a women's military auxiliary unit which helps capture a group of German spies. In *Johanna Enlists* (1918), with Mary Pickford in yet another Great War film, the impact of the conflict on the most remote of American communities is shown.

Pickford, like her fellow stars Douglas Fairbanks, William S. Hart, and Charlie Chaplin, also supported the war effort off the screen by appearing at Liberty Bond rallies and servicemen's benefits. And she told the more than seven hundred artillerymen and aviation corps soldiers who appeared with her in *Johanna Enlists* that she would be their godmother for the remainder of the war. Another actress, Pearl White, posed for the still camera of Howard Chandler Christy and produced the most popular recruiting poster of the war, titled, "Did you think I'd stay home?"

Efforts to support the war by men who were too young, too old, or too frail to join the fight were another popular film subject. In the 1917 movie *The Great Power*, a staunch pacifist chemist is placed in a quandary when he discovers a powerful new explosive. After German agents attempt to steal it, he quickly decides to turn over the formula to the U.S. military. In *An Honest Man* (1917), William Desmond is rejected by the military because of his alcoholism. With the help of a farmer and his daughter, he reforms so he can enlist and do his duty. That everyone, regardless of physical condition, could contribute to the war effort was the subplot of the 1917 release *The Gown of Destiny*. Too frail for induction into the military, a dress designer contributes the profits from his dress shop to purchase ambulances for the front lines.

Even more popular than films about the war's impact back home was a subgenre, the "slacker" movie. Slackers were young men who evaded the draft, and they drew the wrath of the public and filmmakers alike. Typical of the slacker flicks was *Bud's Recruit* (1918), directed by the soon-to-be-renowned King Vidor. Wallis Brennan plays Bud, who organizes neighborhood children into a paramilitary marching unit. When his older brother (Robert Gordon) avoids the military and begins attending pacifist meetings, Bud is so ashamed that he puts on a fake mustache, goes to the recruiting office, and attempts to take his brother's place in uniform. Bud's actions bring his brother to his senses, and in the final frames he answers his call to duty. In *A Little Patriot* (1917), child star Baby Peggy encourages other kids to spit on draft dodgers.

In a rash of films such as *For Valor* (1917), *The Man Who Was Afraid* (1917), *Shame* (1917), and *The Service Star* (1918), slackers were shamed into joining the fighting forces by parents and sweethearts. One of the most popular of the slacker films was the aptly titled *The Slacker* (1917), in which a wealthy young man marries to avoid the draft, while the story plays to a backdrop of patriotic events in United States history.

Films about the conduct of the Great War itself are not so much pro-American, although that label is certainly appropriate, as they are anti-German. Although World War I movies include doughboy battlefield heroics, dastardly spies and secret agents, and comedy centered on life in the military, most of the films concentrate on the inhumanity and brutality of the German army and its Prussian officer corps. "Hate the Hun" was certainly the message of the day. Titles of the films did little to mask their propaganda content. In *The Kaiser, the Beast of Berlin* (1918), German soldiers molest, loot, and slaughter the citizens of Belgium. German-Americans in the United States were portrayed as dangerous in films such as *The Hun Within* (1918). In Raoul Walsh's *The Prussian Cur* (1918), a German agent encourages Americans of German ancestry to sabotage an aircraft manufacturing plant. When the agent and the turncoats he has recruited are captured by "loyal Americans," they are forced to kiss an American flag before being spirited off to jail.

A frequent theme in the anti-German films is the ill treatment of women. In On Dangerous Ground (1917), a French girl is tortured by the Germans for helping an American escape the occupied territories. A seemingly endless number of similar flicks was produced with Austrian Eric von Stroheim playing the role of evil Prussian officer. Stroheim was so effective in the roles that he became known to the U.S. movie public as "the German you love to hate."

Perhaps the greatest, or at least the best received by the American film audience, of the anti-Germany, hate-the-Hun films were D. W. Griffith's Hearts of the World (1918) and William Nigh's My Four Years in Germany (1918). Hearts of the World is basically a love story about a French soldier who goes off to combat, his sweetheart who stays home, and the impact of the war on his family and country. The Germans are shown as barbaric with no compassion for their enemies or for helpless women and children. After the Huns overrun a French village, three young children are shown burying the body of their mother in the family cellar because they are too afraid of the Germans to venture outside their home. In another scene, a French soldier (Bobby Harron) prepares to kill his sweetheart (Lillian Gish) rather than have her fall into the hands of the lecherous Germans. Griffith's film, produced with the assistance of Great Britain, certainly aided the propaganda effort in the United States. In one California city alone, nine hundred army volunteers attributed their enlistment to the film.

My Four Years in Germany was "an authorized film version" of the book of the same title, which detailed the military buildup of Germany as observed by American Ambassador James W. Gerard. When the movie was shown, the subtitle "Fact not fiction" was projected so often that much of the viewing public not only accepted the entire film as the truth but erroneously believed that much of the footage was newsreel rather than re-creation. The film showed German prison camps where captured soldiers and detained civilians alike were starved, beaten, attacked by guard dogs, and summarily executed by firing squads. German leaders were portrayed as maniacal beasts while American soldiers were depicted as heroically slaying the evil Hun in fair fights on the battlefield.

The film succeeded in drawing Americans together to hate the

Germans and provided its makers hefty revenues that rivaled the income produced by *The Birth of a Nation.* In Cleveland, the film so agitated the audience that the kaiser was hung in effigy.*

During the Great War, the American film industry was not limited to its own resources in producing films. It was assisted—some might say hindered—by the Committee on Public Information (CPI), the Federal propaganda agency that was established on April 14, 1917, to sell the war to the American public. The CPI was chaired by former newspaperman George Creel, who was so solidly in charge that the organization was frequently referred to as the Creel Committee.

In addition to producing its own "information" films, the CPI was responsible for overseeing the production of movies made by the commercial studios. The influence of the Creel Committee extended beyond the movie theaters. It printed patriotic posters, displaying them, seemingly, on every fence and barn side in America, and it produced millions of leaflets and booklets supporting the war and the aims of the United States. Joining this campaign of paper were seventy-five thousand registered speakers who'd been recruited by the CPI to orate whenever crowds assembled across the country.

To add realism, the CPI produced films incorporating as much actual military footage as possible. However, because of the difficulties and dangers of filming combat, many of these pictures showed only landscapes, camp life, and marching troops. Three of the most popular CPI films were *America's Answer, Pershing's Crusaders,* and *Under Four Flags.* Typical of the CPI messages, *America's Answer* had an introduction that stated, "The time has come when it is America's high privilege to spend her blood upon the fields of battle already hallowed by the sacrifices of her Allies' stalwart sons. Determined to exercise this privilege, America has called ten million men for military service. Of these, over one million are now in Europe, eager to emulate the heroic deeds of their brothers-in-arms."

---

*It is interesting to note that American demonstrations during the Vietnam War also frequently included the hanging or burning in effigy of world leaders. However, rather than Ho Chi Minh's being the victim of American demonstrators, frequently Johnson, Nixon, or General Westmoreland dangled from the end of the noose or danced at the tip of the flames.

A scene in *America's Answer* shows children standing beside a road greeting marching American soldiers. A subtitle says, "Surely the sanctity of our cause is brought home to these new soldiers by this pathetic group of orphans of France, waving brave little hands to their new friends."

While the CPI films with their repetitious camp and marching scenes were never as popular as the commercial films with re-created battles, the committee did contribute to their commercial counterparts. Scripts were reviewed and revised by the committee, and the CPI staff coordinated the use of military equipment and personnel for the filmmakers. On occasion, the committee provided completed, approved scripts of movies supporting the war for commercial studios to produce.

One resource upon which the CPI could draw was the newly formed U.S. Army Signal Corps Photographic Section, which provided most of the film used in the CPI's releases as well as some of the footage used in commercial movies. Its strength, however, was in filming garrison and camp life rather than actual battle. The Signal Corps' lack of commitment to recording the dangers of combat and the hardships of trench warfare is revealed by the low number of combat photographer deaths. Of more than forty-nine thousand U.S. war dead, only one Signal Corps filmmaker, First Lieutenant Edwin R. Estes, was killed in action, and his death occurred just four days before the war ended.

In the fall of 1918, the Creel Committee and the Signal Corps received a strong indication that the war was nearing an end when a War Department letter directed that they cut back on producing films about German atrocities. A short time later, on November 11, the armistice was signed and peace prevailed.

Although it certainly slowed their production, the end of the Great War did not necessarily mean the end of war movies. The primary difference was that postwar films no longer concentrated on anti-German themes; rather, they showed the horrors of war experienced by both sides. But no war film of great significance was made following the armistice until, in 1925, MGM Studios decided that the viewing public might be ready for another epic combat saga. King Vidor was selected as the director, and Lawrence Stallings, a Marine veteran of the Battle of Belleau Wood, was hired as the scriptwriter. The result, *The Big Parade*, would make MGM into a major studio and add Vidor's name to the list of America's most prominent directors.

The Big Parade offers a simple story about a bartender, a riveter, and a millionaire's son who join the army and become buddies. The story is about individual soldiers, focusing on the loneliness, hardship, and terror of the combat infantryman. Support by the military, in the form of men and equipment, combined with Stallings's personal war experiences and the advice of several other veterans, produced what is still considered one of the most accurate war films ever made. Vidor was so detail oriented that he hired veterans for the many extras' roles because they would know how to "act" like real soldiers.

The next year another film about the Great War was released to such commercial success that the movie industry became convinced that there was a continuing market for the genre. Raoul Walsh's What Price Glory was an adaptation of an antiwar Broadway play originally titled None but the Brave (A Comedy with a Few Deaths), which ended up much more promilitary when brought to the big screen. Its story pivots on the rivalry between a Marine officer and an NCO over a beautiful French girl played by Dolores Del Rio. Although not known for its battlefield or historical accuracy, What Price Glory was well received by the Marines as well as the public and was later credited by the Corps for a marked increase in enlistments.

About the same time that moviemakers were discovering a sustainable market for war films, they also discovered a new type of screen warfare excitement—the aerial combat spectacular. With surplus planes and pilots from the war, and with the extensive assistance of the active military, filmmakers cranked out picture after picture featuring devil-may-care, white-scarf-wearing, hard-drinking, noble young men who could toast their enemies without hatred and erase the name of a downed fellow pilot from the squadron roster without a tear. On the screen the young aviators were so handsome, heroic, and human that the Air Corps never again had recruiting difficulties. In films such as The Power of Wings (1922), Lilac Time (1928), The Dawn Patrol (1930), and Hell's Angels (1930), these heroes of the air became the heroes of the silver screen and of the American public.

In 1926, Paramount Pictures hired William Wellman, the only

director in Hollywood who had World War I flying experience, to direct a film about two friends who enlist in the Air Corps, and the girl they both love. Although Wellman inadvertently used contemporary clothing and automobiles rather than those from the Great War period, audiences did not care, focusing instead on some of the greatest aerial combat on film. The public and critics agreed in their praise of *Wings*, which won the first Academy Award ever presented, as the Best Picture for 1927. *Wings* also has the distinction of being the last of the great silent films. Movies were learning to talk, and audio developments would add to the intensity of future war films.

Less than a decade after the Great War and only thirty years after the first primitive movies made their way to the screen, war films were an important part of the motion picture business. Modern warfare and modern movies came of age almost concurrently with the buildup, conduct, and aftermath of World War I. The mold had been cast for what Hollywood and the public wanted in their war movies. While the occasional movie would focus on the horrors of combat itself, the film industry as a whole concentrated on the valiant American warrior fighting for a pure and just cause against a brutal, evil enemy. The American military man was shown on the screen as honest, patriotic, God fearing, and righteous. It was never doubted that our heroic soldiers and sailors would return home to become productive members of the society they had fought so valiantly to protect. Their women would be waiting at the picket-fence gate, their parents standing at the vine-covered cottage door, and a grateful nation would line the parade routes to welcome home their victorious warriors.

3.   THE GOOD WAR:
WORLD WAR II

WORLD WAR I raised the curtain on war movies, and World War II brought combat films to center stage. The proven Great War themes about the battlefield and home front were extended to a "win at any cost" message in not only traditional war movies but also mysteries, dramas, comedies, and even large-scale victory musicals. As with the Great War, films about what would later become World War II preceded the U.S. entry into the hostilities by several years.

During the 1930s, Hollywood and the rest of the country were unsure where and how America fit into the impending war in Europe and Asia. What moviemakers *were* sure of was that films about the military made for good box office. Using the armed forces as a backdrop for romance, drama, and comedy, a series of films was produced that might as well have been recruiting vehicles for the military. John Ford directed *Men Without Women* in 1930, about the peacetime submarine service. He followed it with *Here Comes the Navy* (1934) and *Devil Dogs of the Air* (1935), both starring James Cagney. The navy got more coverage with *Submarine D-1* (1937) and *Wings of the Navy* (1939), while the army returned to the screen in the 1941 production *Parachute Battalion*. Dedication, romance, and flag waving extended to the military academies. Annapolis was featured in *Shipmates* (1931) and *Shipmates Forever* (1935), and West Point was the setting for *Flirtation Walk* (1934). Most of these films were made with the enthusiastic support of the armed forces.

By the end of the thirties, Hollywood began to take the threat of another world war seriously and concentrated on military-oriented pictures. The preparation of the United States armed forces for future battles was featured in films such as *Flight Command* (1940), *Dive Bomber* (1941), and *I Wanted Wings* (1941).

Films that were more direct in their anti-Nazi themes began to appear at about this same time. Warner's *Confessions of a Nazi Spy* in 1939 was the first American film to directly attack the German government. With Edward G. Robinson as a G-man out to break up a network of German agents in the U.S., the film offered ample opportunity for flag-waving speeches and patriotic oratory. Another Nazi spy movie, *Foreign Correspondent*, by newly-arrived-in-Hollywood director Alfred Hitchcock, made it to the screen in 1940. The same year Charlie Chaplin directed and starred in *The Great Dictator*, which satirized a fictional leader modeled after Adolf Hitler.

Perhaps the ultimate pre-World War II film to rekindle feelings against the Germans was the 1941 release *Sergeant York*, starring Gary Cooper and directed by Howard Hawks. Accusations of anti-German sentiment were answered by its producers with the accurate claim that the film was an honest re-creation of the story of the greatest American hero of the Great War. York, a Tennessee mountain lad about to resist the draft for religious reasons, is shown being told by a preacher that some evils are so horrible that they must be fought regardless of a man's pacifism. Placing his faith in God and on a wind-blown turn of his Bible's pages to an appropriate verse, York goes to France, where he kills and captures Germans in great numbers. He returns home, a much-decorated hero, to a farm bestowed upon him by his grateful neighbors, and to his girl who has waited behind faithfully. The rewards for Gary Cooper were not bad either. He received an Oscar as the year's Best Actor.

Although these films were well received by the public, there were some government officials, particularly those who favored isolationism, who felt that they were too promilitary and so anti-German that they advocated entry by the United States into the war in Europe. In September 1941, several isolationist senators convened a special subcommittee of the Committee on Interstate Commerce to investigate the accusation that moviemakers were deliberately producing propaganda. Several of the major studio heads testified before the committee that their only purpose in making films was to provide entertainment for the public and a profit for themselves. Much was made of the anti-German theme of several films, and it was noted that more than a few of the Hollywood decision makers were immigrants or refugees from countries recently overrun by the German army.

As with most congressional subcommittee meetings, little resulted from the hearings. The senators were in temporary adjournment on December 7, 1941, when the bombing of Pearl Harbor forever ended further need for the subcommittee.

The Japanese attack on Hawaii and the resulting declaration of war against the Axis powers resulted in a total mobilization of all American assets and resources to support the war effort. Government, industry, academia, and the intellectual communities—including the movie industry—united to defend freedom and defeat the Axis threat. Hollywood immediately rushed war-related films into production and updated those already in shooting to include the new developments. In the first eight months of the war, from December 1941 through July 1942, Hollywood released seventy-two films with the war as the primary subject.

Anti-Axis themes dominated the first of those films to be cranked out, and a vengeful American public welcomed the pictures into the movie houses. The sneak attack by the Japanese was a popular target, and films concentrated on the stab-in-the-back tactics of the enemy. Movies that were brought to the screen right after Pearl Harbor included A *Prisoner of Japan,* in which Japanese soldiers kill a boy and a wounded American naval officer. Other films released in early 1942, such as *Danger in the Pacific, Halfway to Shanghai,* and *Secret Agent of Japan,* focused on the brutality of the Japanese soldiers and the treachery of their government. Universal Studios' *Menace of the Rising Sun* brought all these elements together, and the result was promoted with a lurid, colorful advertisement featuring a Japanese soldier with blood dripping from his buck-toothed fangs. The figure is shown rising from the sea as he slaps American planes from the skies and sinks American ships into the briny deep.

Hollywood also concentrated on continuing the anti-Nazi films which had begun before the declaration of war. The treachery of the Germans and the bravery of the European Allies remained popular topics. In *Hitler's Children* (1943), the themes include political indoctrination of young people, the sterilization of "undesirables," and genetic experiments designed to create a super Aryan race. In *Paris Calling* (1941), a brave woman transmits coded messages to the Allies revealing secret German information. German submarines are blown up by Norwegian resistance fighters in *The Commandos Strike at Dawn* (1942).

World War II provided Hollywood with plot ideas for far more than just dramas or combat-action films. On screen, anything related to the war meant profits at the box office, and no film genre was exempt from the draft into the fight against the Axis. Musical comedies—such as *Star Spangled Rhythm* (1942) with Bob Hope, Bing Crosby, and Veronica Lake, and *True to the Army* (1942) with dancer Ann Miller—contained uniforms, tearful farewells, and many more songs and skits than tangible plot. Miller would go on to sing and dance through a long list of Good War movies including *Priorities on Parade* (1942), in which she gives up a Broadway career to work in an airplane plant. In 1943 Miller teamed with Frank Sinatra in a picture about entertaining the troops overseas titled *Reveille with Beverly*. Crosby also appeared in a number of war musicals, such as *Here Come the Waves* with Betty Hutton, wherein the popular tune "Ac-cent-u-ate the Positive" is featured.*

Movies that were little more than patriotic, support-the-troops stage shows were produced as each studio tried to outdo the others with the number of featured stars. United Artists led the way in 1943 with *Stage Door Canteen* featuring William Terry and Cheryl Walker. Although the featured actors were not particularly big, the walk-ons and cameos were headed by Helen Hayes, Benny Goodman, Katharine Hepburn, Harpo Marx, Count Basie, and Edgar Bergen. Warner's followed in 1944 with Bette Davis, John Garfield, Joan Crawford, Ida Lupino, Barbara Stanwyck, and Eddie Cantor in *Hollywood Canteen*. More of the same was presented in Universal's *Follow the Boys* (1944) starring Marlene Dietrich, the Andrews Sisters, Orson Wells, W. C. Fields, Jeanette MacDonald, and Sophie Tucker.

Other musicals of patriotic bent offered examples to American fighting men of what they were fighting for: Betty Grable appeared in *Pin-up Girl* (1944); Carmen "the Brazilian Bombshell"

---

*Although African-Americans played an important role in World War II, they were seldom included in the films of the period—and when they were, it was not always positive. "Ac-cent-u-ate the Positive" was performed in blackface in the film.

Miranda danced in *Up in Arms* (1944); and Dorothy Lamour was featured in *Rainbow Island* (1944).

Comedies without music—although a song or two might still slip in—were brought to the screen to try and get a chuckle out of audiences and provide a brief escape from the real dangers and hardships of the times. *Buck Privates* (1941), the first feature film of the popular comedy team Abbott and Costello, is about men accidentally enlisting in the army. Assisting the funny pair are the Andrews Sisters, singing two of the war's most popular tunes ("Boogie Woogie Bugle Boy of Company B" and "I'll Be with You in Apple Blossom Time"). During the same year, Abbott and Costello gave sailors equal time in *In the Navy*.

Every possible comedian and comedy medium got into the war-picture act. Bob Hope goes from draft dodger to hero in *Caught in the Draft* (1941), and Jackie Gleason made his first starring appearance, as a 4-F barber who is losing business to the draft, in *Tramp, Tramp, Tramp* (1942). Phil Silvers and Jimmy Durante play vacuum cleaner salesmen who find themselves in the army by mistake in *You're in the Army Now* (1941).*

Stories from other media were also brought to the wartime screen. Marion Hargrove's bestseller about basic training kept its original title in the 1944 release *See Here, Private Hargrove*. Cartoon character Snuffy Smith stepped off the funny pages to join the army in *Private Snuffy Smith* (1942) with Bud Duncan in the title role.

Although women generally played supporting roles in the war-oriented musicals and comedies, they took center stage in films about how females furthered the war effort at home. Women were shown performing serious jobs in plants and factories in lighter films such as *Swing Shift Maisie* (1943) and *Rosie the Riveter* (1944). In a more serious look at the same situation, Claudette Colbert appears in *Since You Went Away* (1944) written by David O. Selznick, as a woman who struggles to take care of her family and work in a defense plant while her husband is overseas. The film's music, by Max Steiner, won an Oscar.

No genre of film in the early 1940s was safe from the inclusion

---

*The film is better remembered today for its claim to the longest kiss (three minutes, five seconds) in movie history, shared by Jane Wyman and Regis Toomey.

of plots about evil Nazis or Japanese. Nazi paratroopers invade the jungle in *Tarzan Triumphs* (1943), and an aging Johnny Weissmuller has little trouble rallying his animal friends to combat the hated Germans. Tarzan's chimp, Cheetah, even gets in the act by chattering into a captured radio broadcasting to Berlin. The Nazi officers at the other and salute the receiver thinking they are listening to "der Führer."

In *Phantom Plainsman* (1944), cowboys foil a plot by Nazi agents in the American West to steal horses for the Third Reich. In *Northern Pursuit* (1943), Errol Flynn joins the war effort as a Mounted Policeman chasing a downed German pilot across the wilds of Canada. The Mounties are again pursuing Germans in *Yukon Patrol* (1942), when the Nazis search for a mineral compound to be used in their new secret weapon.

Famous detectives were also brought into the screen war against the Axis powers. Sherlock Holmes (Basil Rathbone) tracks Nazis in London in *Sherlock Holmes and the Secret Weapon* (1943), and William Gargan plays another legendary sleuth battling Germans in *Enemy Agents Meet Ellery Queen* (1942). Even short-subject stars like Bugs Bunny, Daffy Duck, and the Three Stooges contributed anti-Axis films.

Despite the sustained efforts of Hollywood to glorify the American military and vilify the enemy, the United States government concluded early in the war that the power and influence of movies were of too great a magnitude to leave in the hands of the private sector. The government was concerned not only with the content of the stories but also with their propaganda effects. Pro-Ally, anti-Axis propaganda was the objective; however, officials did not want the American viewing public to feel misled by lies and half-truths. Propaganda, in the government's view, had to be well done if films were to sustain their influence over American perspectives. One of President Roosevelt's first official actions after the bombing of Pearl Harbor was to appoint Lowell Mellett as coordinator of government films, on December 17, 1941.

An evolution of various offices and agencies followed over the next few months as the government strove to determine how best the film industry could be utilized to support the war effort. While Washington officials argued among themselves about what moviemakers should and should not do, Hollywood was far from idle. The studios cranked out dozens of war-related films with greatly varying propaganda and/or truth content. Although Hollywood continued to enthusiastically support the Allies without being told to, the filmmakers' primary focus was on making "good pictures," and in Hollywood the definition of a "good picture" was good box office and good profits for the studios and their backers.

On June 13, 1942, the White House finally announced the formation of the Office of War Information (OWI) headed by Elmer Davis. By order of President Roosevelt, the OWI was to enhance public understanding of the war at home and overseas. The office's myriad responsibilities included the motion picture industry, which was to be overseen by the OWI Movie Liaison Office of the Domestic Branch. While the definition would certainly be loosely translated by the government and by Hollywood over the next few years, the official mission of the Movie Liaison Office was "to promote truth and accuracy."

The OWI asked motion picture makers to consider seven questions in making their films. First was the simple question, "Will this picture help win the war?" The remaining questions dealt with how a film would portray the Allies, the Axis, the home front, and the truth of the conflict's issues. Although left unstated, it was understood by all that "Will this picture help win the war?" took precedence over all others. The unofficial rule was that anything was acceptable if it met the intent of question number one.

To supplement the seven questions, the OWI issued a manual, frequently updated, outlining how best to assist the war effort. In addition, members of the OWI staff sat in on studio staff meetings, reviewed scripts, provided dialogue and plot ideas, and ultimately, through the Office of Censorship, determined if a movie could be released for distribution. Censorship itself, however, was rarely necessary. The OWI desired to influence Hollywood rather than censor it, and the office was extremely successful in doing so. Of course, because of the box-office profits generated by the OWI-model movies, in most cases the studios found government control easy to accept—and to welcome.

An important but little-noted contribution by the OWI to the filmmakers was the advisers who assisted in movie production from initial scripting all the way through final editing. Military personnel carefully scrutinized the filmmaking process to insure that uniforms, insignia, and decorations, as well as service etiquette and traditions, were properly portrayed. Only in rare cases did errors make it to the screen.

In addition to assisting Hollywood's commercial productions, the OWI was responsible for its own filmmaking in support of the war. Award-winning director Frank Capra was enlisted to produce a series titled "Why We Fight" as an orientation and a motivational tool for soldiers in basic training. War documentaries were produced by other major Hollywood directors and film crews for OWI's release to the public. John Ford took time from making westerns to direct *The Battle of Midway* (1942), and William Wyler directed *The Memphis Belle* (1944), about the first U.S. bomber and crew to complete twenty-five missions over Nazi-held territory.* The true account of an infantry regiment's fight to capture a village during the Italian campaign was written and narrated by John Huston and released as a half-hour documentary titled *The Battle of San Pietro*.**

Early in the war, the biggest problem the OWI experienced with Hollywood was not liberalism or pacifism but rather an overzealous condemnation of the Japanese and Germans. Racial slurs were a common and accepted part of Hollywood's anti-Axis films. While the Germans were frequently referred to as "krauts" or "squareheads," the more caustic slurs were reserved for the Japanese, who were singled out for more reasons than the fact that they did not look like Westerners: Japan had attacked Pearl Harbor with no warning, and on a Sunday morning. Little was known about the Japanese by the average American, so racial stereotypes and prejudices were much easier to apply to them than to the Aryan Germans.

Whatever the reason, Hollywood pandered to Americans' racial prejudices against the Japanese. The jungle-fighting Japanese soldier was frequently referred to as a monkey, an ape, or a rodent. In the 1944 film *The Purple Hearts*, the Japanese are referred to as "cornered rats." Less directly, the Japanese are likened to animals

---

*Hollywood would remake the film under the same title in 1991 in the same flag-waving spirit of World War II.

**The Battle of San Pietro* is considered such an accurate, intimate account of ground combat that it was still being shown to infantry lieutenants at Fort Benning, Georgia, before deployment to Vietnam as late as 1969.

in *Destination Tokyo* (1944) when American pilots are encouraged before takeoff: "Good luck and good hunting."

Racial slurs against the Japanese were included in films of all types and budgets. George Tobias, playing a bomber gunner in *Air Force* (1943), brags, "Fried Jap going down" as a Zero he has shot crashes in flames. John Wayne, in one of his many World War II films, *The Fighting Seabees* (1944), boasts of looking forward to fighting "Tojo and his bug-eyed pals." In *Guadalcanal Diary* (1943), a Marine's only comment on killing a Japanese soldier is "Scratch one squint-eye." Perhaps the ultimate racial slur is delivered by Humphrey Bogart in *Across the Pacific* (1942) when he comments about his lack of feelings in killing the Japanese, saying, "They all look alike anyway." In these films, as in practically every other World War II movie set in the Pacific theater, the Japanese are referred to as Japs, Nips, and/or slant-eyes.*

Axis treachery was also a popular theme of Good War films, German spies and Japan's sneak attack on Pearl Harbor being common topics. In *Ministry of Fear* (1944), German spies use a charity organization for refugees as a front for their activities. The Japanese are repeatedly taken to task for Pearl Harbor in films such as *Flying Tigers* (1942), *Stand By for Action* (1942), and *So Proudly We Hail* (1943). Ruthlessness on the part of the enemy also received much screen attention. The Nazis' barbarism was shown in the treatment of prisoners of war and concentration camp victims in *The Cross of Lorraine* (1943) and in *The Seventh Cross* (1944), which starred Spencer Tracy. In *Behind the Rising Sun* (1943), Japanese soldiers spear babies with bayonets; in *Back to Bataan* (1945) they beat and torture women and children.

With the direction, supervision, and assistance of the OWI and with the full cooperation of Hollywood, motion pictures settled into a fairly consistent, formulistic pattern as the war progressed. The Allied cause was just; the Axis totalitarian. The Allies fought bravely and fairly; the enemy was sneaky and dirty. American soldiers respected each other, their sergeants, and their officers and

---

*Unlike the movies and day-to-day life on the streets of America during World War II, when much criticism was directed toward the enemy, any soldier in today's films or in polite conversation who refers to the Vietcong or the North Vietnamese Army as gooks or slopes is immediately labeled a bigot or worse.

pulled together for the common cause. The people at home were united in working to support the war effort. Victory would ultimately be achieved by the Allies, but it would require careful cooperation and great sacrifice.

The men depicted on the screen who would achieve this victory on the battlefield, on the sea, and in the air were from a cross-section of ethnic, social, and geographical backgrounds. United States units, whether infantry squad, bomber crew, or navy shipmates, usually consisted of a tall Texan, a wisecracking New Yorker, an innocent midwesterner, and a first-generation Polish, Italian, or other immigrant. All were religious, patriotic, respectful, sentimental, and dedicated. Example after example of these model characters appeared on the screens of movie houses across America throughout the war and continue to reappear with great frequency on late-night television and on rental videos.

Even the films made during the darkest days of the war's first months, when the Japanese and Germans were rolling over their enemies, did not vary from promising better days and ultimate victory ahead. *Wake Island* (1942) and *Bataan* (1943) promised future victories would rise from the ashes of defeat. *Casablanca* (1943) revealed a cynical Humphrey Bogart who was willing to sacrifice all, including his only love, in order to strike back at the Nazis. The film, perhaps the supreme example of this idea, won multiple Oscars and came to be considered one of the greatest films of all times.

Along with *Casablanca, Wake Island,* and *Air Force,* there are many other films from the time—*The Purple Heart* (1944), *Sahara* (1943), and *Thirty Seconds over Tokyo* (1944)—that followed the Hollywood red, white, and blue prescription and which remain popular today. Two films, however, are perhaps the "classics" of the World War II film genre. William Wyler's *Mrs. Miniver* (1942), with Greer Garson and Walter Pidgeon, shows the difficulties of a middle-class English family coping with the war as it delivers its patriotic, sentimental message. A speech by costar Henry Wilcoxon at the end of the picture could have served as the conclusion for almost any Good War film with its emphasis on total involvement. He says, "This is not only a war of soldiers in uniforms. It is a war of the people—of all the people—and it must be fought not only on the battlefield but in the cities and in the villages, in the factories and on the farms, in the home, and in the heart of every man, woman, and child who loves freedom. Well, we have buried our dead, but we shall not forget them. Instead, they will inspire us with an unbreakable determination to free ourselves and those who come after us from the tyranny and terror that threaten to strike us down. This is the people's war. It is our war. We are the fighters. Fight it, then. Fight it with all that is in us. And may God defend the right." *Mrs. Miniver* won seven Oscars, including that for Best Picture.

Three years later, the second "classic" was released. William Wellman's *Story of G.I. Joe* (1945) took several of the newspaper articles written by famed war correspondent Ernie Pyle and wove them into the story of an infantry company involved in the Italian campaign. Wellman showed that the skills he had demonstrated in the silent-era, award-winning *Wings* were only enhanced by the addition of a sound track. Robert Mitchum, in his first starring role, plays a beloved company commander, Lieutenant Walker,* and Burgess Meredith narrates as Pyle in this story of brotherhood, patriotism, and death in the cold, mud, and fear of the front lines.

The victory at the end of World War II brought American soldiers home to parades before discharge and return to work; women left their places in the war plants to return to the hearth. However, as Americans settled into postwar prosperity and the baby boom, their hearts remained loyal to movies about the Good War. John Wayne continued to win the war in films like *Sands of Iwo Jima* (1949), and salutes to the services continued, to the navy in *Task Force* (1949) and the air corps in *Twelve O'Clock High* (1949).

Readjustment to peacetime for combat-hardened veterans also proved popular as an extension of the Good War films. The men of World War II were more than up to the task. In the classic multiple-Oscar-winning *The Best Years of Our Lives* (1946), three veterans return to their small hometown to make the transition. One, a decorated bombardier, follows his desire to build things rather than return to his job as a drugstore clerk. Another, an older ex-infantryman, must learn new ideas and techniques to keep up with younger executives when he returns to his former position at a bank. The third, a double-amputee navy machinist, must adjust to a life with hooks instead of hands. All succeed, in spite of their

---

*The Walker character is based on one of Pyle's best-known columns about the 36th Infantry Division and the death of Captain Henry T. Waskow of Belton, Texas.

difficulties—in business and family life—and live happily ever after as the credits roll and "The End" fades from the screen.

Every year to date continues to see the release of one or more major World War II movie productions. The propaganda may not be quite so blatant but the flag is still waving, and no doubt exists about who is good and who is bad. Nothing has daunted the American movie audience response to World War II film stories— not even other conflicts and armed hostilities. In fact, the reverse has been true. New battles send Hollywood and moviegoers back to Good War films.

The conflict in Korea increased the production of World War II films, and the 1970 release of *Patton* at the height of the Vietnam War proved that the American public's love affair with the Good War was in little danger of being ended by other genres. *Patton* was a tremendous success at the box office as well as an Oscar winner for Best Picture, Best Director, and Best Actor (George C. Scott). Even President Nixon openly admitted that it was his favorite film, and it was rumored that he rewatched the movie before making difficult decisions about the war in Southeast Asia.

Patton opens with Scott, in full dress uniform, delivering a speech which Patton himself presented to his troops during the war. In a scene direct from 1940s Hollywood, and one that could be included in any Good War film (with the possible exception of the profanity), Scott/Patton states, "Be seated. Now, I want you to remember that no bastard ever won a war by dying for his country. He won it by making the other poor bastard die for his country. Men, all the stuff you heard about America not wanting to fight, wanting to stay out of the war, is a lot of horse dung. Americans, traditionally, love to fight. All real Americans love the sting of battle. When you were kids, you all admired the champion marble shooter, the fastest runner, the big-league ballplayer, the toughest boxer. Americans love a winner and will not tolerate a loser. Americans play to win all the time. I wouldn't give a hoot in hell for a man who lost and laughed. That's why Americans have never lost—and will never lose—a war, because the very thought of losing is hateful to Americans."

American films about the Good War continue time and time again to reinforce Patton's sentiments. Unfortunately, somewhere along the way Americans and the movies lost sight of the possibility that things would not always be as Patton predicted.

4. THE NOT-SO-UNKNOWN WAR: KOREA

WHEN THE NORTH Koreans crossed the 38th Parallel early on the morning of June 25, 1950, they surprised more than just the South Koreans and their American allies. Hollywood was caught unaware as well. Before American involvement in the two world wars, the movie industry had years to establish positions and policies and to develop story lines about the anticipated conflict. But few in Hollywood even knew where Korea was located, let alone that this "police action" was to be the first large-scale confrontation between communist and noncommunist forces.

Generally, the film industry was not overly concerned that the cold war had suddenly warmed up. What did gain Hollywood's attention was that an apparent decline in interest in Good War films could be reversed and a new market for war stories would be available. With theater seats to be filled, popcorn to be sold, and money to be made, Hollywood welcomed another war.

All of the major studios immediately dusted off scripts from World War II, modified sets, collected actors, and approached the new war with the same flag-waving zeal and enthusiasm that had led to success and profits in previous conflicts. Although there was no formal organization like the Creel Committee or the Office of War Information, which had controlled Hollywood during the two world wars, Washington and the Pentagon certainly maintained a strong influence on the film industry during the early 1950s. The primary control measure was the offering of equipment, men, and shooting locations for films approved by the Defense Department's Motion Picture Production Office, which had been founded in 1949. Few studios were willing to risk the expenses involved in making a war film without the Pentagon's picking up much of the tab.

Another important influence that kept Hollywood on the patriotic line was the activity of Joe McCarthy and the House Committee on Un-American Activities (HUAC). As early as 1947, a group
of writers and film executives, known as the Hollywood 10, was
jailed for refusing to cooperate with HUAC in investigating communism in the movie business. As a result of the committee's in-
vestigations, by 1954 a total of 212 film people of varying degrees
of guilt and innocence had been blacklisted—effectively barred
from working in Hollywood. With such attention paid to communist sympathizers, it is no surprise that movies about the first war
against the red menace were supportive of the United States and
her allies.

Regardless of the reasons for Hollywood's support, during the
war and in the succeeding decade the fifty-five or so films made
about the Korean Conflict closely followed the well-worn pathway
established by Great War and Good War films. Our side was right,
the enemy treacherous and ruthless, our cause just, and our soldiers dedicated, resilient, and brave.

The first Korean Conflict film to reach the screen was *The Steel
Helmet* (1951), which was written, produced, and directed by Samuel Fuller. Shot in twelve days in Los Angeles's Griffin Park with
an unknown cast at an expense of a mere $100,000, it closely re-
sembles the back-lot productions of World War II. The combat
scenes are indistinguishable from those of Good War films, and although the enemy is North Korean, he is just as barbaric and
bloodthirsty as his Japanese and Nazi forbears. In one scene an
enemy soldier disguises himself as a woman to kill Americans; in
another a North Korean officer hides behind a statue of Buddha.

Along with the usual, Fuller added scenes that make *The Steel
Helmet* one of the few pre-Vietnam films to confront issues of the
future instead of just rehashing the glories of the past. In one
scene a tough sergeant calls a boy who has saved his life a "gook."
The boy angrily replies, "I am no gook! I'm Korean!" The film also
underscores how a lack of understanding can have unpredictable
effects. When a chaplain's assistant plays "Auld Land Syne," he is
surprised when the Koreans proudly sing along in their native language. The soldier is unaware that the tune is also that of the
South Korean national anthem.

Despite cardboard-cutout tanks as props and a tired plot—
experienced, tough sergeant pitted against a by-the-book officer

who must rally his badly outnumbered men against a determined enemy—the weak parts were molded by Fuller into a strong final product. *The Steel Helmet* still manages to make it onto an occasional "best films of all time" list. However, at the time the Pentagon was not so impressed. When Fuller requested actual combat footage to splice into his print, he was turned down with the explanation that the movie was "un-American" because of the depiction of harsh treatment of enemy prisoners. Although the viewing public of the time did not seem to have a problem with American servicemen shooting POWs, the military did not care for it to be shown on the screen.

More than fifty Korean War films followed *The Steel Helmet*, most produced with the support and supervision of the Department of Defense. This interaction between Hollywood and the Pentagon was so important to film production that many of the movies began or concluded with a statement of "grateful acknowledgment" to the Department of Defense, "without which this film would not have been possible."

Early Korean War films were rushed to the screen, and the result usually mirrored their hasty production. General MacArthur was promising to have the troops home by Christmas, and Hollywood producers felt they had to hurry to beat the peace to the box office. The first film to make it to the theaters after *The Steel Helmet* was Lew Landers's Columbia release *A Yank in Korea* (1951). With a plot about as original as its title, the film followed a tried-and-true World War II plot line—a young man sees his duty, joins the army, goes to combat, survives as a hero, and returns home. Along the way he marries his loyal sweetheart and makes mention of the importance of God, country, and responsibility.

Other successful World War II formats were adapted to the Korean Conflict. In the 1951 production *Starlift*, a bevy of Warner Brothers stars, including Doris Day, James Cagney, and Gordon MacRae, teamed up in a remake of the old Hollywood canteen musicals. In a confusing motion picture released the same year, *Tokyo File 212*, RKO Studios resurrected World War II Japanese enemies and placed them as communists supporting North Korea.

The war had been raging for well over a year before any major Hollywood films about Korea reached the screen. Unfortunately, the wait was not worth the trouble, as most of the large-budget films were little better, and in some cases were worse, than the low-cost movies that preceded them. Interestingly, the first major Korean War film was directed by Sam Fuller, who had beaten everyone to the screen with *The Steel Helmet*. This time, for *Fixed Bayonets* (1951), Fuller had a big-name cast and a substantial budget. Increased financing and support by 20th Century Fox did not, however, result in a better motion picture. Offering combat sequences and a plot that could just as well have been from World War II—an infantry platoon composed of all-American boys fights against a superior force that has them surrounded—the film did not nearly measure up to the quality of Fuller's first Korea movie. In fact, the most interesting and memorable aspect of *Fixed Bayonets* may very well be the first screen appearance, in a brief, nonspeaking role, by future Hollywood legend James Dean.

How the war was affecting the homefront was another early major-release subject. Distributed to theaters in time for Christmas of 1951, *I Want You* tells the story of a family facing war for the third time. The head of the family, Robert Keith, is a World War I veteran, and his son, Dana Andrews, fought in World War II. When a draft notice arrives for the third generation (Farley Granger), his mother hides the letter until after the holiday season. Andrews does not approve of the ruse, saying, "Maybe that's the way we are—we think we are on holiday, but somewhere, somebody knows that the holiday is over." In the end, not only does Granger go off to war, but Andrews's character reenlists.

By 1952, Hollywood had settled into a routine similar to that of World War II—producing films that enthusiastically supported the Korean Conflict effort. Most of the films paid little attention to the ideology of the war, merely showing the North Koreans and their Chinese communist supporters as murderous beasts. The military effort was shown as being shouldered primarily by Americans, and there was little acknowledgment of the efforts of South Koreans or the other United Nations forces.

Typical was the 1952 Allied Artists film *Battle Zone*, about two Marines (John Hodiak and Steve McNally) who spend far more time wooing a nurse (Linda Christian) than fighting the enemy. In *Submarine Command*,* released the same year, nearly three-

*Any submarine film about Korea makes for a long stretch, since the North Koreans essentially had no naval force.

quarters of the film is devoted to World War II to show why William Holden is fortunate to have another war in which to prove himself: He was responsible for the death of his captain and quartermaster in the final hours of the Good War.

Another 1952 film, *Retreat, Hell!*, tells the true story of a Marine regiment training in the States, landing at Inchon, and fighting its way out of the encirclement at the Chosin Reservoir.* Frank Lovejoy delivers the line that provides the movie's title when he says, "Retreat, hell! We're just attacking in another direction." Even if hordes of communists were chasing American units down the Korean peninsula in real life, Hollywood still did not acknowledge retreats, or "bug outs" as they were known to GIs of the time.

It was not until after two years of warfare in Korea that films acknowledged and explored the United States/United Nations relationship. In *One Minute to Zero* (1952), Robert Mitchum plays an American colonel carrying on a love affair with a UN representative, played by Ann Blythe. They spend much of the film discussing the evils of communists and the support of the North Koreans by the Chinese and the Soviets. Along with spliced-in newsreel footage of actual combat, it is revealed that Blythe is leery of falling in love with a another military man after losing her husband in World War II.

The Korean Conflict was nearing a close when 20th Century Fox released *The Glory Brigade* (1953), the first film to focus on Americans fighting alongside UN allies. Despite a proven cast of "tough guys" including Victor Mature, Richard Egan, and Lee Marvin, the film did little at the box office, and little to promote understanding of the United Nations alliance in Korea.

By chance, *Battle Circus* (1953) has the distinction of being the last film about Korea to appear before the end of the war. This soap opera set in a combat hospital centers on a romance between Humphrey Bogart and June Allyson—both of whom had far larger reputations and broader abilities than shown in this movie. The most interesting aspect of *Battle Circus* is that its opening se-

Retreat, Hell! was filmed at Camp Pendleton, California, where hillsides were whitewashed to resemble the snowy mountains of Korea. Nearly all of the Korean Conflict movies were filmed in southern California and/or on Hollywood back lots.

quence shows a sign identifying the hospital as the MASH 8666. This served at least as a part of the inspiration for a later film focusing on a Mobile Army Surgical Hospital. The 1970 release *M*A*S*H* uses the unit number 4077 and is also set in Korea. (However, *M*A*S*H* is not really about the Unknown War but about the war in Vietnam.)

In the days immediately following the peace, truce, stalemate, tie, or whatever one cares to call the end of the Korean War, several films that had already been in production about the conflict were released. All continued with the same gung-ho, flag-waving spirit of the past half-century of American war films. In *Take the High Ground* (1953), Richard Widmark and Karl Malden played tough sergeants teaching recruits in infantry basic training at Fort Bliss, Texas. *Sabre Jet* (1953), with Robert Stack and Amanda Blake, focuses on the waiting wives of fighter pilots. Two officers fight over their job responsibilities but unite to fight the communists in *Mission over Korea* (1953) starring John Derek, John Hodiak, and Maureen O'Sullivan. In *Flight Nurse* (1953), two pilots compete for the same girl when not flying missions over North Korea.

Over the next decade, more than two dozen films about the Korean War made their way to the screen. On the whole, they were forgettable and formulistic, differing only by subgenre. One of the most popular subgenres of the post–Korean War films mixed combat with sex—at least the 1950s movie version of sex. Films such as *Target Zero* (1955), *Jet Attack* (1958), *Tank Battalion* (1958), and *Operation Dames* (1959) managed to have nurses, USO girls, and/or other attractive women trapped behind enemy lines with GIs, or supporting soldiers on the front lines. This type of Korean War film pretty well ran its course and came to an overdue conclusion with the 1962 release *The Nun and the Sergeant*, which, in addition to the nun of its title, included a busload of convent girls. Despite the sexual overtones of these films, however, American GIs remained ferocious with the enemy but gentlemen with the ladies.

Another, and a much more serious, subgenre of Korean War movies was the prisoner-of-war film. In addition to the traditional use of this type of film—to show the hardships suffered by prisoners and the brutality of their captors—Hollywood, with prodding from the Pentagon, also attempted to show the adverse consequences of collaboration with the enemy. However, because of the relatively brief duration of the war and the fact that little was known about the North Korean and Chinese communist prisons until the truce was signed, no POW film appeared until the war was over.

First to reach the theaters, in 1954, was the appropriately titled *Prisoner of War* starring Ronald Reagan and Steve Forrest. Reagan plays an officer who deliberately allows himself to be captured so he can report prison camp conditions to his superiors. Initially the Department of Defense supported the film and arranged for a former POW to act as a technical adviser. When MGM failed to make all the changes recommended by the military, support was withdrawn. The primary area of contention was the unrealistic banter between prisoners and captors and Reagan's broadcast of a false confession even though it supposedly contained coded information for his superiors about the POW camp conditions.

Another movie released the same year, *The Bamboo Prison*, followed the same general plot—a loyal American (Robert Francis) poses as an informer to outwit his North Korean captors. Neither film pleased the Pentagon, because it was preparing to prosecute American POWs who had collaborated with the enemy. A few years later, MGM finally released a POW film that the Department of Defense approved. *The Rack* (1956) featured Paul Newman as an officer, son of an officer, and brother of an officer killed in Korea, who is found guilty by court-martial of collaboration. In the final scene Newman looks directly into the camera and says, "Every man has a moment in his life when he has to choose. If he chooses right, then it's a moment of magnificence. If he chooses wrong, then it's a moment of regret that will stay with him for the rest of his life. I wish that every soldier . . . could feel the way I feel now, because if they did they'd know what it's like to be a man who sold himself short, and who lost his moment of magnificence. I pray to God they find theirs."

One postwar subgenre of Korean Conflict film had already proven its box-office draw with *Submarine Command*. These movies relied on plots that featured old soldiers from World War II returning for more action in Korea. After the war, Hollywood added another element to these "two wars" pictures. A series of films was released that not only told of World War II heroes fighting in Korea but were based on the true stories of real men. In *The*

McConnell Story (1955) Alan Ladd plays a real-life test pilot, with June Allyson as his supportive wife. Sterling Hayden portrays Admiral John Haskins, who, despite having lost a leg in World War II combat, returns to sea during the Korean War in *The Eternal Sea* (1955).

The epic of these "return to fight again" features, *Battle Hymn* (1957), starred Rock Hudson as the fighting preacher Colonel Dean Hess. An introduction is provided by General Earle C. Partridge, commander of the Fifth Air Force in Korea, who assures the moviegoer that what follows is a true story. The real Colonel Hess acted as a technical adviser on the film, and a planeload of Korean orphans was flown to the States to use as extras. Except for the Southern Arizona shooting location, the studio spared no expense in bringing an accurate story to the screen.

Hudson's character is known as "Killer Hess" because of his accidental bombing of a German orphanage during World War II. Filled with guilt, Hudson/Hess becomes a parson in Ohio after the war only to reenlist when the Korean Conflict breaks out. In Korea he trains allied pilots, flies 250 ground-support missions, organizes an orphanage, and flies a thousand children to safety. While the hero comes to grips with his experiences of two wars, several patriotic speeches are delivered—complete with "The Battle Hymn of the Republic" as musical background. A fellow aviator, played by Don DeFore, offers his viewpoint about the Unknown War, saying, "I thought you knew what war was about. Just keep this one thing in mind. All that counts is who wins, not how nice a guy you are. You win or you die. You go soft and you're one step from being dead."

The popularity of the Korean Conflict film had mostly faded before Hollywood finally made, in 1959, what may be the most accurate depiction of the war's combat, United Artists' *Pork Chop Hill*. In still another story based on a real man and an actual incident, Gregory Peck plays U.S. Army Lieutenant Joe Clemons, who must lead his company to take and hold a pork-chop-shaped bit of worthless hill in no-man's-land. Peck and his men know that the hill is of no value except to show the communists that the Americans have the resolve to continue the fight despite the continuing truce talks.

Realistic and gritty, the battle for Pork Chop Hill is shown from a foot-soldier's view. While the soldiers ultimately are heroic, no glamor is shown in their heroism. In a final voiceover, Peck explains, "Pork Chop Hill was held—bought and paid at the same price we commemorate in monuments at Bunker Hill and Gettysburg. Yet you will find no monuments on Pork Chop. Victory is a fragile thing, and history does not linger long in our century. Pork Chop is in North Korea now—but those who fought there know what they did, and the meaning of it. Millions live in freedom today because of what they did."

By the beginning of the 1960s, Korean War films no longer drew the viewing public. Those who did remember the war generally had no understanding of what it was all about or that it ended in an armed truce rather than a real peace. Hollywood's interest in the war faded with the decrease of box office receipts.*

Hollywood tried a Korean War film comeback with *MacArthur* in 1977, with Gregory Peck in the title role. The film was uneven, overedited, and unfavorably compared to the earlier, much more popular *Patton*. The Korean War film was more or less (mostly more) laid to rest with the Reverend Sung Myung Moon's production *Inchon* in 1982. Made at a cost of $46 million, it delivered nothing but bad reviews and empty theater seats. Even the legendary Sir Laurence Olivier in the starring role of MacArthur, at a salary of $1.25 million, had no chance of rescuing the Moonies from this one.

Interestingly, *Inchon*, as the last epic Korean War film to reach the screen, did no more to make any sense out of the war than did any of the earlier half-hundred movies about the conflict. Korean War films offered heroic combat action with great speeches about patriotism and service to country without an explanation of cause or purpose of the war. Perhaps the best epitaph to the Korean Conflict and to the films it influenced is provided in *The Hunters* (1958). The film's star, Robert Mitchum, as World War II veteran Major Cleve "Iceman" Saville, remarks, "The only trouble is Korea came along too soon after the big one. It's hard to sell anyone on it."

---

*By the time of the 1975 release *W. W. and the Dixie Dance Kings*, only the most conscientious viewer noticed the Korean War–era Airborne Ranger Company scroll patch on Burt Reynolds's jacket and the brief mention of his character's service during the war.

5. VIET WHAT?: PREWAR MOVIES

PRIOR TO THE mid-1960s, it is doubtful that many Americans could have found Vietnam on a map or had even heard of the Southeast Asian country that would dominate the U.S. news for the next decade and beyond. If asked about Vietnam, the response of most Americans would have likely been "Viet what?" Hollywood, like the American public, had also pretty well ignored that remote part of the world. During the first half of the twentieth century, Vietnam, or Indochina* as it was better known for much of that time, appeared in films only when an exotic-sounding, distant location was needed for a setting.

During the first two decades of American movie production, no mention was made of either Vietnam or Indochina. Interestingly, when the setting was finally used, it was used in two films that appeared within a month of each other. Reaching the screen on May 4, 1929, and thereby earning the honor of "first Vietnam

*The Vietnamese people have been considered a separate ethnic group since as early as the first millennium B.C., when they were identified as several clanlike tribes of people living south of China's Yangtze River. They were then known as the Yüeh. During more than a thousand years of warfare with the Chinese they were pushed south to their present borders. The French colonized Vietnam in 1883 and divided the country into three provinces, Tonkin in the north, Annam in the central region, and Cochin China in the south. In 1887, France united these three regions into what they called Indochina. It would keep this name until 1954, when the Vietminh defeated the French, resulting in the country being divided at the 17th Parallel (the Ben Hai River) into North and South Vietnam. With the fall of Saigon in 1975, the two nations were united into the Socialist Republic of Vietnam.

film," was MGM's *Where East Is East*. Starring the popular Lon Chaney and Lupe Velez, this silent picture featured ferocious tigers, a killer gorilla, and a love affair between the son of an American circus owner and the daughter of a wild-animal trapper. The mother of the bride-to-be, a Vietnamese who had abandoned her daughter at birth, reappears just before the wedding and attempts to disrupt the procedures by seducing the groom.

Less than a month later, First National Pictures brought to the screen a story about love and intrigue in Indochina. Although the plot of *Careers* offered few surprises—focusing on a lecherous French official and the loyal wife of a minor magistrate—the film did gain some following due to its being one of the first "talkies." Not only did the audio track include dialogue by former silent-film stars Noah Beery and Billie Dove, but the theme song of "I Love You, I Hate You" became a semihit. With all the attention given to the talk and singing, the Cochin China setting went pretty well unnoticed.

A little more than a year later, the third film set in Vietnam made its way to the screen. The 1930 production *Lotus Lady* featured a no-name cast in a romantic drama about an American who buys a worthless Indochina swamp in belief it is an operating tea plantation. A Vietnamese girlfriend and the discovery of oil under the swamp add a few twists to an otherwise routine story.

During the next twelve years, Indochina provided the exotic location for two more films, but it would be the pictures' actors much more than the movies themselves who would go on to fame and fortune. In 1932, Clark Gable, Jean Harlow, and Mary Astor appeared in MGM's *Red Dust*. A decade later, Gable returned to Indochina—or at least to the MGM back lot representing that country—to appear with Lana Turner in *Somewhere I'll Find You*. While the two films were well acted and profitable at the box office, both were rocked by tragedy and scandal that brought far more attention to the actors than to the Indochina settings. During the making of *Red Dust*, Harlow's husband, Paul Bern, committed suicide; Gable's wife, Carole Lombard, was killed in a plane crash during production of *Somewhere I'll Find You*.

None of these pioneer Vietnam pictures was filmed outside the studios of Hollywood. In *Red Dust*, MGM went so far as to create a rubber plantation on one of its back lots. Several of the production staff and actors would later recall that the only realistic aspect of the shoot was the unusually hot southern California summer that produced sweat without any special-effects assistance. Vietnamese actors did not appear in these early productions; their roles were usually played by American Chinese or by actors of Hispanic background.

In fact, except for the announced locations of the films, most could have been set in any tropical country. The exception is *Somewhere I'll Find You,** in which some of the action takes place in Hanoi and along the Vietnam–China border, where Gable and Turner go to report on the Japanese occupation of Indochina before the bombing of Pearl Harbor. One of the film's first insights into the fighting abilities of the Vietnamese is offered by a reporter who commends their bravery and tenacity but concludes that they "can't fight (Japanese) tanks with bows and arrows."

Somewhere I'll Find You also has the distinction of being the only film to directly unite the Good War and Vietnam. After the formal entry of the United States into World War II, the European and Pacific theaters would offer far too many exotic locations for Indochina to play any further role. It was not until several years after the Good War that Vietnam once again made its way to the screen. Unfortunately, while the exotic-sounding location stayed the same, so did the plots of the pictures set there.

Paramount Pictures released *Saigon* in 1948,** but the title was the most Vietnamese thing about the film. Rather than being about its city namesake or Indochina, *Saigon* served as a vehicle to team Alan Ladd with Veronica Lake in the last of a series of romantic dramas featuring the duo. Along with the Ladd/Lake love story, the picture offers black marketeers, plane crashes, an aviator with only a few weeks left to live, and action aplenty for everyone. However, all of that is set on less-than-convincing soundstages in an obviously hurried production effort that presents no actual similarity to Saigon or its environs.

Another Vietnam film appeared in late 1948. While not notable for any great production values—with southern California and

---

*Although none of the pioneer Vietnam films has been released on videotape, *Somewhere I'll Find You* does make infrequent appearances on late-night cable television.

**Saigon* is erroneously listed in many motion picture studies as the first Vietnam-oriented film—a distinction that it misses by nearly twenty years.

much wicker and bamboo furniture standing in for Indochina—it did offer several firsts. *Rogue's Regiment,* starring Dick Powell, concentrates on the exploits of an American intelligence officer who joins the French foreign legion in order to pursue a major Nazi war criminal. Along the way Powell and his fellow legionnaires fight the first film skirmishes with the local guerrillas, who would soon become better known as the Vietminh and later as the Vietcong. Several conversations discuss the motivation of the Vietminh; some explanations suggest that they have openly communist aims, while others rationalize, saying that the guerrillas merely want enough food to eat. For a brief time, Powell's character is captured and imprisoned by the guerrillas, earning him the distinction of being the first American POW in Hollywood's version of Vietnam.

The 1950s added only five Hollywood releases to the short list of movies about the country that was soon to so consume and divide the United States. In two of these pictures, Indochina again merely offers an out-of-the-way, exotic location for what is no more than an average action yarn. In *A Yank in Indo-China* (1952), two American fliers destroy guerrilla war supplies and escape through the jungle with two young women. A group of doctors and nurses fairly well repeat this scenario in the 1959 release *Five Gates to Hell.*

Two other 1950s films explored the difficulties of the French in Vietnam. The first was *Jump into Hell* (1955), released only months after the fall of Dien Bien Phu. It was followed in 1957 by *China Gate.* While *Jump into Hell* attempts, with mixed results, to show the war and its background, *China Gate* is just another Hollywood glamorization of the foreign legion. Its sex appeal is represented by Angie Dickinson as a Eurasian jungle guide by the name of "Lucky Legs." Nat "King" Cole, in one of his few screen appearances, has a minor role as an American mercenary with a grudge against communists and a great voice, the better to sing the picture's theme.

The final 1950s Vietnam film, *The Quiet American* (1958)—even though primarily a love story and murder mystery—presents more insights into the nature of the country and the conflict that lay ahead than any other motion picture produced up to that time. It is also the first Hollywood production to be filmed on location in Vietnam and to cast Vietnamese in most of the minor roles. The leading "native" parts, however, are played by American Chinese and an Italian starlet.

Set in 1952 in the midst of the French-Vietminh conflict, *The Quiet American* features an American who imports a vast amount of plastique explosives with hopes of creating a "third front." Excellent observations are made about the communists' being soldiers by night and farmers by day, and about the major difference between the French and the Vietminh being that the guerrillas look like the other Vietnamese.

Along with absolutely wonderful scenes of Saigon and the surrounding countryside, *The Quiet American* presents a preview of what was to come in Southeast Asia. Although it does not go into detail, nor is it nearly as critical of U.S. policy in Vietnam as is the Graham Greene novel on which it is based, the film still pays far more attention to the politics and human turbulence than any other of the prewar pictures. Another interesting aspect is that the title role is played by America's most decorated hero of World War II, Audie Murphy, and the famous real-life warrior of the Good War is one of the first casualties of Hollywood's interpretation of the Vietnam Conflict.

Brushfire! (1962), written, produced, and directed by Paramount's Jack Warner, Jr., follows earlier Indochina plot lines—abducted Americans, demands for weapons and supplies by guerrillas, and a daring rescue led by other Americans. Even though the war in Vietnam was heating up rapidly at the time of its release, *Brushfire!* cooled quickly at the box office and quietly slipped into oblivion, becoming but a minor footnote in Paramount's history.

While most of the prewar films were mediocre at best, one of the period pieces did win an Academy Award. It was not a Hollywood production, however, but rather was made in France* and

---

*Despite the long, costly French efforts in Indochina, fewer than two dozen films were made about or set in Vietnam by the French movie industry. Only *Sundays and Cybele* found an American audience. Except for several documentaries, the only French film about the conflict in Vietnam to be generally circulated (on videotape) in the U.S. since the war is the 1980 production *Charlie Bravo*. Set in the final days before the Vietminh-French truce, it has some interesting re-created combat footage but is most remembered because of the patrol leader's performing oral sex on one of his men. Needless to say, *Charlie Bravo* won no Oscars.

won Oscar honors in 1962 as the Best Foreign Language Film. *Sundays and Cybele* focuses on a French aviator recently returned home from Indochina who befriends a twelve-year-old orphan girl. He is plagued by flashbacks about strafing a Vietnamese village and killing a young girl about the same age as his French friend. In addition to being the first film touching upon Vietnam to win an award, *Sundays and Cybele* is also the first to have as its lead character a crazy veteran, complete with flashbacks of atrocities committed in Vietnam.

The last American film about the prewar period spared no expense on cast, story rights, or location. Filmed in Thailand, starring Marlon Brando, and based on the hugely successful novel by William J. Lederer and Eugene Burdick, *The Ugly American* reached the screen in 1963. Because American involvement in Southeast Asia had greatly increased since the book's publication in 1958, little of the movie version resembles the novel. Brando plays the newly arrived American ambassador to the fictional country Sarkhan, which is clearly based on Vietnam. Most of the picture focuses on the lack of understanding by the American officials of the Sarkhan natives and their politics—which ultimately leads to disaster. Brando's best, and most appropriate, line is delivered to his staff when he says, "The only thing clear at all is that there is no clarity."

The pre–Vietnam War film died with the arrival of the war, and to date, Hollywood has made only two efforts to add to the list of films about the period. Featuring an international cast including Anthony Quinn, George Segal, and Claudia Cardinale, the 1966 release *The Lost Command* follows a unit of the French foreign legion from Dien Bien Phu to the revolt in Algiers. The second did not appear until 1985, and it too features a big-name cast led by Tom Hanks and John Candy. Set in 1962, *Volunteers* is a farcical look at Peace Corps volunteers building a bridge in Southeast Asia and dealing with the natives, communist insurgents, and CIA operatives.

With the exception of portions of *The Quiet American* and *The*

More recent developments show renewed interest in Vietnam by the French. In 1992 two French films set in Vietnam, *The Lover* and *Indochine*, were released. *Indochine* was later awarded an Oscar as the year's best foreign film.

Ugly American, all of the pre–Vietnam War films about the region shared the same tenets. In every case, the Americans were the good guys and the communist insurgents and/or Vietnamese bandits were the bad. On the whole, however, the prewar pictures dabbled little in politics, and the only reason for a Vietnam/ Indochina setting was usually its exotic name and location. Regardless of the setting, most of these motion pictures were filmed on Hollywood soundstages and back lots with the occasional scene filmed in the hills surrounding Los Angeles. Only the production staff of *The Quiet American* actually took its cameras to Vietnam to record real street and countryside activities. During the first three decades of action-adventure and romantic-drama movies set in Vietnam, there was little difference from the "Americans as heroes" standard set by J. Stuart Blackton when he filmed the tearing down of a Spanish flag in 1898.

PRE–VIETNAM WAR FILMS

Brushfire! (1962)
Careers (1929)
Charlie Bravo (1980)
China Gate (1957)
Five Gates to Hell (1959)
Jump into Hell (1955)
Lost Command, The (1966)
Lotus Lady (1930)
Quiet American, The (1958)
Red Dust (1932)
Rogue's Regiment (1948)
Saigon (1948)
Somewhere I'll Find You (1942)
Sundays and Cybele (1962)
Ugly American, The (1963)
Volunteers (1985)
Where East Is East (1929)
Yank in Indo-China, A (1952)

6. VIETNAM: WHERE HAVE ALL THE MOVIES GONE?

By 1969, MORE than 350,000 Americans were serving in Vietnam. Three hundred a week were dying, and the total death toll was nearing fifty thousand. Despite those numbers, not a single moving picture about the war reached the screen during that year, nor was any Hollywood studio in production on a Vietnam film. Where the film industry had embraced America's wars and warriors at the height of previous conflicts, servicemen and battles in Vietnam were being ignored.

Hollywood's primary rationale for this inattention was lack of viewer interest and the consequent low profit potential. While the questionable profitability of movies about the war certainly provides a plausible argument for not producing films, it should also be noted that Hollywood of the 1960s was much different from that of the 1940s. Most of the original, powerful studio heads who had maintained rigid systems of star and production control were retired or dead. Many of their replacements—including producers, directors, and actors—were independent, antiestablishment liberals who opposed the war and the United States' involvement in it. Instead of asking how they could "help win the war," Hollywood decision makers mostly turned their backs on the conflict while it raged on the battlefield.

In all fairness, there was another important reason why the actual war seldom made it to the screen while it was ongoing. Modern technology, without any media censorship, delivered real footage of the war itself to the living rooms of America via the nightly television newscasts. Even a movie with the best of intentions would have had trouble competing with daily war news shot on location and delivered for free into American homes.

Whatever the reason or argument, the fact cannot be contested that Vietnam became the first United States war not to dominate, or even to make an impression on, the silver screen during the actual conflict. America's soldiers went off to war from West Coast airfields and seaports and, if fortunate enough to return, were met in the middle of the night by no bands, parades, or movies about their ordeals, triumphs, and heartbreaks.

Despite this lack of enthusiasm, a few films did make their way to the theaters in the 1960s. The list, however, is short and mostly unremarkable. Marshall Thompson, who began his acting career in *The Purple Heart* (1944) as a young air corpsman whose parachute does not open after his bomber is shot down in a raid over Tokyo, directed and starred in the first movie to feature uniformed Americans in Vietnam. Playing a Marine major helicopter pilot in *A Yank in Viet-Nam* (1964), Thompson is shot down by Vietcong gunners. He is captured but saved by a South Vietnamese patrol that also rescues a kidnapped doctor and his daughter. The aviator and the doctor's daughter fall in love and, with the assistance of Marine paratroopers, safely make it back to Saigon.

Although its plot resembles typical B-movie westerns of the period, *A Yank in Viet-Nam* is notable for more than merely being first. The film is the only Hollywood production about the war to be filmed completely in Vietnam. A small production company of Allied Artists personnel journeyed to Saigon, where they hired technicians and the preponderance of the cast from the local Vietnamese film community. Using Saigon streets and markets along with the rice paddies and jungles of the surrounding countryside, the production did not simulate Vietnam but featured the real thing.

Other than to make a few comments on the long combat history of the region, Thompson, as actor and director, did little to explain the politics of the conflict that was increasing in intensity as the movie was shot. However, it was explained that the American forces at the time were in the country by invitation to advise and observe and to fight only when necessary. Throughout the picture, it is made evident that the Americans are welcomed allies of the South Vietnamese in their struggle to defend their freedom against invading communist forces.

A Yank in Viet-Nam reached theaters in late January 1964, when the country was still "Viet what?" to many. It was greeted by tepid reviews and empty theater seats. In a matter of days it was reduced to the lower half of a double bill with Dean Martin's comedy *Who's Been Sleeping in My Bed?*

Undaunted, two years later Thompson attempted once again to bring the Vietnam War to the movie screen by starring in *To the Shores of Hell*. Backed by massive Marine Corps support by way of troops, weapons, helicopters, and landing craft, the film begins with maneuvers at Camp Pendleton, California, in preparation for a unit's deployment to Vietnam. Unlike *A Yank in Viet-Nam*, which was shot entirely in Vietnam, Camp Pendleton provides all the locations for *To the Shores of Hell*, including the beach sites for the Marine landing near Da Nang and later action in the "jungle."

Once the Marines arrive in Vietnam, the plot closely resembles Thompson's earlier movie about the war as he treks into the jungle in order to rescue his doctor brother who is being held prisoner by the Vietcong. Along the way, he is accompanied by brave South Vietnamese and encounters barbaric VC who rape women, kill children, burn orphanages, and torture captives.

The description of the enemy in *To The Shores of Hell* is not the only similarity to movies about earlier wars. Before Thompson's character sails for Vietnam, he walks along the California beach with his beautiful blonde fiancée, who gives him her scarf to wear in combat and promises to wait for him. When he returns, she has kept her promise and they are reunited at a full-scale USMC parade complete with flags flying and a band playing the Marine Corps Hymn several decibels above the rest of the sound track.

Reaching the screen in 1965 was *Operation CIA*, with a then-unknown Burt Reynolds in the lead role. Reynolds played a CIA agent transferred to Saigon to investigate the death of another agent. Before revealing a communist plot to kill everyone in the U.S. Embassy, Reynolds's character manages to get rolled in a massage parlor and ambushed by the Vietcong during a drive through the countryside.* Other than Marines who guard the embassy, and two army captains dressed in khakis who are the target of a terrorist grenade that kills children instead of the officers, the

---

*Filmed in Hong Kong and Thailand, the movie features right-side-drive automobiles that are on the "wrong side" for Vietnam.

U.S. military plays no role in the picture. In fact, the film is mostly a throwback to Vietnam films of the previous decade, in which the country merely provides an exotic locale for a routine spy story.

An English-made film similar to *Operation CIA* was released to American audiences in 1967. *Some May Live* stars Joseph Cotten as a U.S. intelligence officer in Vietnam whose mission is to identify the communist spy in his command. *Some May Live* was obscure at the time of its release and is even more so today. Unlike *To the Shores of Hell* and *Operation CIA*, it is has not been reissued on videotape.

These four pioneer Vietnam films share more than being the only ones of their kind made during the conflict. Each was produced on a low budget, received limited distribution, and sold few tickets at the box office. Only *Some May Live* was shot in color.

It was not until 1968, nearly a decade after the beginning of American involvement in the Vietnam War, that a big-budget ($6.1 million), large-scale, Pentagon-supported* film was made about the conflict. More has likely been written and said about *The Green Berets* than about any other Vietnam film of its time or since— and most of the comments have been negative. Some of the criticism is deserved; much of it is not. Those opposed to the war singled out the warrior for their wrath, and a motion picture supportive of the war's combatants was also an obvious target for their collective objection. *The Green Berets* is unashamedly patriotic, is played by men too old and, in cases including John Wayne, too fat for their parts, and contains quite possibly every war film

---

*Several scripts were submitted to the Department of Defense before and after *The Green Berets*, but either they were considered unsuitable or the producers were unwilling to make appropriate changes to secure military assistance. What the Pentagon was looking for by way of films was not secret. The requirements were outlined in Department of Defense Instruction 5410.15, "Delineation of DoD Audio-Visual Public Affairs Responsibilities and Policies." This document, dated November 3, 1966, stated in Paragraph V, "The production, program, project, or assistance will benefit the DoD or otherwise be in the national interest based on consideration of the following factors: 1. Authenticity of the portrayal of military operations, or historical incidents, persons or places depicting a true interpretation of military life. 2. Compliance with accepted standards of dignity and propriety in the industry."

cliché ever conceived. Flaws, such as the sun setting in the east and the scrub pine forest of southern Georgia standing in for South Vietnamese jungle, make it that much more vulnerable to criticism. Still, like a stale crumb of bread to a starving man, *The Green Berets* is dear to most veterans' hearts simply because it is all they have.

Based loosely on the Robin Moore novel and the Barry Sadler song by the same titles, *The Green Berets* made it to the screen not because of any effort by a Hollywood studio but because of the support and diligence of John Wayne.* The actor's personal letter to President Johnson secured the support of the Department of Defense in what amounted to a blank check for the use of military advisers, equipment, weapons, shooting locations, and personnel.

Wayne claimed that he wanted to make the film strictly for entertainment; however, his hawkish views on the conflict were well known. "The Duke" had also made an extremely successful career in Hollywood playing military men in the Old West cavalry and as an officer and NCO in World War II and Korean Conflict films. At one time or another, he had acted the part of a member of every branch of the armed services, including the Seabees. Wayne's career really took off during World War II, when he won his spurs not on any real battlefield but on the back lots of Hollywood. The hottest action seen in the Good War by Wayne, who conveniently was able to avoid the largest draft in the history of the country, was under stage lights.

Early filming of *The Green Berets* at Fort Benning was so successful that Wayne and his production company decided to make the rest of the picture there instead of moving to a more tropical jungle setting. The result has been compared to a cavalry-and-Indian film and to the movies of World War II. Although those observations are delivered as harsh criticism by graybeard college cinema professors and deskbound newspaper reporters, those are the same reasons why many Vietnam veterans and their supporters have fond feelings for the picture. The similarities of *The Green Berets* to the cavalry riding to the rescue, or to World War II

---

*Interestingly, the movie, novel, and song share more than just a topic and a title. Each was the only work in its medium to earn popular approval among American consumers while the war was actually fought.

heroics, are images too often missing from films about the Vietnam War.

In addition to its uniqueness in its portrayal of the Vietnam War, the opening scenes of *The Green Berets* provide dialogue that well defines the feeling about the conflict by those who fought it. This "minority opinion" was also shared by a vast number of other Americans—at least during the early years of the war.

The Green Berets opens with a public demonstration by a Special Forces A Team of their functions and capabilities. Following a description of their training and skills, the team fields questions from its audience.* The initial question is directed to Green Beret Sergeant Muldoon (Aldo Ray) by a news reporter who asks, "Why is the United States waging this useless war?"

Muldoon responds most accurately, "Foreign policy decisions are not made by the military. A soldier goes where he is told to go, fights whom he is told to fight."

Another reporter (David Janssen) follows up with a question to a different member of the team, "Do you agree with that, Sergeant McGee? That the Green Beret is just a military robot with no personal feelings?"

McGee (Raymond St. Jacques) ignores the implication by the reporter that he should feel differently because he is black and calmly responds that soldiers do indeed have feelings and do their best to control themselves even though the Vietcong are guilty of the "extermination of the civilian leadership, the intentional murder and torture of innocent women and children . . ."

A woman reporter, with a look of disdain, interrupts, saying, "Yes, I guess horrible things happen in war, but that doesn't mean they need us or even want us."

With seemingly no reaction to the comment, McGee continues, "Let me put it in terms we can all understand. If this same thing happened in the United States, every mayor in every city would be murdered. Every teacher, every professor, every senator, every member of the House of Representatives, and their families. But

---

*Anyone who ever wrote or reported that uniformed members of the military did not agree with the content of the film or were embarrassed by it, never sat in a post theater at Fort Benning or Fort Bragg or others around the world and heard the wild cheering that accompanied much of the movie—especially the opening scenes.

in spite of this, there's always some little fellow out there willing to stand up and take the place of those who've been decimated. They need us . . . and they want us."

By this time, the audience, with the exception of the reporters, is responding positively to the Special Forces NCOs. A woman in the crowd, who introduces herself as a housewife, remarks, "It's strange that we never read of this in the newspapers."

Sergeant Muldoon again takes center stage as he answers, "Well, that's newspapers for you, ma'am; you could fill volumes with what you don't read in them."

After the audience stops laughing, Janssen wades back in with another question. "That's sometimes very true, Sergeant. But how do you know we should be fighting for this present government? They've had no free elections. They have no constitution. Six months ago, a committee was appointed to form a constitution— still no constitution."

Muldoon stands a bit taller as he answers, "The school I went to taught us that the thirteen colonies, with proper and educated leadership, all with the same goal in mind, after the Revolutionary War, took from 1776 to 1787, eleven years of peaceful effort, before they came up with a paper that all thirteen colonies could sign—our present Constitution."

The audience again applauds, but Janssen is not yet finished as he expounds, "There are still a lot of people who believe this is simply a war between the Vietnamese people. It's their war, let them handle it."

Muldoon, who has lost a bit of his cool by now, answers by slamming weapons, ammunition, and equipment on a table as he explains their origins in the Soviet Union, Red China, and their allies and notes that each piece was captured from the enemy in Vietnam. Muldoon concludes, "No sir, it doesn't take a lead weight to fall on me or a hit from one of those weapons to recognize that what is involved here is communist domination of the world."

Despite prejudicial reviews, protests outside several theaters, and the Hollywood wisdom that Vietnam films would not sell, *The Green Berets* was an immediate box-office success. During the first six months of its release, it made $8.7 million in revenues. It continues today to produce profits through frequent television airings and videotape rentals.

Unfortunately, Hollywood ignored the success of *The Green Berets* and avoided controversy on further production of movies about the war. Instead, cameras were focused on the antiwar movement at home, and for the first time in American history, the film industry began a concentrated effort not only to make the war a villain, but also to portray the conflict's warriors and their supporters as equally evil. It is a trend that continued throughout the war and is little changed in present times.

THE WAR DURING THE WAR

Green Berets, The (1968)
Operation CIA (1965)
Some May Live (1967)
To the Shores of Hell (1966)
Yank in Viet-Nam, A (1964)

7. HELL NO! WE WON'T GO: THE PROTEST FILMS

ANTIWAR MOVIES ARE not a phenomenon that originated with the Vietnam Conflict. Before both world wars, films were produced that supported neutrality and the benefits of nonviolent means of settling disputes. The pictures that preceded the Great War are generally labeled pacifist films, while those of later periods are collectively labeled antiwar movies. After decent intervals of several years, antiwar films followed both world wars, with the general focus being the horrors and personal sacrifice of warfare.

A common element of both world wars was that the minute the United States entered the hostilities, antiwar film production ended. Without dissent, the film industry stepped forward and asked, "How can we help win the war?" rather than doing anything to protest the conflict or to disrupt the morale of the troops and those who stayed home. Vietnam, a very different kind of war in many aspects, certainly did not enjoy the kind of support Hollywood had given previous wars and warriors.

From 1965 to 1975, more than forty movies with a central anti–Vietnam War theme reached the screen. These featured deserters or draft evaders as the movies' heroes. Half again that many (more than twenty) were released in the years following the fall of Saigon. Some of these films were produced by independent companies and had limited budgets, but the vast majority were made by the same major Hollywood studios that had amassed their fortunes featuring the brave, heroic fighters of the Good War and their triumphant homecoming.

The majority of the anti-Vietnam films were released not before or after the conflict but while the war was being fought. During the period 1968 to 1970, when more than a thousand Americans were dying each month, Hollywood produced at least one antiwar/protest film every thirty days. Most of these films focused on glamorizing the protests on the campuses of the United States,* supporting the efforts of draft resisters and evaders, and making heroes of deserters from the armed forces.

Four major studio productions of 1970, *Getting Straight, R.P.M., The Strawberry Statement,* and *Zabriskie Point,* provide an excellent look into the campus protest movement on film. In *The Strawberry Statement,* students take over a college administration building to protest the school's receipt of defense research money and the presence of an ROTC detachment on campus. While pretty well trashing the building they occupy, the students sing "Give Peace a Chance" as they pose in front of posters of Cuban communist revolutionary Che Guevara and communist Chinese leader Mao Tse-tung. The students also unite with neighboring militant blacks who are protesting the loss of a children's playground to university expansion. An American flag provides the backdrop for the finale as the students burn candles and sing while the police and National Guard assault them with nightsticks and tear gas.

A similar theme is followed in *Zabriskie Point* as a student, who may or may not have killed a cop during a protest riot, is hunted down and killed by policemen. The student describes himself as a "revolutionary" and compares himself to "Old John Brown" of pre–Civil War notoriety.

In *R.P.M.* (revolutions per minute), protesting students succeed in getting their choice of a laid-back professor (Anthony Quinn) appointed as university president after they demand the ouster of the incumbent. Quinn lets them down, however, by calling in the police to break up their protest when they threaten to destroy a valuable computer.

Getting Straight opens with an inscription on an apple stating, "There is no gravity, the earth sucks." Elliott Gould plays a graduate student who tries to get his life straight and join the faculty establishment. However, he soon sides with protesting students against his stodgy fellow instructors and administrators. Gould

---

*North Vietnamese officials frequently stated that they would win the war not on the battlefield but on the campuses and in the streets of America.

chides the school's and the country's leadership because they are "a bunch of maniacs sending kids to drop napalm on people." Co-star Candice Bergen encourages Gould to join the protesters, claiming, "A man that can't believe in a cause can't believe in himself."

Deserters from the American military provide another source of heroes for the anti–Vietnam War films. In *Deserter USA* (1969) and *Georgia, Georgia* (1972), actual deserters are cast in the fictional roles of soldiers who have fled the war zone. The reasons for their desertion are credited to atrocities they observed or were forced to participate in, or to an overall feeling that the war is unjust. A deserter seeking refuge in Japan in *Summer Soldiers* (1972) explains that he quit the war because a Vietcong prisoner was being tortured and "there was nothing I could do."

The deserter-as-hero theme is expanded to include a love story in *Two People* (1973), starring Peter Fonda (brother of Jane) and Lindsay Wagner (the future Bionic Woman). Fonda, on the run in North Africa after deserting his unit in Vietnam, romances high-fashion model Wagner across several continents before deciding he must return to the United States and turn himself in. Wagner agrees with his desertion but concurs that he must return home. With a crescendo of background music, Fonda declares, "I'm tired of running. . . . I want my life back."

Two People was not, of course, Fonda's first antiwar, anti-establishment movie. In 1969, he roared onto the screen and into the hearts of protesters everywhere in *Easy Rider*. As Captain America, Fonda wears a large American flag on his motorcycle jacket. According to the film, Fonda's and partner Dennis Hopper's characters are the "heroes of our time." Surprisingly, this "bible film" of the alienated-youth movement makes no direct mention of the war in Vietnam. However, when supporting actor Jack Nicholson says, "This used to be a hell of a good country," there can be no doubt in any viewer's mind that he means "before Vietnam."

The most popular, or at least the largest, subgenre of protest film were movies about draft resistance and evasion. These pictures feature draft protests in general, the fear of young men awaiting the draft, evasion techniques such as fleeing to Canada, and methods of beating the draft at the induction center. Oddly, especially when compared to patriotic scenes of men voluntarily marching off to combat in films about earlier wars, the draft, the military, and the Establishment are treated as the enemy in every sense of the word, and the young men out to beat the system and avoid their legal responsibilities are hailed as heroes.

Much of the draft resistance shown in Vietnam protest films is fairly passive. Eligible young men fret over the possibility of being drafted and weigh their options for avoiding conscription. However, this is not true in all protest movies. In *The Edge* (1968), a resister is so angry about the war and the draft that he plans to assassinate President Johnson to "make him pay for all the killing he's done" in Vietnam. Other pictures, such as *Cowards* (1970) and *The Trial of the Catonsville Nine* (1972), show protesters breaking into draft board offices to destroy records.

Legitimate methods of beating the draft, such as marriage, are covered in *Jenny* (1970), and the value of student deferments is mentioned in *Getting Straight* (1970) and *Alice's Restaurant* (1969). Faking mental or physical ailments at the induction center as a last-ditch effort is another popular protest film story line.

Sometimes these desperate measures were unsuccessful and the potential draftee still had to head north to Canada or report to basic training.* In *Greetings* (1968), which featured Robert De Niro in one of his first starring roles, a potential draftee attempts to beat conscription by challenging a group of black militants to a fight in hopes they will break his legs. When this fails, he poses as a homosexual, and when that too is unsuccessful, he assumes the role of a racist Nazi in hopes of being turned down. None of this works, and a final scene shows the young man applying for a passport to leave the country.

Along with the usual ruses to beat the draft, the induction centers are similar in all protest films. The sergeants are fat, ignorant, sadistic brutes; the officers are weak, effeminate martinets. All people in uniform are referred to as baby killers and village burners. In *The Gay Deceivers* (1969), two young friends claim to be homosexuals to secure a draft exemption only to have the captain and sergeant in charge of the induction center also revealed as

*Although a desire to avoid personal dangers and discomforts presented by service in Vietnam was certainly the primary motivation behind most draft resisters' actions, the rigors and hardships of basic training were no doubt other factors in their draft dodging.

gay. A "crazy act" fools the induction center staff into thinking a draftee is insane in *Drive, He Said* (1971), but later the draftee is unable to prove he is sane after all.

Several of these antidraft themes are woven together in the 1969 release *Alice's Restaurant*. Based on Arlo Guthrie's song about his real-life experiences, the film opens with the singer (playing himself) attending college in Montana as a means of draft deferment. When he gets kicked out of school, he returns to Massachusetts and is soon drafted. At his induction physical, Guthrie is none too unhappily informed that he is unfit for military service because of a previous criminal conviction for littering. Amazingly, both Guthrie's arresting officer and presiding judge agreed to appear in the film as themselves.

Other protest films do not treat draft evaders quite so nicely, but nonetheless they remain the pictures' heroes. *Windflowers* (1968) begins and ends with the killing of a draft dodger by the police and FBI. In between, the young man explains he is running from the draft because he is opposed to killing and being killed.

Journey through Rosebud (1972) follows an on-the-run draft evader who wanders onto an Indian reservation as he sings "America the Beautiful." He is befriended by a Vietnam veteran, whom the dodger repays by sleeping with the vet's former wife. The film concludes with a gang of young Indians severely beating the draft dodger; however, the beating is more for his being white than for his political beliefs or sexual conduct.

The antiwar/protest films of the late 1960s and early 1970s shared several other characteristics. Many, such as *The Activist* (1969), *Captain Milkshake* (1970), *David Holzman's Diary* (1968), and *Medium Cool* (1969) (for a complete list, see the end of this chapter), used actual footage of demonstrations, riots, and speeches from politicians and protesters. Real news footage of dead Vietnamese civilians and of GIs burning hooches was also included with explanations that atrocities were standard operating procedure for the U.S. military.

In addition to their political statements, the antiwar/protest films provided excellent starts for young actors and actresses who would become Hollywood's stars of the future. Candice Bergen, Robert De Niro, Harrison Ford, and Michael Douglas are but a few (see the complete list at the end of this chapter) who got their movie starts playing protesters, draft dodgers, and supporters of the antiwar movement.

While most actors and directors tried to deliver their antiwar messages as part of an overall entertainment package, other films, in the form of documentaries, took a more blatant approach. Dozens of these antiwar/protest pictures were produced, usually in 16mm format, for showings on campuses and in community theaters. Some of these documentaries were made in the United States using American sources; some were made in the U.S. using film footage supplied by North Vietnam, Cuba, and East Germany; and others were made in North Vietnam or in one of the countries that supported the communist cause. Many of these documentaries made their way to mainstream movie houses and to television. Several were so well received that they were later transferred to videotape to enable them to more easily deliver their propagandized, one-sided message about the war to future generations.

Director Emile de Antonio opens his 1968 documentary, *In the Year of the Pig*, by comparing the efforts of the Vietcong to those of American Revolutionary War soldiers. Ho Chi Minh is praised as the "greatest patriot of this century," and American university professors, politicians, journalists, and church leaders are shown praising the Vietnamese communist forces and condemning the U.S. military and the South Vietnamese. U.S. and ARVN forces are pictured allegedly committing atrocities. When General Westmoreland is shown stating that prisoners are not being mistreated, the screen fades to torture scenes. The documentary goes so far as to speculate that "the Vietcong may be contributing to world peace by ending the arrogance of power of the United States."

Hearts and Minds (1974), directed by Peter Davis, continues in the same spirit of "a little truth can camouflage a bigger lie." Early in the film, American Daniel Ellsberg is quoted, "We aren't *on* the wrong side, we *are* the wrong side." As in *In the Year of the Pig*, the Vietcong and North Vietnamese are shown as heroic freedom fighters while the American military is portrayed as brutal killers who routinely commit atrocities and pursue genocide. Insight into the feelings of Hollywood toward the Vietnam War was revealed when *Hearts and Minds* was awarded an Oscar as 1974's Best Documentary—despite its poor production quality, inferior writing, and confused editing that make it difficult to follow.

An earlier Oscar-winning documentary, much more deserving of the award, was *Woodstock* in 1970. Music, the counterculture, drugs, the antiwar movement, and more music are included in this story of the three-day 1969 music festival near Bethel, New York, that provided a name for a generation. Although music and just having fun were the real focus of the festival and much of the documentary, the war in Southeast Asia played an important role. Country Joe and the Fish perform "Fixin' to Die Rag," and performers and audience members alike express their feelings about the Vietnam War. The music is great, the documentary well done—and the only thing missing is an acknowledgment that without Vietnam, there would have been no Woodstock.

A final documentary is worth mentioning more for its stars, Jane Fonda and Donald Sutherland, than for its content or production values. During late 1971, Fonda, Sutherland, and company toured the Pacific Rim putting on a stage show for American servicemen in Hawaii, Okinawa, the Philippines, and Japan called "Free the Army" (or "Fuck the Army," as it was more commonly known). Including songs such as "America Lies" and references to the military as prison, the show was filmed and released as *F.T.A.* in 1972.

The evidence of Hollywood's embrace of antiwar/protest themes during the actual conflict is seen in far more films than those linked directly to Vietnam. Although set during the Korean Conflict, the irreverent *M*A*S*H* (1970) is as much about, and inspired by, the war in Vietnam as any film ever made. Vietnam's impact on Hollywood had great influence on movies about other eras and wars that changed former enemies of the U.S. into heroes and former heroes into villains. The 1972 film *Ulzana's Raid* shows Apache Indians in the roles of sympathetic guerrillas but U.S. cavalrymen as bloodthirsty killers. *Little Big Man* (1970) portrays American soldiers as inept fools who rape, murder, and destroy entire Indian villages before being killed, to the man, by the noble red men. Another 1970 film, *Soldier Blue*, again shows American cavalrymen slaughtering women and children and burning their homes. In the same movie, Candice Bergen lectures a soldier in tone and words that closely resemble those used by her later character in the hit television series "Murphy Brown." Bergen's character comments about soldiers, calling them "brave lads, coming out here to kill themselves a real live Indian . . . putting up their forts in a country they got no claim to. What the hell do you expect the Indians to do? Sit on their butts?"

Another picture, *Johnny Got His Gun*, appeared in 1971 after more than thirty years of effort to bring the 1939 novel by Dalton Trumbo, which many consider the most powerful antiwar book ever written, to the screen. Not until the Vietnam era was Hollywood willing to support a film about a World War I soldier who loses all four limbs as well as his speech, sight, hearing, and smell.

Even more remarkable than the influence of the war on movies not directly related to Vietnam are those films that totally ignore the conflict. One of the most highly acclaimed motion pictures of the 1960s, *The Graduate* (1967), featured Dustin Hoffman in his first major role and earned director Mike Nichols an Oscar. Hoffman's character, the son of upper-class parents and fresh out of college, is advised that the future is in "plastics." Other than deciding on his employment, his only real problem is his sleeping with an older woman while he falls in love with her daughter. One problem that is never mentioned or confronted is the draft. This ultimate movie of the 60s fails to make any mention whatsoever of the decade's major event—the Vietnam War.

The fall of Saigon and the end of the war in 1975 did not bring an end to antiwar/protest films. Although the number of releases declined, the same themes continued: righteous protesters, heroic draft resisters, persecuted deserters, and evil men in uniform.

Many of the postwar protest films attempt to create a nostalgic look at the period, to re-create the entire "sixties experience" in a ninety-minute movie. For films such as *'68* and *1969*, both released in 1988, the era even provides the titles. In *1969* a character played by Kiefer Sutherland (son of Donald) says, "It's not my war, it's bullshit." A friend (Robert Downey, Jr.) of Sutherland's character is so afraid of the draft after flunking out of college that he breaks into a draft board to destroy his records. He is caught and jailed. When Sutherland's brother is killed in Vietnam the entire town unites in protest and marches to the jail to demand the release of Downey. At the cemetery, the dead soldier's mother (Mariette Hartley) refuses to accept the American flag from her dead son's casket.

In *'68*, the tribulations of a Hungarian refugee family living in San Francisco are played out against protests in the streets and war news on television and the radio. When the oldest son is drafted, he says things are no better in the United States than they were in Eastern Europe. To avoid serving his new country, he professes to be a homosexual at his induction physical and kisses the army major in charge to prove his claim.

A similar incident at an induction center is included in the 1979 screen version of the musical *Hair*. A board of officers interviews nude draftees and breaks out into a song about "boys" as they wink and flirt. Much more accurate scenes about the draft are shown in *A Small Circle of Friends* (1980), with actual footage of the first draft lottery and a re-creation of Harvard students responding to their birthday numbers being high or low. Screams of anguish and fear are the reactions of the losers of what the students call "Vietnam Bingo." When one of the friends gets a low number and is drafted, a sympathetic doctor is found to falsify his medical records to show a history of asthma. Another of the friends, a former Eagle Scout, responds to the draft and war by going underground and organizing a group to bomb government buildings.

The deserter/draft dodger also continues to be a hero of postwar anti-Vietnam films. In *Wolf Lake* (1978), a deserter, who fled the war because of the killings he witnessed of children, women, and old men, hides in Canada only to become the prey of a hunting expedition of American rednecks, led by Rod Steiger, who do not like cowards. In *White Nights* (1985), Gregory Hines plays another deserter who fled the war zone because of the murder and rape of civilians. Although he claims, "I was a patriot," he provides antiwar statements to members of the world press after his defection to the Soviet Union. Later in the film he proves he really is a hero by assisting the redefection of a Russian dancer who has been detained in Moscow.

In *Running on Empty* (1988), Judd Hirsh and Christine Lahti play a couple who have been on the run for fourteen years for their part in blowing up a military-related research lab and leaving a janitor blind and paralyzed. They explain their protest as "an act of conscience to stop the war." Pursued by FBI agents, the couple and their two sons have to move frequently and assume new identities. Assistance is still provided by members of their old underground network. At each new stop they continue their activism by establishing food co-ops and organizing protests against nuclear-waste dumps. At the film's conclusion, Hirsh's character tells his son, "Go out there and make a difference; your mother and I tried."

Although the number is slowly decreasing, the antiwar/protest film is apparently going to remain a Hollywood staple. As early as 1978, the film industry was setting the trend for the future by filming nostalgic looks back at the glory days of the protest movement. In *The Big Fix*, Richard Dreyfuss plays a former sixties radical who, ten years after the war, drives a VW, smokes dope, and cries when he sees films about protests. He and his friends still occasionally enjoy chanting, "Hey, hey, LBJ, how many kids did you kill today?" One of his radical friends brags about what Hollywood has shown in dozens of films during and since the war: "We were the cult heroes."

ANTIWAR/PROTEST FILMS

Activist, The (1969)
Alice's Restaurant (1969)
Big Fix, The (1978)
Big Wednesday (1978)
Billy Jack (1971)
Blue Movie (1969)
Captain Milkshake (1970)
Cowards (1970)
David Holzman's Diary (1968)
Deserter USA (1969)
Deserters (1983)
Drive, He Said (1971)
Easy Rider (1969)
Edge, The (1968)
Explosion (1970)
Fandango (1984)
Four Friends (1981)
Friendly Fire (1979)
F.T.A. (1972)
Gay Deceivers, The (1969)
Georgia, Georgia (1972)
Getting Straight (1970)
Graduate, The (1967)

Greatest, The (1977)
Greetings (1968)
Hail, Hero! (1969)
Hair (1979)
Head (1968)
Hearts and Minds (1974)
Homer (1970)
In the Year of the Pig (1968)
Jenny (1970)
Joe (1970)
Journey through Rosebud (1972)
Kent State (1981)
Line, The (1980)
Masculine Feminine (1966)
Medium Cool (1969)
Memory of Justice (1976)
Model Shop (1969)
More American Graffiti (1979)
1969 (1988)
No More Excuses (1968)
Nude Restaurant (1967)
Our Winning Season (1978)
Outside In (1972)
Parades (1972)
Prism (1971)
Proud Men (1987)
Purple Haze (1982)
R.P.M. (1970)
Running on Empty (1988)
'68 (1988)
Small Circle of Friends, A (1980)
Sneakers (1992)
Strawberry Statement, The (1970)
Summer Soldiers (1972)
Tell Me Lies (1968)
Thank You, Aunt (1967)
Trial of Billy Jack, The (1974)
Trial of the Catonsville Nine, The (1972)
Two People (1973)
Vixen (1968)

White Nights (1985)
Windflowers (1968)
Wolf Lake (1978)
Woodstock (1970)
Zabriskie Point (1970)

FUTURE STARS WHO BEGAN IN ANTIWAR/PROTEST FILMS

Alan Alda: *Jenny* (1970)
Ellen Barkin: *Kent State* (1981)
Dirk Benedict: *Georgia, Georgia* (1972)
Candice Bergen: *Getting Straight* (1970)
Karen Black: *Easy Rider* (1969)
Kim Darby: *The Strawberry Statement* (1970)
Robert De Niro: *Greetings* (1968)
Michael Douglas: *Hail Hero* (1969) and *Summertree* (1971)
Peter Fonda: *Easy Rider* (1969) and *Two People* (1973)
Harrison Ford: *Getting Straight* (1970) and *Zabriskie Point* (1970)
Terri Garr: *Head* (1968)
Elliot Gould: *Getting Straight* (1970)
Dennis Hopper: *Easy Rider* (1969)
Jack Nicholson: *Easy Rider* (1969)
Lindsay Wagner: *Two People* (1973)

8. COMING HOME:
THE NOT-SO-WELCOME BACK

ALONG WITH THE seemingly endless number of antiwar/
protest films produced during the conflict, Hollywood also provided American and world audiences with its versions of what to
expect when the Vietnam veterans returned home. The returning
Vietnam vet, according to the movies, arrived back in the States at
best disturbed by his war experiences and at worst unable to cease
destroying and killing.

Years before the war was anywhere near concluded, Hollywood
was already depicting the veteran, usually still clad in his faded
army field jacket, as dependent on drugs and alcohol and incompetent to sustain relationships or employment. The veteran is presented in motion pictures as bitter toward the war, his officers,
and his country. He cannot sleep at night or find peace when he
is awake. He is plagued by flashbacks and nightmares and now has
a new enemy—himself.

The initial Vietnam-veteran coming-home films made it quite
apparent that Hollywood had little idea of what to do with the returning warriors. Since the early 1950s, the most loathsome, angry,
and brutal movie characters had been members of motorcycle
gangs—so the early films about veterans arriving home had them
riding motorcycles, either as members of, or fighting against, outlaw biker gangs.

First to reach the screen was the appropriately titled (at least in
Hollywood's opinion) *Born Losers* (1967), with Tom Laughlin as
Billy Jack, a role he would repeat in a series of later films. The
opening narration describes the veteran: "He had just returned
from the war. One of those Green Beret Rangers—a trained killer,
people were to say later." Billy Jack ends up being the only person

in a small California town willing to stand up against a biker gang that is terrorizing the citizens. Despite his help, the townspeople do not care much for the vet and refer to him as crazy. The bikers agree, calling him a psychopath.

A year later, the 1968 release *Angels from Hell* had a Vietnam veteran returning from the war and organizing his own motorcycle gang. Rebelling against all authority and particularly angry at the Establishment that sent him off to war, the vet is soon taking over other gangs, by means of beatings and bloodshed, and uniting them in a campaign against the police. The vet's girlfriend tells him, "You're insane." All of this "badness" is, of course, not allowed to prevail—the film concludes with a deputy sheriff's killing the vet.

During the closing days of 1969, still another Vietnam-veteran-versus-motorcycle-gang film reached the theaters. The plot of *Satan's Sadists* is simple—a motorcycle gang angers a vet, and he spends the remainder of the film hunting the members down one by one and killing them. His methods include slashing with knives, drowning in toilet bowls, and assaulting with a rattlesnake. *Satan's Sadists*, like its two motorcycle-film predecessors, focuses on the extreme violence of a veteran who uses the destructive skills learned in Vietnam in response to his inability to adjust to his homecoming.

In addition to violent, crazy Vietnam veterans, these first three coming-home films also share the commonality of being produced and released by relatively small, minor film companies. The first major Hollywood studio to release a coming-home film was, ironically, the same studio that made *The Green Berets*. In 1969 Warner Brothers brought to the screen *The Big Bounce*, starring Ryan O'Neal in his first leading role. The veteran played by O'Neal opens the film by clubbing a fellow baseball player with a bat over a disputed call. He later admits that he has been "drifting" since his discharge and supplements his wages as a migrant produce picker by breaking and entering. Although O'Neal does not wear a field jacket, he frequently lugs an army duffel bag containing his few possessions.

Two more Vietnam-veteran/motorcycle films, each with a slightly different twist, appeared in 1971. In *The Hard Ride* and *Chrome and Hot Leather*, veterans are the victims of biker violence. Robert Fuller stars in *The Hard Ride* as a Marine escorting the body of a buddy home from Vietnam. The friend's old motorcycle gang does not take kindly to Fuller's trying to get them to go to the funeral and are even less happy that he has a letter saying the dead man's custom cycle is bequeathed to him. After many bloody fights, Fuller's character is killed by the bikers, and the motorcyclists ride into the sunset.

Chrome and Hot Leather begins with the fiancée of a Green Beret sergeant being killed by a motorcycle gang. The sergeant, accompanied by three fellow Vietnam veterans, goes after the bikers and brings them to justice. This film is extremely unusual in that the veterans do not kill or seriously harm any of the bikers and go out of their way to insure a deathless capture. Also not in character with the genre is the fact that the four vets are all reasonably well adjusted and are proud of their Vietnam service.

With the exception of *Chrome and Hot Leather*, the only picture made during the war that remotely shows a veteran as a hero is *Vanishing Point*—and it is quite a stretch to find anything positive in the portrayal. *Vanishing Point* (1971) features a recently returned Medal of Honor winner's attempt, for no explained reason, to race his car from Denver to San Francisco in fifteen hours. Along the way, he garners the support of a disk jockey and the residents of the small towns he speeds through with an army of police in pursuit. The authorities say of the vet, "This guy's nuts," and apparently they are correct, because in the final scene the former soldier deliberately crashes his car into a barricade and dies with a smile on his face.

Neither *Chrome and Hot Leather* nor *Vanishing Point* would establish any trends in Hollywood's portrayal of Vietnam veterans. The revelation in 1969 of the massacre by American soldiers of Vietnamese civilians in the village of My Lai provided Hollywood a focus that extended beyond motorcycles in showing the returning veteran. From 1969 onward, and up to today, this single atrocity has provided the film industry the impetus to picture the returning veteran as a disturbed person who often cannot stop the murder, rape, and mayhem that were supposedly a part of his life in Vietnam.

In the 1970 production *Jud*, an acquaintance of a newly arrived-home vet remarks, "If you ask me, they're all killers." Another film released the same year, *The Ravager*, features a veteran so disturbed that he is kept in an army rehabilitation hospital for six months after he comes home from Vietnam. The treatment does little good, however, because he goes on a rampage of rape and murder as soon as he is discharged.

Major Hollywood personalities joined the "returning vets are killers" trend. Elia Kazan, famed director of A *Streetcar Named Desire* and *On the Waterfront*, put up his own money and provided his Connecticut farm as a shooting location to bring *The Visitors* to the screen in 1972. The plot of Kazan's picture has two veterans, just released from prison for raping and killing a Vietnamese woman, hunting down the man who testified against them. When they find him, they beat him nearly to death and sexually assault his wife.

Another film released in 1972, *My Old Man's Place*, spotlights three Vietnam veterans who continue to rape and murder after they return to northern California. Although fairly routine in delivering what had become the usual Hollywood message, i.e., that American soldiers were murderers and deviates in Vietnam and will continue to be when they come home, this movie is remarkable for a mostly unknown cast that would go on to bigger and better things. In addition to the well-established character actor Arthur Kennedy, the film features Michael Moriarity and William Devane.

Two more 1972 movies took the violent returning vet to new heights—or rather depths. In the horror film *Deathdream*, a soldier reported killed in Vietnam shows up at his parents' home and proceeds to murder his family, friends, and neighbors. Only his own decaying flesh stops the orgy of death, and the film concludes with the veteran's crawling into an open grave.

Welcome Home, Soldier Boys takes a bit more direct approach. Four Green Berets, just back from Vietnam and discharged from the army, begin a cross-country car trip. Along the way, they gang rape a young girl and throw her from their speeding automobile. At a stop for food, a fellow diner remarks to a friend about what he thinks the vets did in Vietnam: "Shit, you watch television, all they do is kill the damn civilians." During another conversation, one of the Green Berets, who admits to killing 113 people, is asked, "Is all that killing hard?" He responds, "Yeah, in the beginning, but I got better at it." A girl listening to the conversation exclaims, "Then you're a killer, a killer," to which the veteran answers, "That's kinda what I've been thinking." The vets later stop for gas in Hope,* New Mexico, and get into a disagreement with the station owner. They kill him and then proceed to rape, kill, and burn until the entire town is destroyed. The film concludes with the four dressed in their Vietnam uniforms, waiting to fight the National Guard.

Black soldiers receive a bit more attention from Hollywood in the coming-home films than they do in other Vietnam films. While black Americans are included in all Vietnam War movie subgenres, their roles are usually minor. Hollywood's exploitation of the black militant and civil rights movements during the 1960s and 1970s did, however, include several films about returning black veterans.

In *Slaughter* (1972), ex-football player Jim Brown, in the title role, portrays a former Green Beret captain who does not like being reminded of his former rank or of his Vietnam service. Nevertheless, when he discovers the Mafia is responsible for the deaths of his parents, he uses the killing skills he learned in Vietnam to stack up bodies on two continents as he pursues the guilty mobsters.

A black vet in *Gordon's War* (1973) comes home to find his neighborhood has been taken over by junkies and pushers—many of whom are also Vietnam veterans. Proclaiming that he will clean up his old block in a manner "just like the Nam," he proceeds to gleefully break the legs of one opponent and kill anyone else who gets in his way. In *Black Gunn* (1972), black Vietnam vets join former convicts to steal money in order to procure guns, ammunition, and explosives to "take on the man" in a people's revolution "that could make Watts look like Disneyland." The ultimate skills and worth of the returning black veteran are shown in the story of *Mean Johnny Barrows* (1976), in which a vet is recruited by rival Mafia families as a contract killer because of the talents he acquired in Vietnam.

The only motion picture made during the war to make any hon-

---

*A place called Hope was popular long before the 1992 presidential campaign and election of Bill Clinton. Two other Vietnam movies feature a Hope, but neither are in Arkansas. In addition to the Hope in *Welcome Home, Soldier Boys*, a Pacific Northwest town by the same name is where Rambo's troubles begin in *First Blood*. Still another Hope, in northern California, is featured in the TV movie *The New Healers*.

est statement about returning black veterans was the 1971 release *The Bus Is Coming*. Produced by a black-owned film company, the movie follows a vet who is torn between joining militants and helping the police as he investigates the murder of his brother. Interestingly, of all the films featuring black veteran characters, *The Bus Is Coming* is the only one not yet released on videotape.

Production of films about returning vets, regardless of race, and movies about any aspect of the war slowed with the fall of Saigon in 1975. In 1978, the multi-Oscar-winning *Coming Home* renewed Hollywood's confidence that movies about troubled Vietnam veterans meant profits at the box office. *Coming Home* focuses on three Vietnam veterans associated with a character played by Jane Fonda—her Marine Corps officer husband, her disabled lover, and the brother of a friend also married to a Marine.

The friend's brother is a patient in a VA hospital psycho ward and refuses to talk about his brief tour in Vietnam. Everyone around him asks. "What did he see?" No one finds out because the confused young man commits suicide by injecting air into one of his veins. The husband (played by Bruce Dern) of Fonda's character goes to Vietnam to further his military career but is disturbed by what he sees there—"My men were chopping heads off." When he returns home, he is decorated for bravery but asks, "How can they give you a medal for war they don't want you to fight?" One of his last comments before killing himself is simply "I'm fucked."

Fonda's character's lover, played by Jon Voight, whom she meets while her husband is in Vietnam, is disabled from his war wounds and uses a wheelchair. He is bitter about being paralyzed and about the war in general. In protest he chains himself to the gate of a Marine Corps Recruit Depot and later gives impassioned antiwar speeches at high schools. His basic message is "I'm a bit smarter now than when I went [to Vietnam]. There is a choice to be made here."

Although Hollywood has focused on other subjects related to the Vietnam War since the release of *Coming Home*, the returning veteran has remained a popular movie topic, with at least one of this subgenre appearing yearly up to the present time. Most of these films continue with the stereotypical disturbed veteran who cannot readjust. Typical of the movies that have continued the coming-home theme are *The Ninth Configuration* (1980), in which a narrator opens the picture by explaining, "Toward the end of the war in

Vietnam an unusually high percentage of American servicemen suddenly manifested symptoms of psychosis." The remainder of the film centers on a Stateside medical center where the crazy vets are confined for treatment. In charge of the facility is a veteran by the name of Killer Kane who is even weirder than his charges.

In the aptly titled *Birdy* (1984), a soldier is so disturbed by what he did and saw in Vietnam that he has retreated into a world of silence in which he perches on the end of his bed and acts like a bird. His childhood friend, who is not in a much better mental state after his combat tour, is brought to the hospital in hopes he can bring the bird man back to reality. About coming home, the friend says, "I feel like one of those dogs no one wanted." He adds, "In any other war, we would have been heroes. We didn't know what we were getting into with all that John Wayne shit. Boy, were we dumb." To his buddy who thinks he is a bird, the vet remarks, "They got the best of us. We're totally screwed up."

A more recent film, *The Indian Runner* (1991), has the father of a soldier in Vietnam state, "They say some of the boys coming back are coming back confused." The soldier's brother adds that his sibling has written him that many GIs are disturbed with all the death they have seen. When the Vietnam vet finally gets home, he disappoints no one. He is quickly jailed for beating a woman and, when released, steals a car, robs a gas station, kills a bartender by beating him with a stool, and then disappears. The brother's only explanation is that the vet "is the angriest person I know."

A rather different look at the plight of the returning veteran is offered in *Search and Destroy* (1981). After coming home to the States, members of a special unit in Vietnam are hunted down and killed by a South Vietnamese officer the vets left behind to be captured by the VC on their last mission. The single vet who manages to survive says of the war, "I loved it. I loved the high of it. I was sorry it was over. No one thought about right or wrong. It was all crazy." At the end of the film, after his final showdown with the revenge seeker, the vet concludes, "The war just never ends."

Several African-American oriented films about returning veterans were made about the same time as *Coming Home*, but this particular subgenre seems to have run its course. *Youngblood* (1978) features a black veteran who leads a Los Angeles ghetto gang that, while not above murder and robbery, fights against neighborhood drug pushers after one of the gang dies of an overdose. The 1982 production *Ashes and Embers* is a film consisting entirely of the flashbacks of a Vietnam vet while a policeman holds a gun to his head. Included in the flashbacks are the horrors he witnessed in Vietnam and the injustices he and his family have experienced back home.

Only two films produced since have made any great attempt to realistically show the honest story of returning veterans. *Cease Fire* (1985) and *Gardens of Stone* (1987) take different looks at returning vets—those who came back to civilian life and those who remained in uniform. In *Cease Fire*, a character played by Don Johnson exclaims, "Coming back, that's the real hell." Johnson's character is told by a potential employer that Vietnam was "nothing but a sucker's war" and that the smart young men got out of going. Although melodramatic at times and containing an obligatory veteran suicide, *Cease Fire* does an excellent job of showing veterans sticking together and learning to depend on each other to cope with an ungrateful country and uncaring neighbors.

A unique look at returning vets who remained in the army is presented in *Gardens of Stone*. Two senior NCOs, played by James Earl Jones and James Caan, believe in their country, themselves, and, most of all, the U.S. Army. While proud of their Vietnam service, both are nonetheless concerned about what the war is doing to "their" army, which they consider "family." The two old sergeants are extremely critical of the lack of commitment to win the war on the part of the country's civilian leadership. At the same time, they are concerned about the gung-ho young men they are training to go to combat. Set against the background of the army's Old Guard funeral-detail unit at Arlington National Cemetery, *Gardens of Stone* is similar to *The Green Berets*. Both received a tremendous amount of production support from the Department of Defense, and neither is really a very good movie—but in the famine of accurate Vietnam films that give the veteran his due, they are simply all that is available.

NOT-SO-WELCOME-HOME FILMS

American Commandos (1985)
Angels from Hell (1968)
Ashes and Embers (1982)

Ballad of Andy Crocker, The (1969)
Bears and I, The (1974)
Big Bounce, The (1969)
Birdy (1984)
Black Gunn (1972)
Born Losers (1967)
Bus Is Coming, The (1971)
Cease Fire (1985)
Chrome and Hot Leather (1971)
Clay Pigeon (1971)
Coming Home (1978)
Crazy World of Julius Vrooder, The (1974)
Deathdream (1972)
Electra Glide in Blue (1973)
Fighting Back (1980)
Gardens of Stone (1987)
Gordon's War (1973)
Green Eyes (1976)
Hard Ride, The (1971)
Indian Runner, The (1991)
Jud (1970)
Mean Johnny Barrows (1976)
My Old Man's Place (1972)
Ninth Configuration, The (1980)
Norwood (1970)
Ravager, The (1970)
Resting Place (1986)
Satan's Sadists (1969)
Search and Destroy (1981)
Slaughter (1972)
Tracks (1974)
Tribes (1970)
Vanishing Point (1971)
Visitors, The (1972)
Welcome Home, Johnny Bristol (1971)
Welcome Home, Soldier Boys (1972)
Youngblood (1978)

9. KILLERS AND CRAZIES: THE SUPERVILLAINS

WHEN VIETNAM MOVIES appeared on the horizon, the western film rode off into the production sunset. The Hollywood motion picture about the Great American West was simple. There was good and there was bad—distinguishable by the white hat of the hero and the black hat of the villain—and the good always prevailed. Westerns were not the only movie format to readily distinguish between good and bad. War films did as well. America and her allies were the good guys, their enemies the bad.

When Vietnam War films reached the screen, they obscured the white and black of good and bad into various shades of gray or completely reversed the two. No Hollywood genre would ever be the same. The western, despite its long-term popularity as one of Hollywood's leading formats, became but another in a long list of casualties of the Vietnam War. Although the Clint Eastwood spaghetti westerns and Mel Brooks's western parody *Blazing Saddles* (1974) mark the official end of the genre, the real death of the western began and ended in Southeast Asia—or at least in Hollywood's interpretation of America's longest war.

In today's Vietnam-related films, the villain is still easy to identify. Rather than wearing the black cowboy hat of the past, today's villain stands out of the crowd in his faded army field jacket, which often bears Vietnam unit patches and badges. Even films made since the late 1960s that are not directly about the war contain easily recognizable bad guys in field jackets who are identified as Vietnam veterans. The disturbed, often criminal, Vietnam-veteran character established in the coming-home films has remained a film bad-guy staple. Distance and time separating the veteran from the war zone make no difference to a Hollywood

that has discovered—or invented—the fact that Vietnam provides
a villain for all circumstances.

Stereotyped as disturbed and/or criminal, the Vietnam vet is
also usually portrayed as jobless and incapable of sustaining a relationship with the opposite sex. If the vet does find employment,
he is unable to hold it. For the few who do stay employed, the job
is a menial position such as a janitor or laborer. In the movies, the
only vocation many veterans seem to cultivate is crime or some
other activity where they can use the skills they acquired in Vietnam, inflicting death and mayhem.

Although women's roles in war movies have generally been minor, there have been no combat stories in which females are so
conspicuously absent as in Vietnam films. Vietnam veterans are
shown without wives, sweethearts, or even mothers. The only
women characters included in the casts of Vietnam combat films
are the prostitutes the soldiers pay, the innocent civilians they
murder, and occasionally the enemy they fight. Veterans who
make it back home fare no better with female partners. If the vet
has a wife or girlfriend, she has left him while he was in Vietnam
or leaves soon after he returns, when she discovers what a monster
he has become. The only replacement for the missing women of
the Vietnam War are the righteous protesters who fill the streets
and meet the returning vets with taunts of "baby killer."*

The Vietnam veteran's criminal activities of murder, robbery,
rape, and drug abuse were well established in the "coming home"
films made during and after the war. Subsequent movies have
shown that the veteran's unlawful actions can begin and/or continue regardless of how long he has been back from the war zone.
Of these, murder and rape are the primary criminal vocations of
Hollywood's Vietnam veteran. Popular secondary crimes include
bank robbery and drug smuggling, with some gun running and
child molestation thrown in for good measure. In the occasional

*While the employment and personal-relationship status of the Vietnam
veteran is easy to note in motion pictures, the differentiation between the
categories of "killer" and "crazy" is a bit more difficult. It may be inferred
that the killers are indeed disturbed; however, many of the mentally unbalanced movie vets are harmful only to themselves. With this in mind,
this chapter marks the difference between "killer" and "crazy" as being the
former's commission of an overt criminal act.

film, such as *The Stunt Man* (1980), all that is initially revealed about the vet's past is that he is "on the run from the law."

Filmland's Vietnam-veteran killers cover a wide range, but the most prevalent is the mass murderer. In *Don't Answer the Phone* (1980), a drug-addicted pornography dealer—a veteran of the 101st Airborne Division—rapes and strangles a succession of women in Los Angeles. After viewing several of the victims, a police officer speculates that the killer's motive "may be a religious cleansing." He concludes that the murderer is "a sick son of a bitch" and speculates, "Maybe we're looking for a Vietnam veteran."

Death on a larger scale is planned by a veteran played by Bruce Dern in *Black Sunday* (1977). Dern's character, who is upset about the treatment he has received from the VA and the navy, attempts to kill the president of the United States and a good part of a Super Bowl crowd with a blimp-mounted bomb.

"After you've hunted men, animals just don't rate," declares a Vietnam veteran who, along with two wartime buddies, goes on an annual hunting trip in *Open Season* (1974). Their prey is the same each year. They kidnap a couple at random, rape the woman and torture both, before releasing them and hunting them down in the woods surrounding their cabin. The 1979 release *Night Flowers* is similar, with two vets going on periodic rampages of rape and murder in Hoboken, New Jersey. A vet in *Fear* (1988) is so mean he kills an entire family, including the dog, before committing a string of rapes and murders.

Veterans who kill for money rather than "just for fun" are also a staple of Vietnam murderer films. In *The Stone Killer* (1973), a gang of veterans is employed by a mob leader to kill his rival gangsters. A psychologist assisting the police combat the gangs warns, "Vietnam does not make heroes, it makes psychopaths." Another vet is hired by organized crime to fly an armed helicopter to protect a drug business in *Harley Davidson and the Marlboro Man* (1991). His talents are available strictly to the highest bidder, and he displays his lack of loyalty by changing sides in mid-firefight, killing his old boss when offered a better price. In *The Package* (1989), a vet is a Cold War assassin. His target is the leader of the Soviet Union, but the killer explains that the money is more important than the politics or identity of his victim.

Although far more films have been made with Vietnam veterans portrayed as drug users than as pushers, vets are occasionally shown on the profit side of the addiction. The involvement of Vietnam veterans in the movie drug trade ranges from running an entire cartel in *Lethal Weapon* (1989) to a troubled vet's selling only enough dope to feed his family in *Combat Shock* (1986). Smuggling heroin from Vietnam into the United States is the subject of *Who'll Stop the Rain* (1978), while *American Commandos* (1985) features vets who are in charge of Southeast Asian drug production as well as its export to the States. *Fighting Mad* (1977) also features vets who smuggle, but the contraband is gold instead of drugs. Coffins from Vietnam battlefields are the mode of transportation to get the booty across the Pacific Ocean.

Bank robbery is the speciality of a gang of Vietnam veterans in *Special Delivery* (1976). They profess to steal as a means of getting back at the system that sent them to war, but eventually they admit that they really do it for the cash. In *Charley Varrick* (1973), money is the only motivation for bank robbery by a vet who is recruited by a gang's leader because of the demolition skills he learned in Vietnam. Another 1973 film, *Two*, has a vet who robs a bank to impress the young woman he has kidnapped and is holding hostage.

Various Vietnam films also have been made with veterans taking over entire towns for illegal activities. In *Vigilante Force* (1976), veterans are hired to clean up crime in a California oil boomtown. They do so but then use the town for their own profit and amusement. Two Clint Eastwood movies feature the character Dirty Harry as he combats vets turned urban guerrillas. In *The Enforcer* (1976), the villain vets bomb police headquarters, kidnap the mayor, and kill helpless women and children for no other reason than to extort a huge ransom. Renegade Vietnam-vet policemen who kill lawbreakers without benefit of arrest or trial are the opponents of Dirty Harry in *Magnum Force* (1973). This "quick justice" is continued in *Zebra Force* (1977), in which vets kill and rob mob members. Although the vets in this movie are proud "to rid society of scum," they readily admit appreciating the financial rewards.

A variety of additional crimes are committed by Vietnam veterans in other motion pictures. *Hi, Mom!* (1970) features a former soldier who kills his pregnant wife by blowing up her home. In *Follow Your Heart* (1990), a veteran sexually molests a child. Gun running is the crime of choice of vets in *Private War* (1990). Murder and the hijacking of a nuclear weapon in order to secure political and financial demands make up the plot of *Twilight's Last Gleaming* (1977).

Little about the motivation behind the criminal activity is revealed in any of these criminal-vet films. Hollywood seems to be saying, "Everyone knows they raped, plundered, and murdered in Vietnam, so why should we expect them to do otherwise when they get home?" To reinforce this perception, the movie criminal vet frequently has flashbacks to his combat days, when he either observed or participated in atrocities. The "American soldiers committing atrocities" theme is also reflected in many of the other subgenres of the Vietnam War film.

The lengths to which the film industry is willing to go to condemn the actions of the individual U.S. soldier in Vietnam are boundless. A succession of movies has gone so far as to compare the American warrior in Vietnam to the Nazi soldier of the Third Reich. The highly acclaimed 1976 documentary *Memory of Justice* focuses much of its four-hours-plus on the Nuremberg trials of Nazi leaders and the difference between individual and collective responsibility in modern warfare. During the final portion of the film, however, the "immoral" actions of the United States in Vietnam are featured. Whatever the legitimate purpose of the juxtaposition, if there is one, any comparison between the brutal "final solution" sought by the Nazis and the U.S. effort in Southeast Asia is unfair and farfetched.

This theme of American soldiers' similarity to Nazis continues in one of the four episodes that compose *Twilight Zone: The Movie* (1983). A comparison of the American soldier in Vietnam to the KKK in the United States is included as a bonus. The story, directed by John Landis, follows a bigoted Korean War veteran who hates everyone and everything. One evening, after making numerous racial insults, he steps out of a barroom into the Twilight Zone. He is first transformed into a Jew hunted by the Nazis, then a black man hounded by southern Klansmen; finally he is a Vietcong who is killed by dope-smoking American infantrymen.

References to Vietnam veterans as Nazis abound on the Hollywood screen. Only one Vietnam film, however, makes reference to the World War II Pacific theater, but it is quite enough. In *Purple Haze* (1982), the destruction by the American armed forces in Vietnam is compared to the atomic bomb attacks against Japan.

Interestingly and, unfortunately, typically, it is implied that the A-bombing was more justified than actions in Vietnam.

While the criminal Vietnam vet in the movies certainly can be considered disturbed, an even larger number of films has been made with the veteran depicted as crazy, unbalanced, and/or simply weird without directly committing crimes. The veteran's aberrant behavior is shown through angry outbursts, withdrawal, and a general inability to readjust to "the world." Flashbacks, nightmares, and hallucinations are the dominant traits of the disturbed movie veteran.

"My mind takes me where I don't want to go," a vet complains in the 1989 film *In Country*. Another character in the same movie remarks about veterans, "Those guys are still back in Vietnam; ain't none of 'em come to nothin'."

Withdrawal to remote locations or simply withdrawing inward and wandering from place to place is a frequent means of escape for Hollywood's version of the Vietnam veteran. *Distant Thunder* (1988) features "bush vets" who retreat to remote forest camps in the Pacific Northwest. There they build bunkers surrounded by barbed wire to re-create the Vietnam fire bases where they felt relatively safe during the war. Unfortunately, they forget they are home, flash back to Vietnam, and kill intruders. One of the bush vets, a self-described "loony," enjoys singing a song that contains the line "Rape the town and kill the people." One of the veterans becomes more despondent than usual and commits suicide by attempting to "kiss" an approaching train. The people in the nearest town merely refer to the vets as "freaks," "crazies," and "weirdos."

Simpler, more traditional places to get away from it all are veterans' destinations in other films. In *Americana* (1981), David Carradine plays a vet, identified only as "the American Soldier," whose aimless cross-country venture is briefly halted in a small Kansas town. He stops to repair and restore an antique merry-go-round just because it seems like the thing to do at the time, and then he moves on. In *Criss Cross* (1992), a Vietnam veteran's sanctuary is a Florida monastery where he works as a gardener. Another vet finds solace from the war in the deep woods, taking care of orphan bear cubs, in the 1974 picture *The Bears and I*. Just sitting in front of a television and drinking beer all day and night is the retreat for a vet in *Bell Diamond* (1987).

The degree of "craziness" of the featured veteran varies greatly from film to film. A normal, well-adjusted veteran is the only kind *not* to be found on the screen. Some movies portray the Vietnam vet as merely a confused failure; others feature vets who are absolute lunatics. In *Suspect* (1987), a vet who lives in the sewers and abandoned cars of Washington, D.C., is arrested for murder. He fights the police, physically assaults his female lawyer, and is so mixed up he confesses to a crime he did not commit. A vet whose only ambition is to establish a worm farm is featured in *Heroes* (1977). He suffers flashbacks that turn peaceful, small-town streets into battlegrounds complete with helicopter gunships, fighting infantrymen, and burning bodies.

Crazy vets in other films occupy equally strange worlds of their own imaginations. In *Jacob's Ladder* (1990), a vet has difficulty distinguishing between reality and flashbacks and encounters hellish monsters in both. Two vets in *Night Wars* (1988) have nightmares so vivid that they awake bleeding from wounds afflicted by their dream opponents. Their solution is to heavily arm themselves, lie down, go to sleep, and return to the war to kill their nemeses and nightmares.

"I ain't one of these burning-baby, flashback fuck-ups you see Bruce Dern playing," brags a vet in *Graveyard Shift* (1990). For the remainder of the film, however, he proves that he is as weird as anyone in or out of the movies as he zealously goes about exterminating rats. He admits, "Maybe I'm a little prejudiced," after talking about seeing rodents eat the bodies of his buddies in Vietnam. Another vet, featured in *Ruckus* (1982), lives like an animal, ordering raw hamburgers and sleeping in trees. He also is easily the filthiest former soldier in any film.

In Hollywood, time separating the vet from the war zone seems to make no difference in behavior. The two dream-traveling vets in *Night Wars* have been home for nine years. In *Jacknife* (1989), two vets are still drowning their flashbacks in alcohol two decades after leaving the war, destroying public property, and punching window panes out with soon-to-be bloody fists.

According to the movies, flashbacks, bad dreams, and various psychoses related to Vietnam War service are not limited to street people and weird wanderers. In *Firefox* (1982), Clint Eastwood plays a top American jet pilot who infiltrates the Soviet Union to steal its most sophisticated fighter plane. Every time Eastwood's character is confronted with stress or adversity, he flashes back to his rescue as a POW, when a Vietnamese child is burned alive by napalm. In *Lethal Weapon* (1989), Mel Gibson plays an alcoholic, suicidal policeman who both fellow cops and the crooks think is crazy. A similar character is portrayed by Mickey Rourke in *Year of the Dragon* (1985). His boss frequently reminds him that he is no longer in Vietnam and therefore must not abuse suspects and prisoners.

Suicidal veterans are stock characters in all the subgenres of Vietnam films. While the success and method of self-termination vary, the reason behind the death wish is always the same: The vet is unable to deal with what he saw and did in Vietnam and cannot adjust to a "normal life" when he arrives home. The message of the Vietnam-veteran suicide film seems to be that the veteran is better off dead by his own hand than alive and attempting to survive with the guilt of the war on his shoulders. (A complete list of suicide films can be found at the end of the chapter.)

In the same manner displayed in the criminal-vet films, little is provided in the disturbed-vet movies to explain the aberrant behavior. Through dialogue and/or the wearing of a field jacket early in the picture, it is established that the character has been to Vietnam—and this alone is considered sufficient motivation for whatever weird or crazy behavior follows. One of the more typical and popular films of the disturbed-vet subgenre is also one of the earliest. In the 1976 movie *Taxi Driver*, a none-to-bright veteran (Robert De Niro), who cannot sleep, becomes fed up with the seedy and undesirable late-night characters of New York City. He clips his hair into a Mohawk, dons his field jacket, arms himself with a number of weapons, and hits the streets to rid them of pimps and pushers.

De Niro's character, while not much different from the other criminal and/or disturbed Vietnam vets depicted on the screen, does have one distinguishing characteristic—he has a job. The usual Vietnam-related film has the vet chronically unemployed or too moody, unpredictable, or violent to hold employment if he secures it. A common scene is for the vet to apply for a job only to be told by a prospective employer that vets are losers and unwanted. In *Green Eyes* (1976), a former soldier is told he did not get a job and is advised not to wear his uniform or admit to being a vet at future interviews.

The unemployment office is a meeting place for veterans who recognize each other by their field jackets in *Cease Fire* (1985). In *Mean Johnny Barrows* (1976), a vet applying for a job refers to the Silver Star he won in Vietnam only to be told that medals do not buy meals.* "The only natural talent I have is for screwing up," states a vet who admits to "blowing two jobs" in as many months in *Electra Glide in Blue* (1973). Even Rambo (Sylvester Stallone), in *First Blood* (1982), laments the difficulties in finding employment. "Over there [Vietnam]," he says, "we had a code of honor. Over there I could fly a gunship or drive a tank; be in charge of a million dollars of equipment. Here I can't even hold a job." In *The Park Is Mine* (1985), still another veteran who complains of being unable to hold a job for more than two weeks says, "I'm sick and tired of hearing what a loser I am."

The movie version of the Vietnam veteran has just as much trouble keeping a woman as he does a job.** According to the movies, simply having served in Vietnam is all the explanation required to portray the vet as divorced or as the victim of an unfaithful wife. Vietnam veterans are shown as divorced either during the war or soon after in a host of movies, including *Black Sunday* (1977), *Jacob's Ladder* (1990), *House* (1986), and *Suspect* (1987). The vet's wife or girlfriend is unfaithful in such pictures as *Bell Diamond* (1987), *Coming Home* (1978), *Cutter's Way* (1981), *My Old Man's Place* (1972), and *The Stunt Man* (1980).

Several "missing women" elements are brought together in the 1987 production *Hamburger Hill*. The only Vietnamese women in the films are hookers at a bathhouse that caters to GIs. "Never happen" is the response of a sergeant when he is asked if his wife still writes. At mail call, two soldiers receive correspondence. One is told in an audio tape by a girlfriend, "Back home, no one cares."

Mean Johnny Barrows is one of the few films to treat more or less sympathetically the veteran's joblessness. It concludes with the statement, "Dedicated to the veteran who traded his place on the front line for a place in the unemployment line. Peace is hell."

**Women are also absent in the films about the war itself. Other than the story of an army-hospital nurse in the 1984 release *Purple Hearts*, Hollywood has shown minimal interest in the role of American women in the war. As for Vietnamese females, on the screen they are relegated to minor parts as whores, atrocity victims, and enemy soldiers.

Another gets a letter from an old college friend who says she can no longer write to him because he is fighting an "immoral war."

An occasional Vietnam film opens with a veteran who has a seemingly happy relationship and home life. However, within the first quarter-hour of the movie, the wife or girlfriend is killed, providing the veteran even more motivation to begin a spree of retaliation and mayhem. Among the "kill the wife off early" films are *Chrome and Hot Leather* (1971), *Outlaw Force* (1988), *Year of the Dragon* (1985), and *Blind Fury* (1989).

There are indeed exceptions to the criminal, disturbed, jobless, relationshipless Vietnam veterans depicted in films—but they are rare. For the past twenty-five years, the black hat of the movie bad man has been replaced by the field jacket of the Vietnam vet. "Villain," "loser," and "Vietnam veteran" are synonymous to the Hollywood film industry. Someday, it is hoped, the Vietnam-veteran film will disappear into the sunset like its western movie predecessor. For 2.5 million veterans who served honorably in Vietnam and came home to be sane, productive citizens and family men, it cannot occur soon enough.

CRIMINAL-VET MOVIES

Alamo Bay (1985)
American Commandos (1985)
Angels from Hell (1968)
Betrayed (1988)
Black Sunday (1977)
Blind Fury (1989)
Charley Varrick (1973)
Chrome and Hot Leather (1971)
Code of Honor (1984)
Combat Shock (1986)
Dangerously Close (1986)
Delirium (1979)
Distant Thunder (1988)
Doberman Gang, The (1972)
Don't Answer the Phone (1980)
Electra Glide in Blue (1973)
Enforcer, The (1976)

Fear (1988)
Fighting Mad (1977)
Follow Your Heart (1990)
Green Eyes (1976)
Hamburger Hill (1987)
Harley Davidson and the Marlboro Man (1991)
Hi, Mom! (1970)
House (1986)
In Dangerous Company (1988)
Indian Runner, The (1991)
Karate Kid III, The (1989)
Lethal Weapon (1989)
Long Journey Home (1987)
Magnum Force (1973)
Mean Johnny Barrows (1976)
My Old Man's Place (1972)
Neon Maniacs (1985)
Night Flowers (1979)
Ninth Configuration, The (1980)
Nowhere to Hide (1987)
Off Limits (1988)
Open Season (1974)
Opposing Force (1986)
Outlaw Force (1988)
Package, The (1989)
Park Is Mine, The (1985)
Presidio, The (1988)
Prince of Tides, The (1991)
Private War (1990)
Purple Haze (1982)
Pursuit of D. B. Cooper, The (1981)
Ravager, The (1970)
Special Delivery (1976)
Stone Killer, The (1973)
Street Trash (1987)
Stunt Man, The (1980)
Suppose They Gave a War and Nobody Came (1970)
Targets (1968)
Texas Chainsaw Massacre 2, The (1986)
To Kill a Clown (1972)

Tough Guys Don't Dance (1987)
Tracks (1977)
Trained to Kill (1975)
Twilight's Last Gleaming (1977)
Twighlight Zone: The Movie (1983)
Two (1973)
Vanishing Point (1976)
Vigilante Force (1976)
Visitors, The (1972)
Welcome Home, Soldier Boys (1972)
When You Comin' Back, Red Ryder? (1979)
Who'll Stop the Rain (1978)
Wild at Heart (1990)
Youngblood (1978)
Zebra Force (1977)

DISTURBED-VET MOVIES

Air America (1990)
Americana (1981)
Angry Breed, The (1969)
Article 99 (1991)
Back to School (1986)
Bears and I, The (1974)
Bell Diamond (1987)
Big Chill, The (1983)
Birdy (1984)
Blue Thunder (1983)
Cage (1988)
Cease Fire (1985)
Choirboys, The (1977)
Choose Me (1984)
Crazy World of Julius Vrooder, The (1974)
Criss Cross (1992)
Cutter's Way (1981)
Deer Hunter, The (1978)
Deserters (1983)
Distant Thunder (1988)
Fandango (1984)

Final Mission (1984)
Firefox (1982)
First Blood (1982)
Fourth War (1990)
Graveyard Shift (1990)
Hardcore and Fist (1988)
Heroes (1977)
House (1986)
In Country (1989)
Jacknife (1989)
Jacob's Ladder (1990)
Journey through Rosebud (1972)
Jud (1970)
Lethal Weapon (1989)
Let's Get Harry (1986)
Looking for Mr. Goodbar (1977)
Men at Work (1990)
Night Wars (1988)
Ninth Configuration, The (1980)
Prince of Tides, The (1991)
Quick Change (1991)
Riders of the Storm (1986)
Ruckus (1982)
Splash (1986)
Stunt Man, The (1980)
Suspect (1987)
Taxi Driver (1976)
Trained to Kill (1975)
Vanishing Point (1971)
Vietnam, Texas (1990)
Welcome Home, Johnny Bristol (1971)
Year of the Dragon (1985)

SUICIDAL-VET MOVIES

Bell Diamond (1987)
Big Chill, The (1983)
Cease Fire (1985)
Coming Home (1978)

Deer Hunter, The (1978)
Distant Thunder (1988)
Don't Cry, It's Only Thunder (1982)
Eye of the Eagle II (1988)
Flatliners (1990)
Full Metal Jacket (1987)
Go Tell the Spartans (1978)
Journey through Rosebud (1972)
Lethal Weapon (1989)
Line, The (1980)
Memorial Day (1983)
Ninth Configuration, The (1980)
Off Limits (1988)
Outside In (1972)
Park Is Mine, The (1985)
Prince of Tides, The (1991)
Tribes (1970)
Vanishing Point (1971)

10. REAL-TO-REEL WAR: SCREEN COMBAT

COMBAT SCENES ARE the greatest challenge for movie-makers to duplicate on the screen. The complications and hardships involved in re-creating the life-and-death action of combat have resulted in what is perhaps the most striking similarity between Vietnam movies and films about earlier wars. Hollywood's combat, Vietnam or otherwise, remains simply Hollywood—with little resemblance to what actually occurs on the battlefield.

In an effort to achieve a degree of realism (and to save production costs), World II films often integrated actual combat footage. This footage was usually shot with gun cameras for air warfare and hand-held cameras for ground combat. The result frequently was poorly framed, grainy, out of focus, and jerky. Video technology had improved by the time of the Vietnam War, but the actual combat footage was still far from the quality of studio productions. The movie audiences of the 1960s and since have been more demanding and too sophisticated to accept the quality inconsistencies inherent in blending actual and studio footage.

Another limitation to the use of combat footage was the nature of Vietnam itself. Most of the pitched battles were fought in thick jungles that greatly restricted the ability of a camera to record anything of cinematic interest. Film footage from gun cameras and bomb sights did provide some spectacular shots. However, because air-to-air combat was extremely rare in Vietnam, the real combat air footage is composed of what appears to be the same jungle or rice paddy exploding over and over again.

The greatest limitation to the use of combat footage in Vietnam War films is one shared by movies of earlier conflicts—very little real combat has ever been caught on film. The reason is quite simple. Cameramen have a natural aversion to being shot, and the enemy in any conflict cares not if he shoots a moviemaker or a soldier. In Vietnam, where combat was frequently preceded by long marches and days of looking before the enemy was found, few journalists were willing to attach themselves to a field unit and share its hardships and dangers. It was much easier to cover the war from the comfortable hotels and bars of Saigon than to venture into the rice paddies and jungles. As a result, insufficient combat footage exists, regardless of quality, to adequately show the intensity and rigors of ground warfare in Vietnam.*

Because of these factors, Hollywood has had to completely recreate combat—usually recasting it in Hollywood's own image of battle, one formed from watching too many of its own John Wayne movies. So, in locations that resemble the war zone, such as the Philippines and Thailand, moviemakers have set scenes *they* perceive to represent Vietnam and yelled, "Action!" All too often, however, the film industry has cared no more for accuracy in location than in content and shot its Vietnam films on Hollywood back lots and in the hills of southern California.

Along with unrealistic filming locations, Hollywood has paid scant attention to accurately portraying the uniforms, weapons, tactics, language, and use of supporting assets such as air power, artillery, and communications. More important, and sadly, Hollywood has almost always attempted to re-create the war and the warrior to fit its preconceptions rather than to mirror reality. According to the Hollywood film, the American soldier in Vietnam was a dope-smoking (or heroin-shooting), racist baby-killer with no morals or patriotic spirit. His leaders are shown as cowardly martinets interested only in themselves rather than the men they are responsible to lead.

The few films produced about the war during the war did make some effort to achieve realism. The bulk of A *Yank in Vietnam* (1964) was actually filmed on location in South Vietnam. *To the Shores of Hell* (1965) includes lengthy scenes of Marine Corps exercises at Camp Pendleton, California, in preparation for de-

---

*Actual Vietnam combat footage is in such short supply that the marketing of videotapes adapted from 8mm and Super 8 film taken by soldiers in the field has emerged as a cottage industry. However low the quality, any real combat footage is readily marketable.

ployment to Vietnam. Both pictures, however, follow B-movie plots that could just as easily have featured cowboys and Indians as the Vietcong and the U.S. armed forces. Despite much assistance from U.S. Army technical advisers and almost limitless support in arms and equipment, which added to the accuracy of detail, *The Green Berets* (1968) still more resembles John Wayne's westerns than any honest portrayal of Vietnam combat.

During the final years of the war in Southeast Asia and those that immediately followed the fall of Saigon, Hollywood flooded theaters with protest films and coming-home movies. The former damned the war as unjust and immoral; the latter "exposed" the conflict's warrior as a criminal and/or a disturbed freak. It was not until three years after the communist victory that Hollywood made any attempt to show what the war was really like. Unfortunately, the film industry had already shown the returning veteran to be deeply disturbed. Now it was time to create Hollywood's version of the war to show why Vietnam veterans had come home such violent losers. A glimmer of combat truth has been revealed in the occasional film since then, and a rare few have neared the edge of Vietnam War reality. Most, however, merely add to the myth of the crazy, hootch-burning, atrocity-committing soldier who will continue his outrageous behavior once he gets home.*

The initial onslaught of "real combat" Vietnam films reached the screen in 1978 and included *The Boys in Company C, The Deer Hunter*, and *Go Tell the Spartans*. Another movie, *Apocalypse Now*, was originally planned for release that same year but, because of production difficulties, did not make it to the screen until 1979. All four pictures had big budgets, major stars, and a great amount of studio support during their making and marketing.

The Boys in Company C, the lowest-budgeted, most inaccurate, and least watchable, was the first to reach theaters around the world. The film follows Marine recruits from boot camp to Viet-

---

*A large number of Vietnam-related movies have been released in the last dozen years as action/adventure films and, either by intent or by accident, have had little or no relationship to reality. Part or all of these films are set in Southeast Asia and follow plots that are not remotely comparable to anything that actually occurred during the war. These action/adventure Vietnam films will be covered in a later chapter, "Ramboesque Films: The Superheroes."

nam. Among them is a black Chicago gang member who volunteers for Southeast Asia in order to send drugs back home in the caskets of "nonviewable" remains. His narcotic connection in Vietnam is an ARVN officer. The drug dealer and his fellow Marines are commanded by a captain who cannot read a map and who does not mind sacrificing his men in order to further his own career. By the middle of the picture, the captain is so afraid of his own men that he does not accompany them on field missions.

Throughout *The Boys in Company C* officers are inept, uncaring cowards. During a mortar attack, officers shield themselves behind Vietnamese women and children. In another instance, a Marine company is placed in great danger to insure the safety of a general's luxury mobile home, and cases of liquor are delivered to his haven. The use of drugs—marijuana and heroin—among the Marines is common, and a unit of the army's 173d Airborne Brigade is shown to be so strung out that it is completely devoid of military discipline. Proper radio procedure, normal military procedures, and correct use of fire and maneuver are nonexistent. Apparently the director's guidance to his actor "Marines" was to respond to danger by yelling loudly at each other. The Philippines* substitute for Vietnam, with Filipino and American Chinese playing the parts of Vietnamese. None of the substitutions is believable to anyone who ever actually visited Vietnam.

Makers of *The Deer Hunter* delivered a much better movie to the screen, but along with a few truths about the war, it also contains numerous inaccuracies. Its excellent cast of Robert De Niro, Meryl Streep, Christopher Walken, and John Savage, and superb direction by Michael Cimino, make it well deserving of its five Oscars, including Best Picture of 1978. *The Deer Hunter*'s strength as a truly great film is also its largest weakness—the wonderful directing and forceful acting only make its inaccuracies and distortions more believable to unwary audiences.

Much of the "in country" action of *The Deer Hunter* focused on

---

*A large number of Vietnam movies have been filmed in the Philippines. Apparently, filmmakers think one rice paddy and/or jungle is like any other. They are wrong. Some areas of the Philippines and other locations that stand in for Vietnam are extremely realistic. Others, such as that used in *The Boys in Company C*, do not remotely resemble any part of the war zone.

the participation of one character in Russian roulette contests. These events are staged in Saigon bars complete with audiences who bet and cheer. This type of activity, with or without the participation of an American soldier, never occurred during the war or since. Another interesting departure from reality is the full beard De Niro's character wears along with his dress green uniform when he returns home.

The Deer Hunter does deserve praise beyond its simply being a great motion picture. It is also the only major Hollywood production to show soldiers departing for Vietnam with the support of their community. Although they receive no parade when they return, their friends who stayed behind do welcome and honor them.

The third 1978 release, *Go Tell the Spartans*, takes place entirely in Vietnam, although it was obviously filmed in southern California. Set in 1964, it does an excellent job of showing the early problems of the war and accurately predicts the difficulties that lay ahead. Although *Go Tell the Spartans* includes the typical Vietnam scenes of prisoner torture, a gung-ho incompetent lieutenant, a suicidal sergeant, and an opium-smoking medic, it goes deeper into the causes and effects of the war than any other film. If this movie had been made early in the conflict instead of several years after it was over, it would have been hailed as the most visionary motion picture of the time. Even with the advantage of hindsight and its stereotypical characters, it is a noteworthy picture of value to anyone attempting to see the real Vietnam.

Apocalypse Now features every negative stereotype of the war and the warrior yet established. When the film was released, director Francis Coppola claimed the movie to be "not about Vietnam; it *is* Vietnam. It is what it was really like."* Nothing could be farther from the truth. Despite Coppola's claims of innovation, all he

*In 1991, the difficulties in the making of *Apocalypse Now* were recorded in a documentary titled *Hearts of Darkness*. Coppola and company brag that making the movie was tougher than the war itself, but in doing so they reveal themselves as arrogant and pretentious. While they undoubtedly know the movie business, actual warfare in Vietnam is foreign to them. The documentary also reports that *Apocalypse Now* has grossed $150 million. That is quite a bit more than the thirty pieces of silver longsince established as the going rate for betrayal of fellow citizens.

really accomplished was an overbudgeted rehash of American soldiers' murdering innocent civilians, smoking dope, ignoring their officers, and violating every law of land warfare and generally accepted levels of morality.

Oddly, the financial success and general audience approval of these first "real war" Vietnam films did not result in a large number of imitations and clones. During the decade after the fall of Saigon in 1975, a mere half-dozen films appeared that attempted to show actual Vietnam combat. The best of these, *The Killing Fields* (1984), is not about the war in Vietnam but rather the takeover and genocide of more than two million noncombatants by the North Vietnamese–supported Khmer Rouge in Cambodia. Its re-creation of the mounds and acres of rotting corpses is the most explicit of any ever filmed. *The Killing Fields* also provides excellent insights into the importance and the abuses of a free press and into the priority which many journalists in Southeast Asia placed on getting the story, ahead of all other considerations.

Another 1984 release, *Purple Hearts*, proved to be the best, if not the only, romantic drama about the war. In what is almost a throwback to World War II films, a doctor and a nurse fall in love in Vietnam while at the same time doing everything possible to take care of their patients. Despite lines such as "We had last night" and Philippine shooting locations that little resemble Vietnam, this is one of the most positive movies about Americans in the war zone.

The only other motion pictures worth mention during this decade-long drought of Vietnam movies about real combat are two 1979 releases, *More American Graffiti* and *The Odd Angry Shot*. Both, particularly the latter, have merit. While the comedy *More American Graffiti* praises the antiwar movement, glorifies the protesters, and shows military commanders as inept bunglers, several scenes are realistically rendered. This sequel to the highly acclaimed *American Graffiti* includes re-created footage of helicopter assaults, fire fights, and support-base activities that are shot in a dark, grainy format that adds to the realism by mimicking actual footage.

Far more accurate in showing the overall actions of the war is the other film, *The Odd Angry Shot*. Produced by an Australian studio, it received advice and support from the Australian Defense Forces. *The Odd Angry Shot* follows the actions of an elite Aussie

Special Air Service (similar to U.S. Army LRRPs and Rangers) from deployment to Vietnam through the rotation back home of the survivors. In between are some of the most authentic ground patrols, ambushes, fire fights, and reconnaissance actions available to the moviegoing public. Although the weapons, equipment, and soldier slang are strictly Australian, any American Vietnam veteran will recognize his Aussie brothers in this film as the real thing. Of particular note are the discussions between the SAS grunts about their countrymen back home not caring about the war or the military. The soldiers also remark that they anticipate their political leaders will sell them out, along with their Vietnamese allies, before it is all over. American vets will also find truth and kinship in the Aussies' comments that only poor men are sent to the war because the fathers of the rich are able to keep their sons out of the army. *The Odd Angry Shot* is the antithesis of virtually every American film made about the Vietnam War—and is absolutely right on target.

It was not until ten years after the end of the war that an American film convinced the majority of the moviegoing public that it was seeing the "real war" on the screen.* *Platoon* was given the Best Picture Academy Award for 1986, and another Oscar went to the film's Vietnam-veteran director, Oliver Stone. It is without a doubt one of the best theatrical releases of the decade and contains some of the most accurate Vietnam War footage yet recreated. Unfortunately, Stone uses his great film to deliver a

---

*Each new release of a "realistic" Vietnam War film results in electronic and print interviews with veterans *ad nauseam*. The interviews are all similar regardless of their origin or the film they discuss. A long-haired, bearded, field-jacket-wearing vet is asked if the film is "like it really was in Vietnam." With a choke in his voice and often a tear in his eye, the purported veteran replies, "That's exactly like it happened." He then usually continues with stories of helicopter crashes and of friends blown away before his very eyes, and if given enough encouragement, he hints of villages burned and civilians murdered. No journalists ever seem to go to the trouble to find a Vietnam veteran in a business suit and/or carrying a briefcase. Neither do they check to see if their "professional veteran" actually served in Vietnam and, if he did, whether or not he ever left his secure supply room or clerk's position in Saigon or Danang. Television and newspapers seem to present only the stereotypical veteran, which they and the movies are responsible for establishing to begin with.

one-sided view of the war and its combatants. Every immoral and illegal act of murder, rape, and wholesale destruction is committed by the rifle platoon of the 25th Infantry Division, which the film follows throughout. Along with committing atrocities that go unreported and unpunished, the platoon's NCOs share dope with their troops and fight—eventually to the death—among themselves.

Director Stone delivers his version of the war in a manner that provides an illusion of validity. The background scenes, day-to-day activities (minus the atrocities), uniforms, equipment; and age and language of the soldiers are as accurate as any yet produced. The Philippine jungle sets are a match for many parts of the Vietnamese jungles, and the viewer can all but feel the heat, humidity, insects, exhaustion, boredom, and fear experienced by the heavily laden infantrymen. Except for the maniacal killing of innocents and the burning of their homes, and sergeants who want to kill each other as much as the enemy, *Platoon* closely delivers what a grunt's life in combat was really like. The final battle and its inclusion of supporting fires and radio communications are re-created as near to reality as one can get without dodging real bullets.

Only Oliver Stone can explain why he portrayed the warrior as evil as the war itself. Artistic license, delivering what the audience wants to see, and merely telling a story are all explanations that have been offered. Whatever the real motivation, Stone's rewriting of history has continued since his success, and tremendous profit, with *Platoon*. In 1989, Stone directed another Vietnam film, *Born on the Fourth of July*. Based on the experiences of disabled Marine veteran Ron Kovic, the movie was presented by both Stone and Kovic to be "as it really happened." Only after several exaggerations and out-and-out fictions were noted in the press did Stone admit to having taken a few liberties to make the film more commercial.

Despite the depiction of his fellow Vietnam veterans as murderous villains in *Platoon* and the revelation of his deliberate fabrications in *Born on the Fourth of July*, it was not until Stone's 1991 release of *JFK* that he received any widespread criticism about his revision of history. Stone's premise in *JFK* is that President Kennedy was assassinated by a conspiracy of defense contractors and the military because he was going to withdraw U.S. troops from Vietnam before the war really got started. Also presented is every other assassination theory, no matter how wild or weird, ever devised. Throughout the movie, actual news footage is so well intercut with Stone's version that it is often difficult to differentiate between fact, conjecture, and distortion.

Immediately upon its release, *JFK* and Stone were panned by the media and many of those involved in the events of the times for taking too much literary license and for intermingling fact and fiction. It is interesting to note that *JFK* is no more a fictional portrayal of actual events than were *Platoon* and *Born on the Fourth of July*. Similar errors, stretching of the truth, and distortion of the facts are common in all three films. More than a few Vietnam vets recognize that lies on film about a popular president generate much more investigation and criticism than lies about soldiers who fought an unpopular war. As for Stone, all the controversy has really meant is much publicity and large profits.

The popularity and resulting profitability of *Platoon* spearheaded a golden age (in financial gain if not quality) of "real combat" Vietnam War films that continues to the present. A larger number of real combat movies were made about the war during the three years following *Platoon* than the total produced in all the years that preceded it. Many of these films are remarkably accurate in showing what the war and warrior were really like. Not surprisingly, however, given Hollywood's past record of re-creating warfare, some of the films are deserving of comment for much-less-than-positive reasons.

Four major productions were released during the first year (1987) of the post-*Platoon* period. Three of these pictures represent perhaps the best one-year triad of Vietnam War movies ever made. The fourth, *Full Metal Jacket*, is by far the most inferior of the group, yet it gained the most attention and box-office revenue. *Full Metal Jacket* is basically two movies presented as one. The first half does a fair job of showing Marine boot camp, but the second part gets totally off track in an attempt to follow a Marine platoon during the battle for Hue during Tet of 1968. *Full Metal Jacket* is much easier to understand when placed into context with the other films of its director. Stanley Kubrick has made a long list of motion pictures that focus on the theme of dehumanization. In this light, *Full Metal Jacket* fits in well with Kubrick's earlier *Dr. Strangelove* (1964), *2001: A Space Odyssey* (1968), and *A Clockwork*

Orange (1971). One of the most unusual aspects of *Full Metal Jacket* also provides insight into the mind of Kubrick. Rather than shoot the film in the Philippines or another tropical, Vietnamlike setting, Kubrick filmed the movie on soundstages and in the countryside of England. Despite the inclusion of palm trees, rice paddies, and burning buildings, it still looks like . . . well, it looks like England.

The other three 1987 Vietnam films are vastly superior in revealing the real war, its participants, and its effects on combatants and those back home. *Gardens of Stone* relates the impact of the conflict on the career army and professional soldiers. *The Hanoi Hilton* provides an extremely accurate look at the life and existence of American POWs in North Vietnam. *Hamburger Hill* recreates some of the best combat scenes and soldier interaction available. Each has great individual merit.

Gardens of Stone follows two career NCOs assigned to the Third Infantry "Old Guard" funeral detail unit at Arlington National Cemetery. They attempt to train young soldiers to stay alive when they get to Vietnam, while at the same time they are burying those killed there. Both NCOs are bright, articulate, and devoted to their profession. Neither uses drugs, commits murder, or supports war crimes or other criminal activity. This picture received full production support by the Department of Defense and was filmed at the home of the Old Guard, Fort Meyer, Virginia. The result is accurate detail, believable characters, and unique insights into how professional soldiers maintained their belief in their army and their country during extremely trying times.

Production of *The Hanoi Hilton* was advised and assisted by seventeen former POWs held in the infamous North Vietnamese prison. Although the film is at times almost as boring as the long days of being a prisoner, it is outstanding in showing the conditions of the POWs' confinement and the ill treatment by their communist jailers. The most remarkable portion of the movie is the re-creation of visits of American pacifist and antiwar groups who praise the North Vietnamese and deny that the American POWs are being mistreated. This accurate portrayal—combined with the movie's communist guards quoting statements by U.S. entertainers, political leaders, and clergy about the immorality of the war and the barbarism of the American military—is credited

by many as the reason the film was greeted by a storm of controversy and attempts to limit its release.

The third film of the great Vietnam War movie triad of 1987,
Hamburger Hill, tracks the actions of one infantry squad as its
men make eleven assaults over a period of ten days to take Hill
937 (better know by the film's title) from the NVA. This fictionalized version of the actual event delivers many truths. Most of the
movie is composed of extremely tight camera shots which reveal
only a limited portion of the battlefield. By not pulling back for a
broad view of the fight, the film lets the viewer see the action on
the screen very much from the same perspective as that of the individual soldiers who actually fought their way up the isolated
mountain. The actors are convincing in appearance and action;
their language, slang, and profanity are accurate; and their weapons and equipment are as they really were. This is an exhausting
movie to watch, and while it may not have received the accolades
of the media or the monetary returns of *Platoon* and *Full Metal
Jacket,* it is a much more realistic portrayal of the war and its warriors.

Real-war Vietnam movies of 1988 covered a wide range of content and greatly vary in their degree of realism and accuracy. The
best of the lot, *The Iron Triangle,* claims to be based on "the diary
of an unknown Vietcong soldier." While its re-creation of the actions of a 25th Infantry Division rifle company during field operations is not remarkable, its portrayal of the Vietcong unit the
Americans face in the jungle is the most detailed and authentic of
any motion picture made to date.

Another 1988 film based on a true story is *Platoon Leader,*
which was adapted from the book by the same name about and by
Lieutenant James McDonough. The film is unusual in that it is
presented sans politics; it shows the difficulties encountered by a
young army officer near the end of the war as he leads his platoon, deals with his superiors, and fights the enemy. While the
picture is positive about the American combatants, neither director Aaron Norris (brother of Chuck) nor his actors apparently understood the military and combat operations well enough to earn
any amount of credibility. *Platoon Leader* ends up being a noble
effort that just does not work as an entertainment or informa-
tional vehicle.

Another 1988 release based on an actual event, *Bat 21*, is about the rescue of a downed air force pilot rather than an infantry officer. Still, it does have similarities to *Platoon Leader*. Again, without praising the war itself, the film is extremely positive toward the American servicemen in Vietnam. However, despite a big-name cast including Gene Hackman and Danny Glover, the believability quotient of *Bat 21* never rises above negative numbers.

When the real-war films of 1988 had plots that were not based on true stories, they grossly strayed from any degree of accuracy. In fact, beyond being set entirely in Vietnam and occasionally making a minor assault on reality, *Off Limits* and *The Siege of Fire Base Gloria* could just as easily be classified as action/adventure (Ramboesque) films. *Off Limits* focuses on the efforts of two military policemen to track down a serial killer of Saigon prostitutes. Their primary suspect is a highly decorated full colonel who likes to throw enemy prisoners out of a high-flying helicopter and who commits suicide when the MPs discover his kinky sex habits. Despite the presence of Willem Dafoe and Gregory Hines in the lead roles and a big production budget, nothing about this film resembles Saigon, Vietnam, or anyone who ever served there. In fact, more than anything else, it resembles a variety of failed television pilots.

The Australian *Siege of Fire Base Gloria* comes complete with a cowardly captain who hides naked and smokes pot in his command bunker, American soldiers who torture prisoners, and some of the most ridiculous dialogue ("It really hurt us to see their heads on stakes") ever recorded. This picture is in no way comparable to the earlier Aussie *Odd Angry Shot* and would not be included among real-combat films except for its portrayal of the Vietcong who are responsible for the siege of the fire base. Their attack is organized and executed in a fashion remarkably similar to VC combat doctrine and tactics in use at the time. The VC chain of command, including the position of the communist cadre, is accurately depicted, as are their weapons, uniforms, and equipment.

In addition to Oliver Stone's *Born on the Fourth of July*, 1989 delivered two other real-war Vietnam films to the screen. *Casualties of War*, like *Born on the Fourth of July*, is based on a true story and has a major-name director, in this case Brian (who earlier directed *Greetings* and *Hi, Mom*) De Palma. De Palma's film be-

gins with a degree of realism and accuracy before deteriorating
into typical Hollywood Vietnam-soldier bashing. Early scenes feature extremely authentic movement through the jungle and the
establishment of a night defensive position. The proper employment of claymore mines and the correct use of radio communications are included. Most remarkable is the display of tracer rounds
crisscrossing the kill zone during a fire fight. The showing of
tracer fire is extremely rare in war films of any era because of the
difficulty and dangers in re-creating the red, green, and white
streaks of fire. *Casualties of War* shows tracers as they were actually used, to track machine-gun bursts and to mark targets for
other fires.

After the initial quarter-hour, the picture focuses on a small patrol of the 23d Infantry Division that kidnaps, gang rapes, and
murders a Vietnamese girl. De Palma attempts to include a great
deal of philosophy about the war, collective guilt, and friendship
between soldiers—to the point where the basic plot becomes
mired in talk unrelated to the action. Ultimately *Casualties of War*
ends up being merely another Hollywood effort to take an isolated, one-of-a-kind brutal event and show it as behavior typical of
American soldiers in Vietnam.

The other 1989 release, *84 Charlie Mopic*, was written and
directed by decorated Vietnam veteran Patrick Duncan, was
filmed on a shoestring budget, and features an unknown cast in
what very well may be the most impressive movie about the Vietnam War yet made. Told through the single view of an army
motion-picture specialist (84-C is the designation of his military
occupation specialty), it follows the cameraman's filming of a patrol of the 173d Airborne Brigade. The soldiers' language, weapons, and equipment are as they were in the real thing. This is
about as close as an audience can get to a one-year tour in Vietnam while safely sitting in a movie theater or in an easy chair in
front of a VCR at home.

The production of real-war films slowed to two releases in
1990—*Air America* and *The Flight of the Intruder*. Combining an
all-star cast, including Mel Gibson and Robert Downey, Jr., with a
script heavy with action and comedy, *Air America* is one of the
few films to take a look at the "secret" U.S. war in Laos. Good detail is provided in the wide variety of aircraft flown by the airline's

CIA pilots, and the Thai shooting locations closely resemble the neighboring Laotian mountains and jungles. The result, however, is mostly an action comedy that reveals little about the clandestine operations outside Vietnam.

The Flight of the Intruder is also about a part of the Vietnam War little covered in the movies—the air war over the North. Cliché-ridden dialogue, delivered through poor performance by actors (Danny Glover, Willem Dafoe, and Brad Johnson) who usually are much better, detracts from what is an honest look at the experiences and feelings of navy carrier pilots who know the only people they can depend on are each other. This film was supported by the Department of Defense, and the scenes filmed about the flight deck and in the ward rooms of the USS Independence are the best available about Vietnam carrier warfare.

Another aspect of real-combat Vietnam films is the training that prepared young men for combat. Basic training (army) and boot camp (Marines) along with induction center activities were popular World War II movie subjects. Vietnam films, however, use induction centers to highlight protests and to glorify the various ruses used to beat the draft (see chapter 7). The re-creation of basic and boot training receives only minor attention in the Vietnam War films.

A 1970 television movie, Tribes, which tells the story of a tough drill instructor trying to make a Marine out of a long-haired, laid-back hippie, is the only Vietnam-era film to focus in entirety on the training environment. Hair (1979), using Nevada National Guard facilities, takes a brief look at army basic training, while The Boys in Company C attempts to re-create Marine boot camp on a Hollywood back lot. The best, albeit somewhat overdone, depiction of boot camp makes up the first half of Full Metal Jacket. Although posed on British soundstages and sets, the look and language are well done. Lee Ermey, a former Marine drill instructor who plays a DI in the film, is particularly believable. The greatest fault of the boot camp scenes in Full Metal Jacket is the general inability of the nonmilitary audience to know just when to take Ermey seriously and when he is merely posturing for effect. There is also a question as to whether or not director Kubrick really understood the DI's role and motivation.

All of the Vietnam movies with basic-training, boot-camp, and induction-center themes share one particular scene—the shearing of the long locks of new recruits and draftees, which is something no director seems to want to leave out. One thing that is good about these haircut scenes is that even Hollywood has difficulty in getting them wrong.

The last subcategory of real-war film provides the most significant contrasts in delivering truth and fiction. By definition alone, documentary films* should present facts and events as they happen. Embellishment, bias, and/or the addition of propaganda should not have a role in their production. However, Vietnam documentaries, like the war itself, do not follow established rules, and the result is some of the very best and some of the most abysmal films to be made about the conflict.

The Vietnam War documentaries that are available today are fairly equally divided between the good and the bad, with merit defined as the degree of accuracy and evenhandness exhibited rather than the production quality. At the top of the list of best documentaries about the Vietnam War is a trio of films that can also easily be recommended as among the most insightful movies about the war and its participants. *The Anderson Platoon* (1967) follows the day-to-day action of a First Cavalry Division infantry platoon over a period of six weeks. *A Face of War* (1968) does the same thing during a three-month span for a company of the Seventh Marine Regiment. There is no better record of the hardships, dangers, and boredom experienced by the American infantryman in Vietnam than what is contained in these two documentaries. Both are in black and white, and picture and sound quality are inferior to commercial motion pictures because of the conditions under which they were filmed. Politics of the war are excluded in favor of showing how nineteen- and twenty-year-old soldiers, led by sergeants and officers a year or two older, actually lived and, in all too many instances, died in Vietnam.

The third of the outstanding documentaries was not released until 1987, but the delay was well worth the wait. *Dear America: Letters Home from Vietnam* blends excerpts of actual correspond-

---

*More than seventy documentaries about the Vietnam War were produced during and immediately after the war. For this study, only those documentaries currently available on videotape and/or those released to movie houses are included.

ence from servicemen in Vietnam with newsreel footage and still photographs backed by the music of the period. The result is an amazingly honest, concise history not only of the war but of the era as well. This documentary portrays the Vietnam War clearly and accurately through the words and pictures of those who served. Its opening announcement is candid as to content: "This film is about young men in war. It is their own story, in their own words. Words they wrote home in letters from Vietnam. Every scene, every shot in the film is real—nothing has been re-enacted."

The only negative attribute, other than some events being out of sequence, of *Dear America: Letters Home from Vietnam* is the selection of narrators/readers of the soldiers' letters. Although their performances are moving in every aspect, it is worth mention that many of them, including Robert De Niro, Martin Sheen, Tom Berenger, and Sean Penn, either began or added to their Hollywood careers by starring in Vietnam films that are not honest toward or positive about the war's veterans.

Two other documentaries made during the war prove that the format can also be awful. In any other war but Vietnam, *In the Year of the Pig* (1968) and *Hearts and Minds* (1974) would have resulted in charges of sedition against their directors and producers. Instead, both were nominated for Academy Awards (*Hearts and Minds* won in 1974) for Best Documentary. Both films praise Ho Chi Minh and the communist forces while showing the American and ARVN military as loathsome institutions bent on murder, rape, and destruction for its own sake. No balance is provided; biased reports distort and manipulate news footage and interviews to tell lies and present blatant propaganda. Daniel Ellsberg sums up the theme of *Hearts and Minds* by saying the United States is the enemy. *In the Year of the Pig* follows a similar track, showing Father Daniel Berrigan and journalist Harrison Salisbury condemning the bombing of the North, praising the communists' passion for education, and stating that the Vietnamese are victims of American colonialism.

Regardless of the positive or negative aspects of Vietnam War documentaries, they play only a minor role in informing the moviegoing/video-renting public about the conflict. America's and the world's major source of information will continue to be the real-war films containing re-created battles, death, and survival recorded on back lots and inexotic tropical locations. Even these

movies may have seen their best days—such as they were. Despite
the use of cheap foreign labor and locations, the re-creation of real
war is an extremely expensive venture. War films of any kind are
pricing themselves out of production, and although several real-
war films are currently in production or in the planning stages, the
number is decreasing.

Costly production of future real-war films will result in two
types of film. The occasional megabudget epic will still be made,
but far more low-budget films will be produced in which accuracy
neither in plot nor in settings and costumes will be an issue. The
only way real-war re-creation movies will continue to be produced
is for Hollywood to request and receive support and assistance
from the Department of Defense. This is occurring in some
cases—particularly with combat films not about Vietnam—but the
relationship between Hollywood and the military is still far from
amiable. Neither trusts or respects the other. Too many in today's
armed services readily recall *In the Year of the Pig* and the hundreds of other antimilitary films churned out by Hollywood over
the past three decades. As for Hollywood, barring a change in studio philosophy, the price of cooperation with the Pentagon, which
includes some degree of script approval, is much too high to per-
mit any great partnership in the near future. The wounds of
Vietnam—especially Vietnam at the movies—are deep and far
from healing.

REAL-WAR VIETNAM FILMS

Air America (1990)
Anderson Platoon, The (1967)
Apocalypse Now (1979)
Bat 21 (1988)
Born on the Fourth of July (1989)
Boys in Company C, The (1978)
Casualties of War (1989)
Charlie Bravo (1980)
Dear America: Letters Home from Vietnam (1987)
Deer Hunter, The (1978)
84 Charlie Mopic (1989)

Face of War, The (1968)
Flight of the Intruder, The (1990)
For the Boys (1991)
Full Metal Jacket (1987)
Gardens of Stone (1987)
Go Tell the Spartans (1978)
Green Berets, The (1968)
Hamburger Hill (1987)
Hanoi Hilton, The (1987)
Hearts and Minds (1974)
In the Year of the Pig (1968)
Iron Triangle, The (1988)
Killing Fields, The (1984)
More American Graffiti (1979)
Odd Angry Shot, The (1979)
Off Limits (1988)
Platoon (1986)
Platoon Leader (1988)
Purple Hearts (1984)
Rumor of War, A (1980)
Siege of Fire Base Gloria, The (1988)
To the Shores of Hell (1965)
Yank in Vietnam, A (1964)

BASIC TRAINING/BOOT CAMP FILMS

Boys in Company C, The (1978)
Dear America: Letters Home from Vietnam (1987)
Full Metal Jacket (1987)
Hair (1979)
Tribes (1970)

VIETNAM DOCUMENTARIES

Anderson Platoon, The (1967)
Dear America: Letters Home from Vietnam (1987)
Face of War, A (1968)

Hearts and Minds (1974)
Hearts of Darkness (1991)
In the Year of the Pig (1968)
Memory of Justice (1976)
Swimming to Cambodia (1987)
Vietnam: An American Journey (1981)
Woodstock (1970)

11. RAMBOESQUE FILMS: THE SUPERHEROES

To THE ORDINARY moviegoer or video renter, it must seem quite incredible that the United States did not handily win the war in Southeast Asia. Without a doubt, characters portrayed by Sylvester Stallone, Chuck Norris, and a long list of Rambo wannabes have killed sufficient Vietnamese on the screen to guarantee overwhelming victory. These same characters have also employed the combat skills learned in Vietnam to become movie superheroes in fighting crime and corruption on the streets and in the cities back home.

The superhero subgenre* of Vietnam War film generally brings to mind Stallone as Rambo or Norris as Colonel Braddock in their series of movies. The success of those films, however, has led to a proliferation of the subgenre, with releases from seemingly every Hollywood and foreign studio, large and small.

Ramboesque films set in Vietnam usually center on an individ-

---

*At times it is difficult to distinguish between the superhero subgenre and those Vietnam movies that feature criminal and/or disturbed veterans. Some superhero films also attempt to mimic the real-war motion pictures. For the purposes of this book, the Ramboesque film is distinguished from the criminal/disturbed film by the superhero's good and/or honorable objectives—even if he does have to resort to illegal means to accomplish his aims, and despite the fact that his mental state might not be considered quite normal by conventional standards. As for comparison of the Ramboesque movies to the real-war films, any veteran, and any nonveteran who has a reasonable grasp of reality, will recognize that the only accurate content of the superhero movies is the end-of-picture disclaimer that announces, "Any similarity between actual people or events and this film is purely coincidental."

ual or a small group of Americans attempting to rescue POWs, or the same personnel performing amazing deeds against overwhelming odds as they fight drug dealers and other street riffraff back home. The makers of Ramboesque films generally claim no political intent, their only objective being to entertain—while, of course, making a profit. This making of Vietnam vets into heroes, albeit of the comic book variety, is not a popular phenomenon among the lingering anti-Vietnam, antiestablishment set, who are still lamenting the extinction of the protest and antiwar film. Many in this group, including a number of professional film critics, credit the popularity of the Ramboesque subgenre of Vietnam War film to the Ronald Reagan era of U.S. militarism and worldwide projection of power.

Of the two explanations—entertainment versus Reaganism—the former is certainly more valid. However, regardless of the explanation for their popularity, the Ramboesque films do provide a commonality of concern for the antiveteran factions and the Vietnam veterans themselves. Both groups share a disdain of the subgenre, but for greatly different reasons. While the antimilitary forces pan the Ramboesque films because of their violence and glorification of warfare, veterans recognize that their screen versions of combat are so far removed from reality that they cannot be compared to actual events. What is a concern is that some viewers of the Ramboesque films, particularly the young, do not have an adequate understanding of the military and of the Vietnam War to keep them from confusing the antics of Stallone, Norris, and company with actual occurrences. The result is that these superhero-film believers do not understand how 2.5 million servicemen failed to win a war when individuals such as Rambo and Braddock are singlehandedly able to accomplish impossible missions against overwhelming odds.

Although it is Sylvester Stallone's character John Rambo who has lent his name to the superhero subgenre of Vietnam War film, the Rambo movies were not the first films to feature comic-book-like warriors fighting communists in Vietnam and street vermin back home. Tom Laughlin, as the director and star in a series of films about the "reluctant" hero Billy Jack, was the first to bring to the screen a one-against-the-world Vietnam veteran who feared no man and, regardless of the odds, stood up for what he thought was right. Laughlin's *Born Losers* (1967), *Billy Jack* (1971), and *The Trial of Billy Jack* (1974) feature a former Green Beret who hated the Vietnam War and has dropped out of society after returning home. Billy Jack claims to be against violence, but he does not hesitate to beat hell out of anyone with whom he disagrees. Most of the tremendous success of the Billy Jack movies, however, cannot be attributed to the superhero's being a Vietnam veteran; rather, they have succeeded in spite of his war service. Billy Jack is not proud of his time in uniform and is antiestablishment in every aspect as he defends oppressed minorities, harassed war protesters, and flower children of all ages.

During the pre-Rambo period of superhero Vietnam-veteran films, the veterans are typically depicted as burned-out, vagrant types with no direction to their lives. In films such as *Clay Pigeon* (1971) and *High Velocity* (1977), veterans are recruited by the police or wealthy Americans to perform difficult, dangerous missions. Their abilities to destroy and kill are their primary marketable skills, and ultimately the vets are shown to have been used and taken advantage of in peacetime in the same manner as they were in Vietnam.

Often in the pre-Rambo films, the motivation of the veteran to lash out against new enemies is generated by the killing of the vet's wife or girlfriend. In *Chrome and Hot Leather* (1971), a Vietnam veteran and his buddies pursue a motorcycle gang that is responsible for the death of the vet's fiancée. A group of Texas toughs who kill a former POW's wife and grind off his hand in a garbage disposal are the targets of the veteran's vengeance in *Rolling Thunder* (1977). In other films, the reawakening of the veteran's warrior spirit is generated by disgust with the deterioration of the old home neighborhood while he was gone. *Taxi Driver* (1976) features a Marine vet who is sickened by the late-night drug dealing, prostitution, and other criminal activity he observes as a cab driver. Although Robert De Niro, in the title role, is about as strange as the crooks and street people he takes on, his vigilante acts make him a local hero.

The Vietnam-vet superhero movies continued to make at least one appearance a year for nearly a decade after the United States had withdrawn from Southeast Asia. It was not, however, until the 1982 release of *First Blood* and its introduction of Sylvester

Stallone as John Rambo that the subgenre really defined itself and found a wide audience. Through *First Blood* and its two sequels, Stallone as Rambo quickly became identified as the ultimate motion-picture Vietnam veteran. Just as John Wayne had assumed the role of the stereotypical western cowboy and World War II soldier during the 1940s and 1950s, Stallone became the public's idea of the superhero warrior who refused to give up the Vietnam fight.*

Rambo's screen introduction occurs on a dark, rainy Pacific Northwest day. He is dirty and long-haired and wears a field jacket with an American flag patch as he tries to find an old friend from Vietnam only to learn he has died of Agent Orange complications. Rambo wanders into the ironically named town of Hope and is stopped by a policeman who warns, "Wearing that flag on that jacket, looking the way you do—you're asking for trouble around here, friend."

Later, the police arrest Rambo for vagrancy and possession of a large knife and place him in a cell, which triggers flashbacks to his days as a POW. Rambo goes crazy, whips the entire police force in hand-to-hand combat, and escapes to the woods. Shortly after, a police report arrives revealing that Rambo is a former Special Forces soldier who received the Medal of Honor for actions in Vietnam. A deputy sheriff remarks, "Those Green Berets, they're real badasses." Over the next ninety minutes the police and the National Guard discover just how much of a "badass" Rambo really is. Wounds slow him only until he can hand-suture the lesions closed. He takes on armed helicopters with a handful of rocks. Soon even the police realize, "We ain't hunting him, he's hunting us."

With more and more police and National Guardsmen in pursuit, Rambo mentally withdraws back to Vietnam as he lives off the land and takes up a feral existence in a cave. Rambo returns to reality, or at least his perception of it, only when his former Vietnam commander calls him using his old Green Beret call sign on a captured police radio. His Vietnam commander advises the cops to give up the chase, saying, "Let him skip through. In a few weeks he will defuse; you'll pick him up in a car wash in Seattle

---

*Interestingly, neither Stallone nor Wayne—Hollywood's ideal military men—ever served a day in the armed services in peace or war.

or somewhere." But the police do not back off, and neither does Rambo. He defeats the cops and the National Guard and returns to Hope to kill the sheriff and destroy most of the town. Rambo is never stopped by the authorities—the film ends with his voluntary surrender.

Three years later, in 1985, Stallone's Vietnam-vet character returns to the screen to provide closure for the first film and to set the standard for all Vietnam-veteran superhero movies of the future. *Rambo: First Blood Part II* opens with the hero in prison serving time making big rocks into little rocks for his actions in Part I. His former Special Forces commander arrives, beret in hand, to recruit Rambo to return to Vietnam to rescue POWs left behind. No explanation is offered as to why the military has to turn to a not-very-stable convicted felon to perform a dangerous mission rather than call on its own active-duty special-operations units— except for the weak excuse that the POW camp is the same one in which Rambo was held during the war. Rambo is reluctant at first, but he finally accepts the mission with only one question: "Do we get to win this time?"

Over the next one-and-one-half hours, Rambo kills a Vietnamese or a Soviet adviser at the average rate of one per minute. He accomplishes this body count of nearly one hundred through use of machine guns, rifles, exploding arrows, knives, and his bare hands. As almost an aside to this spectacular exhibit of killing, he manages to rescue the POWs. The only problem is that he was not supposed to win this time either, so his CIA controllers attempt to stop his return of the prisoners. But not even the CIA can stop Rambo, and with gaping, bloody wounds streaking his rippling muscles, Rambo brings the abandoned prisoners to safety.

In *Rambo III* (1988), Rambo returns from retirement in a Far East monastery to perform another rescue mission. This time his objective is to free his old Special Forces boss from captivity by the Soviets in Afghanistan. Everything in this film mirrors its big budget—big guns, big explosions, big battles. The only cost-saving measure seems to be a limited wardrobe budget; muscular Rambo never seems to have a shirt to cover his oiled body. Where the first two Rambo films were parodies of comic-book heroes, *Rambo III* is a parody of Rambos I and II. By film's end, Rambo has survived more impossible situations, performed more outrageous missions, and killed more enemy soldiers than did all the Vietnam vets in all their tours combined. All that is left for Rambo to do is re- tire and join the ranks of other out-of-work former comic-book heroes.

Even before Rambo reached the screen, Chuck Norris starred in a series of films in which the hero was a tough, no-nonsense Viet- nam veteran. In *A Force of One* (1979) and *Good Guys Wear Black* (1979), Norris's characters identify themselves as Vietnam veterans primarily to validate the tough-guy image they attempt to project. As with other Norris films, plot and dialogue take backseat to any excuse to fight with one's feet and to grunt and yell as loudly as possible. Norris continued his films with *Forced Vengeance* in 1982, the primary difference between it and his earlier films being the Hong Kong setting. Fighting with his feet is still a priority for Norris's character.*

In 1984, *Missing in Action* introduced Norris as Colonel James Braddock, a long-haired, bearded commando who rescues POWs from communist Vietnam years after all prisoners have supposedly been released. Braddock's similarities to Rambo are many. Both are former POWs, both spend much time with their shirts off, and both seem dedicated to wiping the Vietnamese off the face of the earth. The financial success of *Missing in Action* led to a "prequel" that backdates Braddock to the time he was a prisoner of war. *Missing in Action II* (1985) features action so contrived and comic- book-like that one expects *Pow* or *Wham* with stars and exclama- tion points to appear on the screen. In 1988, Norris once again returned to Vietnam and a good payday in *Braddock: Missing in Action III* to rescue his wife and son left behind ten years earlier. All three of the Braddock films share absolutely unbelievable dia- logue, situations, and action. No attention whatsoever is paid to the accuracy of uniforms, weapons, and equipment.

Regardless of their absurdity and unbelievability, Rambo and Braddock have proved as unbeatable at the box office as they are on the screen. Stallone and Norris have had their careers greatly enhanced, and both have become stars in spite of the seeming

*Norris was a three-time world karate champion before beginning his film career. Although he served in the air force in the 1950s and his brother was killed in Vietnam, Norris is not a veteran of the war in Southeast Asia except through the magic of motion pictures.

lack of any real acting talents. Even worse, in addition to spawning profits and advancing the careers of Norris and Stallone, the Rambo and Braddock films have produced a seemingly unending list of superhero clones.*

The Rambo/Braddock wannabe films follow the same two basic superhero scenarios as the movies they emulate. Either they rescue POWs in Vietnam or they fight crime, drugs, and corruption on the streets back home. The in-country superhero films share several additional characteristics. All follow plot lines that are totally lacking in credibility. The acting is poor, and anything extra in the budget goes for additional explosives. No money is wasted on military advisers to provide any degree of accuracy in weapons, uniforms, and equipment. Most of the wannabe superhero actors dress in thrift-shop attire or in uniforms left over from World War II or earlier. Weapons appear to have been borrowed from some third world country or to have been purchased at a confiscated-weapons auction. Ammunition is no problem: Superheroes rarely carry any extra ammo but are still able to shoot all day without reloading. Apparently, they are also so tough that they need to carry no water or rations. Vehicles, artillery, and armor are usually relics that appear to have been borrowed from some small-town park or from in front of the local VFW hall.

Superhero wannabe films are filled with scenes of hand grenade pins being pulled by the hero's teeth, and one machine-gun burst easily eliminates a dozen or so men. Silent kills are made with knife throws of more than a hundred feet, and a single drink of water from a rusty canteen can heal bullet and shrapnel wounds. Superhero wannabe movies deserve no more mention than their titles and include *Eye of the Eagle I* (1987), *Eye of the Eagle II* (1988), *P.O.W. The Escape* (1986), *Saigon Commandos* (1987), *Strike Commando* (1987), *Tornado* (1983), *The Last Hunter* (1980), *War Bus* (1985), and *Dog Tags* (1990). Most of these films received either limited or no theatrical release and went directly to videotape. With garish pictures of explosive combat and printed

---

*Not even Hollywood has had the nerve to team Stallone and Braddock in what would have to be the ultimate superhero film. Beyond the obvious issues of finances and egos, the likely reason is that no screenwriter has been able to conceive any mission so difficult and dangerous as to require the joint skills of such a dynamic duo.

promises of blood and gore, they sit on video-store shelves waiting
to deliver a grossly incorrect, ridiculous message of what Vietnam
was really like to any unsuspecting renter with a few dollars in
hand.

Only one of the Vietnam superhero films deserves any attention
for its merits rather than its faults. *Uncommon Valor* (1983) follows
a POW rescue plot similar to that of other such films, the primary
difference being that it is better acted and a bit more believable.
The performances of the all-star cast including Gene Hackman,
Robert Stack, Fred Ward, and Patrick Swayze, along with attention
to detail in weapons and tactics, are particularly noteworthy. Insights into actual military operations are provided through the
extensive training and rehearsals that the rescue team goes
through before deploying on its mission. Clichéd characters such
as a French gun salesman who sports a parrot on his shoulder and
a Vietnam-veteran team member who wears a hand grenade as a
necklace detract from the film's realism, but good dialogue makes
up for the weaknesses. Hackman's character delivers several long
speeches about Vietnam veterans having only each other to depend on because the country they served thinks they are crazy
and/or criminals. This is one of the few Hollywood portrayals of
Vietnam, especially of the superhero subgenre, after which a veteran will feel good.

The post-Rambo superhero films set in the United States have
stayed fairly true to the earlier standards, with Vietnam veterans
as street vigilantes or as cops with attitude. Ridding the streets of
drugs and pushers is the objective of veteran superheroes in such
films as *American Commandos* (1985). *The Annihilators* (1985), *Exterminator II* (1984), and *Steele Justice* (1987). In some of these
films, such as *Zebra Force* (1977), the vets admit that it is not all
bad if they take a little of the profits from the street scum they are
eliminating.

These superhero-in-the-U.S. films follow a formula—brief
flashbacks to combat and/or atrocities in Vietnam followed by
scenes of a troubled vet returning home and not being able to find
a job or to sustain a relationship with the opposite sex. A gratuitous nude scene during a chance sexual encounter or during a
visit to a topless bar occurs early in the movie. After wandering
aimlessly, the vet finds a purpose to his life, and a use for the com-

bat skills learned in Vietnam, when he confronts the local street toughs, drug pushers, the Mafia, or other ne'er-do-wells. Of course, the avenging vet wears a field jacket for the majority of the picture. Each of these films seems to attempt to outdo the others in devising bloody methods for the vet to kill off his opponents. The police in these films seldom make an appearance unless they are a part of the bad-guy gangs. In a climax consisting of a huge battle with multiple explosions and a megadeath body count, the vet is wounded but victorious and walks into the sunset to heal and, maybe, return for a sequel.

The second type of post-Rambo superhero film features a crazy Vietnam-veteran policeman. Most of the supercop films have bigger budgets than the vigilante movies and feature well-known performers. Mickey Rourke introduced the subgenre in 1985 when he played a New York police detective in Michael Cimino's *Year of the Dragon.* Rourke's character wears a USMC pin and a miniature U.S. flag in his lapel as he shoots and bludgeons first and asks questions later—or not at all. He is described as "selfish, callous, and indifferent to suffering" by his girlfriend. Rourke's character inflicts so many casualties that his boss warns him to remember he is no longer in Vietnam and cannot kill indiscriminately. The motivation behind this film about a veteran cop who is crazy, racist, and violent is much easier to understand when the credits roll and it is revealed that Oliver Stone cowrote the screenplay.

Mel Gibson perfects the role of crazy, suicidal, superhero cop in the extremely popular 1987 release *Lethal Weapon.* Gibson's character comments that all he has ever been good at is killing people. His fellow police officers and the crooks on the street think he is out of his mind and fear him. Another Vietnam-vet cop who does not worry about due process is played by Steven Seagal in *Above the Law* (1988). Although both Seagal and Gibson are their respective films' heroes, Vietnam-veteran drug dealers are also the villains in each.

Unfortunately, the future of the Vietnam-veteran superhero film is bright. As long as Hollywood needs a rationale for heroes with "super" capabilities—super angry, super strong, super mean, and super lethal—the character will continue to be exploited. Millions of Americans and moviegoers around the world will form their image of the Vietnam veteran from what they see on the movie screen. Unfortunately, accuracy and reality will continue to be the first casualities in superhero films, where body count and bloodshed are the primary attractions.

SUPERHERO MOVIES—IN COUNTRY

American Commandos (1985)
Behind Enemy Lines (1987)
Braddock: Missing in Action III (1988)
Dog Tags (1990)
Eye of The Eagle (1987)
Eye of the Eagle II (1988)
Fatal Mission (1989)
Heated Vengeance (1987)
Last Hunter, The (1980)
Losers, The (1970)
Missing in Action (1984)
Missing in Action II (1985)
No Dead Heroes (1987)
Operation Nam (1987)
P.O.W. The Escape (1986)
Rambo: First Blood Part II (1985)
Saigon Commandos (1987)
Strike Commando (1987)
Tornado (1983)
Uncommon Valor (1983)
War Bus (1985)
White Ghost (1987)

SUPERHERO MOVIES—BACK HOME

Above the Law (1988)
American Commandos (1985)
Annihilators, The (1985)
Armed Response (1986)
Band of the Hand (1986)
Billy Jack (1971)
Billy Jack Goes to Washington (1977)

Black Six, The (1978)
Blind Fury (1989)
Blue Thunder (1983)
Borderline (1980)
Born Losers (1967)
Cage (1988)
Chrome and Hot Leather (1971)
Chrome Soldiers (1992)
Clay Pigeon (1971)
Deadly Encounter (1982)
Desperate Hours (1990)
Electra Glide in Blue (1973)
Enemy Territory (1987)
Exterminator, The (1980)
Exterminator, II (1984)
Extreme Prejudice (1987)
Final Mission (1984)
Fireback (1984)
First Blood (1982)
Flashpoint (1984)
Force of One, A (1979)
Forced Vengeance (1982)
GI Executioner, The (1984)
Good Guys Wear Black (1979)
Gordon's War (1973)
Hang Fire (1990)
High Velocity (1977)
Lethal Weapon (1987)
Let's Get Harry (1986)
Malone (1987)
Marked for Death (1990)
Ministry of Vengeance (1989)
Mr. Majestyk (1974)
Nightforce (1987)
Omega Syndrome (1987)
Outlaw Force (1988)
Package, The (1989)
Patriot, The (1986)
Rambo III (1988)
Rolling Thunder (1977)

Satan's Sadists (1969)
Savage Dawn (1985)
Slaughter (1972)
Steele Justice (1987)
Stranger on My Land (1988)
Taxi Driver (1976)
Tiger by the Tail (1968)
Trained to Kill (1973)
Trial of Billy Jack, The (1974)
Vietnam, Texas (1990)
War Birds (1989)
War Dogs (1986)
Year of the Dragon (1985)

12. STRIPES AND BARS: THE POWS

PRISONER-OF-WAR films have played a continuing role in the history of war movies since the beginnings of the genre. Most of these motion pictures, particularly those made during wartime, have focused on the cruel treatment of the POWs by their captors and on the prisoners' efforts to escape. POW films presented during peacetime have also used these plots, as well as adding comedy and the occasional romance between a prisoner and a local girl.

The first POW film, *Escape from Andersonville* (1909), was a brief one-reeler about the Confederate mistreatment of Union prisoners in Georgia during the Civil War. World War I and the post–Great War period provided a variety of films about POWs including an Austrian prisoner of the Italians in *Three of Many* (1916), an American prisoner of the Germans in *After the War* (1918), and a German prisoner of the Americans in *Hell in the Heavens* (1934). Many of these early films included messages promoting harmony and tolerance after the war.

During World War II, POW films joined the propaganda effort to show the brutality and cruelty of the Japanese and the Germans. *The Seventh Cross* (1944) portrays the torture of political prisoners by the Nazis; American bomber pilots are beaten and executed by the Japanese in *The Purple Heart* (1944).

Korean War films continued the plot lines involving cruel captors but also added stories of American collaboration with the enemy in such films as *The Rack* (1954) and *Time Limit* (1957). In two 1954 releases, *Prisoner of War* and *The Bamboo Prison*, American POW collaborators are shown as undercover U.S. intelligence agents seeking information about prison camp conditions.

Vietnam prisoner-of-war movies, like the other films about the conflict, have varied greatly from motion pictures about previous wars. Instead of gallant prisoners resisting barbaric guards and inter-rogators and plotting escape at every opportunity, Vietnam prisoner films feature Rambo-type rescue missions or concern themselves with former POWs who cannot adjust to being home and flash back to captivity whenever confronted with conflict. Few prisoner-of-war films have shown what captivity in North Vietnam was actually like, and even fewer have dwelled on the tribulations and hardships experienced by family members back home.

In a manner similar to other aspects of the war (with the exception of the protest/antiwar movement films), the POWs received little movie notice until years after the conflict had concluded. The few POW films that were produced during the war were made not for theatrical release but for television. Until the late 1960s, the television networks relied on the great number of motion pictures in the vaults of Hollywood studios for their movie broadcasts. Old movies, many dating to the early days of the talkies, were a staple of afternoon and late-night television. After repeated showings of old films and the increased competition offered by the expanding cable industry, network television, as well as some of the new cable stations, began to have a greater demand for movies than were available.*

Instead of turning to the Hollywood studios for a solution to this need for more movies, television looked inward and began making its own motion pictures, premiering them in prime time and using topical, often controversial events as the films' subjects. Made-for-television movies have remained focused on current events over the years, and many of the TV films have rivaled their big-screen competitors in quality. More important, many TV movies are quickly issued on videotape after they air during prime time and share the shelves of video stores with the productions of major Hollywood studios. Unless renters read the video box closely, they can easily be unaware they are watching a film originally made for television.

*Television also had the effect of decreasing the number of moviegoers who paid to see films in theaters. This caused fewer movies to be made—down from five hundred a year in the 1940s to three hundred a year by the 1960s—and as a result, fewer new films were available for television once they had completed the commercial circuit.

It is not surprising that some of the earlier made-for-television films were about Vietnam and in particular prisoners of war in Southeast Asia. While the war and its warriors were not popular with the folks back home watching the conflict on tape on the evening news, POWs were a sympathetic, safe subject that still created enough controversy and interest to gain a movie audience. As a result, the first two movies made about Vietnam POWs were both made for television.

Two 1971 prime-time releases introduced Vietnam POWs to television audiences. In *Welcome Home, Johnny Bristol*, Martin Landau stars as a career officer who is rescued after two years in a POW cage, where he maintained his sanity by recalling every-thing good that ever happened to him in his hometown, Charles, Vermont. When he returns to the States, he discovers no one has ever heard of the town, and it does not appear on any map of any historical period. Landau's character ends up in a military psycho ward convinced that he and his old hometown are a part of some strange government conspiracy or cover-up. Another rescued POW is played by Dennis Weaver in *The Forgotten Man*. Weaver's char-acter has been reported killed rather than captured, and when he gets home he is not particularly welcome. His business has been sold, his wife remarried, his daughter adopted. Throughout their respective films, Weaver's and Landau's characters are plagued by flashbacks to their time as prisoners.

The first nontelevision film about Vietnam prisoners of war, *Limbo* (1972), is not really about the POWs as much as it is about their "waiting wives" back home. Along with its distinction as the first Hollywood production featuring the POW story and the only one made while the war was being fought, *Limbo* is also unusual in that its producer, writer, editor, and many of the production staff are women. This dominance by females in the film's making is appropriate since the movie itself features three wives of POWs who not only wait for word about their husbands but also go to Paris to query North Vietnamese officials about their status. Al-though *Limbo* is generally apolitical, a request for Pentagon sup-port was turned down because one of the wives is having an affair, and the military felt that the film might be used as propaganda against the POWs who were still being held by the communists.

POW films of the late 1970s were similar to the "coming home" movies of the period and featured returning vets as strange, disturbed, and at times violent. *Black Sunday* (1977) has a former POW so angry about the way he is treated by the navy on his return that he plots to kill the president and a large portion of a Super Bowl crowd. In *Twilight's Last Gleaming* (1977), another former POW takes over an air force Titan missile silo and threatens to start World War III if his demands are not met. A POW in *The Deer Hunter* (1978) is so disturbed by his captivity that he stays in Vietnam after his escape and competes in Russian roulette contests.

Rolling Thunder (1977) offers a POW who returns home reasonably well adjusted. He receives a hero's welcome complete with a parade, and his hometown presents him a gift of cash. His calm mental state is broken when a gang of hoodlums—including a Vietnam veteran—steals the money, kills his wife, and grinds off his hand in a kitchen garbage disposal. The former POW responds by sharpening the hook that has replaced his hand, sawing off the barrel of a shotgun, and with the help of another former POW, hunting down and killing the entire gang.

The vast majority of Vietnam POW films focus not on the prisoners themselves but rather on rescue attempts from outside. Most of these movies expound the premise that prisoners were left behind after the war with full knowledge of the United States government. Stallone and Norris as Rambo and Braddock originated this subgenre of Vietnam movie and set the standard of a single individual or a small group led by a former POW who infiltrate North Vietnam, confront an overwhelming number of Vietnamese and their Soviet advisers, kill most or all of them, and escape with a few prisoners. The POW stockade is located in a remote jungle, surrounded by barbed wire and composed of straw huts and a bamboo watchtower. The POWs are detained in wooden cages or holes in the ground where rats are able to freely roam over the hungry, dirty prisoners. Just how these prisoners have managed to survive for ten to twenty years under such harsh conditions is never revealed.

Rambo and/or Braddock clones conduct rescue missions in *P.O.W. The Escape* (1986), *Behind Enemy Lines* (1987), and *Dog Tags* (1990). In similar films the POW rescuers must not only combat the Vietnamese but also are confronted by representatives of the United States government who do not want it revealed that prisoners are still being held. U.S. military personnel actually join the communist forces to halt a rescue attempt in *Operation Nam* (1987). A similar scenario is followed in *The Forgotten Warrior* (1987) and in *White Ghost* (1987).

According to the movies, prisoners who are released instead of rescued are not safe from their own government. In *The Forgotten* (1989), six Green Berets are set free after seventeen years in Vietnam in order to enhance U.S. and Vietnamese trade possibilities. Instead of going home, the six are taken by the CIA to Germany for interrogation and execution so they will not reveal the nature of their last mission in Vietnam, which was to prolong the war so additional profits could be made by the munitions manufacturers. *The Forgotten* is typical of all the POW films in that there is no attention to detail in uniform and equipment accuracy. Judging from the awards and decorations of the Green Berets in *The Forgotten*, it appears the men are all veterans of the Korean Conflict as well as Vietnam. Unless the former POWs fought their first war as pre-grade-schoolers, this is just not possible.

An interesting aspect of Vietnam prisoner-of-war films is that they focus on rescue attempts by outside forces rather than escape from within. Although there were in fact several escape attempts from prisons in North Vietnam and at least one successful escape from a Vietcong camp in the South,* Hollywood seems to prefer to show American prisoners as helpless, complacent inmates instead of the brave, resourceful detainees featured in movies about previous wars, who outsmarted and evaded their captors with no outside assistance. During and after the Vietnam War, Hollywood continued to produce World War II POW escape films—*The Great Escape* (1963), *Von Ryan's Express* (1965), and *Victory* (1981)—while showing that the only way to freedom for POWs in Southeast Asia was through outside rescue efforts.

Without a doubt, the American prisoners of war in Southeast Asia suffered as much as, or more than, any other characters in the long-running drama known as the Vietnam War. Although the prisoners were used as pawns in negotiations during the war, and the possibility that POWs were left behind has been exploited by

*Army Special Forces Lieutenant James N. Rowe was captured in the Delta region of South Vietnam in 1963 and escaped five years later. Although he wrote a successful book about his experiences, Hollywood thus far has not seen fit to make a movie about his captivity and escape.

Hollywood, television, and seemingly every other group and organization, only three motion pictures have come anywhere near telling the real story of prisoners of war in Vietnam.

The most outstanding overview of the POW experience is given in *The Hanoi Hilton* (1987). This re-creation of North Vietnam's most infamous prison, in downtown Hanoi, accurately shows the confinement conditions, the inferior rations, and the brutal organized torture of prisoners.

The other two creditable POW films are based on the true stories of former prisoners. *When Hell Was in Session*, a 1979 made-for-television movie, tells the story of Navy Commander Jeremiah A. Denton, Jr., who was held by the North Vietnamese for seven and one-half years. This is the first film from any source to accurately show the torture of American prisoners and the failure by North Vietnam to honor Red Cross and Geneva Convention accords on the lawful treatment of prisoners of war. The efforts of Denton's wife to establish communication with her husband and her trials in coping with his capture are also included. Perhaps the most interesting segment of *When Hell Was in Session* is a brief conversation between Denton and his jailers that shines some light on what may have happened to some of the more than two thousand Americans who are still missing in action in Southeast Asia. In the scene, Denton, played by Hal Halbrook, is told by a high-ranking North Vietnamese officer that badly disfigured prisoners—those missing limbs or maimed by wounds received before capture or from torture while in prison—would never be released because their injuries would promote negative world opinion about their captors.*

Another made-of-television movie, *In Love and War*, first aired in 1987. It tells the story of the highest-ranking U.S. prisoner held by the North Vietnamese, Commander James B. Stockdale. The mistreatment of Stockdale and his fellow prisoners and his wife's activism back home to encourage President Nixon to publicly admit that POWs were being tortured are clearly and accurately shown. Some of the most telling lines in the film about the POW experience and the conflict itself are spoken by a North Vietnamese of-

---

*In February 1973, Hanoi released 591 POWs and claimed that was all they were holding. Few of the freed men were missing limbs or were otherwise seriously maimed.

ficer who tells Stockdale that what happens on the battlefield and in the prison is not really important because the communists will ultimately win the war in the streets and on the campuses of the United States.

True-to-life, accurate movies about prisoners of war in Vietnam may very well have run their course. Good ones have already been made, and there really are only so many ways a director can tell a story of long confinement and continuous torture. Freeing POWs will undoubtedly continue to be the objective of various Rambo-type characters in low-budget films that offer little realism. The question of whether or not any POWs were left behind will continue to be a subject of great interest as well as a vehicle that groups of all persuasions will use to move to center stage. Ultimately, the POW will continue to be used in much the same way he was during the long years that the United States could neither commit to victory nor give up and come home.

POW MOVIES

Behind Enemy Lines (1987)
Birdy (1984)
Black Sunday (1977)
Braddock: Missing in Action III (1988)
Combat Shock (1986)
Dear America: Letters Home from Vietnam (1987)
Deer Hunter, The (1978)
Dog Tags (1990)
Exterminator, The (1980)
Fireback (1984)
Firefox (1982)
First Blood (1982)
Forgotten, The (1989)
Forgotten Man, The (1971)
Forgotten Warrior, The (1987)
Good Guys Wear Black (1979)
Hanoi Hilton, The (1987)
Heated Vengeance (1987)
House (1986)
In Love and War (1987)

Intimate Strangers (1986)
Iron Triangle, The (1989)
Limbo (1972)
Long Journey Home, The (1987)
Missing in Action (1984)
Missing in Action II—The Beginning (1985)
More American Graffiti (1979)
My Husband Is Missing (1978)
Night Wars (1988)
No Dead Heroes (1987)
Operation Nam (1987)
P.O.W. The Escape (1986)
Private War (1988)
Rambo: First Blood Part II (1985)
Rolling Thunder (1977)
Some Kind of Hero (1982)
Twilight's Last Gleaming (1977)
Uncommon Valor (1983)
War Dogs (1986)
Welcome Home (1989)
Welcome Home, Johnny Bristol (1971)
When Hell Was in Session (1979)
White Ghost (1987)

13. SYMPATHETIC VETERANS: THE ONLY GOOD VET IS A DISABLED VET

SINCE THE END of the Vietnam War, Hollywood and television have presented real-combat and POW films in an attempt to provide realistic images of the conflict. Superhero Vietnam veterans have provided material for all the action and adventure films that theaters and video-rental stores could ever desire, and deranged veterans have supplied the ingredients for thrillers and terror flicks. In the vast majority of these films, accuracy and truth have been ignored or manipulated, and the Vietnam-veteran character is much more often cast as a villain in a dirty field jacket than as a respectable, productive citizen. Only one type of veteran has emerged in the movies as a sympathetic character—the disabled veteran whose life has been forever altered by battlefield wounds suffered in Vietnam.*

There are restrictions, however, on the qualifications for cinematic sympathy. The disabled vet must be in a wheelchair, blind, or have multiple handicaps, but he must have retained his upper-body strength and agility. More important than his physical condition, though, is his mental state. In order to evoke compassion, the disabled veteran must be verbose in his bitterness about the war, violent within his means to express his rage, and lovingly supportive of other disabled vets.

While the Vietnam War was actually being fought, Hollywood could not manage to present any warrior or veteran of the war in a positive role. As a result, the first disabled-vet film is also the

---

*Approximately seventy-five thousand veterans are classified as disabled by wounds suffered in Vietnam. More than five thousand lost a limb, and more than one thousand suffered multiple amputations.

only one to portray a handicapped vet as the villain. In what has to be one of the greatest miscastings of all time, Alan Alda plays a disturbed Vietnam veteran in *To Kill a Clown* (1972). Alda's character, who has limited mobility and must use canes to 'walk because of Vietnam wounds to his kneecaps, terrorizes a young couple who rent a cottage from him on a remote island. Except for being a veteran, no reason for his behavior is offered. More interesting than Alda's character are his two Doberman pinschers, named Rice and Charlie, that assist in harassing the couple.

After the fall of Saigon in 1975, Hollywood slowly eased into developing movies about sympathetic disabled Vietnam veterans. In the initial films, vets are sympathetic crooks rather than admirable heroes. *Special Delivery* (1976) features a bank-robbing gang of Vietnam vets, one of whom hopes to use his ill-gotten gains to purchase a glass eye so he will no longer have to cover the empty socket with a black patch. In *Rolling Thunder* (1977), a former POW returns home physically whole only to lose a hand in a kitchen garbage disposal while fighting a gang of thugs who kill his wife. He then seeks revenge with a sawed-off shotgun and a sharpened hook in place of his missing hand. Another 1977 film, *Zebra Force*, features a badly scarred vet who lost an arm to wounds and who leads his old Vietnam squad against mobsters in southern California. Their primary objective is "to rid society of scum," but they do not at all mind getting rich from stolen mob money in the process.

It was not until 1978 that Hollywood produced a film that would set the standard for sympathetic disabled-Vietnam-veteran movies. *Coming Home* opens in a VA hospital with a group of disabled vets discussing the emotional and physical pain they experienced during the war and since. Eventually the scene shifts to a paralyzed former Marine named Luke (Jon Voight) lying on a hospital gurney. In an Oscar-winning performance, Voight's character moves from the gurney to a wheelchair to a love affair with an officer's wife, played by Jane Fonda. Along the way, Luke chains himself to the gate of a Marine Corps recruiting depot in protest of the war. When the husband (Bruce Dern) of Fonda's character returns from his Vietnam tour and confronts his wife's lover, Luke responds, "I'm not the enemy; maybe the enemy is the fucking war. You don't want to kill anybody here; you have enough guilt to carry around."

At the end of *Coming Home*, the physically whole but mentally disturbed character played by Dern commits suicide while the disabled Luke is speaking out against the war at a local high school. The film concludes with Luke telling students, "And now I'm here to tell you that I have killed for my country, or whatever, and I don't feel good about it 'cause there's not enough reason, man, to feel a person die in your hands or to see your best buddy get blown away. I'm here to tell you it's a lousy thing, man. I don't see any reason for it. And there's a lot of shit that I did over there that I find fucking hard to live with. And I don't want to see people like you, man, coming back and having to face the rest of your lives with that kind of shit. It's as simple as that. I don't feel sorry for myself. I'm a lot fucking smarter now than when I went. And I'm just telling you there's a choice to be made here."

The same year *Coming Home* set the standard for sympathetic wheelchair-bound veterans, the highly acclaimed *Deer Hunter* (1978) added to the definition of the subgenre. Of the three Russian-American steelworkers in the film who go off to Vietnam, one, Steve (John Savage), missing his legs, returns to a VA center. He prefers to stay in the hospital rather than go home because he feels he no longer "fits" in his old environment. Steve's primary contacts with the world outside the hospital are his old friend Nick, who sends him winnings from Russian roulette contests in Saigon, and his wife, Angela, who sends packages containing socks in spite of the fact that her husband no longer has feet. By film's end, Steve has recovered enough to return home and, with Angela at his side, is prepared to attempt to face the future.

Television also picked up on the "disabled Vietnam-veteran hero" and aired movies on the subject before the popularity of *Coming Home*. The first made-for-television disabled-vet movie was actually telecast in March 1975, a few months before the end of the war. *The Desperate Miles* tells the true story of a vet who lost one leg and part of the other to a mine in 1967. Seven years later he sets off from Long Beach in his wheelchair, bound for San Diego, in order to prove to himself and other disabled vets that there is a life outside the VA hospitals.

Another TV-movie, *Just a Little Inconvenience* (1977), features a vet who quits his job to help a disabled war buddy—he'd lost an arm and a leg—to learn to ski and to regain his sense of self-worth. Although both of these made-for-television movies are strictly low budget and neither has been released on video, they are as close as Vietnam veterans can get to having films from their war to compare to those of the Good War such as *The Best Years of Our Lives* (1946).

Two more televised disabled-vet films, both about athletes, aired in 1980. In *Coach of the Year*, a former professional football player confined to a wheelchair because of Vietnam wounds returns home, and the only job he can find is in a boys' reform school. Although one of the students tells him he is a loser, just like the inmates, he coaches their football team to victory over an exclusive private school. The second film, *Fighting Back*, focuses on the real-life story of Rocky Bleier, who, despite serious combat wounds, returned from Vietnam to football's Pittsburgh Steelers to become their fourth all-time leading rusher.

By the early 1980s, television had ceased making disabled-vet films and gone on to more contemporary issues, but Hollywood continues to turn to the subgenre fairly regularly. In the 1981 release *Cutter's Way*, John Heard plays a bitter, cynical Vietnam vet who lost an eye, an arm, and a leg in Vietnam. Heard's character wears a field jacket and is an obnoxious, wife-beating drunk, but he still manages to bring a brutal murderer to justice. *Savage Dawn* (1985) has a vet in a wheelchair who defends his ranch and town against a sadistic motorcycle gang. *Enemy Territory* (1987) has another wheelchair-using veteran who defends his apartment against a violent gang. In *Cage* (1988), because of a head wound suffered in Vietnam, a disabled veteran has the mind of a child, but he has the physique of a giant. He makes his living by fighting to-the-death matches conducted in a locked cage but is so childlike that he expects an ice-cream-cone treat for his victories.

A sympathetic, blind Vietnam vet attempts to adjust to a sightless world in *Ordinary Heroes* (1985); in a rarity for Vietnam films of any genre, he has a loving wife who stays by his side. The ultimate blind character, however, appears in *Blind Fury* (1989), which features a vet who, through teachings from Vietnamese mountain villagers, learns to "see" with his mind rather than his eyes. He fights, and wins, against mobsters armed with clubs, knives, pistols, and machine guns.

For more than a decade, sympathetic disabled-Vietnam-veteran movies rode the coattails of the successful *Coming Home*. It was not until 1989 that Oliver Stone released the next epic version of the plight of handicapped vets. Unfortunately, in *Born on the Fourth of July*, Stone manipulates fact and invents fiction—just as he had in his real-war story *Platoon*—in his attempt to redefine the sympathetic, bitter, antiwar veteran in a movie based on the real-life experiences of Ron Kovic. Kovic, played by Tom Cruise, begins the film as a gung-ho teenager who volunteers for the Marine Corps and Vietnam. On his second tour, he is severely wounded and his legs paralyzed. By film's end he has joined the Vietnam Veterans Against the War* and crashes the Republican National Convention to declare, "This society lied to me. The Vietnamese have been struggling for their independence; we are killing our brothers in Vietnam."

While Ron Kovic is indeed a sympathetic character, both he and Stone claimed as fact and showed as truth many things—such as Kovic's experience at a college war protest and his visit to the family of a fellow Marine he thinks he killed—that have since been exposed as fabrication. Stone's and Kovic's attitudes toward the war and, particularly, its warriors are typified at the end of the film. Rather than a dedication to the dead and maimed of either side, the film credits list an "In Memoriam" to war protester and antiestablishment activist Abbie Hoffman, who made a brief appearance as himself in the film but died before its release.

Another category of disability that receives some movie mention is the effect of the defoliant Agent Orange on the health of Vietnam veterans and their children. The first film reference to Agent Orange was made in the 1974 antiwar, antimilitary documentary *Hearts and Minds*. Against a background shot of a carpenter constructing baby coffins, the documentary denounces the use of the chemical because of its alleged effects on Vietnamese civilians. No mention is made, or sympathy offered, to any possible consequences suffered by American infantrymen and Marines.

Agent Orange plays a small but important role in the introduction of Rambo in *First Blood* (1982). Before Rambo gets into trouble with the local police, he looks for an old friend from Vietnam only to discover he has died from cancer induced by Agent Orange. In *Bell Diamond* (1987) a Vietnam vet is rendered sterile be-

*Of the 2.5 million American men and women who served in the war zone, only seven thousand (or slightly more than one-fourth of one percent) ever joined the Vietnam Veterans Against the War.

cause of his exposure to the chemical, and in *Combat Shock* (1986) a vet is haunted by his belief that his exposure to Agent Orange is responsible for his son's disfiguring birth defects. The failure of the U.S. government to recognize the effects of the chemical and the lack of treatment offered its victims by the Veterans Administration are mentioned in the 1991 film *Article 99*.

Generally, Hollywood films have mixed sympathy for victims of Agent Orange with a bit of an indictment of the vet for having served in Vietnam in the first place. Many of these films also use the plight of the chemical-affected veteran as a grandstand from whuch to denounce the Pentagon and the major chemical companies that produced the defoliant. None of these movies has been much concerned with balance or with defining the real Agent Orange problem. Television, however, has presented, if not good movies, at least something more accurate. *My Father, My Son* (1988) tells the true story of Admiral Elmo Zumwalt, who ordered the use of Agent Orange to defoliate concealing vegetation along Vietnam rivers and inland waterways, and of his son, who served in many of those same areas and later contracted two types of cancer. This is the only film to attempt any explanation of the advantages of the defoliant and the possible lives it saved as compared to the dangers it offered.

Another made-for-television movie, *Unnatural Causes* (1986), is the only film to provide any real information on the background and possible results of exposure to Agent Orange and similar chemical defoliants. This real-life story focused on former navy medic and VA benefits counselor Maude De Victor, who led the effort for medical recognition of the relationship between veterans' exposure to Agent Orange and the health of their children. *Unnatural Causes* includes actual news footage of air force C-123s spraying some of the eighteen million gallons of Agent Orange and related defoliants that were used in Vietnam.

Be he a man in a wheelchair, one who cannot see, or one who is wasting away from cancer, the only sympathetic Vietnam veteran in movies is the disabled Vietnam veteran. According to the messages delivered through Hollywood films and TV movies, only those veterans who have suffered greatly and will never again be physically whole are worthy of the compassion of the viewer and of an ungrateful nation.

SYMPATHETIC DISABLED-VET MOVIES

Blind Fury (1989)
Born on the Fourth of July (1989)
Cage (1988)
Coach of the Year (1980)
Coming Home (1978)
Cutter's Way (1981)
Deer Hunter, The (1978)
Desperate Miles, The (1975)
Enemy Territory (1987)
Fighting Back (1980)
Just a Little Inconvenience (1977)
Ordinary Heroes (1985)
Rolling Thunder (1977)
Savage Dawn (1985)
Special Delivery (1976)
To Kill a Clown (1972)
Zebra Force (1977)

AGENT-ORANGE VIETNAM-VET MOVIES

Article 99 (1991)
Bell Diamond (1987)
Combat Shock (1986)
First Blood (1982)
Hearts and Minds (1974)
In Country (1989)
My Father, My Son (1988)
Unnatural Causes (1986)

14. SUSPICIOUS ALLIES, UNUSUAL ENEMIES: THE VIETNAMESE

DURING THE FIRST six decades of war-film production, the portrayal of America's friends and her opponents was simple and consistent. Allies were presented as valiant on the battlefield and resilient on the home front; enemies were shown as evil, barbaric, and animalistic.

Movies about America's Vietnamese allies and enemies, like all the other films about the conflict, have greatly differed from the standard fare delivered by Hollywood about the two world wars and Korea. South Vietnamese civilians are portrayed as prostitutes, pimps, drug pushers, and black marketeers. The only other function of South Vietnamese civilians in the movies is to serve as the victims of torture and atrocities by American and ARVN soldiers. South Vietnamese government officials are consistently corrupt, and its military men are reluctant warriors prone to slothfulness, cowardice, and treachery.

The portrayal of the Vietcong and North Vietnamese Army soldiers has been more complex. Movies about the Vietnam War have generally presented a role reversal between American and enemy forces. Right and wrong, black and white, and "good guy" and "bad guy" themes have been reversed from movies about earlier wars. For the first time in American film history, the enemy is shown as humble, dedicated, fighting for a just cause against an overwhelmingly superior opponent, and winning. While Hollywood's sympathy has been directed toward the VC and the NVA, the moviemakers have made few inroads into accurately showing how the communist soldiers were organized or how they lived and fought. A particular failing of the movies has been in their version of VC and NVA tactics. Any regular attendee of Vietnam movies surely must wonder just how enough enemy soldiers survived the war to make their triumphant march into Saigon in 1975. In film after film, particularly of the superhero subgenre, the communist forces press the attack despite incoming artillery and air strikes, and they use tactics much more akin to conventional warfare than to guerrilla warfare.

Vietnamese characters have not fared well in the movies since their earliest introduction to the big screen in the 1929 pictures *Where East Is East* and *Careers*. In both films, the Vietnamese are played and treated as serfs to the colonial French. A Vietnamese who is discovered attempting to steal a few trinkets kills a French official in *Careers*. In a later film, *Red Dust* (1932), Vietnamese merely provide colorful background characters who act as servants and rubber-plantation workers.

The first hint at the warlike abilities of the Vietnamese is mentioned in *Somewhere I'll Find You* (1942). A journalist in Hanoi remarks that the natives are fighting furiously against the occupying Japanese, but it is difficult to "fight against tanks with bows and arrows." An interesting comment is also made in the same movie by a Vietnamese woman about a character played by Lana Turner: "She is a pretty girl for a white woman."

Post–World War II films set in Indochina include a backdrop of fighting between the French and the Vietminh, but their primary focus remains on routine action and adventure, with Vietnam merely providing an exotic locale. *China Gate* (1957) and *Five Gates to Hell* (1959) both present the Vietminh as little more than sadistic bandits. An earlier film, *Rogue's Regiment* (1948), does offer some background to the guerrilla movement, French colonialism, and the quest for self-determination, but the majority of the movie tracks an American pursuing a Nazi war criminal. The only film of the period to include any information on Vietnamese communist tactics and operations was the 1955 story *Jump into Hell*, about the siege of Dien Bien Phu. Although this picture does include a decent look at the Vietminh trenching system used to overrun the French garrison, the scale of the battle is not captured, nor is any sense of realism attained.

Two movies with similar titles offer the best insights into conditions in prewar Vietnam, the attitudes of the Vietnamese, and early United States policy in the region. *The Quiet American* (1958) is set in 1952 Saigon and was filmed there and in the countryside near Tay Ninh. Based on the Graham Greene novel by the same name, *The Quiet American* does a good job of showing the various Vietnamese factions and the outside influences—such as France, the U.S., the U.S.S.R., and China—that were attempting to project power into the region.

The Ugly American (1963), based on the Burdick and Lederer novel, was the last film to attempt to show what Vietnam was like before the war escalated beyond reason and retrospect. With Marlon Brando as the American ambassador to the fictitious country of Sarkhan, the film shows many of the misunderstandings and cultural differences that would cause so much trouble in later years.

While the Vietnam War was continuing, the few movies directly about the conflict followed the earlier line of prewar films that portrayed the communist guerrillas more like bandits than soldiers and mostly ignored the South Vietnamese. *A Yank in Vietnam* (1964), *To the Shores of Hell* (1965), and *Operation CIA* (1965) offer no sympathy for the enemy, and they provide no insight into the communist soldiers' way of life or their motivation for fighting.

The Green Berets (1968) was the first film to attempt to bring the South Vietnamese and their VC and NVA enemies to the screen with some degree of accuracy. Support of the Vietcong by communist countries around the world is covered, and an attack against a Special Forces camp includes a hint of realism. In the film the South Vietnamese military is represented by an ARVN captain and his troops stationed at the Green Beret outpost. He is one of the few ARVN officers portrayed as brave and loyal in any Vietnam film. The captain is also aware that some of his men are Vietcong and plans his defenses accordingly.

The sun had barely set—in the *east*—at the end of *The Green Berets* (a scene panned by critics as exemplary of the movie's problems) when the antiwar/protest films came to the forefront of American movie production. Although these films are blatantly antimilitary, antidraft, and antieverything, they show the self-indulgence and excesses of the sixties much more than they provide any accurate portrayals of Vietnam or the Vietnamese. Students chanting, "Ho, Ho, Ho Chi Minh!" and waving National Liberation Front (Vietcong) flags are seen in films such as *Medium Cool* (1969), *The Strawberry Statement* (1970), *Zabriskie Point* (1970), and *Getting Straight* (1970). However, none of these films offers any rationale for why the communists are right and the South Vietnamese government wrong, or just why the U.S. should not be involved. Despite their best intentions, most of the protest films deliver no real insights into the conflict in Southeast Asia.

Two documentaries made during the war that received wide distribution and are still available on video-store shelves are typical of what was presented as the truth to America and the world. *In the Year of the Pig* (1968) quotes an American congressman who says, "Ho is the George Washington of his country." Later Ho is praised as "the greatest patriot of this century," and the Vietnamese communists are said to have attracted "the best of a generation." *Hearts and Minds* (1974) follows the same track, showing Ho Chi Minh as a gentle man surrounded by North Vietnamese children who have "a passion for education." The documentary also reports that "the South is enslaved, the North is free," and that the American "invaders" are fighting a war of genocide while the communist forces fight for unity and freedom.

Both documentaries accuse the Americans of being the aggressors and committing atrocities, including the bombing of peaceful villages and the torturing of prisoners. *In the Year of the Pig* features Americans forcibly relocating South Vietnamese villagers, and scenes of what are reported to be children killed by U.S. air attacks. An American army colonel is shown describing his men as "a bloody good bunch of killers," while a U.S. senator (Fulbright) warns viewers never to trust the State Department. *Hearts and Minds* labels U.S. action in Vietnam as "imperialist policy" and quotes a Vietnamese monk who says, "It is not us who are the savages." An American soldier is quoted as saying he enjoys killing and carnage, while, at the same time, students back home are shown waving VC and NVA flags and chanting for peace.

The South Vietnamese fare no better than the Americans in the two documentaries. *In the Year of the Pig* accuses the South Vietnamese government of corruption and election-rigging. *Hearts and Minds* shows South Vietnamese street venders dealing in the black market, and women prostitutes. Vietcong suspects are shown confined in small "tiger cages," and a narrator reports they are being held with no charges filed.

In the Year of the Pig was nominated for an Academy Award for Best Documentary of 1968. *Hearts and Minds* was nominated and won the Oscar in the same category in 1974. For the first time in

United States history, films praising America's enemies and vili-
fying its military were produced and honored by the movie industry.

During the years following the end of the war, Vietnamese on
either side made few appearances in the "coming home" subgenre
of movies. The superhero subgenre of Vietnam War movie generally ignored the South Vietnamese except to include them in minor, stereotypical roles as corrupt officials or prostitutes.
Communist forces play a larger part in the superhero films, but
their primary role is that of cannon fodder to pad the hero's body
count. None of the superhero films offers any more truth about
the South or North Vietnamese than they do about the American
soldiers they feature in their comic-book roles.

A particular failure of the superhero films is in depicting VC
and NVA uniforms, weapons, and equipment. Many of the costumes appear to be left over from World War II Japanese films or
from remakes of French Foreign Legion movies. Weapons of any
sort or origin are used, and the enemy's equipment appears to
have been purchased at an army surplus store going-out-of-
business sale. In the movies, not even the Vietnamese are
Vietnamese—typically, they are played by Filipinos, Chinese, and
other Asians.

Hollywood has made a greater effort to accurately portray the
enemy in the real-war and POW pictures, but the South Vietnamese remain crooks and whores or victims of American atrocities.
South Vietnamese officials are shown as void of compassion and
unwilling to do anything, including their basic jobs, without the
benefit of bribery in such films as *The Children of An Loc* (1980),
Don't Cry, It's Only Thunder (1982), *Purple Hearts* (1984), and *Last
Flight Out* (1990). Typical of the appearance of Vietnamese
women in real-war films is their portrayal in *Hamburger Hill* (1987).
Although it has nothing to do with the story of the actual assault
on Hill 937, a long sequence occurs early in the film of American
soldiers frolicking with prostitutes in a Vietnamese bathhouse.

The only other role for Vietnamese women in real-war films, as
well as for children and old men, is to serve as victims. Some movies, such as *Casualties of War* (1989), use atrocities against Vietnamese civilians as their central theme; others, such as *The Boys
in Company C* (1978), *Platoon* (1986), and *Born on the Fourth of
July* (1989), include the torture and murder of noncombatants as

secondary plot lines. Still other films weave all the characteristics of the South Vietnamese into a single plot. *Off Limits* (1988) features an American mass murderer of Vietnamese prostitutes and a local police force more interested in arguing with the Americans than in assisting in the investigation.

While not a single Vietnam movie offers any reliable portrayal of the South Vietnamese civilians and military, several films have presented reasonably accurate looks at the organization and conduct of the VC and NVA. Portions of two pictures, *The Iron Triangle* (1989) and *The Siege of Fire Base Gloria* (1988), are viewed from the side of the enemy. *The Iron Triangle*, which claims to be "based on the diary of an unknown Vietcong soldier," provides the most accurate and detailed re-creation of day-to-day life in camp and battle. Interaction among soldiers, their commanders, and the Communist Party political officers is shown, as well as the means for discipline and morale building.

The Siege of Fire Base Gloria offers an excellent look at VC and NVA offensive combat tactics and the defensive measures they employed to counter air and artillery threats. This picture and *The Iron Triangle* are the only two films to show communist troops as ordinary humans with the same fears, expectations, and desires experienced by soldiers of all ages and causes. Other real-war Vietnam films such as *Hamburger Hill* (1987), *Platoon* (1986), and *Platoon Leader* (1988), while not offering an in-depth look at the other side, do show the VC and NVA on the battlefield as many American soldiers actually saw them—as fleeting glimpses of ghostlike figures much more interested in survival than in heroics.

A not-so-sympathetic but extremely accurate look at the Vietnamese communists is offered in the POW films. The inhuman treatment—including isolation, starvation, and torture—of American prisoners of war are vividly exhibited in *The Hanoi Hilton* (1987), *In Love and War* (1987), and *When Hell Was in Session* (1979).

Movie versions of Vietnam that feature the period since the fall of Saigon are few but notable. *Boat People* (1983), produced by the Chinese communist government, is the only film to show the imprisonment and execution of South Vietnamese officials by the victorious Northerners and to picture the poverty and lack of human rights suffered by the defeated Southerners. Another result of the communist victory is shown in *The Killing Fields* (1984), in which the Khmer Rouge, supported by the North Vietnamese, commit murders by the hundreds of thousands against their fellow Cambodians. Both films offer excellent insights into why hordes of Southeast Asians have risked everything, including their lives, in an attempt to escape to the West.

Despite these two commendable films on the war's aftermath, Vietnamese who have found freedom and sanctuary in the United States have not fared well in the postwar films. In *Steele Justice* (1987), *Gleaming the Cube* (1989), and *Vietnam, Texas* (1990), former ARVN officers and South Vietnamese government officials are shown leading "Asian Mafia" mobs that deal in drugs, prostitution, and murder in their new American home. The ultimate evil ARVN officer appears in the 1981 film *Search and Destroy*. Identified only as "the Assassin," he tracks down and attempts to kill four former U.S. soldiers who left him behind to be captured during a firefight.

"Good" South Vietnamese appear only in a few postwar-period films, and their purpose is more to make American Vietnam vets look "bad" than to exhibit merits of their own. *Alamo Bay* (1985) features hard-working Vietnamese fishermen on the Texas Gulf Coast being harassed by racist veterans assisted by the Ku Klux Klan. In *The Lady from Yesterday* (1985), a married veteran finds a former Vietnamese girlfriend and their child on his doorstep.

The movies have taken the same liberties with the actual country of Vietnam as they have with the Vietnamese of both sides. (For a complete list of Vietnam stand-ins, see the list at the end of this chapter.) Only five motion pictures (three of which are documentaries), all produced before 1969, were filmed in Vietnam. Filling in as the film version of the hotly contested country have been various locations in the United States, including Hollywood back lots and the southern California hills and valleys, and such diverse shooting locations as Georgia, Kentucky, and New York. Locales more similar to Vietnam, such as Thailand and the Philippines, have provided some of the more realistic-looking jungles and rice paddies, but filmmakers have also attempted to re-create Vietnam in such odd places as Canada, Spain, and England.

SUSPICIOUS-ALLY
(SOUTH VIETNAMESE) MOVIES

Air America (1990)
Alamo Bay (1985)
American Commandos (1985)
Autopsy (1986)
Blind Fury (1989)
Boat People (1983)
Born on the Fourth of July (1989)
Boys in Company C, The (1978)
Careers (1929)
Casualties of War (1989)
Children of An Loc, The (1980)
Don't Cry, It's Only Thunder (1982)
Girl Who Spelled Freedom, The (1986)
Gleaming the Cube (1989)
Good Morning, Vietnam (1987)
Go Tell the Spartans (1978)
Green Berets, The (1968)
Green Eyes (1976)
Greetings (1968)
Lady From Yesterday (1985)
Last Flight Out (1990)
Lotus Lady (1930)
Off Limits (1988)
Purple Hearts (1984)
Quiet American, The (1958)
Red Dust (1932)
Saigon Commandos (1987)
Search and Destroy (1981)
Somewhere I'll Find You (1942)
Steele Justice (1987)
To the Shores of Hell (1965)
Ugly American, The (1963)
Vietnam, Texas (1990)
Where East Is East (1929)
Wild Eye, The (1968)
Yank in Vietnam, A (1964)

UNUSUAL-ENEMY (VC AND NVA) MOVIES

Air America (1990)
Anderson Platoon, The (1967)
Apocalypse Now (1979)
Backfire (1988)
Bat 21 (1988)
Behind Enemy Lines (1987)
Boat People (1983)
Born on the Fourth of July (1989)
Brushfire (1962)
Casualties of War (1989)
Charlie Bravo (1980)
China Gate (1957)
Deer Hunter, The (1978)
Face of War, The (1968)
Five Gates to Hell (1959)
Flight of the Intruder (1990)
Forgotten Warrior, The (1987)
Full Metal Jacket (1987)
Good Morning, Vietnam (1987)
Go Tell the Spartans (1978)
Green Berets, The (1968)
Hamburger Hill (1987)
Hanoi Hilton, The (1987)
Hearts and Minds (1974)
House (1986)
In Love and War (1987)
In the Year of the Pig (1968)
Iron Triangle, The (1988)
Jump into Hell (1955)
Killing Fields, The (1984)
Last Flight Out (1990)
Last Hunter, The (1980)
Losers, The (1970)
Lost Command (1966)
Missing in Action (1985)
Missing in Action II—The Beginning (1985)
My Husband Is Missing (1978)
No Dead Heroes (1987)

Operation CIA (1965)
Platoon (1986)
Platoon Leader (1988)
P.O.W. The Escape (1986)
Quiet American, The (1958)
Rogue's Regiment (1948)
Siege of Fire Base Gloria, The (1988)
To the Shores of Hell (1965)
When Hell Was in Session (1979)

VIETNAM MOVIE STAND-INS

Australia: *Odd Angry Shot, The* (1979)
Canada: *Distant Thunder* (1988)
China: *Boat People, The* (1983)
England: *Full Metal Jacket* (1987)
Italy: *Last Hunter, The* (1980)
   Operation Nam (1987)
   Strike Commando (1987)
   Tornado (1983)
Malaysia: *Bat 21* (1988)
   Welcome Home (1989)
Mexico: *Missing in Action II—The Beginning* (1985)
   Rambo: First Blood Part II (1985)
   Rumor of War, A (1980)
   Who'll Stop the Rain (1978)
Philippines: *American Commandos* (1985)
   Apocalypse Now (1979)
   Boys in Company C, The (1978)
   Braddock: Missing in Action III (1988)
   Don't Cry, It's Only Thunder (1982)
   Green Eyes (1976)
   Hamburger Hill (1987)
   Missing in Action (1984)
   Platoon (1986)
   P.O.W. The Escape (1986)
   Purple Hearts (1984)
   Saigon Commandos (1987)
   Siege of Fire Base Gloria, The (1988)

St. Kitts: *Missing in Action II—The Beginning* (1985)
Spain: *Autopsy* (1986)
  Lost Command (1966)
Sri Lanka: *Iron Triangle, The* (1989)
Thailand: *Air America* (1990)
  Casualties of War (1989)
  Deer Hunter, The (1978)
  Heated Vengeance (1987)
  Last Flight Out (1990)
  Off Limits (1988)
  Operation CIA (1965)
  Ugly American, The (1963)
  Uncommon Valor (1983)
  Welcome Home (1989)
United States:
  California—
    Cage (1988)
    Fighting Back (1980)
    Five Gates to Hell (1959)
    More American Graffiti (1979)
    Operation War Zone (1989)
    To the Shores of Hell (1965)
  Georgia—
    The Green Berets (1968)
  Hawaii—
    Flight of the Intruder, The (1990)
    Uncommon Valor (1983)
  Kentucky—
    In Country (1989)
  New York—
    Search and Destroy (1981)
Vietnam: *Anderson Platoon, The* (1967)
  Face of Battle, A (1968)
  Quiet American, The (1958)
  Wild Eye, The (1968)
  Yank in Vietnam, A (1964)

15. STRANGERS SELDOM SEEN: COMEDIES, MUSICALS, HORROR, AND MORE

WARS PREVIOUS TO Vietnam infused every genre of Hollywood production—dramas, comedies, musicals, cartoons, and westerns—with messages of sacrifice and victory. In this respect, as in so many others, Vietnam has not played to tradition. No all-star-cast musicals like the "canteen" series of World War II films have been produced about Vietnam, and no slapstick comedies about basic training or sad-sack soldiers have made it to the screen. Vietnam, like the taint of unsure parentage or a relative a bit touched in the head, has remained a subject Hollywood prefers to keep separate from certain film types. However, the Vietnam War and its aftermath do occasionally make their way into types of motion pictures not usually used as vehicles for the conflict and its combatants.

Combat and comedy may seem an unlikely union, but humorous movies about warfare and the peacetime military date back to the beginnings of film. Prior to the Vietnam era, comedies set in wartime generally used the period as a backdrop for slapstick, with the military serving as props for gags delivered by duos such as Abbott and Costello, Martin and Lewis, and Hope and Crosby. Seemingly every Hollywood comedy act, including a talking mule named Francis, got into the wartime picture business.

Vietnam, however, forever changed the military comedy film. Harmless slapstick and the amusing adventures of soldiers and sailors on leave during training or between battles gave way to "message humor," which targets the military system and its leadership, as well as the folly of war itself, for ridicule. Most of these films make little or no direct mention of Vietnam but deliver their anti-

Vietnam War message through earlier conflicts such as Korea in M*A*S*H (1970) and World War II in *How I Won the War* (1967).

Few laughs have been provided in any of Hollywood's stories about the Vietnam War, and the nearest thing to a traditional service comedy about the war did not appear until fifteen years after the American withdrawal from Southeast Asia. *Good Morning, Vietnam* (1987) is loosely based on the experiences of Armed Forces Radio disk jockey Adrian Cronauer in 1965. Robin Williams in the lead role is hilarious for the constant banter that at times resembles more his stand-up club act than movie dialogue. Much of the humor is closer to contemporary than to the Vietnam War period, but Williams keeps the film moving at such a fast, funny pace that the laughs outweigh any inaccuracies in time lines or the many hidden messages about the war.

Other Vietnam films, such as *Some Kind of Hero* (1982), *Air America* (1990), and *Dogfight* (1991), include comic relief but only as a minor part of an overall dramatic picture. Vietnam-veteran characters do appear in more traditional motion picture comedies such as *Back to School* (1986), *Men at Work* (1990), and *Quick Change* (1990), but their role is usually as a stereotypical crazy vet.

Musicals have played an important role in military films since the beginning of the talkies in the late 1920s. The war musical reached its zenith during World War II with major Hollywood stars appearing as themselves along with ordinary servicemen in pictures which, if short in plot, were at least long in song, dance, and escapism from the bleakness of the war years. Not a single World War II musical contains a note sung or a step danced that was not in every way positive about the war and its warriors. Conversely, of the few musicals about the Vietnam War, each is blatantly against the war and negative toward the warrior.

The primary characteristic of Vietnam War musicals is their rarity. Only four films can be remotely considered musicals, and they are extremely dissimilar to the World War II examples. The nearest Hollywood has come to a traditional musical about the Vietnam War is the 1979 film adaptation of the Broadway hit *Hair*. This celebration of the hippie life style contains all the great song and dance ingredients of a fine musical. The only difference is that the film is blatantly anti-Vietnam and antimilitary. Its most positive point, however, is that it does not extend its negativism to the individuals who fought the war and does not automatically equate the war's evils with its warriors.

Two films actually produced during the war that can also be included on the short list of Vietnam "musicals" are *Woodstock* (1970) and *F.T.A.* (1972). *Woodstock* is a well-done documentary that focuses on a concert that lent its name to a generation. In addition to wonderful music, the film delivers a good look at the antiwar feeling of many of the attendees and the overall life style of the period. *F.T.A.*, on the other hand, is a poorly produced documentary of the antiwar entertainment troupe led by Jane Fonda and Donald Sutherland during their tour of U.S. bases in the Pacific.

The final, and most recent, Vietnam musical is also the most remarkable. *For the Boys* (1991) follows two entertainers through three wars (World War II, Korea, and Vietnam) as they perform for the troops. The contrasts of the wars, their times, and the audiences are extremely notable.

While the Vietnam War caused a decline to a near void in the production of war-related comedies and musicals, it and its combatants have emerged as characters in the increasingly popular horror-film genre. Because of the difficulties in competing with the horror of actual combat, these films instead concentrate on the war's veterans in the roles of monsters and victims. Vietnam vets appear as the monsters in *Deathdream* (1972) and *Neon Maniacs* (1985) and as the victims of horrible creatures in *Moon in Scorpio* (1987), *Graveyard Shift* (1990), and *Jacob's Ladder* (1990). In other films, such as *House* (1986) and *Night Wars* (1988), Vietnam veterans fill the roles of both monster and victim. The U.S. military and/or government is responsible for horrors in *Autopsy* (1986), *Piranha* (1978), and *Piranha II: The Spawning* (1983).

The popularity and profit of Vietnam films of the late 1980s caused the war and its combatants to appear in some rather unexpected, if not strange, types of movies. A few triple-X porno films of the period include servicemen in uniforms with patches and decorations indicating Vietnam service. In order to get on with the film's more basic action, the uniforms, usually containing even more mistakes than those of mainstream movies, are quickly shed, with no mention of the war. Only two pornographic films, *Stryker Force* (1987) and *The Platoon: More Than a Company of Men* (1988), include actual combat footage from the war, and both feature all-male casts and explicit homosexual sex.

There are other categories of movies that have never been made about Vietnam or that are rarely seen. No legendary detective or famous cartoon character has been cast in a Vietnam movie. Except for a deserter who returns home to his father's cattle ranch in *Proud Men* (1987), cowboys have avoided Vietnam movies. Unlike previous conflicts, where every film genre joined the fight asking only, "What can we do to help win the war?" Vietnam films have consistently showed the war and the warrior as equally evil. While many types of film have been glutted with disturbed, criminal Vietnam vets and some subgenres such as musicals and comedies have been seldom seen, the real strangers to Vietnam War movies have been balance, truth, and accuracy.

VIETNAM COMEDIES

Air America (1990)
Back to School (1986)
'Burbs, The (1989)
D.C. Cab (1983)
Dogfight (1991)
Good Morning, Vietnam (1987)
Hollywood Shuffle (1987)
How I Won the War (1967)
Men at Work (1990)
Moving (1988)
Norwood (1970)
O.C. & Stiggs (1985)
Quick Change (1990)
Ruckus (1982)
Russkies (1987)
Some Kind of Hero (1982)
Splash (1984)
Stripes (1984)
Suppose They Gave a War and Nobody Came (1970)
UHF (1989)
Volunteers (1985)

VIETNAM MUSICALS

For the Boys (1991)
F.T.A. (1972)
Hair (1979)
Woodstock (1970)

VIETNAM HORROR FILMS

Autopsy (1986)
Deathdream (1972)
Graveyard Shift (1990)
House (1986)
Jacob's Ladder (1990)
Moon in Scorpio (1987)
Neon Maniacs (1985)
Night Wars (1988)
Piranha (1978)
Piranha II: The Spawning (1983)
Street Trash (1987)
Texas Chainsaw Massacre 2, The (1986)

16. WAR ON THE SMALL SCREEN: TV MOVIES AND SERIES

DURING THE WAR, television delivered the real Vietnam conflict into the living rooms of America on the evening news. As the war heated up and the number of Americans committed to Southeast Asia escalated, so did television coverage. When U.S. troops began pulling out of the war zone, so did the TV reporters and cameras. The influence of "the first televised war" on the conduct of the conflict and the perceptions of the American and world publics about Vietnam has been much debated. While most of this attention has been devoted to news coverage, television series and movies have also contributed to the understanding and misunderstandings of the war.

The first TV series to feature a Vietnam-veteran character as a regular cast member was "Route 66," which aired on CBS from October 1960 to September 1964. "Route 66" starred Martin Milner and George Maharis as two young men who traveled the highway in a Corvette in search of adventure and new experiences. In late 1962, Maharis became ill with hepatitis and appeared only intermittently over the next months. When it was determined he was no longer physically able to do the show, a replacement was introduced. As Linc Case, Glen Corbett joined Milner's character on the road in an episode aired on March 22, 1963, and remained a cast member until the program was canceled. It was quickly established that Case was a Green Beret Vietnam War hero from Houston who was unsure of his future and in need of coming to grips with his war experiences. Corbett's Vietnam-vet character remained somewhat confused for the remainder of the series but was generally heroic and sympathetic.

Linc Case would be the last "good" vet to appear on a television series for a long number of years. Television went through its own "coming home" period of using returning Vietnam veterans as ready-made black-hat types wearing field jackets who were bent on crime and craziness. Every cop and detective show—and they were numerous during the Vietnam era and postwar years—readily picked up on Vietnam veterans as stereotypical drug users and pushers, thieves, and murderers. If a script called for an insane character, it was a good bet that a Vietnam veteran would be written into the role. Of particular noteworthiness for their inclusion of loathsome Vietnam veterans were the popular series "Mannix," "Cannon," "Kojak," and "The Streets of San Francisco."

Made-for-television movies, although in their infancy, also featured returning veterans as well as other aspects of the war. Generally, TV movies have followed the same trends as their big-screen brothers. However, made-for-television movies, unlike prime-time TV series and Hollywood films, have been a bit kinder to veterans and also a little more accurate in the portrayal of the war and its warriors.

The first Vietnam television motion picture, *The Ballad of Andy Crocker*, aired on ABC on November 18, 1969. This homecoming film features a vet returning to his Texas home to find his girlfriend married to another man and his motorcycle-repair business in ruin. The overall theme of the movie is one often repeated on the big screen and in some TV films to follow: The Vietnam veteran is a loser.

Not all the early TV movies, however, follow this "loser" theme. *Tribes* (1970) presents a decent look at USMC boot camp, *Terror in the Sky* (1971) features a Vietnam vet who helps prevent an airplane disaster, and *The New Healers* (1972) offers three former Vietnam medics who meet the medical needs of an isolated northern California village.

About an equal number of TV films during the same period followed the usual track of disturbed veterans who are not able to fit into "the world" after their return from combat. Typical of these films is *Welcome Home, Johnny Bristol* (1971), in which a former POW finds nothing, including his hometown, as he remembered. *The Forgotten Man* (1971) features a loser vet who comes home to find his wife remarried, his daughter adopted, and his business failed.

Over the years, TV movies have relied more on true stories for

Vietnam plot lines than have Hollywood motion pictures. The first
of these, aired in 1975, loosely follows the experiences of Jim
Mayo, a vet wounded in Vietnam who rolls his wheelchair from
Long Beach to San Diego to show that his disability is not really
a handicap. Interestingly, the original title of the film was the
same as the sign Mayo hung on the back of his wheelchair—*No
Help Required*. The moviemakers' image of desperate veterans
comes through a bit clearer in the final title, *The Desperate Miles*.

Since the fall of Saigon, TV movies based on true events have
mostly been positive about Vietnam veterans. *Fighting Back* (1980)
tells the story of a wounded vet who goes on to pro-football fame,
and true experiences of POWs are told in *When Hell Was in Session* (1979) and *In Love and War* (1987). Other films, such as
Friendly Fire (1979), which is about an Iowa couple's quest to find
out the truth about their son's death in Vietnam, and *Kent State*
(1981), which centers on the shooting death of four students by
the Ohio National Guard in 1970, provide a decent balance of opposite views of controversial subjects.

Unfortunately, not all made-for-television movies have been so
positive or balanced. In *Code of Honor* (1984), a Vietnam veteran
is a dishonest adulterer; in *Follow Your Heart* (1990), a veteran is a
child molester. Vietnam veterans are suicidal criminals in *The Park
Is Mine* (1985) and *Memorial Day* (1983). The 1987 TV film *Proud
Men* (1987) features a war deserter who returns home to convince
his father that the war is wrong.

Because of production costs, real combat has been an infrequent subject of made-for-television movies. Only one such film
has been made to date, but it is comparable to the better big-
screen releases. *A Rumor of War* (1980) is based on the book of the
same title about the real-life Vietnam experiences of USMC Lieutenant Philip Caputo. The film shows Caputo arriving in country
as a gung-ho Marine who is enthusiastic about the war, only to become disillusioned and eventually court-martialed for atrocities
against Vietnamese civilians.

Several TV movies, including *Fly Away Home* (1981) and *Shooter*
(1988), were produced as pilots for unsuccessful series. It was not
until 1987, however, that a series based on the Vietnam War finally made it to prime time. "Tour of Duty," which followed the
adventures of an infantry platoon of the Americal Division, premiered on CBS and lasted with mild success for a little more than

two seasons. In the same year, Home Box Office aired a trilogy of ninety-minute fictionalized stories set in Vietnam. ABC followed the next year with "China Beach" which, by the time it was discontinued in 1992, had earned well-deserved Emmys for its episodes and performers.

The networks and cable stations continue to air the occasional new made-for-television movie, and old Vietnam films from Hollywood and TV have become a late-night staple across the channels. Vietnam veterans also make rare appearances as villains and even rarer appearances as heroes on the various prime-time series. Mostly, however, Vietnam is old news for television; the war and its veterans have been replaced by more contemporary issues. There is no indication that the Vietnam War will make any resurgence on the small screen in the near future. Unfortunately, future generations will likely develop many of their opinions about the war and its warriors from the same movies that have established the Vietnam veteran as a stereotypical loser bent on crime and insanity.

MADE-FOR-TELEVISION VIETNAM MOVIES

Ballad of Andy Crocker, The (1969)
Children of An Loc, The (1980)
Chrome Soldiers (1992)
Coach of the Year (1980)
Code of Honor (1984)
Deadly Encounter (1982)
Desperate Miles, The (1975)
Fighting Back (1980)
Fly Away Home (1981)
Follow Your Heart (1990)
Forgotten, The (1989)
Forgotten Man, The (1971)
Friendly Fire (1979)
Guts and Glory: The Rise and Fall of Oliver North (1989)
In Love and War (1987)
Intimate Strangers (1986)
Just a Little Inconvenience (1977)
Kent State (1981)

Lady from Yesterday, The (1985)
Last Flight Out (1990)
Long Journey Home, The (1987)
Lost Flight (1969)
Memorial Day (1983)
My Father, My Son (1988)
My Husband Is Missing (1978)
New Healers, The (1972)
Park Is Mine, The (1985)
Promise of Love, The (1980)
Proud Men (1987)
Resting Place (1986)
Rumor of War, A (1980)
Shooter (1988)
Stranger on My Land (1988)
Terror in the Sky (1971)
To Heal a Nation (1988)
Tribes (1970)
Vestige of Honor (1990)
Welcome Home, Johnny Bristol (1971)
When Hell Was in Session (1979)

17. THE ONLY WAR WE HAD: CONCLUSIONS

MORE IMPORTANT THAN what movies show and tell about the Vietnam War is what they do not reveal. The most comprehensive poll of Vietnam veterans' opinions about the war was conducted in a 1980 Harris Survey. Of the veterans queried, fully 91 percent stated they were "glad they served their country," and 74 percent stated they "enjoyed their time in the service." When asked if they felt "the United States took unfair advantage of me," 80 percent disagreed. About the war itself, 72 percent strongly agreed with the statement "the trouble in Vietnam was that our troops were asked to fight in a war which our political leaders would not let them win."

During March 1985, a *Washington Post*/ABC News survey polled Vietnam veterans about their activities since returning from the war. The study revealed that Vietnam vets, when compared to nonveterans of the same age groups, were more likely to have gone to college, more likely to own a home, and more likely to earn more than $30,000 per year. In the same survey, more than seventy percent of the veterans stated that they did *not* "often dream I'm back in Vietnam."

Other studies have also revealed the stereotypical Vietnam veteran portrayed in the movies to be merely a Hollywood myth. According to the Selective Service System, only 25 percent of those who served in Vietnam were draftees (75 percent were volunteers). This is compared to 66 percent of World War II soldiers who were draftees (34 percent volunteers). In the area of employment, Department of Labor statistics collected in 1982 reflect that 90.6 to 92.7 percent, depending on the age group, of Vietnam veterans were employed—numbers about equal to the nonveteran employment figures of the time. Furthermore, the Veterans Administration added that of the employed Vietnam veterans, 31.7 percent were in professional, technical, managerial, or administrative positions; 11.9 percent in other white-collar jobs; and 56.4 percent in blue-collar, service, and agricultural occupations.

A 1981 Bureau of Justice study—after much deliberation and data gathering on the widely held belief that Vietnam veterans were filling America's jails—simply concluded, "On the whole, veterans were less likely than nonveterans to be in prison." Only one comprehensive study has been conducted on the marital status of Vietnam veterans. Announcing the results in 1979, the Veterans Administration's National Survey of Veterans Research Project noted that only 7.3 percent of Vietnam vets were divorced— meaning that 92.7 percent were *not* divorced. As for education, facts again debunk Hollywood's version of the Vietnam veteran. A 1980 VA study states that 79 percent had a high school diploma, compared to 63 percent of Korean War vets and 45 percent of World War II veterans.

Finally, according to the movies, Vietnam veterans are "walking time bombs" suffering a wide range of mental problems, post-traumatic stress disorder (PTSD), and suicidal tendencies. War is indeed a horrifying experience for those who see the brutality of the battlefield and confront the reality of sudden death or disability. Soldiers of every combat generation have had to readjust to a peaceful world and a nonthreatening environment after their return home. Vietnam veterans have had the additional burden of returning to an ungrateful nation that exhibited more contempt than respect for their wartime service. Despite this added hardship, Vietnam veterans, notwithstanding what the movies have presented, have had no more readjustment problems than veterans of previous wars. Studies by the National Academy of Sciences estimate that 25 percent of World War II soldiers experienced emotional difficulties upon return. Similar studies have estimated that 20 percent of Vietnam veterans have experienced emotional difficulties related to their war service.

Several other studies have announced, with great media attention, that Vietnam veterans are more prone to commit suicide than their nonveteran peers. In each case, these studies have been discredited and proved to be incorrect. Regardless of what the movies have provided, there is no verifiable information that Vietnam veterans are killing themselves with any more frequency than nonvets or veterans of earlier conflicts.

Despite the overwhelming volume of positive information about the real veterans of Vietnam, Hollywood continues to propagate the myth of the divorced, jobless, field-jacket-wearing, loser Vietnam veteran who is mentally ill and/or criminally inclined. There is no indication that Hollywood has any intention of ceasing its myth making about the war in Vietnam and the warriors who fought there. Even if there were to be a miraculous change in movie production, the damage has already been done. For the first time in American history, the movie industry has focused on the problems rather than the successes of a war's veterans both during the conflict itself and in the years that have followed. The negative image has been projected and the stereotype delivered to audiences around the world. New movies, along with the hundreds already on the video-store shelves and those in storage awaiting late-night airing on television, will continue to perpetuate Hollywood's version of Vietnam at the movies.

Any list of Vietnam movies recommended to a viewer who wants to learn about the war and to observe accurate images and behavior on the screen must unfortunately be an *extremely* short one. Few movies about the Vietnam War have met the barest of requirements for truth, balance, and reality. It is certainly not impossible for a movie to be an extremely good film while at the same time delivering myths and inaccuracies about the war and its warriors. The opposite is true as well. Just because a picture accurately portrays the war and its combatants certainly does not mean the picture is of overall merit. A film such as *Platoon* may contain the most realistic jungle-combat scenes ever filmed, yet the remainder of the picture may be so filled with errors, exaggerations, and propaganda that it cannot, overall, be recommended. Detailed information and comments concerning the merits and foibles of individual films are included in the reviews that are found in the second part of this book. The most remarkable films for their accurate portrayal of the Vietnam War and Vietnam veterans—those that form the short list of recommended movies—are as follows.

VIETNAM AT THE MOVIES—RECOMMENDED
THE SHORT LIST

PREWAR
Quiet American, The (1958)
Ugly American, The (1963)
Yank in Vietnam, A (1964)

REAL WAR
Anderson Platoon, The (1967)
Dear America: Letters Home from Vietnam (1987)
84 Charlie Mopic (1989)
Face of War, The (1968)
Go Tell the Spartans (1978)
Green Berets, The (1968)
Hamburger Hill (1987)
Odd Angry Shot, The (1979)

THE ENEMY
Iron Triangle, The (1989)
Killing Fields, The (1984)

POWS
Hanoi Hilton, The (1987)
In Love and War (1987)
When Hell Was in Session (1979)

COMING HOME
Cease Fire (1985)

HOME FRONT
Gardens of Stone (1987)

AFTERMATH
In Country (1989)

ROMANCE
Purple Hearts (1984)

PROTEST/ANTIWAR
Woodstock (1970)

PART
TWO

EXPLANATORY NOTES

Films appear alphabetically, with the year of their release and the country of origin (if not the U.S.) in parentheses, followed by the principal performers. Additional information is noted by these symbols:

TVM	Made for television
D	Director
_ M.	Length in minutes
OT:	Other title(s)
[TV]	Available on videotape

Each review is composed of two analyses. The first includes a brief summary of the film's general plot line and an evaluation of it as a motion picture in general. Ratings are from one to four asterisks:

****	Excellent
***	Good
**	Watchable
*	Terrible

The second portion reviews the film in terms of its accuracy in portraying the Vietnam War, its combatants, and the times. Accuracy and believability are scored from one to four crosshatches:

####	Among the best
###	Significant
##	Of some value
#	Worthless

MOVIE REVIEWS

Above the Law (1988) **D:** Andrew Davis, 99m. Steven Seagal, Henry Silva, Pam Grier, Sharon Stone, Ron Dean.

*1/2 A tough Vietnam-veteran Chicago cop (Seagal) exposes a plot involving drugs, explosives, and Central American refugees. At the core of the conspiracy are CIA agents whom Seagal refused to assist in Vietnam when they were torturing and killing prisoners and civilians. Big bangs with little excitement are the only result.

All of the CIA agents are current or former U.S. Army officers or NCOs who served in Vietnam. Seagal's character says the CIA kills off whole cultures and thinks it is "above the law." The film also insinuates that the military and the CIA were responsible for the assassinations of the Kennedy brothers, the opium trade in Southeast Asia, and the cocaine traffic from Central America. [TV]

Activist, The (1969) **D:** Art Napoleon, 87m. Michael Smith, Leslie Gilbrum, Tom Maier, Benbow Ritchie, Brian Murphy.

* A radical student (Smith) organizes protests and marches against the Vietnam War while being opposed by evil, baton-wielding policemen. Encouraged by his girlfriend and a university professor to give up his dangerous activism and rejoin the safe ranks of academia, he refuses and returns to his protests. Gratuitous nude scenes earned this picture an X rating. Filmed on and near the Berkeley campus.

Smith had to stretch little to play an antiwar Berkeley student activist because that is what he was in real life during the time of the filming. In the picture, his character is an absolute hero who is the object of much adoration by campus women. He also has

the respect of his professors, one of whom comments, "You're not an activist, you're a romantic."

Air America (1990) **D:** Roger Spottiswoode, 112m. Mel Gibson, Robert Downey, Jr., David Marshall Grant, Nancy Travis, Lane Smith.

*** Two pilots (Gibson and Downey) work for an airline that does not exist (Air America), which is owned by an agency that does not claim it (CIA), in support of a war that is not happening (Laos). According to Gibson's character, "What is perceived as psychotic behavior elsewhere is company policy here in Air America." Downey is concerned, saying, "I'm used to being the weirdest guy in the room, and here I'm not even in the running." Basically the plot involves a corrupt Laotian general who processes heroin in a Pepsi plant, a U.S. senator who wants the general to support the war against the communists, and the CIA pilots who just want to have fun. Superior flying scenes, a big-name cast, and reasonable humor put this one on the plus side.

\#\# The movie opens with actual television footage of President Nixon proclaiming, "There are no American combat troops in Laos." In fact, of course, Air America *was* in Laos with non-American military pilots—many of whom were discharged from active duty for their CIA tour and then reinstated if they survived. Other pilots were strictly mercenaries. This film offers little insight into what actually occurred in Laos. The wide mixture of aircraft is correct and the Thailand shooting locations closely resemble Laos, but the plot line, although at times funny, adds nothing to the history or the understanding of the war. Best lines include a major's comment: "Business and war are the same." An Air America flight director states, "Vietnam is a war for niggers and no-necks; this (Laos) is a gentleman's war. Vietnam is too public—better if secret." (As a point of interest for those who frequently fly on today's commercial airlines, many of the old Air America pilots went legitimate after the war and are filling the cockpits of various airlines across the United States.) 📺

Alamo Bay (1985) **D:** Louis Malle, 105m. Amy Madigan, Ed Harris, Ho Nguyen, Donald Moffat, Truyer V. Tran.

** In 1979, Vietnamese refugees are settling on the Texas Gulf Coast and through hard work are winning the competition with the locals in fishing, crabbing, and shrimping. The local Texans, led by a Vietnam War veteran and supported by the KKK, fight back by cutting crab traps and blowing up boats. Love interest is provided by Madigan, who supports the Vietnamese, and Vietnam vet Harris, who leads the Texans. Overdone at the conclusion and underdone in earlier scenes, the film fails overall to match the talents of its actors and director.

\# The Vietnamese are courteous, happy, hardworking, family oriented, religious, and honorable. They enjoy playing baseball after church. The American Vietnam vets are hard drinking, womanizing, racist (disliking both Vietnamese and Mexicans), and debt ridden. Believing that the Gulf waters belong to them because their fathers and grandfathers fished there, the vets have no redeeming characteristics whatsoever. Madigan so despises the veterans and admires the Vietnamese that she tells the brave, honest leader of the immigrants, "You've got to be one of the last cowboys left in Texas." TV

Alice's Restaurant (1969) **D:** Arthur Penn, 111m. Arlo Guthrie, Pat Quinn, James Broderick, Michael McClanathan, Geoff Outlaw.

*1/2 Not many movies are based solely on a long song, and this film is a good example of why. Alice lives in a church and, no surprise, runs a restaurant. Hippies, nomads, and other characters wander through each. One visitor is Arlo Guthrie, who, after Thanksgiving dinner in 1967 at Alice's, gets arrested for littering. His conviction for this heinous crime ultimately disqualifies him from the draft. The resulting album chronicling his experiences made both Guthrie and Alice folk heroes of the protest movement. Guthrie plays himself in what is supposed to be a true story.

\# Prior to his arrest for littering, Guthrie's opposition to the draft and the war are reinforced by the return of a friend who lost an arm in Vietnam. The value of educational deferments is shown by the singer's enrollment in a small Montana college to continue his exemption. After he drops out and returns to Alice's in Massachusetts, the draft catches up with him. According to Guthrie's narrative, one of the purposes of the interviews at the induction center is to determine if you are "moral enough to burn women, children, houses, and villages." NCOs and officers are portrayed as fat, loud, dumb bullies. Anyone who ever had to lead a squad or platoon in Vietnam will be happy that Guthrie was exempted from the draft for his littering. He was certainly no loss to the military or to those who had to depend on their fellow soldiers for their survival. 📺

Americana (1981) **D:** David Carradine, 91m. David Carradine, Barbara Hershey, Michael Greene.

*1/2 A troubled Vietnam vet (Carradine) struggles to reconstruct his life by restoring a broken-down merry-go-round in a small Kansas town. His only explanation for the repair is "It's something to do." This is an odd film that works in places and fails in far more. Hershey plays a strange, disturbed young woman whose major role is to run across meadows. Drury, Kansas, provides the setting and many of the extras for people fights, dog fights, and cockfights. It is nothing they should be proud of.

\# Carradine is identified in the credits only as "the American Soldier." Worn-out khakis with a 101st Airborne patch and a faded green beret appear to be his only clothes until he recovers a suitcase from his car in a wrecking yard. In the next scene he reports to a military installation, where the only soldiers seen are women officers, and he wears dress greens complete with captain bars, infantry crossed rifles, and multiple rows of ribbons. The absence of a combat infantryman's badge on his blouse is no stranger than the all-female office staff or his being issued back pay for some unexplained disability. No explanation is given about why these services are provided by the regular army rather than the Veterans Administration. It's a shame the movie is not as good as the merry-go-round. 📺

American Commandos (1985) **D:** Bobby A. Suarez, 89m (OT: *Hitman*). Christopher Mitchum, John Phillip Law, Franco Guerrero, Willie Williams, Ken Metcalfe.

* A former Green Beret (Mitchum) does such a great job killing off junkies in southern California that he is recruited by the police to return to Southeast Asia to close down heroin production in the Golden Triangle. Mitchum takes along members of his old Vietnam Special Forces team only to find that other vets are running the drug factories in the Triangle. Poorly produced, with dialogue of the kind found only in bad movies, *American Commandos* offers "acting" by Mitchum that can only be compared to that of Chuck Norris.

Philippine cities are used as sets for California, the Philippine countryside doubling for Vietnam and Thailand. One short burst of M-16 fire kills dozens every time Mitchum and pals pull the trigger. Vietcong, Thais, and Americans are most often played by Filipinos. The mixed wardrobe of uniforms neither side wore during or after the war confuses viewers as to who are the good and who the bad guys—if anyone could possibly care. Watch (in a Vietnam flashback) for a fat GI who mimics, down to wearing a hand grenade around his neck, the part played by Tex Cobb in *Uncommon Valor*, which was released two years earlier. TV

American Graffiti (1973) D: George Lucas, 110m. Richard Dreyfuss, Ron Howard, Cindy Williams, Charles Martin Smith, Paul Le Mat, Candy Clark, Wolfman Jack, Harrison Ford, Suzanne Somers.

**** Teenagers face the present and future as they come of age in 1962 in a small California town to the tune of the finest fifties/sixties sound track ever put together. Funny, poignant, yet unsentimental, the film never gets off track. This was a career breakthrough for the director and many of the previously unknown cast.

No mention of Vietnam is made throughout the movie until the closing credits, when a synopsis of what happened to the characters appears on the screen. Smith, who plays Terry "the Toad" Fields but would rather be called "the Tiger," is listed as "MIA near An Loc, December 1965." Fields is portrayed as a nerdy loser who is ineffectual with girls as well as automobiles—the two central focuses of the film. For an expansion of this brief mention, see *More American Graffiti*. TV

Anderson Platoon, The (1967-France) D: Pierre Schoendorffer, 65m.

***1/2 For six weeks in 1966 the director, soundman Domenique Merlin, and cameraman Raymond Adams followed and recorded the actions of an infantry platoon of the First Cavalry Division in Vietnam. The result was an Academy Award for Best Documentary. Although narrated by the French director in a heavily accented English that is often difficult to understand, and although shot in black and white under less-than-perfect field conditions, it is still more than deserving of its recognition. Vivid images of the platoon in day-to-day activities, ranging from mail call to evacuating its wounded after a firefight, bring the real war to the screen. Most notable are the documentary's images of the platoon's youth and playfulness when at rest and its dedication when in battle.

This is how it was. No Hollywood action or heroics are added. Men, equipment, and terrain are as they were. The only plot line is the struggle by the platoon for survival—and it is not always successful. Memorable scenes include a helicopter crash, the troops eating in the rain, and a soldier keeping the flies off a wounded buddy. Also noteworthy is the platoon's proper treatment of prisoners and villagers as well as the obvious respect and affection the enlisted men, including a white radio operator from South Carolina, show for their black officer. All of this is presented as honestly as possible, without politics. The closest thing to a political statement is made by the narrator in the opening credits when he says, "The Vietnam War is a tragedy, especially to we French who are partially responsible." ⟨TV⟩

Angels from Hell (1968) D: Bruce Kessler, 86m. Tom Stern, Arlene Martel, Ted Markland, Stephen Oliver, Paul Bertoya.

* A decorated Vietnam hero (Stern) returns home, dumps his wife, and forms a motorcycle gang. Initially he fights other bikers, but after one of his men is killed by police, he unites several gangs to fight the cops in an all-out war. This one contains even more sex, drugs, and violence than the usual biker-veteran film.

The motivation for the vet's violence is his desire to strike back at the Establishment that sent him to war. He does not seem to mind using in his fight the combat methods he learned in Vietnam.

Angry Breed, The (1969) D: David Commons, 89m. Jan Sterling, James MacArthur, William Windom, Jan Murray, Lori Martin.

* A Vietnam veteran (Sterling) goes from the jungle to Hollywood with a script in hand and dreams of stardom. Instead of fame, he finds crooked agents, sleazy producers, and a Nazi motorcycle gang that does not like him. Worse than one can possibly imagine.

Thankfully, no simulated Vietnam footage is included. Sterling, whose character lives in an oceanfront cave, is as believable

as a former soldier as MacArthur is in his role of Nazi motorcycle-gang leader. When a producer is told the would-be actor is a "war hero," he responds, "Why do so many [war heroes] end up on skid row?" If this response ever had any validity, the reason might be to avoid this film. ⟨TV⟩

Annihilators, The (1985) **D:** Charles E. Sellier, Jr.. 87m. Christopher Stone, Andy Wood, Gerrit Graham, Dennis Redfield, Lawrence Hilton-Jacobs.

* Vietnam veterans, former squadmates, use their combat skills against gangs, drugs, and crooked cops on the streets of an Atlanta suburb. Featured are shootings, knifings, and bloodshed, including breaking fingers with pliers and assaulting people with meat cleavers. The bad guys the vets fight are so mean they kick a teddy bear and take a school bus full of children as hostages. In an obvious rip-off of the opening of *Baatan* (1943), the opening credits are "shot" on the screen with a machine gun.

\# The film opens with the squad in Vietnam exchanging lines such as "I haven't been shot at in two days; I was starting to feel a little edgy." The VC/NVA wear uniforms that appear to have been left over from a safari movie. Nothing of value or interest here. ⟨TV⟩

Apocalypse Now (1979) **D:** Francis Coppola, 153m. Martin Sheen, Marlon Brando, Robert Duvall, Frederic Forrest, Dennis Hopper.

*** An army captain (Sheen) treks across Vietnam and into Cambodia in pursuit of a renegade Special Forces colonel (Brando) who has withdrawn from the U.S. military to fight a war of his own. Along the way, Sheen encounters every apocalyptic horror committed or imagined during the Vietnam War. A cavalry squadron destroys a village and its inhabitants, a navy patrol boat massacres women and children in a sampan, American soldiers attempt to assault a USO tour of Playboy bunnies, and leaderless, stoned soldiers giggle and swear as they defend a bridge. Sheen's character, as narrator, assures that there is enough "insanity and murder" to go around for everyone. He also questions why he is sent to kill Brando, who has been accused of murder. According to Sheen, "Charging a man in this place for murder was like giving speeding tickets at the Indy 500." Based on Joseph Conrad's *Heart of Darkness*—which is about Africa, not Vietnam—Coppola spares no expense and avoids no slander in condemning the war and those who fought it. Frequently, Coppola's message becomes so surreal and/or cerebral that it obscures the plot line. Still, if one is seeking a story about a man in search of himself, the result is an above-average film. If, however, the viewer seeks a realistic movie about the Vietnam War, this one falls far short of the mark. The Oscar-winning photography of Vittorio Storaro deserves to be considered apart from the plot.

Giving credit where it is due, and damn little is, this movie does offer the most realistic helicopter assault available (even if it is without Cobra gunships), aside from actual footage. Coppola rented the entire assets of the Philippine army and air force and got his money's worth, although it was one of the reasons the film went so far over budget. However, if viewers buy the remainder of the film, they will think American soldiers murdered, raped, and took drugs in Vietnam with impunity while the "war was being run by four-star clowns who were going to give the whole circus away." They will also think that cavalry squadron commanders (Duvall) massacred villages so they could ride the nearby waves, and justified the killing by saying, "Charlie don't surf" and "I love the smell of napalm in the morning." Apparently Coppola does not think much of the level of education of the war's enlisted men, either. A navy crewman (one of the participants in the sampan killings) states, "I didn't get out of the eighth grade for this kind of shit." Finally, surrealism or not, anyone believing that Brando and his men would hang bodies and body parts around their camp has never smelled a ripe corpse on a warm Southeast Asian afternoon. Brando's dying words are more appropriate for how Vietnam veterans are treated in this movie when he utters, "The horror, the horror." 📺

Armed Response (1986) **D:** Fred Olen Ray, 86m. David Carradine, Lee Van Cleef, Mako, Lois Hamilton, Ross Hagen.

*1/2 A former cop and his three Vietnam-veteran sons battle a Japanese gang in L.A.'s Chinatown over a stolen jade statue. Campy lines such as "He's a two-bit thug in a three-piece suit" and "We're thieves, not double-crossers" almost make the film watchable. Van Cleef, as the head of the family, appears in his first Vietnam film since the 1957 *China Gate*.

Vietnam merely provides a rationale for the three sons' tough-

ness and fighting abilities. The dying words of one of the vets, as he is tortured by a Japanese gang member, is, "Thank God I was born in America." Another of the brothers (Carradine) suffers flashbacks about killing women and children in a Vietnamese village. In the flashbacks, American soldiers are played by old, fat guys in uniforms that do not remotely resemble those actually worn in the conflict. 📺

Article 99 (1992) **D:** Howard Deutch, 99m. Ray Liotta, Kiefer Sutherland, Forest Whitaker, Lea Thompson, John Mahoney.

** Young doctors at a midwestern VA hospital fight regulations and bureaucrats to treat their patients. The film's title and much of the plot line are based on the VA authorization to treat only service-connected illnesses and injuries. With little success, Sutherland, as one of the doctors, does his best to mimic his father's performance in *M*A*S*H*.

Although the VA has many shortcomings, it does not deserve this film's treatment, which includes lab animals being given priority over veterans. A Vietnam veteran remarks to a Korea vet, "This is the VA, soldier; the enemy is behind those desks." Veterans of all wars are included as patients, but the Vietnam vets are the weirdest. One goes crazy in a hallway, fighting nurses and attendants as he shouts Vietnamese names and "Kill for peace." 📺

Ashes and Embers (1982) **D:** Haile Gerima, 120m. John Anderson, Evelyn A. Blackwell, Norman Blalock, Kathy Flewellen, Uwezo Flewellen.

* A black Vietnam veteran in Los Angeles deals with racial prejudice and hatred as well as his own nightmares from the war. Much of the film takes place in flashbacks while the vet (Anderson) has a gun held to his head by a policeman. With minimal results, Ethiopian-born director Gerima tries to relate the loss of Anderson's grandmother's land to a tax court to the destruction of the countryside in Vietnam by American soldiers. There is too much dialogue—much of which cannot be understood.

Anderson plays the stereotypical Vietnam veteran—black or white. Unable to find a good job, his character is haunted by bad dreams and flashbacks to combat. Anderson does make one good point, however. When a black activist condemns the war as white

imperialism, the veteran responds that those who did not serve in Vietnam have no right to criticize those who did.

Autopsy (1986-Spain) **D:** None credited, 90m. Vicente Acitores, Pedro Alonzo, Felix Gallego, Eva Leon, Jack Taylor.

* A war correspondent tires of covering the Vietnam War and returns to his native Spain to research the end of life. He wanders across the country asking people of all walks of life, "What do you think of death?" The film concludes with the reporter's observing an actual autopsy consisting of the opening of the chest cavity and the removal of the internal organs. Shots are also included of the top of the skull being sawed off to reveal the brain. This film will appeal to those who enjoy Stephen King novels and to those with a basic morbid curiosity—and a strong stomach.

\# The first half of the film contains a large amount of actual Vietnam footage—mostly of dead villagers, burned children, and alleged barbarisms of all kinds. There is little dialogue or plot as the correspondent narrates the horrors of war and relates that the "Vietnamese only want to live." He concludes, "Hunger, misery, and especially peace have been converted to publicity campaigns as if they were some soft drink commercial being played on TV." The entire movie was filmed in Spain, and there is absolutely no reasonable excuse for it's having made its way out of that country and into American video stores. 〔TV〕

Backfire (1988) **D:** Gilbert Cates, 90m. Karen Allen, Keith Carradine, Jeff Fahey, Bernie Casey, Dean Paul Martin.

** An unfaithful wife and her draft-dodger lover plot to kill her disturbed Vietnam-veteran husband. Many gruesome flashbacks (some complete with dead Americans whose eyeballs have been removed and placed on stakes), a mysterious stranger, multiple plot twists, a good cast, and scenic location shots in British Columbia make for a watchable film.

\# The most unusual aspect is that the Vietnam veteran is extremely wealthy—albeit with inherited riches. Nonetheless, he has a wife who rigs the shower to spout blood and places eyeballs and more blood in his bed. When the vet is finally driven into catatonia, she states, "He was in the war; some guys just can't take it." 〔TV〕

Back to School (1986) **D:** Alan Metter, 91m. Rodney Dangerfield, Sally Kellerman, Burt Young, Robert Downey, Jr., Sam Kinison.

** A self-made millionaire owner of a chain of tall and fat men's stores (Dangerfield) decides to return to college when his son threatens to drop out. Not only is Dangerfield a "big" man on campus, he is the party leader as well. Many sight gags and one-liners, mostly about sex, make this mildly entertaining.

There is good news and bad news concerning the Vietnam War in this movie. The good is that a history professor (Kinison) is a veteran. The bad is that, according to the students, he either has been, or should be, committed to a mental institution for his conduct in the classroom. Most of his classes consist of his screaming at his students about why the United States should not have pulled out of the war. Except to stretch the length of the film, there is no apparent purpose for this one-joke scene. [TV]

Ballad of Andy Crocker, The (1969) TVM, **D:** George McCowan, 73m. Lee Majors, Joey Heatherton, Agnes Moorehead, Jimmy Dean, Marvin Gaye.

** A decorated soldier returns from Vietnam to his small Texas hometown, but no one cares. Corporal Andy Crocker (Majors), met by no parade or band, learns that his girlfriend has married someone else and that his business partner has made a mess of their motorcycle shop. Even his old friends do not seem to want to be around him. This is Moorehead's TV-film debut as the girlfriend's shrewish mother. *Ballad* is really not too bad for a TV film, though not remarkable.

Made-for-television movies were in their infancy in 1969, and this film has the distinction of being the first with the Vietnam War playing a central role. Although Majors, the veteran, is treated sympathetically overall, it is made very obvious that he is a loser for going to the war—he loses his girl, his business, and his friends.

Band of the Hand (1986) **D:** Paul Michael Glaser, 109m. Stephen Lang, Michael Carmine, Lauren Holly, John Cameron Mitchell, James Remar.

* A Vietnam veteran takes a multiracial group—five Miami street punks—into the Everglades to teach them discipline and values. The band then returns to Miami to rid their old neighbor-

hoods of drugs and crime. Bob Dylan sings the title song in this moronic film from the creators of TV's "Miami Vice."

The Vietnam vet is a Medal of Honor winner and the sole survivor of his fire team. He is believable in neither of these roles nor in anything else he does in the movie. As with many Vietnam-vet film heroes, the veteran dies at the end of the picture. 📺

Bat 21 (1988) **D:** Peter Markle, 105m. Gene Hackman, Danny Glover, Jerry Reed, David Marshall Grant, Clayton Rohner.

** Hackman plays a middle-aged, new-to-combat air force officer who is shot down during the early stages of the 1972 Easter Offensive and must be rescued from enemy territory. In addition to the usual urgency involved in the rescue of a downed aviator, this attempt is more frenzied because the officer is an expert on missile intelligence who would be a prize catch for the communists. Glover plays an observation pilot who leads the rescue. None of the actors is particularly believable, least of all Reed, who plays the commander of the rescue force as if he were in a *Smokey and the Bandit* sequel. The film is loosely based on the true experiences of LTC Iceal Hambleton, who served as a technical adviser.

The intent of this film is nothing but the best. All the U.S. participants are shown as brave, dedicated, and resourceful. Hackman shows sincere emotion when he learns that killing on the ground at eye level is very different from killing at thirty thousand feet. The picture is positive and accurate in its portrayal of the U.S. war effort, and it shows the brutality of the North Vietnamese. Unfortunately, the execution is not as good as the intent. The East Malaysian locations are adequate in representing Vietnam, but the mixture of aircraft and equipment from various eras and countries detracts from authenticity. Model planes are obviously substituted in several scenes. The film suffers, too, from improbability and lack of attention to detail. For example, Glover decides to fly a helicopter for the "first time in fifteen years" after his spotter plane is damaged, the only refresher training coming from an enlisted crew chief. In addition, the airmen drink American beer from glass bottles rather than from the cans in which all American beer was delivered in country. (It is also worth noting that Glover's character is a composite of the many air observers who participated in the actual rescue—a fact that is hidden until the final pages of the book by William C. Anderson on which the film is

based. It is also notable that while the U.S. military made every reasonable effort to rescue Hambleton and took significant casualties in doing so, there was much criticism at the time and since that with his highly sensitive, classified knowledge of missile warfare, he should never have flown in hostile skies to begin with.) 📺

Bears and I, The (1974) **D:** Bernard McEveety, 88m. Patrick Wayne, Andrew Duggan, Chief Dan George, Michael Ansara.

** A Vietnam veteran hikes into the northern Rockies to see the father of his best friend, who was killed in the war. He ends up staying on to raise three orphan bear cubs and to help the local Indians in their conflict with the Park Service, which is trying to take their land. Another reason, he explains, is that the mountains seem a good place for "a strung-out veteran" to get it back together. The bears are cute, the scenery magnificent, the movie mediocre.

This is the only Disney-produced Vietnam movie and the only one of its genre with a G rating. It is so squeaky-clean that the theme song is sung by John Denver. The actual word "Vietnam" is avoided in the film; references are only to "combat" or "the war." If the movie had not been based on the real-life story of veteran Robert F. Leslie, the returning-warrior theme might not have been used at all. Still, the movie ends on a high note with the veteran exclaiming that he now knows that he wants to return to college and become a park ranger. 📺

Behind Enemy Lines (1987) **D:** Cirio Santiago, 91m. Robert Patrick, William Steis, Robert Dryer, Lydie Denier, Morgan Douglas.

* A Special Forces patrol goes into North Vietnam to rescue POWs, is captured, escapes via motorcycles, returns to assist a high-ranking North Vietnamese officer defect, fights Russian advisers along the way, and finally joins up with a French captain and a beautiful girl in a wet T-shirt. This film is a farce in its every aspect.

Typical GI dialogue (at least that which is understandable at all) includes "Motherfucking gooks—kill them all and let the devil sort them out." The NVA leader wears a hat that must have belonged to Douglas MacArthur, and the patrol leader has to tell his men to "take cover" when caught in an ambush. Anyone seeing

this film will wonder how anyone could have won the war, because both sides are so inept. 🖵

Bell Diamond (1987) **D:** Jon Jost, 96m. Marshall Gaddis, Sarah Wyss, Terrilyn Williams, Scott Andersen, Pat O'Connor.

* An unemployed Vietnam-veteran mine worker (Gaddis) in Butte, Montana, argues with his wife until she leaves him. Gaddis then spends his time drinking beer, watching television, complaining about his situation, and thinking of suicide. Eventually his wife returns, and, although she is pregnant by another man, Gaddis welcomes her back. This movie was produced with a grant from the National Endowment for the Arts (NEA) and is an excellent example why that organization's giveaways should be curtailed.

\# One of the difficulties between the couple is that Gaddis's character is sterile because of exposure to Agent Orange in Vietnam and his wife wants a baby. All of his other problems are also attributed directly or indirectly to the war. It is important to remember while watching this movie that it is your tax dollars at work.

Betrayed (1988) **D:** Costa-Gavras, 128m. Debra Winger, Tom Berenger, John Heard, Betsy Blair, Ted Levine.

** An undercover FBI agent (Winger) infiltrates an American heartland farming community to reveal white supremacists responsible for the murder of a radio talk-show host. Winger's character ends up falling in love with the racist leader (Berenger) in this overly melodramatic film that, except for the performance of Winger, fails in every aspect.

\# Berenger's character is a highly decorated Marine Vietnam veteran. His wife has left him, and he explains, "Maybe it was that goddamn war." Berenger also brags that, unlike Vietnam, in the battle against blacks, Jews, and other minorities, "We're going to win *this* one." One of Berenger's henchmen had a son killed in Vietnam. He bitterly remarks, "The bank took my farm, Vietnam took my son." 🖵

Big Bounce, The (1969) **D:** Alex March, 102m. Ryan O'Neal, Leigh Taylor-Young, Lee Grant, Van Heflin, James Daly.

* A Vietnam-veteran drifter becomes involved with a thrill-seeking girl and hardworking produce pickers after his return from Vietnam. O'Neal is the drifter. So is the movie, as it and its characters lack direction.

\# Little is said about Vietnam by O'Neal except that he "didn't hang around very long" and that all he did was "try and stay alive." He admits to taking risks because it confirms his nerve, while the girl claims there is no fun without risks. The only unusual twist is that the girl is crazier than the vet. 📺

Big Chill, The (1983) **D:** Lawrence Kasdan, 103m. Glenn Close, Tom Berenger, Kevin Kline, Meg Tilly, William Hurt, Mary Kay Place.

*** Seven former sixties-radical University of Michigan housemates get together in the eighties for the funeral of a peer who has committed suicide. Over a weekend they discuss the past, how they have joined the mainstream, and the ways values and beliefs change with the passage of time. An outstanding cast and a wonderful sound track made up for a somewhat weak script.

\# The seven friends have become lawyers, doctors, actors, businessmen, journalists, and homemakers. Only one, Nick (Hurt), is directionless and confused—and, of course, he is the group's only Vietnam veteran. Nick, stoned for much of the movie, is described as a "changed man" after his return from the war. He "hates his life" and has quit or been fired from a series of jobs. It is unclear if the suicide victim is also a Vietnam vet. All that is mentioned is that he was the type of person who saved everything and that his induction notice was found in the papers he left behind. 📺

Big Fix, The (1978) **D:** Jeremy Paul Kagan, 108m. Richard Dreyfuss, Bonnie Bedelia, Susan Anspach, John Lithgow, F. Murray Abraham.

** A former Berkeley revolutionary and antiwar protester turned private eye is hired to track down a legendary underground leader. Although Dreyfuss in the lead role assures his woman friend that "the sixties are over," he still drives a VW bug, smokes grass, and cries when he watches old footage of campus protests. Big cast, little movie.

\# According to the underground radical character who assisted draft resisters and violently protested the war, "We were cult heroes." Dreyfuss admits to having married to avoid the draft, and the old radical still enjoys occasionally chanting, "Hey, Hey, LBJ, how many kids did you kill today?" and "Ho, Ho, Ho Chi Minh." [TV]

Big Wednesday (1978) **D:** John Milius, 120m (OT: *Summer of Innocence*). Jan-Michael Vincent, Gary Busey, William Katt, Lee Purcell, Patti D'Arbanville.

** Three legendary surfers who originated the "hotdog" style in southern California come to terms with the ocean, the Vietnam War, adulthood, and themselves between 1962 and 1974. Spectacular surfing scenes are mixed with the friends' difficult realization that "the beach didn't change, people did."

When the three surfers get drafted in 1965, only Katt's character accepts the responsibility and does not fake a medical or mental condition at his induction physical. While his friends claim to be homosexuals or put on acts of blindness, paranoia, or other afflictions, Katt passes his exams and goes off to Vietnam. Most refreshing is that Katt returns from the war zone with no more personal difficulties than his buddies who have stayed on the beach. Katt's only problem seems to be with his wardrobe assistant, who has placed a Ranger Tab on the right rather than the left shoulder of his uniform jacket. [TV]

Billy Jack (1971) **D:** T. C. Frank (Tom Laughlin), 114m. Tom Laughlin, Delores Taylor, Clark Howat, Bert Freed, Julie Webb.

* A Vietnam hero, who hated the war and turned his back on society after his return, comes forward to defend a "freedom school" of flower children and Native Americans against local rednecks in Arizona. Great southwestern scenery and Jinx Davis's rendition of the song "One Tin Soldier" do not make up for poor acting and a disjointed script. Praised to cult status, *Billy Jack* was never as good as rated. This is an extremely violent film for one that purports to deliver a message of peace.

Students at the freedom school compare the U.S. involvement in Vietnam to that of Hitler in World War II. Only the kids are good; everyone in a position of authority is bad. Typical of Billy Jack's few lines is "I'm itching to kill somebody; it might as well be you." [TV]

Billy Jack Goes to Washington (1977) **D:** Tom Laughlin, 155m. Tom Laughlin, Delores Taylor, Lucie Arnaz, E. G. Marshall, Sam Wanamaker.

* This rip-off of Frank Capra's *Mr. Smith Goes to Washington* (1939) has Billy Jack (Laughlin) appointed to fill an unexpired term in the U.S. Senate. Oddly, this is the same state in which, in a previous Billy Jack film, he was seriously wounded by the National Guard and tried for murder. Laughlin fights nuclear power plants and government corruption for nearly three long hours. The only positive feature of this film is that unlike his earlier films, in which he fought with his feet and hands, all he does in this one is talk— and talk and talk. Similarities to Capra's film stop with the title. Fortunately, numerous lawsuits and countersuits with creditors kept this one from wide distribution.

\# Billy Jack's motivation in the film is the then-recent Watergate scandal and his lingering anger about his part in the Vietnam War as a Green Beret. Billy Jack is no friend of the veteran or apparently of anyone other than himself.

Birdy (1984) **D:** Alan Parker, 120m. Nicolas Cage, Matthew Modine, John Harkins, Sandy Baron, Karen Young.

**** All Modine's character ever wanted to be was a bird. Now, in a near-catatonic state in a VA hospital after returning from Vietnam, he is acting out his feathered fantasy. A fellow veteran and childhood friend (Cage) is brought in by an army psychiatrist to try to bring Modine back to reality by talking about their youthful adventures before the war. Intriguing, funny, sad, and thoroughly engrossing, this strange story is an updated version of an allegorical World War II novel by William Wharton.

\#\# Cage has the flashbacks and bad dreams about being wounded typical of movie Vietnam vets. However, he also experiences flashbacks about himself and Modine as boys playing sports and fantasizing about being birds. Even though the two friends, particularly Modine, are certainly not average young men before the war, Vietnam is still credited with being the root of their problems. "They [the army and the war] got the best of us; we're totally screwed up," states Cage. He continues, "In any other war we would have been heroes. We didn't know what we were getting into with this John Wayne shit. Boy, were we dumb." Although Cage recalls the war as horrible, he admits that being home and seeing Modine is worse. "I am more scared than I was in the war, and I was more scared there than anyone I know," he says. ⊡

Black Gunn (1972) **D:** Robert Hartford-Davis, 98m. Jim Brown, Martin Landau, Brenda Sykes, Luciana Paluzzi, Vida Blue.

* A group of Vietnam vets and former convicts take on the mob. Brown plays a nightclub owner out to avenge the death of his Vietnam-veteran brother who stole from gangsters to outfit his Black Action Group with guns and explosives. The group intends to take on "the Man," and the police predict, "This could make Watts look like Disneyland." The result is a routine action flick typical of the period.

\# There is little to distinguish between the veterans and the former convicts. The only effort at balance is that the honest black police lieutenant also served in Vietnam. 📺

Black Six, The (1978) **D:** Matt Cimber, 84m. Mercury Morris, Gene Washington, Lem Barney, Carl Eller, Willie Lanier.

* A group of black Vietnam veterans who "just want peace" ride around the country on their motorcycles. They encounter a racist white biker gang who killed the brother of one of the vets, and the fight is on. Most of the cast, black and white, are professional football players, and neither their bodies nor their talent has ever been closer to Vietnam than a 50-yard line in California.

\# The vets are called a new breed of Uncle Toms by other blacks because of their having fought in Vietnam. None of the former soldiers feel like he fits in anymore; all believe Vietnam was "a strange kind of war" and that they didn't know why they were fighting. The veterans admit, however, that they have no regrets. All the black vets are apparently killed in the final scene, but a trailer warns, "Honkey . . . look out . . . Hassle a brother and the Black Six will return." 📺

Black Sunday (1977) **D:** John Frankenheimer, 143m. Bruce Dern, Robert Shaw, Marthe Keller, Fritz Weaver, Steven Keats.

*** An international terrorist organization, Black September, plots to blow up the Super Bowl while the president of the United States is in attendance. A hijacked Goodyear blimp equipped with a giant 200,000-dart claymore-mine-like bomb is the weapon of choice. At the blimp's controls is a former Vietnam POW (Dern). Great flying sequences, suspenseful action, and Dern at his weirdest make for an exciting film.

\# Dern plays a navy lieutenant commander who seeks revenge

for the court-martial imposed on him after his release for the torture-induced antiwar statements he was forced to make during his six years as a POW. (In fact, no returning POW was court-martialed for such statements.) After his homecoming to an unfaithful wife and an uncaring Veterans Administration, Dern decides he wants his wife, their kids, her lover, and the whole country to remember him for something. To explain his joining the terrorist plot, he says, "If they [the U.S.] can do it to me, why can't I do it to them?" During the airborne blimp assault on the Super Bowl (Steelers vs. Cowboys, for those interested), Dern wears his navy uniform complete with Vietnam service ribbons and the Silver Star. 📺

Blind Fury (1989) **D:** Phillip Noyce, 86m. Rutger Hauer, Terrance O'Quinn, Lisa Blount, Randall "Tex" Cobb, Meg Foster.
*1/2 A blind MIA returns after twenty years to aid an old friend. Hauer plays a soldier blinded and left behind in a firefight. Rescued by Vietnamese jungle tribesmen, he learns martial arts, including sword fighting. Two decades later—with no explanation of what has happened in the meantime—Hauer arrives at an army buddy's home in Miami to find the friend's wife dead and his son kidnapped by mobsters. Hauer pursues them cross-country, taking on hordes of bad guys who are armed with pistols, rifles, and machine guns, and he wins—despite his inability to see.
The director of this film asks the viewer to accept that an American MIA could be taken in by villagers without either friendly or enemy forces finding him. Then the film would have us believe that, through Oriental techniques, the blind can be taught to "see" without vision—while also implying that the U.S. military does not take care of its infirm. Although the gangsters Hauer fights commend him by saying, "You're a walking advertisement for the handicapped," they also threaten "to put that blind guy in a wheelchair." The only difference between this movie and the others of the superhero-vet genre is that blindness is added to the usual returning-soldier baggage of flashbacks and weirdness. 📺

Blue Movie (1969) **D:** Andy Warhol, 90m (OT: *F**K* and *Fuck*). Viva, Louis Waldon.
* A Manhattan couple spend an afternoon lounging in bed, tak-

ing a bath, preparing dinner, making love, and talking. Discussions include drugs, art, growing old, New York's Mayor Lindsay, oral sex, athlete's foot, gonorrhea, and the war in Vietnam. The final scene has Viva staring into the camera and asking, "Is it on? Is it on?" Unfortunately the answer is yes. Warhol makes even sex boring.

Vietnam is only a part of the couple's, New York's, and the world's problems. The war receives short mention as being futile and immoral, and then the couple are on to other subjects.

Blue Thunder (1983) **D:** John Badham, 108m. Roy Scheider, Malcolm McDowell, Candy Clark, Daniel Stern, Warren Oates.
*1/2 A troubled Vietnam veteran (Scheider) is selected to test an ultrasophisticated police surveillance helicopter. When he discovers a government conspiracy to use the chopper against rioters, he steals the aircraft and the chase begins. The airborne pursuit is all that is worthwhile in this otherwise ridiculous movie. McDowell, as a wimpish army colonel complete with British accent, has to be one of the most ridiculous, unbelievable characters ever cast.

Whenever things get tough, Scheider's character flashes back to a time in Vietnam when interrogators threw a prisoner out of his helicopter. McDowell's character was Scheider's commander in the war and ordered him to commit atrocities. An NCO who briefs the police on the helicopter's capabilities wears fatigues with basic errors such as jump wings on top of his combat infantryman's badge. It is obvious that no one connected with the film, in front of or behind the cameras, has any idea how military personnel look, think, talk, or act. 📺

Boat People (1983-Hong Kong-China) **D:** Ann Hui, 106m. Lam Chi-Cheung, Cora Miao, Season Ma, Andy Lau, Paul Ching.
*** A Japanese journalist visits Vietnam to see how the united country is faring under communism in 1978, three years after the fall of Saigon. Initially, seeing only what his hosts want him to see, he is most impressed. He finally breaks away from his guides, however, to find summary executions, mass arrests, concentration camps, abject poverty, corruption at all levels, and an overall aggressive, offensive militarism. In one scene he visits a Danang orphanage to find naked children stacked in piles resembling those in Nazi death camps while the two attendants pass their time by dancing the tango. Powerful, well made, and intriguing in every aspect.

Heavy-handed at best, the film still is the most insightful thus far recorded in showing what Vietnam has been like since the departure of the Americans. However, it should be noted that China (which funded and approved the picture) was all but at war with Vietnam at the time of the film's production. Still, this film is extremely accurate in showing why Vietnamese continue to risk their lives in a variety of leaky boats to escape their native land. The movie was filmed in Hong Kong and mainland China, and most of the cast are Chinese.

Borderline (1980) **D:** Jerrold Freedman, 106m. Charles Bronson, Bruno Kirby, Ed Harris, Bert Remsen, Wilford Brimley.
   *1/2 A border patrolman hunts the killer of a fellow officer and uncovers an illegal alien–smuggling operation. Bronson is his usual one-dimensional, stone-faced self in this routine action drama.
   # Harris, in his film debut, plays a character called "the Marine," who is in charge of getting aliens across the border. He is also the murderer of Bronson's fellow patrolman. Harris's character attributes his abilities as a killer and other illegal skills to what he learned while serving in Vietnam. ⬜TV

Born Losers, The (1967) **D:** T. C. Frank (Tom Laughlin), 112m. Tom Laughlin, Elizabeth James, Jeremy Slate, William Wellman, Jr., Robert Tessier, Jane Russell.
   * In the role that introduces Vietnam vet Billy Jack, Laughlin is the only person in a small California town with the guts (or crazy enough) to stand up against the members of a vicious motorcycle gang that is raping the village's girls, among other dastardly deeds. Typical scenes include a motorcycle-gang member, after being spat on by his father, wiping off the spittle and licking it from his fingers.
   # Billy Jack's war service is incidental except to establish his willingness to fight for lost causes. Even the motorcycle gang says that Billy is a "psychopath," and one biker asks, "Do you think you can get away with Green Beret heroics in here?" ⬜TV

Born on the Fourth of July (1989) **D:** Oliver Stone, 145m. Tom Cruise, Willem Dafoe, Tom Berenger, Raymond J. Barry, Caroline Kava.
   ***1/2 Powerful, riveting drama based on the Vietnam experi-

ences of Marine Ron Kovic and his mental and physical readjustments after the war. The picture is vivid in showing the horrors of combat and the plight of the wounded as well as one man's disillusionment with the war, his country, his family, and his religion. Watch for cameos by the real Kovic in an early parade scene and by Stone as a television reporter.

This is a good movie, but the viewer should be forewarned that it is far from the documentary nonfiction that the author and director would like the audience to believe. Both Stone and Kovic greatly alter the facts or out-and-out invent new ones to support their effort to make the consummate anti–Vietnam War movie. Not until after the film's release did Stone and Kovic admit (after being confronted with the facts) that they had taken great license with actual occurrences. Some of the antiwar messages are subtle. Watch for a paperback copy of the acclaimed World War I antiwar novel *Johnny Got His Gun*, first published in 1939, on a hospital bed. Other messages, such as Abbie Hoffman's speaking at a campus antiwar rally, are a bit more straightforward. Also note during the end credits that there is no dedication to the dead, wounded, or veterans of either side of the war, but there is an "In Memorial" to Hoffman, who died shortly after his appearance in the film. [TV]

Boys in Company C, The (1978) D: Sidney J. Furie, 127m. Stan Shaw, Andrew Stevens, James Canning, Michael Lembeck, Lee Ermey.

** A group of Marine recruits progress from boot camp to the paddies and jungles of Southeast Asia. This first postwar Vietnam film by a major studio is extremely similar to the later *Full Metal Jacket*—Lee Ermey plays the drill instructor in both—and it also borrows from *M*A*S*H* in unsuccessful attempts at humor. Subplots include the efforts of a black Chicago gang member who enlisted in the Corps and volunteered for Vietnam to set up a drug-smuggling operation. The entire film is a sequence of clichés and stereotypes of every antiwar protester's image of the war. The director is so unsure about how men react in combat that his instructions to his actors seem to be "The tougher it gets, the louder you yell." A thoroughly irritating film that is not remotely similar to actual events.

Boot camp, despite an unrealistic barracks set, is depicted fairly accurately. Of course, showing heads being shaved for a re-

cruit's first haircut is difficult to get wrong. Vietnam scenes focus
on dope sales and use. Officers are pompous, dishonest, cowardly, and uncaring about their soldiers. During a mortar attack,
officers run to bunkers using Vietnamese civilians and children
as shields. Risking—and losing—Marines to deliver a general's
mobile home, air-conditioner, and liquor is a typical mission for
the film's grunts. One Marine goes so far as to say that his company commander is the enemy and the gooks are more trustwor-
thy. Vietnam and Vietnamese are played by the Philippines and
Filipinos, with neither resembling reality. 📺

Braddock: Missing in Action III (1988) **D:** Aaron Norris, 101m.
Chuck Norris, Aki Aleong, Roland Harrah III, Miki King.
    * Twelve years after the fall of Saigon, Colonel Jim Braddock
(Norris) returns to Vietnam to rescue his wife and son. Between
car chases, plane crashes, boat races, torture scenes, and "one man
against the world" firefights, Norris rescues several dozen
Amerasian children and a priest. The plot, dialogue, and acting
are so atrocious and contrived that long before the film is over, the
viewer is pulling for the communists in hopes that no Braddock
IV will be produced.
    # Despite the fact that the 101st Airborne Division was with-
drawn more than three years before the fall of Saigon, Braddock
appears in the opening scenes with a 101st patch on his left sleeve
to catch one of the last choppers to leave from the U.S. Embassy
roof. More difficult to believe is Norris's shoulder-length hair,
which, even though tied back with a headband, hardly meets military standards for a colonel at any point of the war. Neither does
Norris talk like a soldier. His "best" and most typical line is "I don't
step on toes, I step on necks." Norris returns to Vietnam via a daylight parachute jump and seems surprised to be captured by a
Vietnamese general, played by Aleong. The general, most of
whose lines are unconvincing sadistic laughs, is dressed in a uniform that appears to be left over from one of the remakes of *Beau
Geste*. Aleong may be typecasting himself; he played an almost
identical character in *Rambo: First Blood Part II*. Assuming the
role of both Thailand and Vietnam is the Philippines. The most
accurate part of this film is a disclaimer at the end of the final
credits which states, "Any similarity to actual persons, living or
dead, is purely coincidental." 📺

Brushfire! (1962) **D:** Jack Warner, Jr., 80m. John Ireland, Everett Sloane, Jo Morrow, Al Avalon, Carl Esmond.

** An American couple is kidnapped by communist guerrillas in Southeast Asia and held for a ransom of guns and ammunition. The guerrilla leader is so bad that he rapes the female captive in front of her husband. Two American World War II veterans, now running a nearby plantation, organize a rescue mission that kills the rebels and frees the captives. This is strictly B-movie, low-budget fare.

Although the setting is obviously Vietnam, only Southeast Asia is mentioned as the actual location. Apparently the film makers did not foresee the future scope of conflict in Vietnam. After the rescue, one of the plantation owners remarks that the loss of one of the captives killed during the fray was worth it because the raid kept the guerrilla action from developing into a full-scale revolt.

'Burbs, The (1989) **D:** Joe Dante, 101m. Tom Hanks, Bruce Dern, Carrie Fisher, Rick Ducommun, Corey Feldman.

*1/2 Three bored suburbanites become convinced their new neighbors are up to no good and begin to investigate. A big-name cast produces minimal laughs in a plot that delivers few surprises.

One of the suburbanites (Dern) is a Vietnam veteran who still wears jungle boots and camouflage clothing. He warns, "I was eighteen months in the bush, and I could snap your neck in a heartbeat." Dern's character is by far the most humorous in the picture as he satirizes the many disturbed Vietnam vets he has played in previous films. About the new neighbors burying bodies in their backyard, he says, "In Southeast Asia, we'd call this type of thing bad karma." [TV]

Bus Is Coming, The (1971) **D:** Wendell James Franklin, 108m. Mike Simms, Stephanie Faulkner, Burl Bullock, Tony Sweeting, Jack Stillman.

** A black Vietnam veteran tries to learn the truth about his brother's death at the hands of the Los Angeles police. Caught between equally volatile whites and blacks, the vet does his best to remain neutral and fair in his investigation. Although slow at times and obviously suffering from a low budget, this film is interesting because it records racial strife as seen through the eyes of blacks rather than the usual white view. Its maker, K-Calb Productions, is black owned and operated.

The black vet, played by Simms, is honest, calm, and level headed—almost an aberration for a movie Vietnam veteran. Simms uses his head instead of his fists, and his thoughts are not clouded by flashbacks to Vietnam combat. Maybe this is the reason the film received a limited release and earned little at the box office.

Cage (1988) **D:** Lang Elliott, 101m. Lou Ferrigno, Reb Brown, Michael Dante, Mike Moroff, Marilyn Tokuda.

* A brain-damaged Vietnam veteran is forced to participate in to-the-death fights in a steel cage. Ferrigno, playing the role of a man with the mind of a child and the body of a giant, goes from the Incredible Hulk to the Incredible Olive-drab Hack. If you like your heroes to ask for ice cream before they beat their opponents to death, this one is for you.

The film opens with a USMC patrol fleeing from a force of North Vietnamese in an area that appears to be southern California. As their rescue helicopter lifts off, Ferrigno is shot in the head. Despite massive blood flow, he does not release his grip on his dangling buddy. The scene fades to twenty years later with the two friends running a sleazy saloon called the Incoming Bar. Painted explosions adorn its sign. Little further is mentioned about Vietnam, except for when Ferrigno is warned that he might be killed in the cage. He responds, "It doesn't matter . . . I died a long time ago." 📺

Captain Milkshake (1970) **D:** Richard Crawford, 89m. Geoff Gage, Andrea Cagan, David Korn, Ron Barca, Evelyn King.

* A Marine returns from Vietnam on emergency leave to attend his father's funeral. While in San Diego, he becomes involved with a college girl and her hippie friends and their efforts to smuggle drugs across the border from Mexico. Despite the drugs, sex, and encouragement of his new friends not to return to Vietnam, the Marine does so and is immediately killed in action. This dated film contains poorly accomplished transitions between black-and-white and color scenes, along with psychedelic light shows.

The message seems to be that war-bound troops should accept the hippie life style or be doomed to die in Vietnam. Protest

scenes are shots of actual antiwar demonstrations held in Berkeley's People's Park.

Careers (1929) **D:** John Francis Dillon, 92m. Billie Dove, Antonio
Moreno, Thelma Todd, Noah Beery, Holmes Herbert.

** A young French magistrate (Moreno) in Cochin China plans
a trip to see the colonial governor of Indochina to protest his being passed over for promotions. Unwittingly, his wife (Dove)
reveals the plans to his boss (Beery), who has been holding her
husband back because of his own desire for her. Just as Dove is
about to submit to the lecherous Beery to keep her husband out
of trouble and to insure his promotion, a Vietnamese native is surprised in the midst of burglarizing the quarters and kills Beery.
Moreno arrives to help clear his wife of any implication in the
death, and the two depart Vietnam for Paris and the start of a new
career.

Although released only a month after the first film set in
Indochina (the silent *Where East Is East*), *Careers* not only talks
but sings as well. Beyond a geography lesson on French colonialism and the placement of Cochin China as a part of Indochina,
the movie adds little to an understanding of the region. As usual
in films of that era, and later ones as well, the Vietnamese/
Oriental is pictured as an ignorant criminal who is much inferior
to the white-suited Frenchmen.

Casualties of War (1989) **D:** Brian De Palma, 120m. Sean Penn,
Michael J. Fox, Thuy Thu Le, Don Harvey, John C. Reilly, John
Leguizamo.

**1/2 A patrol of the Twenty-third (Americal) Division kidnaps,
rapes, and murders a Vietnamese girl as a "portable R&R, to break
up the boredom and to keep up morale." Michael J. Fox, as the
only member of the squad who does not participate and who ultimately reports the incident, is so innocent and decent that he
appears to have Vietnam and his old television series confused.
Penn, while at times acting reasonably like a young sergeant, ex-
pends most of his energy playing Sean Penn rather than the
ultraevil squad leader. Basing the film on an actual incident, the
director allows philosophizing to get in the way of drama and
drama to interfere with philosophy as the soldiers discuss guilt, innocence, friendship, the war, and the army.

For what ultimately turns out to be such a bad movie, this one gets off to a reasonably good start. A platoon on patrol moves cautiously through the jungle before establishing a night defensive position. Claymore mines are put out, leaders consult maps using red-lens flashlights to minimize the light exposed, and radio handsets are wrapped in plastic bags to keep out the moisture. In the ensuing firefight, Penn uses tracer rounds from his AR-15 to mark a target for an M-79 grenade launcher. The major problem is that nearly everyone remains standing during the entire battle. The remainder of the film is marred by a total lack of attention to posting security or maintaining noise discipline. At the patrol base where the kidnapped girl is assaulted, members of the squad yell at each other and ignore any possibility that the enemy might be in the area. The surrounding jungle, like the opening scenes filmed in Thailand, resembles no part of Vietnam a native or veteran would recognize. When the patrol finally does look for the enemy, it finds them, untypically, in the open, during daylight, receiving supplies by river sampan. In the final battle, which begins with more screaming and yelling among soldiers only a few meters from the enemy, the squad exposes itself on an abandoned railway trestle in a fire fight that more resembles range target firing than actual combat. Although great effort is made to use GI language and phraseology, they often do not fit properly into the remainder of the dialogue. It seems the writers wanted to include every expression and profanity related to the war. The few sentences without these clichéd phrases, and many of those that include them, conclude with "man," which has to be the most overused word in the film. [TV]

Cease Fire (1985) **D:** David Nutter, 97m. Don Johnson, Lisa Blount, Robert F. Lyons, Richard Chaves, Chris Noel.

*** Johnson plays a Vietnam veteran still having trouble adjusting to peacetime fifteen years after the war. "Coming back, that's the real hell," he says. Although uneven at times, this is one of the fairest screen portrayals of post-traumatic stress syndrome (PTSD). Due to the lack of a "market," this film was shelved for several years after production and was released only after Johnson achieved recognition for his performance in television's "Miami Vice." Johnson has nothing to be ashamed of; his acting is surprisingly solid throughout.

Dialogue and kinship among veterans are well done. Vietnam flashback scenes are supplemented with enough actual footage to be noteworthy. The film is also remarkable for showing the impact of returning veterans on wives and girlfriends. Finally, the film is worth watching if for no other reason than to see Chris Noel (of Armed Forces Vietnam Radio fame) in a minor role as the former wife of Johnson's fellow-vet buddy. [TV]

Charley Varrick (1973) **D:** Don Siegel, 111m. Walter Matthau, Joe Don Baker, Andy Robinson, Sheree North, John Vernon.

*** Small-time crooks rob a small-town New Mexico bank and get in big-time trouble, because the loot turns out to be mob money being illegally laundered. The thieves, under the leadership of Matthau in the title role, seek to escape the police and appease the Mafia in this exceptionally well-crafted and -acted film. Everything is tied together in a riveting final scene.

Among Matthau's fellow robbers is a young punk who is quick on the trigger and not very bright. One of his jobs is to use explosives to destroy evidence such as the getaway car. He brags that he knows what he is doing because he had "blown up a lot of gooks with black powder." This would be very difficult because more modern explosives such as TNT, C-3, and C-4 had replaced black powder in military arsenals several decades before. [TV]

Charlie Bravo (1980-France) **D:** Rene Demoulin, 94m. Bruno Pradal, Karine Verlier, Jean-François Poron, Gerard Boucaron, Bernard Cazassus.

** A few days before the cease-fire in 1954, an elite French paratroop squad jumps into Vietminh territory to rescue a captured nurse. In the process, the squad massacres an entire village, including Vietminh, women, and children, and burns it to the ground. For the next few days hordes of Vietminh pursue the Frenchmen as they attempt to reach safety. Excellent (i.e., realistic) lines such as "Soldiers are always the losers" and "We have to keep laughing or we would all die of fright" make this a fairly realistic, albeit gruesome, portrayal of warfare. Dubbed, but dubbed well.

Battle scenes, field living conditions, and relationships among soldiers in combat are well above average. This film offers an interesting reflection that the French had the same problems

in Vietnam as did their American followers. Interesting also is that the director and writer chose to show massacres and war crimes rather than the regular warfare that predominated. In fairness, the Vietminh are shown to be just as ruthless, with particular devotion to cutting off the genitals of their adversaries. The Vietminh's use of camouflage and their carrying of rice in tubelike containers around the neck are extremely accurately portrayed—practices continued by their Vietcong and NVA progeny. Pay close attention to what the French lieutenant does for one of his wounded men by way of a homosexual favor near the end of the picture—similar treatment by a U.S. lieutenant would not be likely! 📺

Children of An Loc, The (1980) TVM, **D:** John Llewellyn Moxey, 104m. Shirley Jones, Ina Balin, Beulah Quo, Alan Fudge, Ben Piazza.

** An American actress (Balin, who plays herself) leads an effort to evacuate children from the Saigon An Loc (Happy Place) orphanage to the United States in the final days before the fall of the city in 1975. This true story wallows in sentimentality and encourages tears, but perhaps that is the only way the story can be told. Manila plays the role of Saigon.

\#\# Balin visited Vietnam in 1967, 1969, and 1971 as well as at the end of the war. She was not a part of the pampered, protected Bob Hope shows but toured the country on her own, hitching rides on trucks and helicopters to visit as many GIs as possible at some of the war's remotest outposts. A former *Life* magazine cover girl, Balin was never a major Hollywood actress, and the most unbelievable line in the film comes from a Vietnamese official who supposedly recognizes her and says, "It's a pleasure to meet you. I'm a big fan of American movies." Still, among the veterans who met her in the war zone, and among the 217 children she helped rescue from the Happy Place, she will be remembered as a superstar. 📺

China Gate (1957) **D:** Samuel Fuller, 97m. Gene Barry, Angie Dickinson, Nat "King" Cole, Lee Van Cleef, Paul Dubov.

** An American (Barry) in the French foreign legion serving in Indochina leads a patrol to destroy a communist ammunition base. His former wife (Dickinson), a beautiful Eurasian with the appropriate name of "Lucky Legs," serves as a guide for the mission. Cole, in addition to singing the title song, plays another American in the legion who joined the French because "What I started out to do in Korea, I didn't finish. There are lots of live commies around." This film continues Fuller's reputation, which began with *The Steel Helmet* during the Korean War, for getting to the screen first with movies about emerging wars.

This film is antienemy and pro-American in a manner much more like the films of World War II than like those that would follow about Vietnam. It opens with actual news footage outlining the history of the war and the region up to 1954. Included in this prologue is likely most Americans' first look at Ho Chi Minh. Opening with a scene of workers laboring in a lush rice paddy, the film has a narrator who reports, "This motion picture is dedicated to France. More than three hundred years ago, French missionaries were sent to China to teach love of God and love of fellow man. Gradually French influence took shape in the Vietnamese land. Despite many hardships, they advanced their way of living and the thriving nation became the rice bowl of Asia." Later the importance of Vietnam is highlighted by its being labeled the "barrier to communism and the free world." The communist guerrillas are depicted as evil and sinister. Van Cleef, as Major Cham, the guerrilla leader, explains why he has not killed the local Buddhist monks: "It's smarter to let them wander around the temple grounds. It looks more peaceful from the air, and those French pilots are as stupid as the Americans were in the other war. They don't bomb temples or churches. That's why we will win all of Asia. We bomb everything." 📺

Choirboys, The (1977) **D:** Robert Aldrich, 120m. Charles Durning, James Woods, Louis Gossett, Jr., Perry King, Randy Quaid.

*1/2 This screen version of Joseph Wambaugh's bestseller follows the on- and off-duty antics of members of the Los Angeles Police Department (identified only as "Metro" in the film). Much of the picture focuses on the after-work "choir practices" where the cops unwind with booze, women, and other debauchery. The humor is dark, and parts can be understood and appreciated only by those who have been there. Despite the huge all-star cast, the movie is vastly inferior to the book.

The film opens with two soldiers being pursued into a cave by Vietcong with a flamethrower. They survive to become Metro

cops and choirboys, but their flashbacks to the cave end disastrously for the vets. All the policemen in the film are screwed up enough without adding Vietnam to their troubles. The entire Vietnam segment could have easily been eliminated from the final cut. 📺

Choose Me (1984) **D:** Alan Rudolph, 106m. Genevieve Bujold, Keith Carradine, Lesley Ann Warren, John Larroquette, Rae Dawn Chong.

**1/2 A bar owner, a radio talk-show host, and an escaped mental patient share sex, insecurities, and dreams in a late-night, seedy section of Los Angeles. This is a sexy, funny, thoroughly different film that is filled with strange and interesting characters.

\# The mental patient is a Vietnam vet who claims he "flew jets down south." Actually he is such a pathological liar that he may only be a psycho claiming to be a veteran. 📺

Chrome and Hot Leather (1971) **D:** Lee Frost, 91m. William Smith, Tony Young, Michael Haynes, Peter Brown, Marvin Gaye.

* A Green Beret veteran enlists the help of three of his Special Forces buddies to bring to justice the motorcycle gang responsible for the death of his fiancée. For a biker movie, there is surprisingly little sex or violence, and the picture even takes a humorous look at the soldiers' learning to ride motorcycles. Most notable here is the film debut of Gaye as one of the Green Berets.

\#\#\# If you ignore the uniform errors, such as jump wings worn on top of combat infantryman's badges, no right-shoulder patches, and Green Berets worn like soda-jerk hats, this film is far kinder to Vietnam veterans than most. All four of the Green Berets are intelligent, well adjusted, and proud of their Vietnam service. They use military tactics and equipment to capture the bikers but kill none of them in the process. At one point, the leader of the soldiers warns his team to be careful not to kill anyone. In an early scene, a Green Beret sergeant tells a recruit to be careful, saying that the "army can afford to lose ammo, but not to waste you." All and all, this film offers a refreshingly positive view of Vietnam vets—even if set in a poor film and not available on videotape.

Chrome Soldiers (1992) TVM, **D:** Thomas J. Wright, 99m. Gary Busey, Ray Sharkey, Norman Skaggs, Yaphet Kotto, David Morin.

** Five Vietnam veterans roll into town on motorcycles (the same ones they bought to tour the country as "therapy" after returning from the war) to avenge the death of a war buddy who was killed by a drug gang led by the local banker and sheriff. Leading the veteran bikers is a full colonel (Busey) who has just returned from flying jets during Operation Desert Storm. Busey has such great lines as "We are going to make things right around here." Not even the actors seem to buy the dialogue and story line.

What is totally different and refreshing about this film is that each of the six veterans is well adjusted, has a reasonably stable family life, and is doing well economically. Everyone *but* the vets is either a dope dealer or a user! Despite their combat service, they are not superheroes—they even lose a barroom fight against not-too-superior odds. This is the first film to make a Desert Storm/Vietnam link. The only fault—except the film's being so rotten overall—is that Busey plays a colonel in the air force, but the patches on the group's old uniforms indicate that they all served with the army's 199th Light Infantry Brigade. No explanation of how the colonel went from army green to air force blue is offered.

Clay Pigeon (1971) **Ds:** Tom Stern and Lane Slate, 97m. Telly Savalas, Robert Vaughn, Tom Stern, Burgess Meredith, Peter Lawford.

* A decorated Vietnam War hero returns home, becomes a hippie (in one quick dissolve shot), and is recruited by the police to help bust a gang of drug pushers. Violence, blood, gore, sex, and nudity are featured far more than any actual story line. A big-name cast does not overcome the lack of any real drama beyond who will die or take their clothes off next.

The veteran plays what is apparently a continuing role of being taken advantage of by the U.S. government—first as a soldier by the army in Vietnam and then as a stool pigeon for the CIA and fascist police in the States. Several references are also made to marijuana being cool and not evil like heroin and other hard drugs.

Coach of the Year (1980) TVM, **Ds:** Don Medford and Andy Sidaris, 100m. Robert Conrad, Erin Gray, Red West, Daphne Maxwell, Ed O'Bradovich.

** A disabled Vietnam veteran and former pro football player
cannot find a coaching job anywhere except at a state confinement facility for juvenile delinquents. Conrad plays the
wheelchair-bound coach who turns "loser" kids, including his
nephew, into winners. This is typical made-for-the-small-screen
fare, with a plot that could happen only on television.

One of the reform-school boys remarks to Conrad, "You're a
loser, same as us." Conrad's best friend, who makes his living as a
bookie, is also in a wheelchair. The most interesting point is that
Conrad's character played for the Chicago Bears before Vietnam. In
fact, pro football players who went to Vietnam were as rare as good
TV movies. Nearly all of the gridiron heroes were able to find sympathetic doctors who signed medical waivers, or were allocated one
of the coveted local "hide in the National Guard" slots. 📺

Code of Honor (1984) TVM, **D**: David Greene, 105m (OT: *Sweet
Revenge*). Alec Baldwin, Kelly McGillis, Wings Hauser, Kevin
Dobson, Helen Hunt.

* Coincidence leads to an opportunity for revenge after a married Vietnam-veteran major gets his commanding general's teenage daughter pregnant. When the girl dies during a back-alley
abortion, the major places the blame on a captain who is
drummed out of the service and commits suicide. Fourteen years
later, the captain's sister (McGillis) marries an officer (Baldwin)
who works for the major, who is now a full colonel with a reputation as the "best in the army." McGillis seeks and gets revenge.
Only diehard McGillis and Baldwin fans who want to see them in
early roles will stick this one out till the final credits.

The Vietnam veteran is an adulterer; he is blatantly dishonest;
yet he is called the army's finest. One of the major's subordinates
tells him, "You had Vietnam, it's just a hell of a lot tougher in
peacetime." The major states, "Without the army, I wouldn't be
anything." In fact, he would be nothing in the real army as
well. 📺

Colors (1988) **D**: Dennis Hopper, 127m. Robert Duvall, Sean
Penn, Maria Conchita Alonso, Randy Brooks, Trinidad Silva.

** Two Los Angeles policemen (Duvall and Penn) join a special
detail to combat street gangs. Duvall plays a wise old cop near retirement, and Penn portrays his gung-ho rookie partner. Actual

gang members used as extras add, but an unconvincing love affair between Penn and Alonso detracts. Hopper as director is much like Hopper the actor—the dialogue grossly overuses "man," "homes," and "motherfucker."

At a community meeting, several concerned citizens compare gang activity and drive-by shootings to combat in Vietnam. One man states, "I know all about being outgunned; I was in Vietnam." (This may be a good line in a movie, but in the vast majority of firefights, it was the VC/NVA who were "outgunned.") No other mention of the war is made. 📺

Combat Shock (1986) **D:** Buddy Giovinazzo, 90m (OT: *American Nightmares*). Ricky Giovinazzo, Nick Nasta, Veronica Stork.

* A Vietnam veteran feels guilt for the brutal killing of a Vietnamese girl, has nightmares about his time in a POW torture cage, and has a son terribly disfigured (one of the poorest special-effects efforts on film) as a result of the father's exposure to Agent Orange. Forced to become a drug dealer to feed his family, the vet falls back on the fighting skills he learned in Vietnam to survive. This was released by Troma, Inc., whose other films include *The Toxic Avenger* and *Girls School Screamers*. Bad plot, bad acting, bad musical score—even the popcorn tastes bad with this one.

This film has what is perhaps the longest lead-in of actual Vietnam footage of any movie yet released. The only thing that could make it worse would be to shorten the real-film portion. To call this movie exploitative would be a compliment to its content. 📺

Coming Home (1978) **D:** Hal Ashby, 128m. Jane Fonda, Jon Voight, Bruce Dern, Robert Carradine, Penelope Milford.

**** While a Marine Corps officer (Dern) is fighting in Vietnam, his waiting wife (Fonda) falls in love with a paralyzed veteran (Voight) in a VA hospital. An extremely powerful drama and a touching love story, it is explicit in its anti–Vietnam War message. Fonda, Voight, and the writers received Academy Awards.

One can only expect anti-Vietnam sentiments from a Fonda movie, and she and the film deliver in spades. Opening with a roomful of disabled vets (many of whom are actual war veterans) in wheelchairs and hospital beds debating the justification for the war, a more subtle message is incorrectly delivered in that most of

the vets are blacks and Hispanics (whites and minorities shared death and wounds on a proportionately equal basis in the war). Marine officer Dern's only interest in the Vietnam War is in boosting his chances for promotion to major and in becoming a "hero." All the other usual cheap shots at veterans are included— through references to the enemy's ears being cut off, inflated body counts, phony valor awards, suicidal vets, extremely poor treatment in VA hospitals, and the government and the military spying on American civilians. After Voight is arrested for protesting the war, Fonda even discovers that sex with a disabled protester is better than with her Marine officer husband. Regardless of the merits of the film, anyone seeing it will understand why Vietnam veterans are not "fonda" Jane. The movie concludes with Fonda going shopping while Dern commits suicide and Voight addresses high schoolers, telling them, "There is a choice to be made here." 📺

Cowards (1970) **D:** Simon Nuchtern, 88m. John Ross, Susan Sparling, Will Patent, Thomas Murphy, Philip B. Hall.

  * Facing the draft and Vietnam, Phil Haller (Ross) cannot decide whether to flee to Canada or to stay and fight against the war at home. After his girlfriend's brother is killed in Vietnam and a friend is made an invalid by war wounds, Haller decides to fight back—while remaining reasonably safe himself. With the help of an antiwar priest, he invades and wrecks a draft-board office, is arrested, and is jailed. The title is most appropriate.

  # The director, and producer Lewis Mishkin, pull no punches (including those below the belt) in their quest to support draft resistance and to encourage protest against the war. Entertainment is far down on their list of objectives. The film is subtitled "A Primer in New Patriotism." Advertising for the movie featured an Uncle Sam character with President Nixon's face and hands clutching a rifle complete with a bayonet dripping blood.

Crazy World of Julius Vrooder, The (1974) **D:** Arthur Hiller, 98m. Timothy Bottoms, Barbara Seagull (Hershey), Lawrence Pressman, George Marshall, Albert Salmi.

  * Bottoms plays the title role of a Vietnam veteran in a hospital psycho ward. Withdrawn from the world, Bottoms is a "happy crazy" who would rather be insane than deal with his actions in

Vietnam. He spends much of his time in a booby-trapped hooch that he has built on the grounds of the veterans hospital. A love affair is also managed with a nurse (Hershey), and the two make plans to escape to a remote Canadian cabin where they will live off the land. The film was produced by the short-lived screen company owned by Hugh Hefner of *Playboy* magazine.

At the core of the insanity of Bottoms's character is an incident where he was in a hooch full of dead children and the body of an old woman who had earlier befriended him. Other Vietnam vets in the hospital have similar stories. The only redeeming aspect of the film is that the hospital is not limited to crazies from Vietnam. Disturbed soldiers from earlier, more popular wars are also patients.

Criss Cross (1992) **D**: Chris Menges, 101m. Goldie Hawn, Arliss Howard, Keith Carradine, Paul Calderon, Steve Buscemi.

*1/2 After her husband "freaks out" from his experiences as a navy pilot in Vietnam, a woman (Hawn) is forced to become a topless dancer in Key West in 1969 to support her son. The boy becomes involved in a drug-smuggling operation so his mom will not have to take her clothes off in front of strangers. The beautiful Florida scenery and news coverage of the first moon landing playing on radios and TVs in the background do not make up for what is a really bad picture.

The preteen son narrates the film and explains that his father was a bomber pilot in the war. "On one of his missions, he hit a hospital full of kids," he reports. The boy continues that, initially, his mother was for the war but that she turned against it after seeing what it did to his dad. The boy adds that after his father came home, he burned his uniforms, saying that the uniform was nothing but a "killing costume." It is later revealed that the father, an Annapolis graduate, took a vow of silence and joined a monastery. 📺

Cutter's Way (1981) **D**: Ivan Passer, 105m (OT: *Cutter and Bone*). Jeff Bridges, John Heard, Lisa Eichhorn, Ann Dusenberry, Stephen Elliott.

** A cynical, alcoholic, self-destructive, disabled Vietnam veteran (Heard) helps a friend reveal—or at least blackmail—a wealthy, influential citizen who murdered a teenage girl. A

strange, drab, seedy film, it offers no one and nothing of any redeeming social value, with the possible exception of the Santa
Barbara, California, shooting locations.

Heard's character—missing an eye, an arm, and a leg from
combat wounds—beats his two-timing wife and drinks his way
through the entire story. His friend (Bridges) explains the crazy
and obnoxious behavior: "It was the war, man." Heard's basic gar-
ment is a field jacket. 📺

Dangerously Close (1986) **D:** Albert Pyun, 96m. John Stockwell,
J. Eddie Peck, Carey Lowell, Bradford Bancroft, Madison Mason.

* A paramilitary group called the Sentinels terrorizes misfit students at an exclusive high school by means of survival games.
When a student is killed, the school's newspaper editor investigates. Lots of pop music, pop lighting, and pop philosophy make
for a movie of no interest to anyone over sixteen. The most appropriate line is delivered by one of the Sentinels, who says, "It makes
no fucking sense . . ."

The faculty adviser to the Sentinels is a fascist Vietnam vet-
eran. When the dead student is discovered, the vet is an immediate suspect because "He's killed before, taking out VC." 📺

David Holzman's Diary (1968) **D:** Jim McBride, 74m. L. M. Kit
Carson, Eileen Dietz, Louise Levine, Lorenzo Mans, Fern McBride.

** A young New York filmmaker, who has just received his draft
notice, sets out in 1967 to film the events of his life to discover the
"truth." During the nine days of filming, Holzman (Carson) focuses on his relationship with his lover and various discussions
with friends, acquaintances, and strangers. By the end of the project, Holzman's camera equipment has been stolen and he admits
that he has learned nothing. Considered by many to be one of the
best independent films of the 1960s, it was produced at a cost of
only $2,500.

The draft and Vietnam obviously serve as Holzman's motiva-
tion for his project and possibly for its failure as well. Included on
the sound track is news about the war on New York radio
stations. 📺

D.C. Cab (1983) **D:** Joel Schumacher, 100m. Adam Baldwin,
Mr. T, Irene Cara, Max Gail, Anne DeSalvo.

** A Washington, D.C., cab company staffed by "the eight stooges" must clean up its act to survive. The laughs are not as good as the tour of our nation's capital, but the film is mildly entertaining.

The good news is that a Vietnam veteran is shown owning his own business—the bad news is that it is the D.C. Cab Company. Gail, as the vet, is just as crazy as his drivers, has an unfaithful wife, and lights his fireplace with a military flamethrower. [TV]

Deadly Encounter (1982) TVM, **D:** William A. Graham, 100m. Larry Hagman, Susan Anspach, James Gammon, Michael C. Gwynne, Jose Chavez.

** Hagman plays a Vietnam-veteran pilot running the Y.G.H. (Yankee Go Home) Helicopter Service in Mexico. The action begins when an old girlfriend (Anspach), whom he met when she was a nurse in Vietnam, shows up running from mobsters who want a black book full of names left behind by her murdered husband. Hagman and helicopter take on bad guys in airplanes, in cars, on foot, and even on a bicycle. Dialogue is uninspiring, with Hagman, who is fleeing drug charges of his own, mumbling lines such as "It's murder seeing you, honey." The action, though, is nonstop and, if you turn the sound down, exciting.

Most notable are the helicopter flying sequences, and there are a lot of them. Much of the flying is done by real Vietnam-vet chopper pilots, and coordinator Larry Kirsh does his best to get every RPM possible out of the machines and pilots.

Dear America: Letters Home from Vietnam (1987) TVM, **D:** Bill Couturie, 87m. Narration by Robert De Niro, Michael J. Fox, Ellen Burstyn, Kathleen Turner, Robin Williams.

**** This is the state-of-the-art documentary on the history of the Vietnam War as told through the letters of the men who fought, actual news footage, and the music of the time. Still pictures, video, words, and headlines are as they were then in this HBO production based on the book by the same title by Bernard Edelman. Stories vary from a young soldier's writing that he had "never regrett[ed] coming over here" to another's stating that he "can't understand the war, period." Images of day-to-day boredom and terror are intermixed with coverage of the POWs, Tet, Kent State, and Khe Sanh. Other portions of the documentary recog-

nize and honor the tough plight of the infantry, the importance of
mail, the youth of the combatants, and the camaraderie of soldiers. This is a must-see for anyone remotely interested in the real
truth about the war.

There is more accuracy in this documentary than in all the
Rambo and Braddock films and their clones put together. The soldiers are real, the situations are real, the feelings are real, the war
is real. In less than one and one-half hours, this film provides an
amazingly complete, balanced history of the war and its
warriors. 📺

Deathdream (1972-Canada) **D**: Bob Clark, 90m (OT: *Dead of
Night*). John Marley, Richard Backus, Lynn Carlin, Henderson
Forsythe, Anya Ormsby.

* A Vietnam vet returns home "from the dead." After notification that their son has been killed, a grieving family is shocked
when he appears at their door in his dress uniform. Only the family dog is unhappy to see the veteran, who greets the pet by stran-
gling it to death. Later he kills the family doctor and drinks the
blood out of his body. His girlfriend and his sister's boyfriend are
the next victims, and the killing is stopped only by the soldier's
own decomposing body. At film's end, his putrid flesh is falling
from his bones as he pulls himself into an open grave and, it is
hoped, a final rest.

This film succeeds in being horrible, scary, and repulsive—
which is its apparent purpose. Somewhere its makers must have
intended to make a statement about the difficulties of Vietnam
veterans adjusting to returning home, but they lost their way. 📺

Deer Hunter, The (1978) **D**: Michael Cimino, 183m. Robert De
Niro, Meryl Streep, Christopher Walken, John Cazale, John Savage.

**** Three Russian-Americans go from a Pennsylvania steel
town to Vietnam and return, only to find that their home is the
same but that they have changed. One (Savage), with no feet, is in
a wheelchair at the VA hospital, yet his wife sends him socks. Another (Walken) stays in Vietnam to bet and participate in Russian-
roulette contests. The third (De Niro) attempts to sort out their
collective experiences. This is the first of the "epic" Vietnam movies and is deserving of its five Oscars including Best Picture, Best
Director, and Best Supporting Actor (Walken). The final scene

with a confused De Niro being toasted by his friends, who stayed at home, as they sing "God Bless America" may very well be the best, or at least the most memorable, scene of the war's aftermath yet put on film.

This is a great movie in spite of its Vietnam content rather than because of it. There were, and are, no Saigon clubs that host Russian-roulette matches—and if there were, the patrons would not surround the contestants because, unlike the situation in this movie, bullets fired into the temple tend to come out the other side, with lots of messy stuff as well. Just why De Niro runs around at film's end in a dress green uniform (which is surprisingly accurate) with a full beard is not explained or explainable. Also, Savage is the only one of the three who looks young enough to be a Vietnam draftee or enlistee. Unusual to Vietnam films is the accuracy of the warriors' small-town send-off and welcome home. Rather than the usual Hollywood film fare of departures being marked by protests and homecomings that include spittle, at the men's departure party the musicians play "The Stars and Stripes Forever" and the bandleader hails the three as "going off to proudly serve their country." Later they are welcomed home with handshakes and offers of free drinks. 📺

Delirium (1979) **D:** Peter Maris, 86m. Debi Chaney, Turk Cekovsky, Terry Ten Broeck, Barron Winchester, Nick Panouzis.
   * A Vietnam veteran organizes an underground vigilante group that executes criminals who slip through the court system. Everything goes well until the group's lead assassin—another veteran— begins killing noncriminals as well. This was filmed in 16mm and blown up to 35mm for theatrical release. The result is a grainy print that is almost as bad as the acting.
   # Several flashbacks to Vietnam are included to show why the gang leader and his prolific killers are so mean and bloodthirsty. 📺

Deserter USA (1969-Sweden) **D:** Lars Lambert, 97m. Bill Jones, Mark Shapiro, John Ashley, Jim Dotson, Steve Gershater.
   * Produced by graduates of the Swedish Film School and performed by American deserters and draft dodgers running from the Vietnam War, this documentary-style film is far from actually being one. Mostly it is a dramatization of Americans touting Marx-

ism and criticizing the United States. While some incidents are likely based on the truth, others are wholly fictitious. Only the most anti-U.S., antimilitary, anti–Vietnam War fanatics would like this picture, and even they would be bored beyond belief by characters so wimpish it is doubtful that even their mothers would claim them.

One of the deserters (Jones) claims the United States is prolonging the war because it is a profitable venture. Another offers as fact that his poor relatives have been offered money by the CIA to try and trick him into returning to the United States. Even their Swedish hosts are panned as being in league with the imperialist Yankees.

Deserters (1983-Canada) **D:** Jack Darcus, 93m. Alan Scarfe, Jon Bryden, Barbara March, Dermot Hennelly, Ty Haller.

* A three-tour Vietnam-veteran drill sergeant follows two AWOL trainees who have fled to Canada to avoid the war. The three eventually end up together at the home of a liberal Canadian immigration officer and his wife, who harbor draft dodgers and deserters. One of the deserters ultimately decides to return home to face Vietnam and sure death; the tough NCO sees the error of his ways and stays in Canada.

#1/2 This is one of the few films to take a look at the manner in which many Canadians viewed the war and the Americans who fled north instead of facing the draft. Its Canadian producers also go beyond the war issue and focus on the identity conflicts between Americans and Canadians. The best dialogue is an exchange between the drill sergeant and a captain. When the NCO states he is going after the two AWOL soldiers because "they're my best men," the officer replies, "If those are your best men, the country's in trouble."

Desperate Hours (1990) **D:** Michael Cimino, 106m. Mickey Rourke, Anthony Hopkins, Mimi Rogers, Lindsay Crouse, Kelly Lynch.

*** Three killers, led by Rourke and pursued by the FBI, take a suburban family hostage. Hopkins plays the estranged husband and father who is home only for a visit and now must defend his family. Suspense, interesting plot twists, and excellent performances by all make for a good movie based on the novel by Joseph Hayes and first filmed in 1955 with Humphrey Bogart.

Part of the update from the novel and the original film has to do with Hopkins's background. Rourke, who comes across pictures and medals from Vietnam, mocks Hopkins, saying, "Looks like you won the Vietnam War all by yourself, Timmy." Although Hopkins's estrangement from his family fits the Hollywood stereotype of the Vietnam veteran, nothing else about him does so. He is a wealthy, successful, well-adjusted lawyer. In fact, his calmness, bravery, and resourcefulness are ultimately what save the day. [TV]

Desperate Miles, The (1975) TVM, Daniel Haller, 78m. Tony Musante, Joanna Pettet, Jeanette Nolan, Lynn Loring, John Larch.

** In August 1967, Jim Mayo (Musante) lost a leg and part of his other foot in a mine explosion in Vietnam. Seven years later, Mayo travels 130 miles from Long Beach to San Diego in a wheelchair to prove to himself and other disabled vets that there is life outside the hospitals and VA centers. Along the way, Mayo is comforted by a woman and run off the road by a psychotic truck driver.

Released in March 1975, less than two months before the fall of Saigon, this was the only movie on television or motion picture screens remotely positive (or, for that matter, accurate) about the Americans who had fought the war. The most remarkable aspect of this film is that the story is true—and even though the acting and the script are not up to the subject, it is difficult even for television to mess up facts.

Die Hard (1988) D: John McTiernan, 132m. Bruce Willis, Alan Rickman, Bonnie Bedelia, Alexander Godunov, Reginald Veljohnson.

*** A New York cop (Willis) visiting Los Angeles takes on a gang of international thieves who have seized control of a high-rise office building and are holding its occupants hostage. Amazing stunts, nonstop action, and spectacular special effects make for an exciting film.

Vietnam rates but one brief mention. As an FBI armed helicopter makes an assault on the building, an agent laughs and wildly screams, "Just like fucking Saigon!" He seems little con-

cerned that his rescue plan will result, by his own estimate, in the deaths of at least one-fourth of the hostages. 🖥

Distant Thunder (1988-U.S./Canada) **D:** Rick Rosenthal, 114m. John Lithgow, Ralph Macchio, Kerrie Keane, Reb Brown, Dennis Arndt.

** Troubled "bush vets" hide out from society and their Vietnam memories in the forests of the Pacific Northwest. One of the veterans (Lithgow) attempts to rejoin the mainstream after a fellow vet commits suicide and his own son (Macchio), whom he has not seen in more than fifteen years, comes to visit. Despite a big production budget and star performers, the only results are violence, sappy clichés, and a soap-opera ending. Beautiful British Columbia substitutes well for Washington's Olympic Peninsula, but the birch forest used for the Vietnam flashbacks looks strictly Canadian.

The only discernible difference between the various veterans is in their level of craziness. They are referred to by the townspeople, as well as each other, as "fucking freaks," "loony tunes," and "nuts." Their remote huts resemble Vietnam base camps complete with barbed wire, booby traps, and a sign that reads "Trespassers will be executed." One of the vets sings a song to the tune of "Wake the town and tell the people" with lyrics changed to "Rape the town and kill the people" as he laughs merrily. 🖥

Doberman Gang, The (1972) **D:** Byron Chudnow, 88m. Hal Reed, Byron Mabe, Julie Parrish, Simmy Bow, Jojo D'Amore.

** Thieves train six dobermans to rob a bank at fang-point and haul off the loot in doggie saddlebags. The canines steal the picture as well as the cash and are by far the film's most interesting characters.

To train the dobermans, the thieves recruit a Vietnam veteran who was a scout dog handler in the war. Initially the clean-cut air force vet is reluctant to join the scheme but changes his mind once he learns how much cash is involved. 🖥

Dogfight (1991) **D:** Nancy Savoca, 94m. River Phoenix, Lili Taylor, Richard Panebianco, Anthony Clark, Mitchell Whitfield.

**1/2 Four Marine buddies celebrate their last night in San Francisco before shipping out for Okinawa by participating in a "dogfight"—a contest to see who can bring the ugliest date to a party. Phoenix takes Taylor but regrets it once he realizes that he is attracted to her inner beauty. They spend the rest of the night together discussing such things as his idea that "shooting changes the world" and her belief that music, not war, is the key to change. Despite a plodding pace at times, the period and the music are captured exceptionally well in a film that does not quickly leave one's mind.

Although the movie is set in 1963 (evidently so the impact of the JFK assassination can be included), Phoenix's character is already looking forward to going from Okinawa to Vietnam, where he plans to "kick ass, take names, and be back in a few months." A flash-forward to 1966 at film's end shows Phoenix as the only survivor of the four buddies after a Vietnam mortar attack. Wearing his field jacket, he returns to San Francisco with a limp, to be welcomed by a hippie asking, "How many babies did you kill?" Casting and wardrobe did an excellent job in making the young actors look like Marines of the 1960s. The writer also gave them lines that are authentic and believable. [TV]

Dog Tags (1990-Italy) D: Romano Scavolini, 100m. Clive Wood, Mike Monty, Baird Stafford, Robert Haufrecht, Peter Erlich.

* Two "commandos" rescue POWs from Vietnamese tiger cages only to find themselves pawns in an unexpected twist. En route to the helicopter pickup zone, they are diverted by their superiors to make a side trip into Cambodia to secure some mysterious documents. Along the way, the POWs are killed off one by one in spectacular explosions of flesh and fountains of blood. The documents end up being gold ingots—the vets have been duped again. Dialogue includes such riveting phrases as "Relax, okay? Just mellow out." The best line, however, is delivered in the prologue and aptly describes the remainder of the film. The narrator states, "The whole episode stank worse than rotten eggs."

\# Instead of attempting to reveal anything factual about the Vietnam War, director Scavolini appears to want to incorporate snippets of every cliché, inaccurate description, and Hollywood death scene ever recorded on film. The American soldiers, one speaking with an Australian accent, have beards and wear headbands. The Philippines stand in for Vietnam.

Don't Answer the Phone (1980) **D:** Robert Hammer, 94m (OT: *Hollywood Strangle, The*). James Westmoreland, Flo Gerrish, Ben Frank, Stan Haze, Nicholas Worth.

* A crazed Vietnam veteran stalks, rapes, and kills the clients of a radio talk-show psychologist, laughing merrily as he conducts his mayhem. The best advice is "Don't watch this movie."

\# The killer wears his camouflage-pattern jacket with a 101st Airborne Division shoulder patch. His occupation, other than murdering, is selling pornography. Describing the suspect as a "sick son of a bitch," the police decide that they are looking for a Vietnam veteran when they discover the killer strangles his victims with a stocking-and-coin device which is an old "VC trick" (which must indeed be old, because no real veteran of the war has ever heard of it). The homicide detectives also ponder that perhaps the rape-and-murder spree is a "religious cleansing" process for the vet's deeds in the war zone. [TV]

Don't Cry, It's Only Thunder (1982) **D:** Peter Werner, 108m. Dennis Christopher, Susan Saint James, Roger Aaron Brown, James Whitmore, Jr., Lisa Lu.

** An army medic, transferred from an evacuation hospital to the Saigon morgue in 1967 after being caught dealing drugs and black marketing, experiences a different aspect of the war. Honoring a promise to a dying friend, he takes care of an abandoned Vietnamese girl and eventually uses his skills on the black market to support two nuns and a growing group of orphans. Based on a true story, on occasion the plot bogs down in sentimentality. But it does provide fine drama. Gallows humor of the operating room and the morgue—"Where do you find the morgue on an army base?" Answer: "Dead center."—keeps the film on a realistic track.

\#\# Despite drug abuse, racial tension, and martinet officers in the early frames, all characters eventually come around to support efforts to help the orphans. Christopher is young enough to be believable as a combat medic as he displays a unique combination of innocence and hardness. Watch near the end of the movie when he wears a T-shirt that states, "Death before reenlistment." Although the Philippine and Clark Air Force Base sets certainly do not look like Saigon, the Vietnamese actors, who were mostly recruited from the Manila Refugee Center, add to the film's authenticity. [TV]

Drive, He Said (1972) **D:** Jack Nicholson, 90m. William Tepper, Karen Black, Michael Margotta, Bruce Dern, Robert Towne.

* A star basketball player (Tepper) at an Ohio college is having trouble deciding whether to play pro ball or to join campus radicals against everything including the Vietnam War. He manages to carry on an affair with a professor's wife (Black) and to console his roommate (Margotta), who is "freaking out" about the draft. Dern is great in his role as the basketball coach, but overall it is easy to understand why Nicholson is better known for his acting than his directing.

\# Along with the usual antimilitary, anti-Vietnam rhetoric, this film contains the stereotyped induction center scene in which potential draftees will try any method to beat the system. Margotta does a crazy routine so well that he avoids the draft, but the pressures of the act and worrying about being inducted drive him over the deep end into real insanity. All in all, he really would not have made much of a soldier anyway.

Easy Rider (1969) **D:** Dennis Hopper, 94m. Peter Fonda, Dennis Hopper, Jack Nicholson, Karen Black, Luke Askew.

** Captain America (Fonda) and Billy (Hopper) make a big dope sale, hide the money in Fonda's motorcycle gas tank, and head across the country from Los Angeles to New Orleans to see the "real America." Accompanied by a drunken, disillusioned lawyer (Nicholson) whom they pick up along the way, they find more drugs, free love, and violent, antihippie rednecks. Made for less than $500,000, the film made fortunes for the producers and careers for the participants. Extremely dated and never as good as many claimed, it is worth seeing to feel the alienation of sixties youth and the spirit of the generation.

\# One of the biggest surprises of this film is that Vietnam is never mentioned. Nicholson notes that "this used to be a hell of a good country" but that today we "kill and maim to prove we are free." Although the war is not directly referenced, it is in the background and perhaps the foreground of every scene. Without Vietnam, this movie would not have been made nor seen—nor so highly acclaimed. ⊺ⱽ

Edge, The (1968) **D:** Robert Kramer, 100m. Jack Rader, Tom Griffin, Howard Loeb Babeuf, Jeff Weiss, Sanford Cohen.

* A group of burned-out New Leftists withdraws from civil rights activism and the antiwar movement to drink coffee, to be paranoid about FBI surveillance, and to discuss the good old days of draft resistance. One of the radicals (Rader) finally decides to come out of retirement to assassinate the president (although he is not named, a picture of LBJ is displayed at one point) in order to "make him pay for all the killing he's done [in Vietnam]. And then I'll take my own life. Otherwise I'd be just another killer." Rader's assassination attempt fails, and he kills himself rather than be captured alive. A new member of the radical retirees (Griffin) goes to Washington and retrieves Rader's body for burial. Griffin regains his radical motivation and goes to Chicago to organize students against the draft and the war.

\# Released during the 1968 Tet Offensive, this film's message is that to stop violence and the war in Vietnam, any course of action, no matter how violent, is justifiable. Though not stated, some of the radicals' burnout may be due to the fact that most are over twenty-six years old and therefore past draft age. In fact, the only one acknowledged to be under twenty-six is the one played by Griffin, who resumes his activism.

84 Charlie Mopic (1989) **D:** Patrick Duncan, 95m. Jonathan Emerson, Nicholas Cascone, Jason Tomlins, Christopher Burgard, Glenn Morshower.

**** This is a simple, low-budget film in which a reconnaissance patrol of the 173d Airborne Brigade is seen from the point of view of a combat cameraman. Everything is recorded through the single camera lens operated by a soldier whose military occupation specialty 84C, motion picture specialist (Mopic), also provides the movie's title. Without exception, the cast of unknowns offers outstanding performances. Written and directed by Duncan.

\#\#\#\# One of the best. Although there are a few flaws in uniforms, equipment, and operations, this is without a doubt the most accurate portrayal of a Vietnam patrol filmed to date. The soldiers are believable, their language and thoughts authentic, and day-to-day and hour-to-hour action as it really was. Radio communications, use of air and artillery support, and the brotherhood of combatants are right on target—as close as you can get to the real Vietnam in a movie theater re-creation. The variety of hats and headgear worn by the patrol members is the most detracting weakness, but it does help the viewer distinguish among the heretofore unknown actors. Technical adviser Captain Russ "Gunny" Thurman (USMC, retired), director Duncan, and the entire cast and crew deserve a "mention in dispatches." 📺

Electra Glide in Blue (1973) **D:** James William Guercio, 106m. Robert Blake, Billy Green Bush, Mitchell Ryan, Jeannine Riley, Royal Dano.

** A short Vietnam veteran attempts to be a big cop by using his brain. His honesty does not fit in with the crookedness of his police brothers in their harassment of hippies and druggies. There is enough violence and typical Blake posturing to keep this one interesting, but only barely. Note that "Electra Glide" is a model of Harley-Davidson motorcycle. Other, deeper meanings in the film, if any, are not as obvious.

This is one of the few films of the 1970s to acknowledge the existence of Vietnam and of veterans without taking cheap shots or going into antiwar commentary. Blake's character is certainly weird, but it is not the stereotypical Hollywood crazy vet. It is established early that Blake is a Vietnam veteran, but that is not the essence of his character. He stops a truck for a traffic violation and the driver tries to get out of the ticket by saying he is just back from the war, is having trouble readjusting, and has already "blown two jobs." The driver admits that since he got back, "The only natural talent I have is for screwing up." Blake replies that he was with Marine Force Reconnaissance in the war and will "do for you what has been done for me—nothing" as he writes the ticket. Except for this initial scene and a brief mention by a biker that he had been busted for dope in Nam, no more mention of the war is made. Blake ends up being both the hero and the victim. 📺

Enemy Territory (1987) **D:** Peter Manoogian, 89m. Gary Frank, Ray Parker, Jr., Jan-Michael Vincent, Frances Foster, Tony Todd.

*1/2 A vicious gang of black thugs terrorizes a high-rise housing project. When a naive white insurance salesman crosses their turf, his only chance for survival depends on the help of an old woman and her granddaughter, a telephone repairman, and a wheelchair-bound Vietnam veteran. Mildly interesting if you like this sort of film.

When the salesman screams for help, a black telephone repairman comes to his aid. The repairman explains he is a Vietnam veteran and learned in the army that if someone yells "help," you have a responsibility to assist. He adds, "I don't care if he's white, black, or fucking fudge ripple." The insurance salesman, who sat out the war with a college deferment, is also helped by a bitter disabled Vietnam vet (Vincent) whose apartment is armed with automatic weapons and reinforced like a Vietnam bunker. Vincent's character is paranoid about deadly gases and poison food getting into his home. Although Vincent represents the stereotypical crazy Vietnam vet, the repairman is refreshingly different. He is resourceful, brave, intelligent, and has no flashbacks to Vietnam. He is by no means a superhero, but rather a concerned citizen doing what he thinks is right. It is a shame that such a "good" vet is in such a bad film. 📺

Enforcer, The (1976) **D:** James Fargo, 97m. Clint Eastwood, Tyne Daly, Harry Guardino, Bradford Dillman, John Mitchum.
** Dirty Harry is after a gang of urban-guerrilla Vietnam veterans who have kidnapped the mayor and bombed police headquarters. All of the usual Eastwood blood, guns, and killing is included, with the only variation being that this time his partner is a woman (Daly).
# The Vietnam vets are described as "liking combat." They wear their field jackets as they indiscriminately kill unarmed women and men and admit they are fighting not for political beliefs but for money. 📺

Explosion (1969-Canada) **D:** Jules Bricken, 96m. Don Stroud, Richard Conte, Gordon Thomson, Michele Chicoine, Ann Sears.
* An American draft dodger (Thomson) in Canada goes crazy after his brother is killed in Vietnam. Teaming with a hippie (Stroud), he begins a crime spree that leaves two policemen and a gas station attendant dead before he is shot himself. The entire film is contrived and melodramatic. The only remarkable parts are the British Columbia and Vancouver settings.
# Thomson's brother goes to Vietnam instead of Canada at the insistence of his father and girlfriend, who remind him of duty, responsibility, etc. The result, of course, is death. Apparently, at least according to this movie, just the threat of going to Vietnam,

or knowing someone who has, is enough to make you a homicidal maniac. Of many flaws, the biggest is Thomson's concern about being drafted. Once his brother was killed, as a "surviving son" he would have been exempt from combat duty.

Exterminator, The (1980) **D:** James Glickenhaus, 101m. Christopher George, Samantha Eggar, Robert Ginty, Steve James, Tony DiBenedetto.

* A veteran (Ginty) returns home to New York to work with the black friend who saved his life in Vietnam but finds himself back in combat. After his buddy is beaten and paralyzed by gang members, Ginty takes revenge on the hoodlums, the Mafia, and crooks in general in gory deaths by means of rifles, pistols, machine guns, fire, a giant meat grinder, flesh-eating rats, and even an electric kitchen knife—all while having flashbacks to his days in Vietnam. The vet explains that the killing is "like back in Nam; it doesn't matter if it's right or wrong." An absolutely horrible movie in every aspect.

\# Opening with a Ranger team attempting a helicopter extraction, the screen is filled with huge fireball explosions that have no similarities whatsoever to actual combat. For no apparent reason, the team surrenders and is taken to a VC camp—which is built in the open and illuminated by torches in total disregard of any air or ground threat. After several of the prisoners are tortured (scenes include a throat-cutting), one man manages to loosen his bonds, strangle his guard, take the guard's machine gun, and kill the entire camp—while rescuing the surviving members of his team. Another helicopter appears, again amid huge balls of fire, and the Rangers scramble aboard. As it flies away, one of the soldiers removes his fatigue shirt to expose a white vest embossed with three-inch black letters that state, "U.S. Army Flak Jacket." No explanation is given why the VC have allowed him to keep this bit of protection. Of course, that fits the situation, since flak jackets were actually labeled, in tiny letters on olive-drab cloth, "Body armor, protective." As for the set that doubles for Vietnam, it makes as much sense as white flak jackets. 🄣

Exterminator II (1984) **D:** Mark Buntzman, 88m. Robert Ginty, Mario Van Peebles, Deborah Geffner, Scott Randolph, Frankie Faison.

* If you think *The Exterminator* was horrible, wait until you see the sequel. This time Ginty's character teams with a New York garbage-truck-driving black Marine vet who wears his dog tags because "the war is still going on." To the usual array of weapons of death, the two add a flamethrower to wreak their vengeance. Running over thugs with the garbage truck is just another method to pad the body count.

No scenes of the war in Vietnam are offered. However, both "heroes" go about their business wearing field jackets and/or boonie hats. A brief shot is even included of a passed-out wino in an alley wearing the ever-present field jacket. 📺

Extreme Prejudice (1987) **D:** Walter Hill, 104m. Nick Nolte, Powers Boothe, Maria Conchita Alonzo, Rip Torn, Michael Ironside.

** A Texas Ranger (Nolte) finds himself at war with a childhood friend turned drug lord (Boothe). Complicating the matter is that both are in love with the same woman (Alonzo). Double crosses, triple crosses, and a space-age, high-tech group of Vietnam-veteran government undercover commandos muddle the plot to a nearly incomprehensible state. Final scenes have more than a passing resemblance to *The Wild Bunch*.

The Vietnam vets are a special team used around the world for dirty, deadly, clandestine missions. Although a bit crazy and bloodthirsty, the vets are loyal, disciplined soldiers—except for their officer leader, who sells them out to the drug czar. The traitorous leader explains, "There are no heroes." 📺

Eye of the Eagle (1987) **D:** Cirio H. Santiago, 84m. Brett Clark, Robert Patrick, Ed Crick, William Steis, Cec Verrell.

* A three-man Special Forces "Eagle Team" fights the North Vietnamese and a "lost command" of Americans made up of deserters and junkies. The lost command is headquartered in what appears to be a World War II shore-battery complex. One of the team's missions includes a raid on an NVA military train, to eliminate a fat general, and an escape by motorcycle. Look up "ridiculous" in the dictionary and you will find a listing for this film.

The team members wear black uniforms with nonsubdued (gold) sergeant stripes on the sleeves. They carry neither water nor extra ammunition, and one is armed with an Old West six-gun and a lever-action rifle. Firefights are characterized by the pulling of

grenade pins with teeth. The best line, and the most fitting of this movie, is delivered by a team member who says, "This war seems a bit farfetched." 📺

Eye of the Eagle II: Inside the Enemy (1988) **D:** Carl Franklin, 80m. Todd Field, William Field, Andy Wood, Ken Jacobson, Ron Lawrence.

* The sole survivor of a jungle ambush falls in love with a Vietnamese girl who is kidnapped and forced into prostitution by the soldier's commanding officer to cover his drug-smuggling operation. All the viewer can hope is that the Eagle does not develop a third-eye sequel.

\# The evil officer wears a Panama hat and carries a cane during field operations. A fire base contains a single piece of artillery, which appears to be a five-inch World War II deck gun taken from a small-town park. The rest of the film is as authentic. 📺

Eyewitness (1981) **D:** Peter Yates, 103m. William Hurt, Sigourney Weaver, James Woods, Christopher Plummer, Irene Worth.

** In order to meet a television news reporter (Weaver), a New York City office-building janitor (Hurt) claims to have witnessed a murder. The two soon become involved in a complicated conspiracy involving Vietnamese gangsters, Russian Jews, and Israeli patriots. It is a bit confusing and uneven at times, but surprises and a great cast make the picture worthwhile viewing.

\#\# Hurt's character and his janitor buddy (Woods) are old Vietnam War buddies. Neither is very bright, and Woods makes comments about gooks and slopes, but both men are basically honest and end up heroes. Despite using lines such as "Do your floors need buffing or something?" Hurt even gets the girl. 📺

Face of War, A (1968) **D:** Eugene S. Jones, 72m. Cameramen: Eugene S. Jones, J. Baxter Peters, Christopher Sargent.

**** In 1966 producer/director/cameraman Jones and a crew of two spent ninety-seven days in Vietnam with M Company, Third Battalion, Seventh Marine Regiment. During that period more than half of the company was killed or wounded. Jones himself was wounded twice, and one of his crew once. This black-and-white documentary of three months with the Marine grunts takes no political stance in its absolutely outstanding effort to show ordinary infantrymen going about their day-to-day tasks in a combat zone.

Vietnam is shown as it really was. There is no narration or musical score. Scenes are what any Vietnam infantryman—army or Marine—would recognize: ambushes, dawn raids, helicopter assaults, long patrols, the death of a village child and the birth of another, and the absolute boredom punctuated by moments of stark terror that only combat soldiers really understand. This film is authentic and fair. It is hard to find on the video-store shelves but worth the effort. 🖵

Falcon and the Snowman, The (1985) **D:** John Schlesinger, 131m. Timothy Hutton, Sean Penn, Lori Singer, Pat Hingle, Dorian Harewood.

** Two sons of upper-class California families sell secret government information to the Soviets in Mexico. Based on the true story of Daulton Lee and Christopher Boyce, the film is dramatic, with a particularly fine performance by Penn. Although no clear motivations are presented, at least the two traitors are not made out to be heroes.

Neither of the sellers of secrets is a Vietnam veteran, but Boyce's coworker (Harewood), who operates in a classified security area, is. He keeps a bottle of booze in his desk and prefers playing games to working. Harewood's character frequently expresses his disdain for "college boys" and brags about killing fourteen communists in Laos. Another minor player, a buddy of Penn's, talks about his Vietnam service to a Korea-vet guard as he smuggles drugs across the border. The border guard should have paid closer attention, as the Vietnam vet claims to have served at Pleiku with the 82d Airborne—which was never assigned there. 🖵

Fandango (1984) **D:** Kevin Reynolds, 91m. Kevin Costner, Judd Nelson, Sam Robards, Chuck Bush, Brian Cesak.

*** Five fraternity brothers go on one last road-trip fling across west Texas before facing the draft, Vietnam, and the real world. Reynolds, who would later direct Costner in *Robin Hood*, began this film as a student project and later expanded it with the assistance of Steven Spielberg. Funny, sensitive, poignant, and overall excellent performances by Costner and Nelson before their fame make this a good film throughout.

This is one of the best films in showing the individual strug-gles and conflicts among friends as they faced or did not face their responsibilities in the 1960s and early 1970s. No great debate about right or wrong is made beyond one character's saying, "I'm not sure I can go" and another character's willingness to do any-thing (including jumping out of an airplane) to keep his friends from running off to Mexico or Canada. The only real cheap shot is that a parachute-school owner/pilot is a Vietnam veteran who admits to being a "space cadet" and smokes dope while flying. Still, he ends up being a "hero" by helping the five friends solve some of their problems. The most memorable scene is a fireworks fight in a Marfa, Texas, cemetery when two of the participants trip on a new grave with a headstone of a Marine killed in Viet-nam. Play and war are quietly distinguished. This is the best of the "last days before going to war" films and teaches that if getting drafted does not make you crazy, at least it gives you an excuse to act that way. 📺

Fatal Mission (1989) **D:** George Rowe, 84m. Peter Fonda, Tia Carrere, Mako, Ted Markland, Jim Mitchum.
     * A navy commander (Fonda) poses as a French journalist in or-der to assassinate a general in North Vietnam; then he must fight the NVA, Chinese agents, and his own intelligence network dur-ing his escape to South Vietnam. Anyone who can possibly accept any of this film as being even remotely feasible probably has a col-lection of deeds to bridges in Brooklyn and oceanfront property in Oklahoma.
     # Aside from Fonda's cavorting with a female Chinese agent in a jungle pool, the most interesting shots are of Fonda's ineptness in handling an M-16 rifle and his apparent fear of the weapon—all the while attempting to appear cool and in control. Also watch for Fonda, after leaving a city in North Vietnam and entering the jun-gle, tie an olive-drab scarf around his head though he wears a white jacket for the remainder of the film. 📺

Fear (1988) **D:** Robert A. Ferretti, 96m. Cliff DeYoung, Frank Stallone, Kay Lenz, Robert Factor, Scott Schwartz.
     * Four escaped convicts, led by a former Green Beret soldier who thinks he is still in Vietnam, kidnap a family, including the fa-ther who is also a troubled Special Forces veteran. The convicts

kill prison guards, each other, and just about anyone else who crosses their path. Multiple shotgun blasts, strangulations, death by fire, and dialogue that includes "I'll bite your nose off and spit it in your face, man" make this a film to avoid.

The villain veteran is a mass murderer who killed his sister, her husband, their children, and even the family dog while flashing back to Vietnam. One escapee describes him simply by saying, "That's a sick fuck, man." The most interesting scene is when the veteran convict is confronted by a storekeeper who brags about his Korean War service and laments the poor treatment of returning Vietnam vets. The convict's response is to think the merchant is a Vietcong and to blast him with a shotgun in front of a large, wall-mounted American flag. Although the "good" veteran, who heads the kidnapped family, is having trouble with his wife and his adjustment to civilian life, he still retains enough of his killing skills from Vietnam to defeat the convicts. Apparently this film's message is that the only person who can whip a crazy Vietnam vet is another crazy Vietnam vet. ⊡

Fighting Back (1980) TVM, **D:** Robert Lieberman, 100m. Robert Urich, Art Carney, Bonnie Bedelia, Howard Cosell, Richard Herd.

** A professional football player overcomes his Vietnam wounds in this film based on the true story of Rocky Bleier. Bleier (Urich) was selected out of Notre Dame in the next-to-last round of the National Football League draft by the Pittsburgh Steelers. Before he could make the team, he was drafted by a larger organization— the U.S. Army. Suffering leg and foot wounds in Vietnam, Bleier is given little chance to walk again, much less play professional football. This is the story of his comeback, based on the actual events that led to Bleier's going on to become the fourth all-time leading Pittsburgh rusher. Bedelia plays Bleier's love interest and provides a good balance in showing that football is not a substitute for life or, for that matter, really all that important.

This is a great story that is unique in illustrating how a Vietnam veteran faced great adversity and achieved tremendous success. Unfortunately, the film does not show that pitifully few pro football players shared Bleier's experiences. Pro football—that bastion of America's strongest, fittest, and most beloved athletes— was also a means of avoiding the real draft and service in Vietnam. When team doctors could not verify "old football injuries," team

management was able to find the players safe positions in the National Guard or Reserves. Even this film admits that it was only a mix-up that prevented Bleier's being accepted into a National Guard unit. One can but wonder if a greater effort would have been made by the Steelers to keep him out of combat if Bleier had made a better impression in his initial training camp. The film's Vietnam scenes are ridiculously southern California, complete with a coffered rice paddy. Despite the film's generally positive portrayal of Vietnam vets, it still manages a few cheap shots. In one scene, Bleier is shown stopping another GI from murdering an old Vietnamese man.

Fighting Mad (1977 U.S.-Philippines) **D:** Cirio H. Santiago, 83m. James M. Iglehart, Jayne Kennedy, Leon Isaac, Joonie Gamboa, Leo Martinez.

* A trio of vets smuggle gold to the United States in coffins of Vietnam combat dead. During a transfer of the bullion on a yacht off the Philippines, two of the conspirators knife their partner (Iglehart) and throw him overboard. He washes ashore on an island inhabited by two Japanese still fighting World War II, and they teach him to become a samurai warrior. Iglehart's character returns to the United States, lops off many heads with his sword, and reunites with wife Kennedy. Poorly produced and acted, it seems much longer than its eighty-three-minute running time.

\# Although made in 1977, the film was not released until 1981 when Kennedy became a minor television star as a sports announcer and was the subject of a *Playboy* pictorial. In the early scenes, the actors wear khaki uniforms with subdued Twenty-fifth Infantry Division patches and hair so long that they do not attempt to wear hats. Watch during the middle of the film when a street sequence briefly pans a marquee advertising *The Born Losers*—another Vietnam movie of the dog variety. [TV]

Final Mission (1984) **D:** Cirio H. Santiago, 101m. Richard Young, John Dresden, Kaz Garaz, Christine Tudor.

* A Vietnam-vet Los Angeles SWAT team member (Young) is suspended from his job for using excessive force in defending his home against a gang of thugs—he literally breaks their necks with his bare hands. The remainder of the gang, led by a former war buddy who changed sides and fought with the enemy, pursues him into the countryside. Young's character kills them all with a machine gun he conveniently steals from a small-town gun shop window. Soon the police and the National Guard are in pursuit of the vet, who, by now, is convinced that he is back in Vietnam and everyone is the enemy. The final half-hour is a poor clone of *Rambo*. Not surprisingly, Young's other films include *Friday the 13th* V and *Night Call Nurses*.

This is another of the "only man who can stop a crazy vet is another crazy vet" genre. A brother of one of the veterans explains his weirdness, saying, "Something horrible happened to him in Vietnam." The only Southeast Asia footage is an opening-credit raid on a village where Young and the turncoat toss aside their respective M-16 and AK-47 so they can fight with their fists. Only a dentist could appreciate this painful film—especially the final scenes, in which Young actually pulls hand grenade pins with his teeth. 📺

Fireback (1984-Hong Kong) **D**: Teddy Page, 90m. Richard Harrison, Bruce Baron, Gwenolyn Hung, Ruel Vernal, James Gaines, Mike Monty.

* A former Vietnam POW returns home to find his wife has been kidnapped by a jealous mob member. The vet, who is so tough "he can make an ordinary soft-drink straw into a weapon," goes after his spouse and revenge. Produced in Hong Kong, the film has dubbing that is terrible, acting that is even worse, and a plot so disjointed as to be ridiculous. Absolutely horrible in every aspect.

The few flashbacks do not remotely resemble Vietnam or anything that ever happened there. Nothing in this film makes any sense whatsoever. 📺

Firefox (1982) **D**: Clint Eastwood, 136m. Clint Eastwood, Freddie Jones, David Huffman, Ronald Lacey, Warren Clarke.

* An American officer (Eastwood) goes deep into Russia to steal "the most devastating war machine ever built"—the MIG-31. Code-named Firefox, the superjet travels at six times the speed of sound, eludes radar, and navigates and fires its weapons systems by reacting to the pilot's brain waves. Eastwood's directing proves to be equal to his one-dimensional acting, resulting in a slow-moving, predictable film.

For reasons that have no apparent connection to the plot, Eastwood's character is haunted by flashbacks to his flying days over Vietnam, including his being taken prisoner and seeing a young girl killed by napalm during an attempt to rescue him. The immediate response of Eastwood's character to conflict or danger is to hallucinate about the child going up in flames. The only accurate Vietnam content is actual footage of air strikes and a pilot's bailing out of a crippled F-4 fighter. ☐

First Blood (1982) **D:** Ted Kotcheff, 97m. Sylvester Stallone, Richard Crenna, Brian Dennehy, David Caruso, Jack Starrett.

** John Rambo (Stallone), a former Green Beret and Medal of Honor winner, wanders into the misnamed town of Hope in the Pacific Northwest to find that his Vietnam War buddy has died of an Agent Orange cancer and that the local sheriff does not like vagrants. After being arrested and abused by the small-town cops, Rambo flashes back to being a POW in Nam, destroys the police station, and escapes. Soon the local authorities, townspeople, and the National Guard are in pursuit. The poor unfortunates eventually have the jungle fighter, who is "trained to ignore pain and live off the land," surrounded. Rambo utters few words, at least few that anyone can understand, and communicates with grunts and his biceps. All he wants is to be left alone—and soon the people of Hope wish the same thing. Great, albeit mindless, adventure and action. Any film whose credits list an exotic-knife maker, a dog handler, and a rat wrangler can't be all bad. This is the first of the Rambo series and the forerunner of a massive number of clones and rip-offs.

Vietnam provides the excuse for Rambo's destructive behavior. Although he is a sympathetic character, he does veterans no favors by establishing the superhero-vet film genre. Anyone who believes that Rambo could jump from a cliff onto rocks and receive only a minor cut probably also believes that a club fighter named Rocky from Philadelphia could go the distance with the world's heavyweight champion. Regardless, there are lines that will warm the hearts of Vietnam vets. When told by his old commanding officer that they can't have Rambo wasting friendly civilians, Rambo responds, "There are no friendly civilians." In one of his few speeches of more than a half-dozen words, Rambo laments that in Vietnam he could fly a gunship, drive a tank, and be re-

sponsible for millions of dollars of equipment, while in the States
after his return he can't even hold down a job. 📺

Five Gates to Hell (1959) **D:** James Clavell, 98m. Neville Brand,
Patricia Owens, Dolores Michaels, Benson Fong, Shirley Knight.
   ** A group of Red Cross doctors and nurses and a nun are kidnapped by communist guerrillas to treat their ailing leader during
the French Indochina War. The guerrilla leader (Brand) nails the
nun to a tree and allows his men to sexually molest the nurses. In
broken English he boasts, "Soon I warlord of whole Vietnam." The
prisoners finally rebel and kill their guards as well as Brand, but except for a few nurses, all also die in the process. Besides being the
only survivors, throughout the film women are touted as being
better organized and more resilient than men. In addition to
directing the film, Clavell also produced it and wrote the screenplay, and some of the insight into Eastern customs and thoughts
that he gained during five years as a prisoner of the Japanese during World War II is evident.
   # The communist guerrillas are portrayed more like brigands
than as freedom fighters or nationalists. Summary executions,
rape, and torture are routine for *these* "communists." Other than
the fairly accurate depiction of the ruthlessness of the guerrillas,
little is provided that offers any insight into how they would sustain jungle warfare for the next two decades. The hills around
Malibu, California, provide the shooting locations, and while certainly not Southeast Asia, they are not as far off as many of the
southern California film sites often substituted for Vietnam.

Flashback (1990) **D:** Franco Amurri, 104m. Dennis Hopper, Kiefer
Sutherland, Paul Dooley, Carol Kane, Cliff DeYoung.
   ** Sutherland plays an FBI agent escorting a sixties radical
(Hopper) from San Francisco to Spokane twenty years after his going underground. Subtle as well as direct references are made to
earlier Hopper films, such as *Tracks* and *Easy Rider*. Amusing in
places—but it's a real stretch.
   # The first introduction to Hopper's character is a *Life* magazine cover from the FBI file that shows him in front of a banner
that reads, "US Get Out of Vietnam Now." At one point, an audio
tape of Hopper's old antiwar speeches is played to a small-town
Oregon audience. They react by helping him escape and chanting

old anti-Vietnam slogans. Although cloaked in humor, this is merely another movie in which the protesters, hippies, and anti-war activists are the good guys and the police, FBI, and military are the bad. Its major significance is to add to the list of antiestablishment films that have made Hopper a wealthy man. Here he resembles his character when he brags, "I'm too old to grow up." ⟦TV⟧

Flashpoint (1984) **D:** William Tannen, 95m. Kris Kristofferson, Treat Williams, Rip Torn, Tess Harper, Jean Smart.
*1/2 Two Texas border patrolmen (Kristofferson and Williams) discover a long-hidden hoard of money that leads to the revelation of a high-level cover-up of the JFK assassination. The basic story idea is good, but it fails to mature under the direction of Tannen, who is better known for making television commercials. Although set in Texas, the saguaro cactus in the background are a sure sign it was actually filmed in Arizona.
Early in the movie, the border patrolmen emplace sensors to detect illegal aliens. One of the patrolmen comments, "We tried them sons of bitches in Nam; didn't work then, ain't going to work now." Although it has nothing to do with the plot, it is later revealed that Kristofferson's character is a West Point graduate and earned three Silver Stars in Vietnam. He explains that he became a border patrolman because he likes the peace and quiet. ⟦TV⟧

Flatliners (1990) **D:** Joel Schumacher, 111m. Kiefer Sutherland, Julia Roberts, Kevin Bacon, William Baldwin, Oliver Platt.
**1/2 A group of medical students experiment with inducing their own deaths and then bringing themselves back to life in order to see what is on "the other side." In this well-acted drama, they find horrors from their past and in their future.
When Julia Roberts's character crosses over to the other side, she is greeted as a little girl by images of her father returning from Vietnam. She sees what she has suppressed since childhood—her father mainlining dope and killing himself with a .45 pistol. ⟦TV⟧

Flight of the Intruder (1990) **D:** John Milius, 115m. Danny Glover, Willem Dafoe, Brad Johnson, Rosanna Arquette, Tom Sizemore.
** Two Navy A-6 Intruder pilots (Dafoe and Johnson) are tired of only being allowed to attack unmanned jungle targets during

the bombing halt of 1972. Johnson's character is upset about the loss of his bombardier to ground fire, and Dafoe's character is on his third tour because he likes the work. The two team together and, after the loss of their wingman, decide to fly an unauthorized mission "downtown" against a SAM missile park in Hanoi. After the successful flight, they are threatened with court-martial but receive only a slap on the wrist before returning to action to rescue their downed commander (Glover). This first look by Hollywood at the air war over North Vietnam and carrier operations in the Gulf of Tonkin tries hard but misses the mark with cliché-ridden dialogue and obligatory barroom fights and a brief love affair.

Unfortunately, the bomb strikes, zooming missiles, and exploding buildings look like the Hollywood miniatures that they are. Much of the dialogue and its delivery more resembles that of enthusiastic ROTC cadets than real carrier pilots. Still, the film has its merits. It is one of the few that show the war from the view of career officers. Glover best expresses the widespread opinion of professionals in the closing stages of the war by commenting that there are riots and protests at home and soldiers get spit on in airports, and "all we've really got is each other." Even more pertinent information is given by the head of the Board of Inquiry investigating the unauthorized bombing when he strongly reminds Dafoe and Johnson that following the orders of the elected civilian leadership is the cornerstone of the military and the country. Despite its flaws, this is the type of film that veterans of previous wars were provided and that Vietnam vets deserve. Carrier interior and flight-deck shots aboard the USS *Independence* alone are worth the price of admission. ⊡

Fly Away Home (1981) TVM, **D:** Paul Krasny, 104m. Bruce Boxleitner, Tiana Alexandra, Michael Beck, Brian Dennehy, Lynne Moody.

* This TV pilot, set in Saigon during the Tet Offensive of 1968, attempts to introduce ten American and Vietnamese characters for a series that was a quick failure. The primary actors are a journalist (Boxleitner) and his cynical (is there any other kind on the screen?) news-bureau chief (Dennehy). Other characters include American medical and military personnel and both good and bad Vietnamese. Overall it plays like a dull soap opera.

The most noteworthy aspect is that this was the initial at-

tempt by a TV network (ABC) to air a regular series based on the war. It failed as drama and did not succeed in conveying any real accuracy about the conflict and times.

Follow Your Heart (1990) TVM, **D:** Noel Nosseck, 96m. Patrick Cassidy, Frances Sternhagen, Catherine Mary Stewart, Jane Alexander, Nichole Francois.

* A Marine, fresh out of the service and duty in Central America, is stranded in a small, remote western town after he wrecks his vehicle. Taken in by a kind widow rancher, he eventually adopts an abandoned Vietnamese girl and finds inner peace for himself as he pursues a Vietnam veteran who has molested the girl—all before the local garage is able to repair his four-wheeler. With the exception of the veteran, everyone is so sweet that the viewer will know this was made for television without asking. The only redeeming aspect is the excellent portrayal of the widow by Sternhagen.

\# The Marine vet of the conflicts in Central America is able to cope with his war; the Vietnam vet is not. Described as a "sick maniac," the Vietnam veteran is also said by the locals to have been "a sickness in this town for twenty years." When the Vietnam vet first meets the orphan girl, he leers and laughs as he says she reminds him of a woman he knew in Saigon and that maybe he is her father. Later he kidnaps and molests the child and attempts to place the blame on the mentally disabled son of the widow rancher. He is caught only because the girl tears the Fourth Infantry Division patch from the vet's field jacket during the assault.

Forced Vengeance (1982) **D:** James Fargo, 90m. Chuck Norris, Mary Louise Weller, Camilla Griggs, Michael Cavanaugh, Seiji Sakaguchi.

* A Vietnam veteran (Norris) protects the daughter of a casino owner-boss who has been slain by a rival gambling syndicate. The primary purpose of the film is to give Norris the opportunity to do a lot of bad acting and to fight with his feet. The only plus is the Hong Kong background scenes.

\# Norris's character and a Special Forces buddy first met the casino owner when they tore up his establishment while on R&R from Vietnam. No reason is offered as to why Norris dons his old dress-green uniform (not exactly a great fighting suit) for his final showdown with the rival gang. Also unusual is that along with the captain bars and rows of ribbons, the uniform sports the insignia of a general's aide-de-camp—much more a "horse holder" job than one of a combat soldier. 📺

Force of One, A (1979) **D:** Paul Aaron, 90m. Chuck Norris, Jennifer O'Neill, Clu Gulager, Ron O'Neal, James Whitmore, Jr.

* This follow-up to *Good Guys Wear Black* has Norris teaching his karate skills to the police force of a small California town to combat a martial-arts expert who's also a cop killer. Norris explains his motivation: "I fought for the law at dirty little places along the South China Sea you never heard of." However, he also says that he fears the assassin may be "one of the guys who were with me in Nam." Norris spends lots of boring time in the kick-boxing ring, which is about as interesting as the rest of the film.

Vietnam, as in most of Norris's pre-Braddock movies, plays only the minor role of validating the toughness and dedication of the blond hero. Whether or not Norris's black adopted son Charlie has any meaning in the picture is anyone's guess. 📺

Forgotten, The (1989) TVM, **D:** James Keach, 96m. Keith Carradine, Steve Railsback, Stacy Keach, Mimi Maynard, William Lucking.

* Six Green Berets held captive for seventeen years are released just prior to trade talks between Western powers and Vietnam. National Security Council and CIA representatives first cloister the former prisoners in Germany and then mark them for death so they will not reveal the purpose of their final mission in North Vietnam. *The Forgotten* is best forgotten.

This is another in the genre of "high American officials sold out to prolong a profitable war" films. Uniform detail is equally unrealistic, as the combat infantryman's badges the six Green Berets are wearing have a star, meaning they are also veterans of the Korean War. Given their apparent ages, it would have been necessary for them to have gone AWOL from kindergarten to have fought. Watch for such gaffes as the Green Berets toasting the 101st Airborne instead of the Special Forces and all wearing "leg" boots rather than those of paratroopers. Filmed in Great Britain and Yugoslavia. 📺

Forgotten Man, The (1971) TVM, **D:** Walter Grauman, 73m. Dennis Weaver, Anne Francis, Lois Nettleton, Andrew Duggan, Pamelyn Ferdin.

VIETNAM AT THE MOVIES

* An American POW (Weaver) escapes from North Vietnam and returns home to find he has been reported killed in action and that his family is not particularly glad to learn otherwise. His wife has remarried, his daughter has been adopted, and his business has been sold. The rest of the film focuses on Weaver's attempt to readjust while flashing back to the hell of his capture and days as a prisoner.

Weaver, although a good actor, is not convincing as a veteran or former POW. Of course, the entire story lacks veracity; not a single American POW escaped from North Vietnam. While the theme is not entirely overt, *The Forgotten Man* is no more than another of the "loser for having gone to Vietnam in the first place" scenarios. Only its early release as among the first of its kind earns it any mention.

Forgotten Warrior, The (1987) **Ds:** Nick Cacas and Charlie Ordonez, 76m. Ron Marchini, Quin Frazier, Sam T. Lapuz, Joe Meyer, Vilma Vitog.

* An American POW escapes to the Vietnamese jungle, joins local tribesmen, marries, has a family, and just wants to be left alone to practice his martial arts. Vietnamese and American soldiers are soon in pursuit, and the forgotten warrior is forced to fight once more. The only possible purpose in making this film must have been to use up some of the *pop!* and *smack!* sound effects left over from the old Bruce Lee movies. Even when heavily armed, the combatants welcome the chance to drop their rifles and grenades and fight with feet and hands.

Many questions go unanswered in this movie, the major one being "Why was it made?" Also, why are the Vietnamese questioning American prisoners on U.S. troop strength after all the Americans have already gone home? And why do the North Vietnamese welcome American soldiers to join in the hunt for the forgotten warrior? It is not even worth questioning the ridiculous Vietnamese uniforms, their lack of AK-47s, and how one burst of M-16 fire can wipe out an entire platoon. ☑

For the Boys (1991) **D:** Mark Rydell, 145m. Bette Midler, James Caan, George Segal, Patrick O'Neal, Christopher Rydell.

**1/2 Two entertainers perform for the troops of three wars while carrying on a relationship that often rivals the combat they are trying to get off the minds of their audiences. Caan's character, Eddie Sparks, is described by Midler's as a "world-class, solid-gold son of a bitch." Sparks earns the description for such actions as firing one of his writers (who is dressed in a Santa suit) on Christmas night. Midler's character narrates the story to a Hollywood awards-show escort sent to pick her up for a reunion with Caan. Good music, reasonably funny jokes of the kind only soldiers long away from home appreciate, and close attention to detail of the times make for an enjoyable film despite Caan's apparent attempt at film's end to imitate George Burns.

The contrasts of World War II, Korea, and Vietnam in the nature of warfare and combatants are well conveyed. However, the innocence and flag-waving popularity of World War II are a bit overdone, as is the attempt to show the soldiers in Vietnam as embittered and undisciplined. During one show, the Vietnam GIs attack a go-go dancer; in another instance, a soldier is pointed out as being the nineteen-year-old son of a schoolteacher who now collects the ears of his dead enemies. The Vietnam scenes center on a visit to a fire base—interestingly and illogically set in a desert environment—where the son of the two entertainers is stationed as a captain. The officer is confused about the war, but when his mother says she can get him out of Vietnam, he responds that he must stay and face his responsibilities. He states, "I'm a captain, Mom; I've got men under me." Most interesting and unusual for a Vietnam film is that the captain's men respect him and even give him a cheer. The Vietnam segment concludes with an attack on the fire base that is not remarkable except for an extremely realistic exploding bunker—and for the fact that the captain dies in his mother's arms, a bit Hollywood even for Hollywood. TV

Four Friends (1981) **D:** Arthur Penn, 114m. Craig Wasson, Jodi Thelen, Jim Metzler, Michael Huddleston, Reed Birney.
*** A Yugoslavian immigrant comes of age in the America of the 1960s. He and his two best friends spend their youth and early adulthood all in love with the same girl. This is a sentimental, old-fashioned film, and one of the few of its genre to show that the sixties were not necessarily as much fun as depicted in other movies. Thelen states she is tired of "being young." Penn's effort is not nearly as good as his earlier *Bonnie and Clyde*, but it is quite watchable nonetheless.

One of the boys gets their shared girlfriend pregnant and joins the army, leaving a buddy to marry her. The new soldier, as noted in the dialogue of those who stay behind, goes to Vietnam. When he reappears near the end of the film, he has a Vietnamese wife and two daughters and seems to be happy and well adjusted. 📺

Fourth War, The (1990) **D:** John Frakenheimer, 90m. Roy Scheider, Jurgen Prochnow, Tim Reid, Harry Dean Stanton, Lara Harris, Dale Dye.

*1/2 An individual war between American (Scheider) and Soviet (Prochnow) colonels along the West German–Czechoslovakian border threatens to escalate to a much bigger conflict. The film's basic premise is that professional soldiers of any cause like so much to fight that they will make their own wars to practice their deadly skills. As Scheider's executive officer, Reid is badly miscast, but compared to Stanton's portrayal of a senior officer, he looks like General Patton.

As the film opens, a narrator states that the American colonel's dangerous, erratic behavior might be a result of his failed marriage, or "maybe it was the war." The colonel's boss tells him, "You are the offspring of the war in Vietnam." He later calls him "a war-mongering son of a bitch." Former Marine Dale Dye served as technical adviser and plays a small part as a sergeant major. Dye keeps the uniforms and equipment reasonably accurate, but the plot is beyond anyone's help. 📺

Friendly Fire (1979) TVM, **D:** David Greene, 147m. Carol Burnett, Ned Beatty, Sam Waterston, Timothy Hutton, Dennis Erdman.

*** An Iowa farm couple become obsessed with finding the truth behind their son's death by "friendly fire" in Vietnam and emerge as leaders in the antiwar movement. Based on the book by C.D.B. Bryan, this Emmy winner does an excellent job of showing how parents' love of their son and their sense of helpless loss over his death become all-consuming. Beatty is exceptional as the father. Burnett, whining and unable to accept the truth, is completely believable in her prejudices against the military and her campaign against the war.

Author Bryan in the book and in the film (Waterston) is

out to find the true cause of the friendly-fire mishap. He begins with sympathy for the family and a distrust of the army, only to be convinced there was no military conspiracy to cover up; he finds the incident to have been a "stupid accident of war." Overall the film shows the mistakes and strong points of both the parents and the army. Burnett's portrayal of Peg Mullen is poignant in displaying how a person with a few facts and some preconceptions can avoid the truth. Other details are also well presented. Particularly notable are the airport departure scene, the "green sedan" death notification to the parents, and the procedures and efforts of the military to assist surviving family members. Also of interest is the farm boy's battalion commander, whom the Mullens blame for the death of their son. Identified in the film as a Lieutenant Colonel Shindler, in the book he is accurately identified as H. Norman Schwarzkopf, of Desert Storm fame. [TV]

F.T.A. (1972) **D:** Francine Parker, 96m. Jane Fonda, Donald Sutherland, Len Chandler, Holly Near, Pamela Donegan.

* This semidocumentary records the antiwar "F.T.A." tour of American bases in the Pacific. Songs and skits are interlaced with interviews with service members and include such truths as "They [the military] don't want you to be an individual." This is certainly not Bob Hope. The most lasting impression made by the film is the firm understanding of why Vietnam vets are still not fans of Fonda, Sutherland, et al.

"F.T.A." officially stood for Free Theater Associates and unofficially for "Free the Army." The intended meaning of "Fuck the Army" was no secret to anyone. According to the screen credits, the film "was made in association with the servicewomen and men stationed on the United States bases of the Pacific Rim, together with their friends whose lands they occupy." Throughout the film the message is clear: "America lies." Sutherland rails against all "who take the peace from any of us." One of the cast adds, "Free Angela Davis."

Full Metal Jacket (1987) **D:** Stanley Kubrick, 116m. Matthew Modine, Adam Baldwin, Vincent D'Onofrio, Dorian Harewood, Lee Ermey.

**1/2 Two movies are delivered for the price of one. The first part is Marine boot training with Ermey as a profane drill instructor who puts the Corps first, last, and always. Ermey tells his platoon of recruits, "Every Marine is your brother. Marines die, that's what we are here for, but the Marine Corps lives forever. Therefore, you live forever." He not only rants but also makes his men believe that "If you survive, you will be a weapon; you will be a minister of death praying for war." The second part is seemingly a different movie altogether. Following a few of the boot platoon to the war in Vietnam, the film focuses on the battle to retake Hue during the Tet Offensive. Whereas the first part is riveting, the second is clichéd and routine. Despite the letdown in the last half of the film, Kubrick adds to his acclaimed list of films about dehumanization (*Dr. Strangelove, A Clockwork Orange,* and *2001*).

Lee Ermey's molding of reluctant civilians into Marines is far and away the strength of this film. Ermey, an actual Marine DI before beginning his acting career, anchors the most accurate portrayal of Vietnam-era basic training on film. Although there is more physical abuse—slapping, hitting, rifle-butt stroking—than was allowed or actually administered, every Marine will recognize and not so fondly remember his time as a boot during the first half of the film. The only negative aspect to Ermey's performance is that the nonveteran viewer will not understand what is serious, what is a joke, and what is strictly for effect. Unfortunately, the second part is nowhere near as good or accurate as the first. Much of the dialogue is authentic—as it is in the book on which it's based, Gustav Hasford's *The Short Timers,* adapted by Kubrick and Michael Herr (author of *Dispatches*). However, as portrayed, "Hue" and the countryside do not resemble Vietnam or the usual stand-ins of Thailand or the Philippines. Kubrick decided to recreate Vietnam in England, and he failed miserably. [TV]

Gardens of Stone (1987) **D:** Francis Coppola, 111m. James Caan, James Earl Jones, Anjelica Huston, D. B. Sweeney, Dean Stockwell, Mary Stuart Masterson, Peter Masterson, Carlin Glynn.
    **1/2 Two career NCOs (Caan and Jones) are faced with what Vietnam is doing to "their" army as they supervise burial details of the Old Guard in Arlington National Cemetery (the "garden"). Their views are influenced by an old comrade's enthusiastic son (Sweeney), who wants to go to Vietnam to earn a combat infantryman's badge, and an antiwar newspaper reporter (is there any

other kind?) from the *Washington Post* who becomes Caan's girlfriend. Mary Stuart Masterson is wonderful as the girlfriend of Sweeney, who learns the difficulties of loving a soldier during an unpopular war. In an interesting twist, her screen parents are played by her real-life father and mother (Peter Masterson and Carlin Glynn). Overall, the film offers an extremely interesting look at the effect of the war on the home front and the professional army. Based on the novel by Nicholas Proffitt, which is even better than the film.

The U.S. Army, Fort Meyer in Virginia, and the Old Guard lent official support and were heavily involved in the film's production. The barracks, orderly rooms, and service clubs are real. Details include how to properly spit-shine shoes (with cotton balls, polish, and water) along with an excellent depiction of the influence of the low-ranking but powerful company clerk. The naiveté and the gung-ho spirit common to many young soldiers are particularly well done. The film raises the interesting and accurate point that no one hates war more than those who have to fight it, and it illustrates the concern among career soldiers about how the war was tearing apart the country and the military service. Also remarkable is the depiction of how the military was in the lead in equal rights and race relations—Caan and Jones play best friends, and Jones, the black NCO, is the senior in rank. The most atypical part of the film is the life style of Caan. As a sergeant first class in the Washington, D.C., area, he lives in a luxury apartment, complete with a fireplace and furnished with fine Persian carpets and classic and first-edition books. He serves gourmet meals and fine wines to his guests. He does redeem himself a bit when he breaks the jaw of an attorney who calls him a baby killer at a party. Officers rarely appear, and when they do, they are stereotypically pompous and uncaring about their men. Despite the faults, this is one of the most positive, sympathetic films about military life in the 1960s. The best and most accurate lines have to do with the army taking care of its own because no one else will. 📺

Gay Deceivers, The (1969) **D:** Bruce Kessler, 97m. Kevin Couglin, Brooke Bundy, Larry Casey, Jo Ann Harris, Michael Greer.

   * Two straight buddies pose as homosexuals at an induction center to avoid the draft and Vietnam. The army officer in charge declares them unfit but then follows the two to check out their

claim. Forced to act out their ruse, they move into a homosexual neighborhood and are so convincing they fool their gay friends, but they also lose their girlfriends and their jobs. The two finally return to the induction center to admit their fakery but have posed so well that no one believes them. As they leave, the story offers its final twist when the army colonel embraces his sergeant assistant with much more than a straight hug.

The original intent of the film was to reveal the hypocrisy of the draft system, but it ends up going for the easy laugh. The best and most satisfying scene is when one of the acting gays is about to bed the sister of his friend. He looks out the apartment window, sees the army colonel spying on him, and immediately becomes impotent. The remainder of the film is equally impotent and, beyond showing one of the many ruses used to avoid the draft, adds nothing to an understanding of the period. 📺

Georgia, Georgia (1972) **D:** Stig Bjorkman, 91m. Diana Sands, Dirk Benedict, Minnie Gentry, Terry Whitmore, Roger Furman.

* A black woman (Sands) billed as "The Most Popular American Singer in Europe" tours Sweden and has an affair with a white American photographer (Benedict) who is a deserter from the Vietnam War. Her black traveling companion (Gentry) hates whites and wants Sands to romance and support a group of black deserters instead. There is much black-versus-white conflict, anger about Vietnam, and some scenic shots of the Swedish countryside that have nothing to do with the picture.

Bobo (Whitmore), the leader of the black deserters and draft dodgers, was an actual deserter hiding out in Sweden when the film was cast. Several others in the picture had the same status. Their acting mirrors their inexperience, and their participation in the film is the only real reason for it to be set in Sweden. Despite the film's attempt to make them into oppressed heroes, little is accomplished to convince anyone that the deserters are interested in anything beyond their own self-interest and safety. 📺

Getting Straight (1970) **D:** Richard Rush, 124m. Elliott Gould, Candice Bergen, Harrison Ford, Jeff Corey, Max Julien.

** Gould, as a former "ban the bomb" leader, returns to campus as a graduate student with intentions of "getting straight" and pursuing academic endeavors instead of joining the protests and rioting against the draft and the war in Vietnam. He makes a game effort but eventually rebels against the inflexible school administrators and joins the protesters. Better than the usual "protest" genre film, this one is noteworthy also for the early performances of Bergen and Ford.

According to this picture, the draft, the military, the war, the police, and the establishment are all wrong, and only the students can perceive the real truth. Actually, the movie takes fewer cheap shots than many of its type and goes so far as to include light criticism of the protest movement, noting that campuses are a safe place to riot, that demonstrations are "sexy," and that the "kids are turned on by it." References are made to giving Ds and Fs to female rather than male students because women are not drafted if they flunk out of school. Gould still caustically remarks, however, that "The Marines want guys crazy about killing, not just crazy." [TV]

GI Exectioner, The (1984) **D:** Joel M. Reed, 86m. Tom Kenna, Vicki Racimo, Angelique Pettyjohn, Janet Wood.

 * A Vietnam-veteran nightclub owner in Singapore is hired by mercenaries to rescue a kidnapped Chinese scientist. Very little of the plot makes any sense, and often it seems that the reels must be out of order. Other than the usual exploitation of Vietnam vets, the primary purpose of this film seems to be to show as many nude Asian women as possible.

Kenna, as the amoral Vietnam veteran, smokes dope and shoots without asking questions before or after. The only value of this movie whatsoever is in its location shots of Singapore, where many American soldiers went on R&R from Vietnam. [TV]

Girl Who Spelled Freedom, The (1986) TVM, **D:** Simon Wincer, 100m. Wayne Rogers, Mary Kay Place, Kieu Chinh, Kathleen Sisk, Jade Chinn.

** Based on the true story of a Cambodian refugee who became a spelling-bee champion after only four years in the United States, this film is designed to tug at the heartstrings—and it succeeds. A nice added touch is the introduction of the actual characters at film's end as they discuss the movie's events and production.

Set in 1979–1983, the film makes no mention of the Vietnam War except when a boy, referring to the refugees, asks, "Didn't we fight them in the war?" He is assured that the family is Cambo-

dian and not Vietnamese. The refugees are described as having been "slaves of the communists" and escaping "from their brutal homeland to the land of the free." The film ignores the fact that the refugees' sponsors and helpers were veterans. Also of note: Among the first English phrases learned by the champion speller are "soldier kill" and "bad soldier."

Gleaming the Cube (1989) **D:** Graeme Clifford, 105m. Christian Slater, Steven Bauer, Ed Lauter, Micole Mercurio, Min Luong.
   ** A rebel skateboarder seeks revenge against the mobsters who killed his Vietnamese foster brother. This "Hardy Boys adventure on skateboards" will appeal to no one above the age of fifteen—but young "thrashers" will love the skating stunts. For those who care, the title is skateboard jargon for achieving the ultimate or perfection—to neither of which this film comes close.
   # The murdering mobsters are Vietnamese led by a former ARVN colonel. Several of the Vietnamese are played by actors from other Asian countries. Apparently the casting director agreed with one of the movie's lines: "They all look alike." [TV]

Good Guys Wear Black (1979) **D:** Ted Post, 96m. Chuck Norris, Anne Archer, James Franciscus, Lloyd Haynes, Dana Andrews.
   ** The CIA is out to eliminate Norris's character and other members of his wartime Project Phoenix team to protect the appointment of a new secretary of state who "wrote off" MIAs in Vietnam. This is standard Norris action fare that is a bit above his usual because of an excellent supporting cast.
   # Vietnam footage has Norris and team throwing knives great distances to "silently" take out enemy guards. A later firefight on a Squaw Valley ski slope is much more interesting than the Vietnam scenes. Watch for Norris telling a college class studying Vietnam, "It was a war that should have never begun, in a country we should have never entered, and thousands of victims died without really knowing why. The reasons for the war were beyond any rules of logic." [TV]

Good Morning, Vietnam (1987) **D:** Barry Levinson, 121m. Robin Williams, Forest Whitaker, Tung Thanh Tran, Chintara Sukapatana, Bruno Kirby.
   *** Williams plays unconventional army disk jockey Adrian

Cronauer in 1965 Vietnam. The film has a weak story line, but hilarious monologues and quips by Williams keep it rolling—even if the jokes about New York, gays, and "Crockpot cooking" are much more contemporary than the mid-1960s. The film contains a noteworthy performance by Whitaker as Cronauer's buddy. This is hands-down the best comedy filmed thus far about the war—never mind the lack of competition. Still, a two-hour stand-up routine by Williams would have been as good or better.

There really was a Vietnam War. Adrian Cronauer was a disk jockey with Armed Forces Radio, and he did begin his air time by shouting, "Good morning, Vietnam." Other than those three facts, little else in the film is anything beyond funny. Saigon is pictured as surrounded by mountains. Vehicles, uniforms, and equipment are either clearly wrong or of a vintage more recent than 1965. Officers and NCOs are Hollywood stereotypes: dumb, rank abusing, red-necked, and humorless. Some efforts, however, are made to achieve accuracy. Everyone drinks Vietnamese "33" beer, and in one scene Cronauer verbally spars with soldiers of the just-arrived First Infantry Division, which did make its entrance into Vietnam at that time. Watch this one for the laughs, not for any real understanding of the war. Cronauer commented in an interview after the film's release that it would have been fun, but impossible, to get away with the antics that Williams displays in the movie. 📺

Gordon's War (1973) **D:** Ossie Davis, 89m. Paul Winfield, Carl Lee, Tony King, David Downing, Grace Jones.

* A Vietnam veteran (Winfield) returns to his Harlem home to find that his wife has died from a drug overdose and that his old neighborhood is overrun with addicts and pushers. Winfield, along with three of his war buddies, declares war on the drug lords with a lot of resulting car chases, shootings, and explosions.

Winfield hits the streets wearing his field jacket and tells his troops that they will clean up the city just the way they fought in Vietnam—an approach that includes the graphic breaking of the legs of one of the drug dealers. One of the drug bosses is also a Vietnam veteran, to which he credits his heroin addiction. 📺

Go Tell the Spartans (1978) **D:** Ted Post, 114m. Burt Lancaster, Craig Wasson, Jonathan Goldsmith, Marc Singer, Joe Unger, Dolph Sweet.

*** Lancaster leads an American advisory group in the early days of the Vietnam War. Everything that was wrong at the time or was going to be wrong in the future about the conflict is shown with candor and humor. Unlike the usual Vietnam movie fare that is full of cheap shots and/or inaccurate portrayals, this film explains the problems of the war accurately and reasonably fairly— but keep in mind it had the advantage of hindsight, being produced three years after the fall of Saigon. The best line is from a gung-ho lieutenant who says, "We won't lose, because we are Americans." Lancaster adds a strong second best by telling a young draftee who volunteered for Vietnam because he wanted to see what war was really like that it is a "shame we couldn't have shown you a better war, like Anzio, or Bataan; this one's a sucker's tour, going round and round in circles."

Based on Daniel Ford's novel *Incident at Muc Wa,* this film is unusually accurate in its dialogue and its presentation of the situation in Vietnam in the early 1960s. Although the southern California filming locations do not resemble Southeast Asia, uniforms and weapons of the period are on target. Characters are believable, from the old, burned-out first sergeant who has seen too much death to the second lieutenant who believes he can kill communists as well as any first lieutenant. Lancaster mutters the most accurate dying words of any soldier in any war film ever made when, with his last breath, he sighs, "Oh, shit." ⬛TV

Graveyard Shift (1990) **D:** Ralph S. Singleton, 89m. David Andrews, Kelly Wolf, Brad Dourif, Stephen Macht, Andrew Divoff.

*1/2 Giant rats are killing textile workers in a Maine mill basement, and a Vietnam-vet exterminator is hired to end the rodent problem. Based on a short story by Stephen King, this is typical bloody fare from the best-selling horror writer.

The veteran pest exterminator, in the film's best line, describes himself: "I ain't one of them baby-burning, flashback fuckups you see Bruce Dern playing." Yet, the veteran is wild-eyed, has long, greasy hair, dresses in black, has various killing devices attached to his belts, and is really not the type a father would like dating his daughter. The exterminator admits he may be prejudiced against rats after seeing them eat the dead and torture prisoners in Vietnam. It is interesting to note that King, the undisputed monarch of this genre, avoided the draft and duty in

the war. Perhaps he prefers the safety of horror fiction to the real thing. ⟦TV⟧

Greatest, The (1977) **D:** Tom Gries, 101m. Muhammad Ali, Ernest Borgnine, Robert Duvall, James Earl Jones, Ben Johnson.

* Ali plays himself in this biographical film about his boxing career from his early days as Cassius Clay through his title fight with George Foreman. Actual fight footage provides the high points, as Ali proves he is a much better pugilist than thespian. This was Gries's last film, but despite a remarkable cast, it is not in the same league as his earlier *Will Penny* and *Breakheart Pass.*

\# The major portion of the film deals with Ali's refusal to be inducted into the army because, as he said, he had no argument with the enemy and "no Vietcong never called me no nigger." He also delivers a long speech on why black people should not be fighting yellow people. The result of his refusal to serve in the military was his being stripped of his boxing title. He is treated as a hero for his draft refusal, although the story neglects the fact that someone else, who likely also had no argument with the VC, ended up having to take his place in combat. Neither does the film mention that Ali was one of the few professional athletes— and certainly one of the few stars—ever to have to worry about the draft in the first place. The movie does note that Ali's conviction for draft refusal was eventually overturned by the Supreme Court.

Green Berets, The (1968) **Ds:** John Wayne and Ray Kellogg, 133m. John Wayne, Jim Hutton, David Janssen, Aldo Ray, Raymond St. Jacques.

*** Special Forces in Vietnam struggle to defend a fire base and to neutralize a Vietcong general. Complete with a hard-core colonel, dedicated sergeants (including one who is an Eagle Scout), selfless soldiers, slick scavengers, and an orphan kid with a dog, this film includes every war-movie cliché ever contrived. Too long by at least a half-hour, this was the only big-budget film made about Vietnam during the war that was positive about U.S. involvement in Southeast Asia. It is typical John Wayne fare tied up in red, white, and blue, the only things distinguishing it from classic World War II movies being the location and the enemy. Despite its many shortcomings, including the now-famous scene of the sun setting in the east, this is a film that will bring pride to any Vietnam veteran—even if the song really is better than the movie.

A letter from John Wayne to President Johnson resulted in almost unlimited military support for the production of this picture. Uniforms and equipment are authentic due to the multitude of military advisers who oversaw each shot. Many of the extras (both American and Vietnamese) were played by active-duty servicemen and their families. Use of artillery and air support are shown well, and the Special Forces camp is worthy of positive mention despite the fact that it and surrounding jungle scenes were filmed at Fort Benning, Georgia. Alone, the first few minutes of the picture, in which a Green Beret NCO answers the questions of a belligerent newspaper reporter about why we are in Vietnam, are worth the price of admission. Among other good remarks, the best statement by the sergeant comes when he responds, "Foreign-policy decisions are not made by the military; a soldier goes where he is told and fights who he is told to fight." [TV]

Green Eyes (1976) TVM, **D:** John Erman, 98m. Paul Winfield, Rita Tushingham, Jonathan Lippe, Claudia Bryar, Royce Wallace.

** A black Vietnam veteran with a leg crippled from wounds returns to Saigon in 1973 to find the son he left behind with his prostitute girlfriend. Winfield does an excellent job in playing the vet, who, after returning from combat, is no longer welcome at his old workplace or at the VA hospital. At job interviews he hears no employment offers but is advised not to wear his uniform. His return to Saigon is even tougher as he wanders the streets seeking his son among the Amerasian and homeless children known to the Vietnamese as the "dust of life."

Winfield's character comes across as the last honorable man—either military or civilian—in the States or in Vietnam. His convictions and dedication to do the right thing are attributes rarely depicted on the screen by Vietnam veterans. It is a shame that the director went to so little trouble to show Winfield's uniform (sans combat badges and decorations) and flashback battle scenes (World War II trucks and equipment) as accurately as the Saigon streets and markets (shots of which include some real footage mixed in with adequate Philippine reproductions). [TV]

Greetings (1968) **D:** Brian De Palma, 88m. Robert De Niro, Jonathan Warden, Gerrit Graham, Richard Hamilton, Megan McCormick.

* Counterculture scenes of sex, drugs, and New York's Greenwich Village provide the background for three friends' efforts to beat the draft and stay out of Vietnam. Included is satire of computer dating, porno movies, and conspiracy theories about the assassination of John F. Kennedy. A young De Niro does not help this comedy, which was not funny when released and has not improved with age.

\# While the draft is the film's centerpiece, events occurring in Vietnam are included. A recently returned vet drones on and on about the abundance of cheap dope in Vietnam and how the South Vietnamese steal from the Americans and sell to the Vietcong. Although intended as satire, the best (or at least the most accurate) part of the film is actual television footage of President Johnson stating, "I wonder why we Americans enjoy punishing ourselves so much with our own criticism" and "We would be a threatened nation if we let freedom and liberty die in Vietnam. We will do what must be done." TV

Guts and Glory: The Rise and Fall of Oliver North (1989) TVM, **D:** Mike Robe, 200m. David Keith, Barnard Hughes, Annette O'Toole, Peter Boyle, Amy Stock-Poynton.

** This telefilm covers the life of Marine Lieutenant Colonel Oliver North from his days as a midshipman at the Naval Academy to the eve of his testimony before the Irangate congressional hearings. Based on the Ben Bradlee, Jr., book by the same title, it was rushed to the screen to coincide with the hearings. Included in the picture is a scene of Ronald Reagan calling North on the phone to fire him but remarking that someday his story would make "a hell of a movie." Reagan is partially correct, but the film, like real life, leaves much unanswered.

\# A great part of North's motivation in the film is attributed to his frustrations about the limitations placed on him and the U.S. military in fighting communism in Vietnam. North refers to the communists as "those hordes of Satan" and rails that the "liberal politicians, gutless judges, and left-handed journalists" are his enemies.

Hail, Hero! (1969) **D:** David Miller, 97m. Michael Douglas, Arthur Kennedy, John Larch, Louise Latham, Teresa Wright, Peter Strauss.

* Douglas plays a young man who drops out of an Eastern college to enlist in the army and be sent to Vietnam. Before induction, he returns to his parents' Arizona ranch. Although he comes from a long line of war heroes, Douglas tells his mother and father that he opposes the war and wants to go to Vietnam only so he can meet and "love the enemy." This was the first film for both Douglas and Strauss. The music includes two songs by Gordon Lightfoot in one of his few movie contributions.

\# In one scene Douglas presents to his hawkish brother a mummified Indian baby, which he has found in the cliffs above his parents' ranch house. He tells his brother, "Take a good look before you envy my chance to kill." By film's end, Douglas's parents and brother have adopted his peaceful viewpoint. 📺

Hair (1979) **D:** Milos Forman, 122m. John Savage, Treat Williams, Beverly D'Angelo, Dorsey Wright, Annie Golden.

**1/2 An Oklahoma farm boy (Savage) travels to New York to experience the Age of Aquarius before being drafted and sent to Vietnam. The subtitle could easily have been "Hippies Just Want to Have Fun." Not nearly as good as the stage version, but it wins by default as the best musical about the war.

\# Although this film is a celebration of the hippie life style and the antiwar movement, it is surprisingly fair in its treatment of the young men drafted for service in Vietnam. It attacks the war and not the warrior. Cheap shots still abound, however. According to the script, "The draft is white people sending black people to kill yellow people to defend land stolen from red people." Yet a few moments later Williams tells guests at a formal dinner party (which he and fellow hippies have crashed) that Savage is going to Vietnam to fight for them. The cheapest shot, but the most amusing, is when a board of army officers which is interviewing nude draftees breaks into song, singing in girlish voices about "Boys." The most accurate line, however, is delivered by Savage when he tells Williams, "You don't understand, this isn't a game." 📺

Hamburger Hill (1987) **D:** John Irvin, 110m. Anthony Barrile, Michael Patrick Boatman, Michael Dolan, Don Cheadle, Don James.

*** This fictional account of the battle by the same name follows the actions of one infantry squad. In the spring of 1969, elements of the 101st Airborne Division made eleven assaults over a period of ten days to take the heavily fortified Hill 937 from the NVA. By battle's end, the fight was aptly known as Hamburger Hill. Panned by many as limited in overall plot, the film presents an authentic look at battle at its best—or its worst. Along with the fighting, the film offers excellent insights into what the infantrymen thought about the war, the protesters and politicians back home, and each other. By film's end, the viewer is as exhausted as the tired grunts who have fought, crawled, and clawed up Hamburger Hill for ten long days.

This picture is extremely accurate in weaponry, equipment, and the use of artillery and air support. The dialogue is real, the age of the actors believable, and the Philippine shooting locations make for a passable Vietnam. Most remarkable is the camaraderie of the soldiers, their horseplay and discussions between assaults, which include remarks about how they respect the enemy more than the American press. The ultimate response to any difficulty is "What are they going to do, send me to Vietnam?" The strongest aspect of the film is the way it concentrates on a single squad and its individual members. The camera does not pan the battlefield but rather focuses on extremely small areas of the fight, which moves the viewer into the action and the emotion. 🖵

Hangfire (1990) **D:** Peter Maris, 91m. Brad Davis, Kim Delaney, George Kennedy, Jan-Michael Vincent, Yaphet Kotto.

* A busload of escapees from the New Mexico State Penitentiary takes over a small town and holds it despite the efforts of a martinet National Guard commander (Vincent) and his troops. The cons win until the local sheriff and his buddy, both Vietnam veterans, accomplish what the Guard has failed to do. The best line in the film goes to Vincent when he says, "I don't negotiate with the enemy; I ain't no goddamn Henry Kissinger." This one is not good enough for television—even late-night local cable television.

The sheriff and his buddy are "good vets" by Hollywood standards because they talk bad about the Vietnam War and the military. On the other side is the "bad vet" portrayed by Vincent, whose name is "Hawks." Hawks does not care how many of his own men are casualties as long as the mission is accomplished. "Twenty years

later [after Vietnam], and the clowns are still running the circus," proclaims one of the "good" vets. Watch for Vincent flying his own helicopter into combat wearing dress greens complete with Vietnam combat decorations and a combat infantryman's badge— unfortunately, his uniform is sans aviation wings that would show he is qualified to be in the pilot's seat. [TV]

Hanoi Hilton, The (1987) **D:** Lionel Chetwynd, 126m. Michael Moriarty, Paul LeMat, Lawrence Pressman, Jeffrey Jones, David Soul.

** American POWs in North Vietnam are tortured by their captors and ignored by their own country. This well-meaning effort to tell the POWs' story ends up too long, too clichéd, and, considering the subject matter, surprisingly dull. Although certainly not a great movie, it does accomplish the director's stated objective: "It was my goal to render a motion picture which would pay tribute to their sacrifice."

Seventeen former POWs served as technical advisers. On seeing the film, former prisoner Everett Alvarez said, "It was real. They had taken me back." Well worth watching for the accuracy of prison life and lines from the Vietnamese commander who remarks, "The real war is in Berkeley, California; the Washington, D.C., Mall; in the cities of America; and what we do not win on the battlefield, your journalists will win for us on your very own doorstep." The role of journalists and personalities such as Jane Fonda, as pawns of the North Vietnamese in their propaganda efforts, is among the film's most memorable aspects. It is doubtful that anyone could see this movie, regardless of its overall merits or the viewer's feelings about the war, without becoming extremely angry at the Vietnamese and their supporters for the treatment of the POWs. [TV]

Hardcase and Fist (1988) **D:** Tony Zarindast, 92m. Ted Prior, Carter Wong, Christine Lunde, Maureen Lavette, Tony Zarindast.

* An honest cop is framed on drug charges and sent to prison to prevent his testimony against a mob leader. Accompanied by a martial-arts expert, he escapes to punish all concerned. This is the type of movie in which the bad guys wear black shirts and white ties.

The cop is a Vietnam veteran, one of the mobsters out to kill

him is also a vet, and so is another character who gets in their crossfire by happenstance. The jailed cop is referred to as "some kind of crazy maniac." Flashbacks, composed of real combat footage, suffered by the mob hitman are the most interesting aspects. 📺

Hard Ride, The (1971) **D:** Burt Topper, 93m. Robert Fuller, Sherry Bain, Tony Russel, Marshall Reed, William Bonner.

** A Marine veteran (Fuller) escorts the body of his black buddy home from Vietnam only to face the task of getting the dead man's old motorcycle gang and white girlfriend to attend the funeral. A good sound track and above-par acting make this better than the average motorcycle film.

The dead vet's old gang buddies are much more interested in who gets his custom motorcycle than in his funeral or his war. Even though Fuller's character is the hero of the film and a dedicated friend to his Vietnam buddy, in keeping with the general theme of this genre (i.e., that veterans are losers), Fuller is killed near the end of the picture. One of the more watchable scenes has Fuller in full Marine uniform riding his dead friend's motorcycle.

Harley Davidson and the Marlboro Man (1991) **D:** Simon Wincer, 98m. Mickey Rourke, Don Johnson, Chelsea Field, Tom Sizemore, Vanessa Williams.

** In the lawless days of 1996, a pair of buddies (Rourke and Johnson) rob an armored truck to help a friend keep his business open. When the stolen goods turn out to be not money but mob-owned designer drugs, the chase is on—complete with the usual crashes, explosions, and exotic weapons. For a film with two top brand names in the title, the result is nothing but brand-X generic.

With the bad guys using an attack helicopter to pursue Rourke and Johnson, one of the gangsters tells the pilot that he is seven kilometers from the landing zone. The pilot remarks that was the same message and last words of his copilot when he was killed going into Khe Sanh. Apparently the Vietnam-veteran pilot has little allegiance to his present boss, because he is soon flying for Rourke and Johnson in exchange for a higher wage. He even does the dirty work of hosing down the mob's headquarters with the chopper's automatic weapons, killing his old employers. 📺

Head (1968) **D:** Bob Rafelson, 86m. The Monkees, Teri Garr, Victor Mature, Annette Funicello, Frank Zappa.

** This film debut of the TV rock group is a plotless collage of intercut scenes with psychedelic color and a wild sound track. Scenes include The Monkees jumping from the Golden Gate Bridge, then performing an underwater ballet, and later attacking an inoperative soft drink machine in the middle of a desert. In an another sequence, an Italian regiment of World War II soldiers surrenders to one man. Strange, fast paced, and oddly watchable. Jack Nicholson coproduced and wrote it.

Several inserts of American soldiers committing atrocities in Vietnam are flashed on the screen. No real analysis of the footage is attempted, but neither are there scenes of soldiers doing lawful deeds, either. 📺

Heartbreak Ridge (1986) **D:** Clint Eastwood, 130m. Clint Eastwood, Marsha Mason, Moses Gunn, Everett McGill, Mario Van Peebles.

** Eastwood plays a Medal of Honor winner, a veteran of Korea and Vietnam, who on his last tour of duty before retirement trains a platoon of misfit Marines into a fighting force. His commanding officer is a martinet, his platoon leader a naive buffoon, and the soldiers rebellious. Despite these hindrances, Eastwood prevails and takes his men on to victory in Grenada. This film is extraordinarily clichéd and the action is contrived. One of the few interesting aspects is Eastwood's reading of women's magazines in an attempt to better understand the opposite sex so he can win back his former wife (Mason).

There is discussion of the U.S. military tying in Korea and losing in Vietnam. Mason comments about watching the war on television in 1968, hoping to see her husband but dreading that she might see him killed. Of three survivors in Eastwood's platoon in Korea, one is killed in Vietnam. Much more interesting than the brief mention of Vietnam is the leeway Eastwood takes as a director. Heartbreak Ridge in Korea was an army (Twenty-third Infantry Regiment) battle, not a Marine action. This is acknowledged in a brief barroom scene that was added after the film was in production because of protests by the actual participants. Also, the actions by Eastwood's Marines in Grenada—freeing American

students from the Cubans—was, again, an army achievement—this time by the Seventy-fifth Ranger Regiment. 🖵

Hearts and Minds (1974) **D**: Peter Davis, 112m.

** According to this Academy Award–winning documentary, five U.S. presidents lied to the American people about Vietnam, the bombing of the North destroyed primarily hospitals and peaceful villages, and American soldiers tortured, burned, and killed with relish. Not a single incident of any brutality by the VC or NVA is evidenced in this documentary. A returning POW is shown as a buffoon in his support of the war and his country while the welcoming crowd is portrayed as naive and/or brainwashed. Davis readily admits that he deliberately set out to make the ultimate anti–Vietnam War film. That is sad; even more so is the way Hollywood and the viewing public fell at his feet in honor of this half-truth—or less—effort.

Everything pictured or quoted in this documentary actually occurred. The problem is not with what is shown so much as what is shown out of context or not at all. Few veterans will be able to watch this one-sided tripe without becoming extremely angry—at Davis for making it and at the movie production system for allowing it and praising the result. 🖵

Hearts of Darkness (1991) **D**: Fax Bahr, 96m. Francis Coppola, Martin Sheen, Larry Fishburne, Eleanor Coppola, Dennis Hopper, George Lucas, Robert Duvall.

*** This revealing documentary traces the genesis and long, troubled, expensive production of the 1979 film *Apocalypse Now*. Included are interviews conducted at the time and recently with the cast and supporting staff. The documentary incorporates film clips from the movie and footage shot by Eleanor Coppola during the production. The process of getting the film from the idea stage to the screen is shown in fascinating detail. Interesting tidbits, such as Orson Welles's wanting in 1938 to make a movie of the book upon which *Apocalypse* was based (*Heart of Darkness*), only to do *Citizen Kane* instead, are revealed. The major negative aspect of an otherwise extremely good documentary is the arrogance of Coppola and company. In their attempt to show the tough and at times dangerous filming conditions, the cast and staff come off much more wimpish than heroic—and almost laughable to those who experienced the real Vietnam.

The documentary opens with a 1979 interview with Coppola in which he states that the picture "is not about Vietnam, it *is* Vietnam; it is what it was really like, it was crazy." To justify the behavior of the characters in *Apocalypse*, actual footage of GIs' burning villages amid weeping old women is included in the documentary. The scene of a massacre of a family aboard a sampan, where the only survivor is a puppy, is followed by a real photo of an American soldier in Vietnam *holding* a similar-looking canine. A trailer to the documentary maintains a "politically correct" theme by apologizing for the scenes of animals being butchered with the explanation that the deaths were a part of ritual religious ceremonies and not performed strictly for the camera. Coppola made a good movie in 1979. Bahr made a good documentary in 1991. Unfortunately, neither has a clue as to what the war in Vietnam was really like. 📺

Heated Vengeance (1987) **D:** Edward Murphy, 91m. Richard Hatch, Michael J. Pollard, Jolina Mitchell-Collins, Robert Walker, Denny Patrick.

* A Vietnam veteran returns to Southeast Asia to find a girlfriend left behind a decade earlier. His reunion is blocked by drug-dealing Americans still living in the jungle and led by a child-molester whom the vet put in jail during the war. Other than great shots of Thailand countryside, nothing is memorable except to note the decline in the quality of parts for Pollard since his role in *Bonnie and Clyde* (1967).

This film is based on the premise that many of America's Vietnam MIAs are really drug-trafficking deserters. Lots of flashbacks, bad dreams, and the usual crazy-veteran stuff are included. 📺

Heroes (1977) **D:** Jeremy Paul Kagan, 119m. Henry Winkler, Sally Field, Harrison Ford, Val Avery, Olivia Cole.

** Winkler, in his first starring big-screen role, plays a confused Vietnam veteran who escapes from a New York VA hospital and then travels to California, where he intends to make his fortune with a worm farm. Along the way he visits old army buddies and meets Field, who is skipping out on her own wedding. Winkler is totally unbelievable as a veteran. Field does a good job as the girlfriend and confidante. All told, the film works about as well as worm farming.

\# Winkler is in the VA hospital for attempting to prevent recruiters from doing their business. He has recently lost his job and hates the military so much he gives a bus driver a hard time because he is wearing a uniform. Field relates, "The war was terrible; it went on forever. I was against it; I protested it." Winkler's veteran buddies are not in much better shape than he is. One friend (Ford) lives in a remote trailer and drives like he has a death wish. Another friend is not at home. His wife says that "he drifts" and that he "went out for a beer and hasn't returned." When Winkler finally makes it to the West Coast, he has flashbacks as he imagines explosions, bodies, and helicopters in the streets of Eureka, California. 📺

High Velocity (1977) **D:** Remi Kramer, 105m. Britt Ekland, Paul Winfield, Ben Gazzara, Keenan Wynn, Alejandro Rey.

** Two Vietnam vets (Gazzara and Winfield) are recruited by a beautiful woman (Ekland) to rescue her international-executive husband from Filipino guerrilla kidnappers. Lots of action, intrigue, and double crossing, but the quality cast is deserving of a much better script.

\#\# Gazzara and Winfield play somewhat reluctant warriors until threatened with deportation if they do not accept the mission. An offer of $100,000 is also a strong influence. Despite their initial lack of enthusiasm, the two former Marines soon admit they enjoy the risk and danger. Winfield's character simply states that he loves it. Gazzara responds that he also loves it but doesn't like loving it. An unusual aspect of this film is that neither vet experiences flashbacks, bad dreams, or regrets about his Vietnam service. Both are able, professional soldiers who are reasonably honest and well adjusted. The most different ingredient for a Vietnam film, or for any other movie for that matter, is that at the conclusion both heroes are killed, while the unsympathetic executive and many of his captors escape. Perhaps the message is that vets can be "normal" in a film as long as they die in the end. 📺

Hi, Mom! (1970) **D:** Brian De Palma, 87m (OT: *Confessions of a Peeping Tom*). Robert De Niro, Allen Garfield, Lara Parker, Jennifer Salt, Gerrit Graham.

* This uneven sequel to De Palma's *Greetings* is a continuation of his satirizing and glorifying the 1960s. De Niro plays a Vietnam veteran who has trouble finding a job and turns to making porno films. His mentor (Garfield) claims to want to make "the first children's exploitation film—nothing dirty, nothing smutty." De Niro's character also works with a militant revue called "Be Black, Baby" that performs in whiteface, blackens the faces of whites in the audience, and then robs and beats them. Finally, De Niro, after arguing with his wife, places a large charge of explosives in the laundry room of their building and blows it up. His pregnant spouse is one of the victims.

\# So many sixties issues are brought up that the De Niro character's Vietnam service can be credited as responsible for only part of the film's mayhem. Vietnam, however, is obviously a priority on the director's list of wrongs because, in the final scene, De Niro is interviewed on TV while wearing his army uniform in front of the building he has just destroyed. He speaks of the increase of violence as he waves to Mom in television land. 📺

Hollywood Shuffle (1987) **D:** Robert Townsend, 81m. Robert Townsend, Anne-Marie Johnson, Starletta Dupois, Helen Martin, Craigus R. Johnson.

* An actor (Townsend) trying to get a break in Hollywood keeps running into stereotypes as he dreams of success. Some of the satire works, most does not. Townsend also wrote and produced this film, which is based on his own experiences as an aspiring actor.

\# In one of Townsend's dreams, he is the star of *Rambo: First Youngblood*, in which he is a Vietnam superhero. This sequence is closely copied in the later *UHF* (1989). 📺

Homer (1970) **D:** John Trent, 90m. Don Scardino, Tisa Farrow, Trudy Young, Lenka Peterson, Ralph Endersby.

* A small-town rock singer named Homer has trouble with his music, parents, girlfriend, and the Vietnam War. Everyone is so stereotypical and the plot so clichéd that the viewer will be happy only with the fact that a good name was not wasted on the title. It is set in Wisconsin but was filmed in Canada. The only remarkable aspect is the sound track, which includes the Byrds, Cream, Led Zeppelin, and Buffalo Springfield.

\# When Homer's best friend is killed in Vietnam, he chains himself to a parking meter in front of the local VFW hall and wears a sign around his neck stating, "Down with death/End war!" When his father queries him about his actions, Homer replies, "You just don't understand, Pop. This is just something I have to do."

House (1986) **D:** Steve Miner, 93m. William Katt, George Wendt, Richard Moll, Kay Lenz, Michael Ensign.

* A horror novelist (Katt) moves to a creepy Victorian house, where his aunt committed suicide, to write about his experiences in Vietnam. The disappearance of his son and the breakup of his marriage add to his troubled war memories. Katt no sooner gets page one of his memoirs written than demons begin coming out of the closet (literally)—the ugliest and most evil being the rotting corpse of a buddy (Moll) he left behind in the jungle to be captured and tortured by the Vietcong. Only a devoted television fan of Wendt ("Cheers") and Moll ("Night Court") would want to see this one.

\# Although many evils are portrayed in this movie, Vietnam is the most evil and the basis of the novelist's hysterical fantasies. The writer says he has "got to write this book" despite his agent's telling him, "Nobody wants to read about the goddamn Vietnam war anymore, they want to read a good horror story." In the flashbacks to Vietnam, the novelist and his fellow soldiers smoke dope in the field and openly refuse the orders of their platoon leader. Interestingly, the least scary of any of the scenes are those of actual combat. [TV]

How I Won the War (1967-Great Britain) **D:** Richard Lester, 111m. John Lennon, Michael Crawford, Roy Kinnear, Jack MacGowran, Michael Hordern.

** A mistake-prone officer reminisces about leading his men in North Africa to build a cricket field. This World War II satire is well made and funny in a British black-humor sort of way. It is better known for Lennon's first solo movie performance, as Musketeer Gripweed.

\# Vietnam definitely provides the motivation for this antiwar, antiofficer, antimilitary picture. Only at film's end is Vietnam specifically mentioned, when a soldier asks a buddy, "There's a new war shaping up in Vietnam; do you think you'll be in it?" The friend responds, "No, I don't like the director." [TV]

I Feel It Coming (1969) **D:** Sidney Knight, 75m. Sammy Cole, Dandy Thomas, Jean Parker, David Marcus, Linda Shall.

* A Vietnam veteran returns home so disturbed by the war that he is impotent. His understanding wife tries a variety of techniques to arouse him, including a striptease, a lesbian show, and group sex. Nothing works until a girl delivering marijuana to the couple reminds the vet of a woman he knew in Saigon. Only after he rapes the delivery girl is he able also to perform with his wife.

Vietnam in this instance merely offers a background for what is little more than a sex film. The fact that it was released in 1969 at the height of the war and is an absolute insult to every person who served in Vietnam is merely coincidental.

In Country (1989) **D:** Norman Jewison, 120m. Bruce Willis, Emily Lloyd, Joan Allen, Kevin Anderson, Peggy Rea.

*** Lloyd plays a recent high school graduate who wants to know more about a parent whom she never met because he was killed in Vietnam. Talking to a picture of her father she remarks, "You missed Watergate, *E.T.*, Bruce Springsteen concerts. God, you missed everything, and you even missed me." Willis plays Lloyd's Vietnam-veteran uncle who suffers from mental and physical problems as a result of the war. To his niece, Willis says of Vietnam, "You ain't never going to understand it. You don't want to." Closing footage of Lloyd, Willis, and Lloyd's grandmother (wonderfully portrayed by Rea) at the Vietnam Veterans Memorial in Washington, D.C., is among the best on film of that location, which appears so often in Vietnam movies. Great lines and good acting make for fine parts; however, the whole of the film is uneven and not nearly as good as the Bobbie Ann Mason book on which it is based.

Every Vietnam veteran in the film is screwed up in one form or another. It is offered that Lloyd's grandfather was in World War II and came back all right but that Vietnam was a different war in different times. A little balance would have made this an excellent rather than just a good film. Still, the dialogue

is accurate, and anyone who does not get a lump in the throat and/or mist in the eyes at the closing must be one hard-hearted individual. Small-town scenes have the look and feel of reality, provided by the Paducah and Mayfield, Kentucky, shooting locations. The Ballard County Wildlife Recreation Area, where the Vietnam flashbacks were shot, looks much more like a sanctuary for ducks and raccoons than it does Southeast Asia. [TV]

In Dangerous Company (1988) **D:** Ruben Preuss. Tracy Scoggins, Cliff DeYoung, Chris Mulkey, Henry Darrow, Dana Lee.

*1/2 The mistress of the leader of an art forgery ring plots a double cross to steal the fake paintings and go into business for herself. To assist in her plan, she enlists a former lover who is a Vietnam veteran currently employed as a killer for hire. The film has some interesting concepts, but director Preuss fails to bring them all together.

Part of the picture takes place in a Los Angeles Little Saigon bar that caters to American and South Vietnamese veterans of the war. Along with the killer who helps the art thief is another Vietnam vet who runs a hitman employment service. One of the more interesting characters is a Vietnamese who laments that during the war he led a force of three hundred Nung mercenaries and now is responsible only for running the bar's dishwasher. [TV]

In Love and War (1987) TVM, **D:** Paul Aaron, 96m. James Woods, Jane Alexander, Haing S. Ngor, Richard McKenzie, Concetta Tomei.

***1/2 Based on the true story of Commander James B. Stockdale and his wife, Sybil, this film graphically displays the eight years of captivity of the navy's highest-ranking Vietnam POW. While Stockdale is tortured and questioned about his role in the Gulf of Tonkin incident, Sybil organizes the wives of other POWs back home and presses President Nixon to denounce the North Vietnamese treatment of American prisoners. The title tells it all—this is a magnificent story of love and war. It also predates Stockdale's selection by Ross Perot as his 1992 vice-presidential running mate.

Accuracy is a rare commodity in Vietnam War films, but this one rings true. Anyone who believed, however slightly, Jane Fonda and various international newscasters when they said that

the POWs were not tortured should see this picture. Broadcasts to the POWs of Harrison Salisbury praising the North Vietnamese and the Vietcong, coupled with the guards' quoting Senator Fulbright's statements against the war, bring home the realization that to the prisoners, their captors were not their only enemies. The best quote is from an interrogator who tells Stockdale, "We will win the war on the streets of New York." Watch for Haing S. Ngor as an NVA officer in a much less sympathetic role than his portrayal of a victimized translator in *The Killing Fields*. 📺

In the Year of the Pig (1968) **D:** Emile de Antonio, 103m.

** This Academy Award–nominated documentary opens with a comparison of the Vietnam War to America's Revolutionary and Civil Wars and closes with "The Battle Hymn of the Republic" played with Oriental instruments. In between is skillfully blended news footage, combat scenes, and individual interviews that deliver nothing less than Hanoi's view of the war. Included are statements by Harrison Salisbury, Father Daniel Berrigan, and other Americans, all praising the valiant efforts of the freedom-fighting Vietcong and North Vietnamese. According to the documentary, the "best of a generation" was attracted to the communist forces; the Americans are depicted, according to one of their own generals, as "a bloody good bunch of killers." Ho Chi Minh is touted as "the great patriot of the century," and the Vietcong are praised for "contributing to world peace by ending the arrogance of power." Nothing is subtle in the directing, though it is extremely well done. Semitruths and partial facts are blended with misconceptions, fantasies, and out-and-out lies to deliver nothing but anti–United States, antimilitary propaganda.

This documentary was released and viewed by the American public at the height of the Vietnam War. Without a doubt, in any other war but Vietnam, it would have been considered sedition rather than being praised by the film community and the viewing public. 📺

Indian Runner, The (1991) **D:** Sean Penn, 127m. David Morse, Viggo Mortensen, Charles Bronson, Sandy Dennis, Patricia Arquette, Dennis Hopper.

** A highway patrolman and his Vietnam-veteran brother have trouble getting along in a small town. An interesting cast and some good photography cannot make up for a story too long and, basically, boring. For much of the film the actors merely sit staring and smoke cigarette after cigarette. One really should not expect too deep a plot from a film that touts itself as being based on a song by Bruce Springsteen ("Highway Patrolman"). This was Dennis's last film.

The policeman kills a man in the line of duty and is able to cope, while the Vietnam vet is troubled by his combat experiences to the extent that his brother describes him as "the angriest person I know." The vet beats women, including his spouse, robs a gas station, steals a car, and finally abandons his wife the night she is giving birth to their child. He also manages to beat a sleazy bartender (Hopper) to death with a barstool. Director and writer Penn provides a brief insight, that Vietnam may not be the cause of all the vet's problems, by allowing the policeman to remark that his brother, the town's biggest hell raiser, was confused before the war. [TV]

Intimate Strangers (1986) TVM, **D:** Robert Ellis Miller, 100m. Teri Garr, Stacy Keach, Cathy Lee Crosby, Max Gail, Justin Deas.
* A Vietnam POW escapes after ten years of captivity and has spouse troubles after returning home. The different slant to this one is that the former POW is a woman nurse (Garr). Her husband, a successful doctor (Keach) with a beautiful girlfriend (Crosby), must adjust not only to the return of his wife but also to the adopted son who helped her escape.
# The usual POW adjustment problems are included. In one instance, Garr's character huddles in a closet grasping a butcher knife as she suffers prison-camp flashbacks. The biggest flaw to this film (and there are many to choose from) is that there were no American female POWs during the war—captured, released, or escaped.

Iron Triangle, The (1988) **D:** Eric Weston, 91m. Beau Bridges, Haing S. Ngor, Johnny Hallyday, Liem Whatley, James Ishida.
*** Bridges plays a company commander captured by a seventeen-year-old Vietcong (Whatley). Much of the story is seen through the eyes of the "enemy," and both Bridges and the viewer learn to "understand that on the other side of the gun was a man like me." A subplot about a French veteran of Dien Bien Phu and

his beautiful Vietnamese mistress detracts from an otherwise unique film.

Although the portrayal of U.S. forces is rather routine, the depiction of Vietcong organization, motivation, and life in the jungle and underground is well done and the most detailed of any picture produced thus far. Insights into the influence and control of the Communist Party cadre members and the system of criticism/ self-criticism as a means of discipline and morale building are particularly well done. Opening credits state that the film is "based on the diary of an unknown Vietcong soldier." What follows certainly supports the claim and does not disappoint. A Sri Lanka shooting location offers a passable set for Vietnam. 📺

Jacknife (1989) **D:** David Jones, 102m. Robert De Niro, Ed Harris, Kathy Baker, Charles Dutton, Loudon Wainwright III.

*** A Vietnam veteran (De Niro), who is not all that stable himself, journeys to Connecticut to help a friend (Harris) deal with the death of a mutual buddy in the war fifteen years earlier. De Niro falls in love with Harris's sister (Baker) and, despite many difficulties, all ends well. This adaptation of an off-Broadway play, "Strange Snow" by Stephen Metcalfe, works on the big screen only because of the power and talent of the three leading actors.

No veteran is presented who is not disturbed from the war in one form or another. De Niro's character (called "Jacknife" because of all the trucks he has wrecked), according to Harris, was crazy before he went; Vietnam made him crazier. De Niro frequently smashes his fist through windows when he gets angry. Harris, although a hard worker during the week, stays drunk on the weekends and is withdrawn all of the time. Baker, who often wears a field jacket, is also affected by the war in that she must take care of her brother. 📺

Jacob's Ladder (1990) **D:** Adrian Lyne, 116m. Tim Robbins, Danny Aiello, Elizabeth Pena, Matt Craven, Jason Alexander.

**1/2 Robbins, as a wounded Vietnam veteran living in New York, sees demons and monsters on the subway, coming out of the walls, and just about everywhere else. When he discovers that his old platoon mates are experiencing the same troubles, he begins to think that perhaps an army experiment gone awry is the source of his problems. Along with the demons, he is soon pursued by government agents. Pena plays his girlfriend. Apparently the film had a low costume budget, as Pena is rarely clothed. Long before the film's conclusion, the viewer will suspect bad dope rather than a bad war. This is confirmed along with the strong implication either that the entire film is a dream or that Robbins was killed in Vietnam and none of what has been seen is real.

This is far beyond the usual crazy-veteran fare that Hollywood likes so much. Robbins is crazy, but this time instead of the war driving him crazy, the army takes a more direct role. Supposedly, Robbins and his platoon were used in an LSD-like drug experiment in an attempt to enhance their viciousness and fighting spirit. The experiment backfired with the soldiers' killing each other instead. A postscript even claims, "It was reported that the hallucinogenic BZ was used in experiments on soldiers during the Vietnam War. The Pentagon denied the story." This denial is quite reasonable, since it never occurred. The army did do some limited experimentation with LSD in 1958, when the drug was still legal, but that had nothing to do with combat effectiveness or the war in Vietnam. 🖵

Jenny (1970) **D:** George Bloomfield, 88m. Marlo Thomas, Alan Alda, Marian Hailey, Elizabeth Wilson, Vincent Gardenia, Stephen Strimpell.

* Pregnant Jenny (Thomas) and film maker Delano (Alda) marry for convenience, she to acquire a father for her baby, he to avoid the draft and Vietnam. Despite Alda's statement of "We agreed to be married. Now don't try to turn it into something else," they, of course, fall in love. The film concludes with an interesting twist to an otherwise predictable, uninteresting story. Just before the baby is born, Alda learns his draft board is not honoring his marriage deferment, and he plans to take off to Canada, leaving Jenny and the newborn behind. A single tear rolls down Jenny's cheek. The best part of the film is a brief clip from *A Place in the Sun* (1951).

Vietnam is the cloud hanging over the Alda character's head, preventing his success as a film maker and his commitment to Jenny. This midwar release apparently supports any life style as long as it does not include honoring one's obligation of service to country. Watch for a brief shot of President Nixon's official photo

staring down from the wall of the marriage bureau in the wedding scene.

JFK (1991) **D:** Oliver Stone, 189m. Kevin Costner, Tommy Lee Jones, John Candy, Sissy Spacek, Donald Sutherland, Joe Pesci.

*** Every conspiracy theory about the assassination of John Kennedy is presented as New Orleans prosecutor Jim Garrison sets out to solve the murder of the president. Actual footage and recorded dialogue are woven together with re-creation—and fabrication—to the extent that it is extremely difficult to determine what is real and what is Stone. A tremendous cast in starring roles and in cameos, combined with outstanding filming and production, make for an excellent movie—as long as the viewer keeps in mind that it is not a documentary. Stone went so far in delivering "the world according to Stone" that even the liberal Hollywood community and the press were critical of his looseness with fact and his attempt to rewrite history.

\# Although Stone offers many possibilities about who was behind the assassination, by far the most prevalent, and the one on which Garrison focuses, is a conspiracy by the military and the military-industrial complex to kill Kennedy because of his plans to end the Vietnam War before it really got started. The Pentagon and the CIA worry that peace will not bring accelerated rank, profit, and the plain old amusements of war. Garrison states that Kennedy was killed "because he wanted to change things." Lyndon Johnson is shown saying, "Just get me elected. I'll give you the damn war." Sutherland's character goes as far as to call the assassination a "coup d'etat." 🄃🅅

Joe (1970) **D:** John G. Avildsen, 107m. Peter Boyle, Dennis Patrick, Susan Sarandon, Patrick McDermott, Audrey Caire.

**1/2 Boyle magnificently plays a hardhat who hates "niggers, queers, liberals, welfare workers, peace marchers, white kids, hippies, and current music." He teams with a wealthy businessman (Patrick) who has accidentally killed his daughter's drug-pusher boyfriend. The two eventually share sex and drugs with a host of hippies before killing them all. This role launched Boyle's career and also introduced Sarandon.

\# Vietnam plays an underlying role in this story of alienation between classes and between the young and old. Boyle's and Pat-

rick's characters, angry about the antiwar movement, are veterans
of World War II who support the troops in Vietnam. In a switch
from other films of the genre, neither Boyle nor Patrick wears a
field jacket; many of the hippies do. 📺

Journey through Rosebud (1972) **D:** Tom Gries, 93m. Robert
Forster, Kristoffer Tabori, Victoria Racimo, Eddie Little Sky, Roy
Jenson.

* This film focuses on the plight of the American Indians in the
early 1970s. The story follows the wanderings of a white draft
dodger (Tabori) and a cynical Indian Vietnam veteran (Forster) and
his former wife (Racimo). The rambling script includes dialogue
such as Racino's "I'm an Indian, and I'm going to walk in the
beauty like the medicine men say." The one bright spot here is the
scenic location photography on the South Dakota Rosebud Sioux
Indian Reservation.

\# Forster, as the Vietnam vet, is a belligerent alcoholic. The
draft dodger ends up in bed with the vet's former wife. Forster, because of his former wife's antics, and/or because of being an Indian, and/or because of the Vietnam War, commits suicide by
drunkenly driving his car off the road at a high speed. The only
really satisfying scene in the film comes when the final credits began to roll and a group of young Indians is seen beating hell out
of the draft dodger. 📺

Jud (1970) **D:** Gunther Collins, 80m. Joseph Kaufmann, Claudia
Jennings, Bonnie Bittner, Robert Deman, Norman Burton.

* A soldier returns from Vietnam haunted by his role in the
slaughter of a village, the death of his friend, and the breakup
with his fiancée. This is just another "troubled vet" film, except it
is even more poorly executed than most. Its only different stroke
is that the vet flashes back to combat even while making love. See
this movie only if the weather channel is on the blink.

\# An acquaintance of the mixed-up veteran remarks about Vietnam vets, "If you ask me, they're all killers." Everything else in the
film is just as ridiculous. 📺

Jump into Hell (1955) **D:** David Butler, 93m. Jacques Sernas, Kurt
Kasznar, Peter Van Eyck, Pat Blake, Norman Dupont.

**Four French officers volunteer to parachute into Indochina

to support the defense of Dien Bien Phu. Their reasons for volun-
teering are covered in flashbacks, but, despite a script by Irving
Wallace, it is difficult to care about or sympathize with the paratroopers. Even though it is liberally padded with news footage, the
film leaves the impression that only a few fought the battle rather
than the fifteen thousand Frenchmen and sixty thousand Vietnamese who participated. The scope and importance of the fight
are not delivered.

If nothing else, this film was timely (some might add exploit-
ative), its release coming less than a year after the actual battle.
However, except for its good re-creation of the Vietminh's trenching and fire-support systems that were responsible for their victory, and except for the actual footage included, the film is no
more than basic action fare.

Just a Little Inconvenience (1977) TVM, **D:** Theodore J. Flicker,
100m. Lee Majors, Barbara Hershey, James Stacy, Charles Cioffi,
Jim Davis.

** A veteran (Majors) tries to help rehabilitate a buddy (Stacy)
who is withdrawn and bitter after losing an arm and a leg from a
Vietnam land-mine explosion. Majors's character leaves a good job
to become a ski instructor in hopes of teaching his friend to ski on
his one remaining leg. This film marks Stacy's return to television
after being seriously disabled in a motorcycle accident. His performance earned him an Emmy nomination.

This is an unusual Vietnam War film. Majors's character is
well adjusted and employed as an aerospace engineer. Vietnam is
treated apolitically, and the film is much in keeping with movies
of earlier wars, in which veterans are reasonably welcomed home
and given a chance to succeed. The combat flashbacks are forgettable at best, but they do not detract from this being a positive
film. Although *Just a Little Inconvenience* is light-years away from
the World War II classic *The Best Years of Our Lives*, it is the most
comparable of its war.

Karate Kid III, The (1989) **D:** John G. Avildsen, 112m. Ralph
Macchio, Noriyuki "Pat" Morita, Robyn Elaine Lively, Martin
Kove, Thomas Ian Griffith.

* Macchio, as the kid, defends his karate title against a "ringer"
hired by his nemesis (Kove) and Kove's Vietnam War buddy. Since

his student's defeat by Macchio's character in the first *Karate Kid* film, Kove has become "broke and going nowhere" until his old Green Beret friend steps in to make "the boy" suffer. Macchio, at twenty-seven years of age and carrying more than a few extra pounds since the first film, still cannot act, nor is he helped by his supporting cast and a script that is even worse than can be imagined.

\# The two Vietnam vets refer to Morita as a "gook" and are so mean that they smoke cigars and hit women. Neither vet wears a field jacket, but in a reversal of the stereotype, Morita does. Another reversal from usual Vietnam War films is that one of the vets is extremely wealthy. However, he gained his riches through the disposal of hazardous waste—often illegally and with the help of bribed judges and law enforcement officials. 📺

Kent State (1981) TVM, **B:** James Goldstone, 152m. Jane Fleiss, Charley Lang, Talia Balsam, Jeff McCracken, Ellen Barkin.

*** On May 4, 1970, students and hangers-on at Kent State University protested against the Vietnam War and the Cambodian invasion. In a tragic confrontation with the Ohio National Guard, four students were shot dead and nine wounded. This television docudrama based on the incident won an Emmy for director Goldstone. Originally filmed at four hours in length and aired at 180 minutes, the film's current copies vary from 120 to 156 minutes.

\#\# Although the film is heavy-handed in support of the students, who are shown as peaceful innocents, and against the National Guardsmen, who are depicted as red-neck martinets, there is an effort to show both sides of the incident. Barkin, in one of her early major roles, is a campus agitator who wears a T-shirt with an NLF (National Liberation Front) logo throughout the entire movie. Listen for the usual student chants of "Ho, Ho, Ho Chi Minh, the NLF is going to win" and "One, two, three, four, we don't want your fucking war" and "Hell no, we won't go." Since so much was never determined about what happened that day in May, any great degree of accuracy in the picture should not be expected. In a quick postscript, the film makers acknowledge their artistic license with the statement "In this dramatization, some fictional characters have been introduced and some incidents modified for dramatic purposes." The movie was filmed at Alabama's

Gadsden Junior College, which is at least similar to the Kent State campus. 📺

Killing Fields, The (1984-Great Britain) **D:** Roland Joffe, 141m. Sam Waterston, Haing S. Ngor, John Malkovich, Julian Sands, Craig T. Nelson.

**** This powerful drama about the fall of Cambodia to the North Vietnamese–backed Khmer Rouge is told through the real-life experience of *New York Times* reporter Sydney Schanberg (Waterston) and his Cambodian assistant, Dith Pran (Ngor). Pran's escape from the "reeducation camps" through the bleached-bone and rotting-corpse covered killing fields is the most explicit and authentic ever filmed. The movie is well deserving of its Academy Awards for supporting actor, editing, and cinematography.

Costuming of the Khmer Rouge and the Cambodian populace is extremely well done, as are the location shots in Thailand and the stage sets in Canada. This is one of the few films that pull no punches in depicting the savagery of the communist forces in Southeast Asia. Also remarkable is the depiction of news reporters' drive to get the story, preferably of the front-page variety, at whatever the cost or consequence. Unlike most actors, who know no more about war than what they have seen on the screen, and whose portrayals display this lack of understanding regardless of their abilities in the craft, Ngor survived Cambodia during its ravage. His having participated in the actual events brings an authenticity to his role that is not often seen in films about Vietnam and its aftermath. 📺

Lady from Yesterday, The (1985) TVM, **D:** Robert Day, 104m. Wayne Rogers, Bonnie Bedelia, Pat Hingle, Barrie Youngfellow, Tina Chen.

** Rogers plays a Vietnam veteran who is living comfortably in Houston with his wife and two daughters. With no warning, a son he fathered ten years before in Saigon arrives on his doorstep accompanied by his fatally ill mother. Needless to say, Rogers—and his wife—are surprised. With the Vietnamese mother about to die, the decision is whether or not Rogers and his wife and children accept the boy into the family. The city of Houston plays well, but overall the film is rather shallow.

Somewhere in the movie there is an effort to make an issue

of the Amerasian children left behind in Vietnam, but the film is never really able to focus on it. The most positive aspect is that Rogers as the Vietnam veteran—even though the actor is his usual whiny self—is reasonably successful, a nice guy, and a man who faces up to his responsibilities. 📺

Last Detail, The (1973) **D:** Hal Ashby, 104m. Jack Nicholson, Otis Young, Randy Quaid, Clifton James, Carol Kane, Gilda Radner.

**** Two career navy petty officers (Nicholson and Young) escort an eighteen-year-old sailor (Quaid) to the brig as a result of his having received an eight-year prison term and a dishonorable discharge for stealing $40 from the favorite charity of his base commander's wife. Along the way, the tough escorts begin to sympathize with the young sailor's plight and manage to get him drunk, get in a fight with Marines, get in bed with a young hooker (Kane), go to a hippie party (with Radner in her first screen appearance), and have a picnic in a snow-covered public park. Nicholson plays Nicholson at his profane best. He and Quaid both received Oscar nominations.

While certainly far from sympathetic, this is one of the better looks at career NCOs of the Vietnam War era. Young's character admits that "the navy is the best thing that ever happened to me." When a hippie asks him how he felt about going to Vietnam, he replies, "The man says go; got to do what the man says. We are livin' in the man's world, ain't we?" Both Nicholson and Young wear ribbons for Vietnam service—with their occupational ratings, they would have almost certainly served not in country but offshore, aboard ship. Nicholson, who laments, "We're just a couple of lifers," still feels superior to Marines of any rank. He says, "It takes a certain kind of sadistic temperament to be a Marine." 📺

Last Flight Out (1990) TVM, **D:** Larry Elikann, 96m. James Earl Jones, Richard Crenna, Eric Bogosian, Haing S. Ngor, Soon-Teck Oh.

** During the final days before the fall of Saigon, officials of the only commercial American airline still flying into the city (Pan Am) attempt to assist as many Vietnamese as possible to escape before the arrival of the NVA. Overall, the acting and direction are good.

Although filmed in Thailand, this picture offers insights into

the end of the war in Saigon. No attempt is made to paint the invading North Vietnamese as liberators: the NVA's death lists and their plans for reeducation-camp motivate the airline employees to help the South Vietnamese. United States diplomats seem less interested in providing assistance—except for their girlfriends. ARVN and South Vietnamese officials are shown as bureaucratic, corrupt, and inept. [TV]

Last Hunter, The (1980) **D:** Anthony M. Dawson, 97m. David Warbeck, Tisa Farrow, Tony King, Bobby Rhodes, John Steiner.

   * Accompanied by a female war correspondent, an army captain leads a small patrol to silence a Vietcong radio transmitter that is "destroying troop morale." This is a meritless film with extremely graphic violence, putrefying corpses, protruding entrails and eyeballs, exploding bodies, and rats' eating prisoners alive. As horrible as the sights are, they are nowhere nearly as bad as the movie itself.

   # While few Vietnam War films make any great effort to accurately depict uniforms and equipment, this movie is strongly in the running for the poorest overall performance. Soldiers are shown wearing different rank on opposite sleeves of the same uniform jacket, and the captain hero sports the patch of an armored division that served the entire war in Germany. With the excuse that "it has been a long time since we've seen a woman," several GIs attempt to rape the correspondent. Other soldiers smoke dope and kill each other or themselves. At movie's end, the hero discovers that the "voice of Vietcong radio" is an old girlfriend from the States who is doing the broadcasting because of her "ideas" about the war. How she got to the jungles of Vietnam is not explained. The movie's shooting location makes as much sense as the rest of the movie—much was filmed in Italy! [TV]

Last Rites (1988) **D:** Donald P. Bellisario, 103m. Tom Berenger, Daphne Zuniga, Chick Vennera, Paul Dooley, Dane Clark.

   *1/2 A priest (Berenger), the son of a Mafia godfather, falls in love with his sister's husband's lover. To further complicate the issue, the sister has killed her husband and is out to do the same to her brother's new bedmate. This soap opera skipped the theaters and went straight to videotape. See it and understand why.

   # Berenger's character is wounded early in the film, and aid is

given by a fellow priest (Dooley) who recognizes the injury as a bullet wound. "I saw enough of them in Vietnam to know," he explains. The priest stutters but says he talks normally when shocked. He adds that he "never stuttered in Nam." The veteran priest plays no further role in the film, and his inclusion and brief comments on the war make no more sense than the rest of the picture. 📺

Latino (1985) **D**: Haskell Wexler, 105m. Robert Beltran, Annette Cardona, Tony Plana, Ricardo Lopez, Luis Torrentes.

** Two Chicano Green Beret veterans of Vietnam advise U.S.-backed Contras against the Sandinistas in Nicaragua. Much more a propaganda piece than entertainment, nevertheless the "story is fiction, the events fact," according to the lead-in. U.S. officers refer to the locals as spics, drink beer while prisoners are tortured, draft children wearing Disneyland T-shirts into the Contras, and do nothing while the Contras loot, rape, and kill peaceful villagers. This film's message is simple—everything wrong that happened or did not happen in Vietnam occurred again in Central America. Although praised by the liberal media and film industry, at best this is a mediocre movie by any standard.

The politics of this film are easily sorted out: It was produced in Nicaragua with Sandinista support at the height of the rebellion. Other details are just as subtle. The Green Beret sergeant carries a swagger stick (likely the first American soldier, especially an NCO, to own one in the past quarter-century) and wears dark glasses even in the shade. It is also unusual that Beltran's character is still only a lieutenant after three tours in Vietnam and fourteen years of service. As for the ridiculous parachute commands of "ready, set, go," they are as humorous as they are dangerous. 📺

Lethal Weapon (1987) **D**: Richard Donner, 110m. Mel Gibson, Danny Glover, Gary Busey, Mitchell Ryan, Tom Atkins, Darlene Love.

*** Two Vietnam-veteran police detectives, one a stable family man (Glover) and one a past-borderline psychopath (Gibson), assist a fellow Vietnam veteran against a drug operation run by still another vet. Big-name actors, a large production budget, and a fast-paced script make for a big-box-office high adventure that is fun but does not require much brainpower on the part of the viewer.

Glover, with a loving wife, a happy family, and a successful career, seems out of place as a Hollywood version of a Vietnam veteran. Gibson's character, however, more than meets the usual stereotype. He is a hard-drinking, suicidal, anti-everybody-and-everything cop who even the street weirdos think is crazy. A police department doctor states that Gibson has a death wish; his own partner asks him if he has ever met anyone he did not want to kill. Gibson admits that killing is all he was ever good at and boasts of a kill at a thousand yards in the wind in Laos. The vet whom the two cops help has a daughter who snorts coke and makes porno films. Opposing the police is a gang of Vietnam vets and ex-CIA agents led by a former American general who, after Vietnam, is convinced that "there are no heroes left." Interestingly, in *Lethal Weapon 2*, released two years later, Gibson is crazy as ever and is still courting a death wish, but no mention is made of either cop being a Vietnam veteran, and the bad guys are South Africans rather than Vietnam vets. 📺

Let's Get Harry (1986) D: Alan Smithee (pseudonym), 107m. Robert Duvall, Mark Harmon, Gary Busey, Michael Schoeffling, Glenn Frey.
** The brother and friends of a pipeline worker attempt to rescue him and an American ambassador from South American drug-dealer kidnappers. Financed by a used-car dealer (Busey), the group hires a Vietnam-veteran soldier of fortune as its adviser. Except for the usual expected fine acting by Duvall and Busey, nothing in this film works. Director Stuart Rosenbery had his name removed from the credits, and the film received limited release.
# In interviewing for the adviser position, several Vietnam veterans are considered. One washes down multiple pills with alcohol "for my malaria"; another shouts, "Kill them all and let god sort them out." At least their ultimate choice (Duvall) is somewhat normal, despite being troubled by leaving several of his men behind in Laos on the mission for which he earned a Medal of Honor. On the humorous side, Busey laments that he would have been in the war except that his "damn knee kept me out of Vietnam. That pissed me off." 📺

Limbo (1972) D: Mark Robson, 112m. Kate Jackson, Kathleen Nolan, Katherine Justice, Stuart Margolin, Hazel Medina.

** Three wives of POWs/MIAs in Vietnam become friends while waiting in limbo for word of their husbands. One of the women is the mother of four and wife of an officer confirmed as a POW for many years. Another is a socialite who refuses to believe her spouse is likely dead despite much evidence. The third is a young woman who was married for only two weeks before her husband left for Vietnam and who now has another man in her life. The plot is played out with the three women on the way to an airport to meet one of the returning husbands. In addition to its nearly all-female cast, the film is notable for the large number of women on the other side of the camera as producer, writer, editor, and other positions.

This is one of the few films to take a look at the home front during the war. It is generally apolitical, but the picture was turned down for Department of Defense support because the women are shown as being against the war, and one of the women is having an affair. The Pentagon justified its refusal on the reasonable assumption that the film might be used as a propaganda tool against the POWs still held in North Vietnam at the time.

Line, The (1980) **D:** Robert Siegel, 94m. Russ Thacker, Brad Sullivan, Jacqueline Brooks, Lewis J. Stadlen, David Doyle.

* Loosely based on an actual incident at the Presidio, California, in 1969, this is the story of the killing of a soldier prisoner, the resultant riot by fellow prisoners, and the support of the fracas by protesters who gather just outside the stockade—some of whom are ultimately shot themselves by bayonet-wielding, gas-mask-wearing soldiers. Much of the demonstration footage consists of outtakes from previous films by director Siegel mixed with actual video of war protests. Complete with sadistic, cigar-smoking sergeants; pompous, paranoid officers; and young, near-angelic prisoners, this film is so blatantly antimilitary that it loses any credibility for portraying actual events.

Vietnam is shown but briefly, as a patrol crosses a swamp, its men carrying weapons but no ammunition or equipment. Their helmets, without camouflage covers, are of World War II vintage at best. The patrol is ambushed by a young girl with an antique rifle, whom, of course, they kill. Typical lines include comments that the U.S. Army "uniform represents murder" and that the Army gave marijuana to the troops in Vietnam "to keep them happy and

calm." Throughout the film there are not-too-subtle efforts on the part of the director to compare the U.S. Army with that of Nazi Germany. The sign above the stockade gate does not state, "Work will make us free," but it does say, "Adherence to law is freedom." This movie is not so much anti-Vietnam as it is antimilitary—and anti-Army in particular. [TV]

Long Journey Home, The (1987) TVM, **D:** Rod Holcomb, 96m. Meredith Baxter Birney, David Birney, Ray Baker, James Sutorius, Kevin McCarthy.

* Baxter Birney plays a successful young businesswoman whose husband (David Birney, her real-life spouse at the time) has been missing in action in Vietnam for eleven years. Just as she is about to have him declared dead and remarry, he mysteriously reappears, asking her to flee with him to the Bahamas. He is pursued by a weird hitman. There is talk of a secret mission and a drug frame-up amid exploding airliners, poison-tipped umbrellas, and other impossible-to-believe situations. The most interesting aspects are the multiple unresolved subplots and odd turns of events, such as a car wrecked in one scene reappearing minutes later in the same chase, completely repaired.

\# Vietnam really has little to do with this picture other than to provide an excuse for the long absence of Birney. Still, the vet ends up being the bad guy—all he is really after is his wife's money.

Looking for Mr. Goodbar (1977) **D:** Richard Brooks, 135m. Diane Keaton, Richard Gere, Tuesday Weld, Tom Berenger, Richard Kiley.

** A good Catholic girl whose spirit was repressed by illness and her family attempts to find her own identity as a liberated young woman. By day she teaches deaf children, and by night she seeks uninhibited sexual encounters. This is a very "seventies" movie. Keaton is great in the lead role, but the film is not nearly as good as the Judith Rossner novel on which it is based. Weld, as Keaton's sister, has the best line when she says, "We all need someone who doesn't blame us."

\# One of Keaton's lovers (Gere) is unemployed and on welfare and dope. Keaton describes him as "crude, vain, vulgar, and a liar."

He shows her his scars from Vietnam and talks about killing people during the war. 🔲

Losers, The (1970) **D:** Jack Starrett, 96m. William Smith, Bernie Hamilton, Adam Roarke, Houston Savage, Ana Korita.

* Five members of the Devil's Advocates motorcycle club are recruited by the army to do what the military cannot—go into Cambodia to rescue a presidential adviser who has been negotiating with the Chinese to keep them out of the Vietnam War. Using armor-plated bikes with machine guns mounted on the handlebars, the self-proclaimed "scooter trash" fight not for money but because they are "red-blooded, patriotic Americans." This is a worthless Vietnam film. In fact, it is not even a good motorcycle movie—if there is such a thing.

A hint of the film's attention to detail, and its budget as well, is provided in the first minutes when the motorcycle gang mounts Yamahas rather than Harleys. Uniforms and equipment are from a time several decades before Vietnam. 🔲

Lost Command (1966) **D:** Mark Robson, 130m. Anthony Quinn, Alain Delon, George Segal, Michele Morgan, Claudia Cardinale.

*** Quinn leads French paratroopers from defeat and captivity at Dien Bien Phu to more trouble and fighting in Algeria. Rising from peasant recruit to general, Quinn trains and fights by but one rule—"Don't die." Excellent performances are delivered by all, with particularly noteworthy acting by Delon, who actually served as a paratrooper in Indochina before becoming an actor in 1957. Based on Jean Larteguy's book *The Centurions*.

Only a small portion of the Battle of Dien Bien Phu is shown, but parachuting, artillery, fortifications, chain of command, leader/subordinate relationships, and tactics are extremely accurate. The only flaw is that the valley location of the fight is depicted as dry and dusty with blue skies, rather than muddy, rainy and overcast as it actually was. Spanish locations work well for Algerian scenes but not for Vietnam. The Vietminh are arrogant, mean, and prone to shooting prisoners. There is no doubt as to who the bad guys are. Parallels between Vietnam and Algeria are interwoven throughout. It is noted that when the "yellowskins" defeated the French in Indochina, the Moslems in Algeria began to think of independence. Quinn's regiment is forced to use unusual tactics, which include

atrocities, to fight the guerrillas. Much of the Algerian rebels' fighting methods mimic those of the Vietminh. ⟨ᴛᴠ⟩

Lost Flight (1969) TVM, D: Leonard J. Horn, 104m. Lloyd Bridges, Billy Dee Williams, Anne Francis, Ralph Meeker, Andrew Prine.

   * A trans-Pacific airliner crashes near a remote island. Survivors include a quick-tempered pilot, a mean businessman and his mistress, a brash nightclub performer, a racist, a medical student, a pregnant woman, a black Marine Vietnam veteran, and assorted attractive young women. After much strife and violence, the group realizes they will not be rescued and that they must learn to live and work together. This failed television pilot has little going for it except the scenic background provided by Kauai, Hawaii.

   ## Williams, as the Vietnam vet, is a militant but is ultimately looked upon by the others as a leader and a provider. Using his military survival skills, he sets animal traps in the jungle for food. Throughout the film he sides with the reasonable, peaceful faction, and overall the minor role is played positively.

Lotus Lady (1930) D: Phil Rosen, 68m. Fern Andra, Ralph Emerson, Betty Francisco, Lucien Prival, Frank Leigh.

   * An American (Emerson) goes to Indochina, where he buys a tea plantation that is actually a worthless swamp. He marries a local girl (Andra) only to have an old flame appear and try to break up the marriage. Emerson finally realizes that his wife is his true love and, with the discovery of oil on his swampland/tea plantation, finds happiness. This is one of the early talkies about Vietnam but is not worth listening to or watching.

   # Vietnam/Indochina's only real role is to provide an exotic location. Still, the film makes one wonder: If oil really had been discovered in Indochina, perhaps the resolve of the United States government and its people might have been a bit more intense (as in Operation Desert Storm) during the ten-year-long war.

Magnum Force (1973) D: Ted Post, 123m. Clint Eastwood, Hal Holbrook, Mitchell Ryan, David Soul, Robert Urich.

   ** Dirty Harry (Eastwood) returns to the streets and alleys of San Francisco to stop a renegade police death squad whose members are executing criminals who slip through the court system. This is usual Eastwood fare played with a straight face and a big gun.

The four killer cops are Vietnam combat veterans who are "Airborne, Ranger, Special Forces soldiers." Their nonveteran leader is not too concerned when Harry kills the four killer-vets, because there are "a lot more where they came from." 📺

Malone (1987) **D**: Harley Cokliss, 92m. Burt Reynolds, Cliff Robertson, Kenneth McMillan, Cynthia Gibb, Lauren Hutton.

** A tough, cynical CIA hitman (Reynolds) tries to drop out of government service only to cross paths with a right-wing group that is planning on taking over the country. Explosions, bullets, and bodies are soon flying in all directions. The Reynolds character's wounds heal remarkably quickly—at about the same speed you will forget this movie.

The CIA hitman supposedly learned his craft while serving in the army in Vietnam from 1961 to 1967. A gas station attendant who befriends Reynolds is also a Vietnam vet. He has a crippled leg from the war and wants only to be left alone. On the positive side, neither vet experiences flashbacks. On the negative, neither is convincing as a veteran. 📺

Marked for Death (1990) **D**: Dwight Little, 93m. Steven Seagal, Keith David, Joanna Pacula, Basil Wallace, Tom Wright.

*½ A burned-out DEA agent (Seagal) drops out of law enforcement to "try and find the gentle self inside"—until Jamaican drug dealers attack his family. Seagal's character takes no prisoners as he beats, maims, and kills without discretion in this absurd action film. Fifty-three stunt men and women are listed in the credits—most of whom fake violent deaths at the hands or feet of Seagal. Without a doubt, Seagal is the most unconvincing tough guy on the screen. His acting is so bad he makes Stallone and Norris look like great thespians.

Assisting Seagal is an old Vietnam War buddy. The friend, recently divorced, says that "Cambodia was more fun" than his marriage. Other than to lend background to the two vets' killing abilities, Vietnam plays no further role. 📺

Masculine-Feminine (1966-France-Sweden) **D**: Jean-Luc Godard, 103m. Chantal Goya, Jean-Pierre Leaud, Marlene Jobert, Michel Debord, Catherine Isabelle Duport.

* A public-opinion pollster has an affair with an aspiring rock

singer in Paris. They drink coffee, go to movies, dance, and talk. Their conversation includes sexual subjects such as techniques and perversions, the merits of communism, military excesses, and James Bond. The pollster is unsure about his future but buys a building with an inheritance from his mother. At the end of the film, he either jumps or falls from the building to his death, leaving behind his pregnant girlfriend.

In one of their discussions, the couple agree that the United States is the aggressor in Vietnam. They also watch a street demonstration against the war where LBJ is compared to Hitler. A young radical at the protest screams, "Give us TV and cars but spare us liberty" as he burns himself to death.

Mean Johnny Barrows (1976) **D:** Fred Williamson, 90m. Fred Williamson, Jenny Sherman, Elliot Gould, Aaron Banks, Anthony Caruso.

* Williamson plays a Vietnam veteran kicked out of the army for striking an officer. When he can't find a job, he gets involved with two feuding Mafia families, both of which are interested in him because he "killed many men" in Vietnam. During most of the film, Williamson either walks or drives around Los Angeles, accompanied by much-too-loud background music. Gould's cameo as "the professor" is out of place and makes no sense at all.

The uniforms in the military scenes are apparently from an army surplus store's going-out-of-business sale. The actors did not trouble to get military haircuts or to shave. Williamson is credited with winning a Silver Star for "singlehandedly taking on the whole Vietcong army." The commanding officer he punches out is a racist red-neck who refers to Williamson as "boy." The only noteworthy portion of this picture at all is a postscript that states the film is "Dedicated to the veterans who traded their place on the front line for a place in the unemployment line. Peace is hell." [TV]

Mean Streets (1973) **D:** Martin Scorcese, 112m. Robert De Niro, Harvey Keitel, Robert Carradine, David Proval, Amy Robinson.

** A small-time hood (Keitel), his irresponsible friend (De Niro), and their neighborhood buddies drink, fight, cuss, and go to the movies in what is supposed to be an insightful look at New York's Little Italy. The ordinary "nonneighborhood" viewer is left wondering why anyone, including critics who rate the film highly, would care. This story of "the neighborhood," organized crime, and strong family ties won Scorsese his first acclaim.

A brief bar scene includes a welcome home for a Vietnam veteran wearing his dress-green uniform complete with a 199th Light Infantry Brigade patch and a Silver Star. Keitel's character gives him a flag, and "the neighborhood" seems proud of its veteran. The vet gets drunk and goes crazy but does little damage. Except to add to the film's early-1970s setting, this scene has little to do with the movie. 📺

Medium Cool (1969) **D:** Haskell Wexler, 111m. Robert Forster, Verna Bloom, Peter Bonerz, Marianna Hill, Peter Boyle.

* A TV cameraman who has covered the assassination of Robert Kennedy, construction of Resurrection City, and day-to-day life in the black and white ghettos of Chicago begins to question his detached reporting of the news during the Democratic National Convention of 1968. Actual footage of the convention, the riots, and the Illinois National Guard training to stop the demonstrations is used liberally. Unfortunately, the cameraman's fictional relationships and problems do not fit in with the rest of this disjointed, ultimately boring script. Wexler won an Oscar as the cinematographer for *Who's Afraid of Virginia Woolf?* (1966) and in this first effort as a director is obviously more interested in photography than in having the picture make any sense. The title is from sixties guru Marshall McLuhan's description of television as a "cool" medium, as opposed to "hot" media such as movies.

Although references to Vietnam abound throughout, and the usual protester chants of "Hell no! We won't go!" and "Peace now!" provide the background for the final quarter of the film, the movie does do a good job of showing that there were far more problems in the America of the 1960s than just the war. Race, poverty, politics, police brutality, and random violence are all included. 📺

Memorial Day (1983) TVM, **D:** Joseph Sargent, 100m. Mike Farrell, Shelley Fabares, Bonnie Bedelia, Keith Mitchell, Robert Walden.

** A veteran (Farrell) becomes a lawyer after the war because, he explains, "Coming out of Vietnam, law seemed so dependable to me." Although he is successful in his practice and with his family, secrets from his combat days haunt him. Not until he represents a crooked construction firm at the same time he is visited by several army buddies does he begin to talk of a dark day in Vietnam when the rules of warfare were forgotten. Only after one of his veteran friends commits suicide is Farrell able to confront his past. He quits the law firm, punches out the crooked contractor, and takes a job as a laborer as he attempts to get on with his life.

The message seems to be that regardless of success, Vietnam veterans have a past that must be dealt with—and some will resort to suicide instead. At least Farrell is shown to be able to keep a job and a marriage together and ultimately to make correct moral decisions. The film also contains some of the insensitive—and dumb—questions often asked of returning vets by those who did not go, such as "Did you have to shoot people?" 📺

Memory of Justice, The (1976 U.S.-Germany) **D:** Marcel Ophuls, 278m.

*** This massive, extremely well-done documentary studies the differences between individual and collective responsibility in modern warfare. The Nuremberg trials of Nazi war criminals are the primary focus, but the French efforts to retain Algeria and the American involvement in Vietnam are also included. Actual footage of the times is intermingled with current interviews of major and minor characters. At more than four hours in length, the film is still not too long to retain the viewer's interest.

The major problem with this documentary is the juxtaposition of Nazi Germany and the Vietnam War. Comparing the German "final solution" to the U.S. war aims in Southeast Asia is a crime in itself, but the picture adds to the slander early on by way of an interview with Yehudi Menuhin, who states, "I go on the assumption that everyone is guilty." In an attempt at balance, however, one American Vietnam War widow speaks of her pride in her husband's service. In another case, though, parents of a Vietnam War casualty express their regrets about not encouraging their son to refuse to serve. Colonel Anthony Herbert (Retired), who is not considered by many vets to be a reliable source about Vietnam, relates how he finally refused to be a part of a war he considered to be immoral. 📺

Men at Work (1990) **D:** Emilio Estevez, 98m. Charlie Sheen, Emilio Estevez, Leslie Hope, Keith David, Darrell Larson.

** Two garbage men (Sheen and Estevez) get mixed up with a murdered politician, his killers, a beautiful woman, a crazed Vietnam vet, inept cops, and other strange characters—none of which are particularly interesting or amusing.

Sheen and Estevez are accompanied by a work inspector who got his job because he is related to the boss. The inspector arrives wearing a field jacket with staff sergeant stripes, parachute wings, and a combat infantryman's badge and talks about his glory days in Vietnam. During the vet's initial briefing by the garbage duo, he draws pictures of an armored trash truck accompanied by an attack helicopter which strafes tourists along a beachfront boardwalk. He is declared to be "a lunatic" and "a madman" and lives up to his billing when he imagines a pizza delivery boy is a Vietcong and takes him prisoner. 📺

Ministry of Vengeance (1989) D: Peter Mares, 96m. John Schneider, James Tolkan, Arthur Kennedy, Ned Beatty, Apollonia, Yaphet Kotto.

* A Vietnam veteran (Schneider) has become a peaceful clergyman after the war, but when Arab terrorists kill his wife and daughter, he puts aside his clerical collar, picks up a machine gun, and goes after revenge. The preacher is assisted by his old commander from Vietnam, who now runs a CIA-sponsored "candyass Rambo" special-operations training camp. Schneider is devoid of acting talent, but the movie is up to his skills. Beatty and Kennedy must have lost a bet to appear in this turkey.

An opening Vietnam firefight and a tunnel exploration are repeated as flashbacks for the remainder of the film. Soldiers, wearing rank on their hats differing from that on their collars, seem to have no idea how to sight or shoot an M-16 rifle. In the hot Vietnam jungle, the soldiers are bundled up in field jackets. 📺

Missing in Action (1984) D: Joseph Zito, 101m. Chuck Norris, M. Emmet Walsh, David Tress, Lenore Kasdorf, James Hong.

*1/2 Norris, as former POW Colonel Jim Braddock, returns to Vietnam to rescue other prisoners whose existence neither the Vietnamese nor the Americans acknowledge. This is typical Norris fare, with extremely unbelievable fight scenes and multiple opportunities for him to remove his shirt and flex his muscles. The worst aspect of this terrible film is that it spawned two sequels.

The Philippines substitute for Vietnam and Filipinos play Vietnamese—and the mismatches are obvious. Everything else in the film is equally authentic. Most interesting is a rip-off of the Pink Panther movies, a scene in which a bad guy leaps from a closet to attack Braddock. Unfortunately, the villain fails to eliminate him. 🖵

Missing in Action II—The Beginning (1985) **D**: Lance Hool, 96m. Chuck Norris, Soon-Teck Oh, Steven Williams, Cosie Costa, Bennett Ohta.

*1/2 This "prequel" shows why Braddock so hates the communists as he endures the harshness of a jungle POW camp. Watch for Braddock as he is hung by his heels from a tree with a sack over his head, a hungry rat inside. The rodent loses! In addition to "conventional" torture and harassment, see a sex-starved ARVN officer prisoner tormented by being tied to a stake and fondled by jungle lovelies wearing garter belts. Fight scenes are reminiscent of televised professional wrestling's "hold of the week" demonstrations.

Norris apparently does not believe in roughing it while he makes movies. This one was filmed in Mexico and St. Kitts. Although reality has never been a factor in Norris's films, it does seem strange that after ten years in a jungle prison, the POWs are fat, healthy, and still wearing their U.S. uniforms complete with patches and decorations. Also note in the opening scenes before his capture that Norris has not bothered to get a haircut for his role as a career army colonel. With hair like that, he would fit in better with a rock group than with a military organization. 🖵

Model Shop, The (1969-France) **D**: Jacques Demy, 95m. Gary Lockwood, Anouk Aimee, Alexandra Hay, Carole Cole, Tom Fielding.

* A young architect (Lockwood) who is about to be drafted quits his job and wanders aimlessly around Los Angeles—until he spots a beautiful girl (Aimee). He follows her to her place of business, a "model shop" where men pay to photograph seminude women. Using money borrowed to make his car payment for a modeling session with Aimee, he learns she has been abandoned by her boyfriend, who has returned to France. Lockwood and Aimee meet after work and spend the night making love and exchanging long

speeches. The next morning Lockwood gives her his remaining
cash so she can return to France. He goes home to find his car being repossessed and his girlfriend gone. The French director's look
at the sleazier parts of L.A. is much more interesting than the remainder of this generally boring film.

Although it is difficult to believe that a twenty-six-year-old,
well-educated professional would be in any great danger of being
drafted, there is a positive aspect to the film. Lockwood expresses
his fear of going to Vietnam but ultimately realizes that he must
cope with and face his fears. When his draft notice actually arrives, he accepts his responsibility.

Moon in Scorpio (1987) D: Gary Graver, 90m. Britt Ekland, John
Philip Law, William Smith, April Wayne, Lewis Van Bergen.

* Three Vietnam veterans and their significant others cruise
aboard a luxury sailboat to Mexico. No sooner are they under way
than somebody, or something, begins killing them off one by one.
"My honeymoon turned out to be a nightmare on a ghost ship,"
states the lone survivor. Found in the horror section of video
stores, this film could just as easily be classified simply as horrible.

The film opens with a Vietnam firefight in which the three
vets, wearing what appear to be civilian duck-hunting vests, kill
Vietcong who are protecting women and children. They then
murder the helpless civilians. One of the slaughtered villagers becomes a "killer spirit" who stalks the veterans and their mates on
the sailboat. Another scene has a psycho-ward nurse saying,
"Damn Vietnam War has certainly provided us with plenty of patients." Later in the film one of the veterans talks about his sister,
who was raped and stabbed to death by "a vet like us" who claimed
"the war made him crazy." [TV]

More American Graffiti (1979) D: B.W.L. Norton, 111m. Ron
Howard, Cindy Williams, Charles Martin Smith, Candy Clark, Bo
Hopkins, Paul Le Mat.

*** Two years after the events in *American Graffiti*, the characters are facing the real world after high school. Two are in Vietnam, one is leading protests in college, one is racing cars, two are
married and becoming aware of current issues, and one is a flower
child in San Francisco. The use of multiple and split screens to
bring all the stories together results in what is, although not as

good as its predecessor, delightful nonetheless—a difficult task, since a trailer at the end of the original film showed the fate of each character. In addition to another fine sound track, the most lasting impression of the film is the demonstration of differences between the lives of those who went to Vietnam and those who stayed home—often accomplished on the same screen or in rapid switches back and forth.

** Terry "the Toad" Fields, as announced in the original, is MIA at An Loc, where he was serving as a helicopter crewman with another soldier from his hometown. The buddy is not one of Toad's friends who went to college or who was marked for success; he was the leader of the town's gang of hoods, the Pharaohs. Apparently only the losers in small California towns ended up in the war zone. When the former Pharaoh is killed and his commander is more interested in impressing congressmen than in taking care of his troops, Toad fakes his own death and begins walking out of Vietnam. We are not informed of his success or lack thereof. Good helicopter-flying scenes mixed with an adequate base camp, all shot in a grainy, dark format, are reminiscent of the real thing. Actual footage of the war helps add to the realistic appearance, even though the action is farfetched. Although Toad wears the rank of a warrant officer (normally a pilot's rank), the director apparently cannot decide if he is a pilot or a doorgunner. His commander also assigns him various duties, such as latrine cleanup, which would not have been done by a warrant officer. 📺

Moving (1988) **D:** Alan Metter, 89m. Richard Pryor, Beverly Todd, Randy Quaid, Dana Carvey, Dave Thomas.

*1/2 A mass-transit engineer (Pryor) loses his job in New Jersey and accepts a new position in Boise, Idaho. His reluctant wife and rebellious kids are none too happy. The personnel of the moving company are all psychos, and everything that can go wrong with a cross-country transfer does. Laughs are few and far between—especially for anyone who has ever made a similar move.

Quaid plays the "neighbor from hell" with an oversized lawnmower, a dilapidated house, and unsavory friends, including the movers. Wearing military clothing, he brags about his fifteen years in the Marine Corps and exhibits all the other characteristics of the "crazy Vietnam vet" stereotype, though Vietnam is not directly mentioned. 📺

Mr. Majestyk (1974) **D:** Richard Fleischer, 103m. Charles Bronson, Al Lettieri, Linda Cristal, Lee Purcell, Paul Koslo.

* Bronson plays a Colorado watermelon farmer who crosses a Mafia hitman and his pals. The mob loses and Bronson never changes expression in this Elmore Leonard script.

\# A policeman describes Bronson's character as an ex-con whose wife divorced him while he was in prison. To further explain the mounting number of Mafioso bodies, the cop reveals that the simple farmer was a captain in Vietnam, where he won the Silver Star, and then was a Ranger instructor at Fort Benning, Georgia. TV

My Father, My Son (1988) TVM, **D:** Jeff Bleckner, 100m. Keith Carradine, Karl Malden, Michael Horton, Jenny Lewis, Billy Sullivan.

** A veteran combats two forms of cancer likely caused by his exposure to Agent Orange in Vietnam. In an ironic twist to this true story, the spraying of the chemical in the war zone was ordered by the victim's father, Admiral Elmo Zumwalt. Mostly the film is about love and support in confronting the tragedy shared by the elder Zumwalt (Malden) and his son (Carradine). The result is an effective tearjerker that reveals much more of a father-son relationship than anything about the war or Agent Orange.

\#\# The most positive aspect of this movie is the lack of any railing against the war or the use of the defoliant. Both Zumwalts recognize and admit the responsibilities and realities of warfare and react as professional naval officers. This is one of the few pictures in which, despite great horror and hardships endured, the Vietnam veterans involved do not have nightmares, turn to drugs, or end their lives with suicide. Maybe the reason for these omissions is that it is based on a true story rather than a Hollywood writer's version of the war and its combatants.

My Husband Is Missing (1978) TVM, **D:** Richard Michaels, 104m. Sally Struthers, Tony Musante, Martine Beswick, James Hong, Nam Loc.

* The wife (Struthers) of a missing American flier goes to Hanoi to find out what happened to her husband. Granted permission by the Vietnamese to make a jungle search, she is accompanied by a communist official and a Canadian journalist. Struthers finds proof of her husband's death and falls in love with the journalist, and everyone—with the exception of the dead aviator—lives happily ever after. Nothing about the acting or production is worth mentioning except to note that there is little wonder that the whiny Struthers has all but disappeared from TV and movies.

The very idea that the Vietnamese would allow the Struthers character to search the jungle—especially in 1978—is ludicrous. It's also a bit hard to believe that she is able to penetrate the harshest jungle and cross steep mountains to find out what happened to her husband. Instead of one Rambolike soldier accomplishing what the American military could not, this film has a short blonde woman doing the same thing.

My Old Man's Place (1972) **D:** Edwin Sherin, 93m (OT: *Glory Boy*). Mitchell Ryan, Arthur Kennedy, William Devane, Michael Moriarty, Topo Swope.

* Moriarty plays a Vietnam veteran who returns from the war along with two friends (Devane and Ryan) to visit his father's rundown northern California ranch. The three veterans have all been deeply affected by the war, and rape and murder continue to be a part of their personalities and actions. Despite the violence and sex, the film moves slowly. Exploitation is its only apparent objective.

Moriarity's character is troubled by having killed a woman in Vietnam. Devane is a moronic loser who wants to hunt down his cuckolding wife. Ryan so misses the "action" in Vietnam that he reenlists despite the fact that he seems to be doing fine in California, raping and murdering just as well there as in the combat zone. Early in the film the three veterans bind their friendship by jointly beating a San Francisco transvestite. ⟨TV⟩

Nashville (1975) **D:** Robert Altman, 159m. Henry Gibson, Karen Black, Lily Tomlin, Ned Beatty, Keith Carradine, Scott Glenn.

** Greed, politics, sex, and everything wrong with America in the 1970s is shown through country music and a political rally in the title city. There is a huge cast, with some actors (Elliot Gould and Julie Christie) appearing as themselves. Altman's nearly free-form effort was highly lauded and honored by critics and movie academics. However, it is irritating and much too long. Anyone with a remote appreciation for country music will detest the seemingly endless songs by such "great" singers as Tomlin and Gibson, and even Keith Carradine's "I'm Easy," which won the Academy Award for the year's best original song, is hard to take.

Since Altman attempts to include all of America's ills in the film, it is most appropriate that Vietnam has a role—despite the fact that the director does not seem to know what to do with it. Glenn plays a veteran who for the entire movie wears his khaki uniform, complete with Vietnam service ribbons and a blue infantry shoulder cord but no combat infantryman's badge. At times he also wears an overseas cap at least two sizes too large as he pops in and out of scenes at irregular intervals. At one point he is asked by Carradine's character, "How are you doin', sarge? Killed anybody this week?" Later a British journalist asks him if he was in Vietnam, only to answer herself, "Yes, I can see it in your face." At least Glenn is not the assassin who shoots the political candidate but rather is the first to wrestle the killer to the ground. Just what it all means is not remotely understandable. 📺

Neon Maniacs (1985) **D:** Joseph Mangine, 90m. Allan Hayes, Leilani Sarelle, Donna Locke, Victor Elliot Brandt.

* Monsters, described as the "ugly, killing type," emerge from their lair under the Golden Gate Bridge to terrorize San Francisco. The only thing that will stop them is water—and the stop button on the VCR.

\# Each of the monsters is a ghoul with dripping blood and irregular body parts. One, who seems to be the most prolific killer and who enjoys it the most, is dressed in jungle fatigues and combat gear and carries an M-16. Vietnam is not mentioned, but there can be no doubt in the viewer's mind that this horrible monster is fresh off a jungle tour in Southeast Asia. 📺

New Healers, The (1972) TVM, **D:** Bernard L. Kowalski, 99m. Kate Jackson, Burgess Meredith, Leif Erickson, Robert Foxworth, Jonathan Lippe.

** Two medics and a navy nurse just back from Vietnam help a small northern California town in need of medical help. Initially they are anything but welcome until their response to a natural disaster puts the town behind them. Although average at best, this is an exceptional film in that the Vietnam veterans are intelligent, sensitive, dedicated, well-adjusted citizens who are attempting to contribute to their community.

The vets are plagued by flashbacks—not of Vietnam but of the town council telling them they are not welcome because they are not real doctors. Not a single word is uttered by the vets against the war or the military. One of the medics states that he dropped out of medical school because he felt a responsibility to serve in Vietnam. The film concludes with a town official saying, "I just want to say that I'm very glad you're here and am grateful for your help." One of the medics responds for all Vietnam veterans: "That's all we ever really wanted." 📺

Night Flowers (1979) **D:** Luis San Andres, 92m. Jose Perez, Gabriel Walsh, Sabra Jones.

* Two Vietnam veterans readjust to their Hoboken, New Jersey, hometown by committing various acts of rape and murder. For some reason known only to the director and writer, it is important to also clearly identify one as Irish-American and the other as Hispanic. Along with the plot and acting, the background and interiors can only be described as grim.

\# This is just another of the "all Vietnam veterans are crazy" films; it does add several nouns to the usual description—"rapist" and "murderer." The only real question raised by the film (other than why it was made) is "Which is more bleak, being a Vietnam vet or living in Hoboken?" 📺

Nightforce (1987) **D:** Lawrence D. Foldes, 82m. Linda Blair, James Van Patten, Richard Lynch, Chad McQueen, Dean R. Miller.

* Five college students drive a "very fancy Jeep" pulling a U-Haul trailer from southern California to Central America to rescue a friend held by terrorists. Along the way, they are joined by a Vietnam veteran who has withdrawn to a remote, camouflaged jungle hut. An attempt to enhance a ridiculous plot with plenty of nudity and bloodshed is unsuccessful.

\# The most prolific killer is the Vietnam veteran. When the rescuers need information about the terrorist camp, the vet takes a prisoner and tortures him using "a little something I learned from the Vietcong." 📺

Night Wars (1988) **D:** David A. Prior, 94m. Brian O'Conner, Dan Haggerty, Cameron Smith, Steve Horton.

* Nine years after the war, two Vietnam vets are still haunted by their experiences as POWs. Nothing new here—except that in their dreams they return to the war zone, and when they awake they suffer from the wounds—mental *and* physical—of their journey. Finally they prepare for their dream trip by loading up with weapons and explosives, go to bed, and return to Vietnam to take care of unfinished business with their captors. This actually *sounds*, if not interesting, at least different. In fact, it is neither. The film is poorly done, with a believability quotient of zero.

\# The vets are jobless and heavy drinkers. Worse yet is another POW who has sided with the North Vietnamese and tortures his former comrades with a hot iron bar. Combat scenes more resemble children playing war in the backyard than actual battle. Watch the final scenes (or better still, don't watch at all) in which the dreaming GIs carry hand grenades attached to their belts by the pull-to-detonate O-rings. That is a sure way to prevent a sequel. ☖

1969 (1988) **D:** Ernest Thompson, 93m. Robert Downey, Jr., Kiefer Sutherland, Bruce Dern, Mariette Hartley, Winona Ryder.

** Downey and Sutherland play college students pursuing sex, drugs, and rock and roll while avoiding the draft and "getting their face shot off in Vietnam." But when Sutherland's brother is killed in Vietnam, the death brings the entire town to the realization that the war is wrong, and all unite in protest. Except for the offbeat cuteness of Ryder, the cast seems wooden and little involved. Turbulent year, big-name cast, famous director (wrote *On Golden Pond*), great music—disappointing movie.

\# The war is wrong, its participants misled or downright evil; the military and the draft are the true enemies. According to Sutherland, "It's not my war, it's bullshit." Whatever accuracy might be contained in these sentiments is lost in the unconvincing acting by all concerned in this bitter film. Watch for the movie marquee near the end, which advertises *Easy Rider* and *ur Grit* (sic) on the same bill. ☖

Ninth Configuration, The (1980) **D:** William Peter Blatty, 115m (OT: *Twinkle, Twinkle, Killer Kane*). Stacy Keach, Scott Wilson, Jason Miller, Robert Loggia, Moses Gunn.

*** During the final days of the Vietnam War, a new director (Keach) takes over an asylum for disturbed military personnel in a Pacific Northwest castle—only to prove himself crazier than his charges. Humor ranges from slapstick and sight gags to the extremely sophisticated and is delivered so rapidly that it is impossible to absorb or appreciate it all. In an extraordinarily violent ending, Keach takes on an entire motorcycle gang in a barroom and kills them all—women included. Based on the novel *Twinkle, Twinkle, Killer Kane* by director Blatty, who also wrote the screenplay and produced. (Various prints ranging in length from 99 to 140 minutes are in circulation.)

\# The film begins with a very officious narrator relating, "Toward the end of the Vietnam War, an unusually high percentage of American servicemen suddenly manifested symptoms of psychosis." The remainder of the film goes to great and somewhat successful lengths to show that all Vietnam veterans are crazy, with the difference among them being that some are more crazy than others. 🔲

No Dead Heroes (1987) **D:** J. C. Miller, 86m. Max Thayer, John Dresden, Toni Nero, Nick Nicholson, Mike Monte.

* At the end of the war, a Soviet adviser on prisoner interrogation takes an American POW from North Vietnam to Russia, implants a mind-control computer chip into his brain, and sends him home to kill his own family before dispatching him to El Salvador to kill the visiting Pope. To stop the "bioelectronic" man, the CIA counters with the POW's best friend from Vietnam. It's just as bad as it sounds.

\# This is the type of Vietnam War film where grenade pins are pulled with teeth and one shotgun blast kills five men at a hundred meters. It includes such regretfully unforgettable dialogue as the former GI's telling a CIA recruiter, "Fuck you. I'm not one of your pawns anymore" as he throws the appropriate chess piece at the agent from a board on his desk. The Soviet adviser is noteworthy for two points in addition to his terrible acting: He thoroughly enjoys pulling out prisoners' fingernails, and his name is Ivan Dimanovitch—pronounced De-*mean*-o-vitch. 🔲

No More Excuses (1968) **D:** Robert Downey, 55m. Robert Downey, Alan Abel, Lawrence Wolf, Prentice Wilhite, Linda Diesem.

* A slightly wounded Confederate soldier flees a Civil War battlefield and ends up in modern-day New York. There he observes the action in a singles bar, meets a man campaigning to clothe animals, trades his rifle for the services of a prostitute, and goes to a Yankee baseball game. Parallel stories have a priest as a rapist and flashbacks to the assassination of President Garfield. Finally, the soldier tires of his new world and returns to the conflict of the Civil War. Weird, and not nearly as good as it might sound.

\# Documentary footage of the Vietnam War is spliced in on what seems to be random basis. In one scene, an ABC news reporter questions the rapist priest and his victim about their opinions on the war in Vietnam. They don't approve of it.

Norwood (1970) **D:** Jack Haley, Jr. 96m. Glen Campbell, Kim Darby, Joe Namath, Billy Curtis, Carol Lynley, Dom DeLuise.

** A Marine Vietnam veteran (Campbell) travels by stolen car, bus, and his thumb from Texas to New York to Arkansas (although actual shooting locations are in Corona and Lake Elsinore, California) in pursuit of a music career. Along the way he encounters an old Vietnam buddy (Namath) who owes him money, a pregnant hippie (Darby), a midget (Curtis), and an "educated," trick-performing chicken by the name of Joann. This lightweight comedy is Namath's first screen appearance and reunites Campbell and Darby after their success in *True Grit*.

\# The characters played by Campbell and Namath are Marine Vietnam vets, as is Darby's mean boyfriend, but the war has little to do with the story. All concerned seemed to be confused and directionless enough on their own. Interestingly, in real life Namath could be a football star *and* make movies but was physically unable to serve in Vietnam. For those who think this film resembles Elvis's "returning home from the army" films, note that the producer is Hal Wallis, who turned out nine Presley movies before giving singer Campbell a chance.

Nowhere to Hide (1987-Canada) **D:** Mario Azzopardi, 100m. Amy Madigan, Daniel Hugh Kelly, Robin MacEachern, Michael Ironside, John Colicos.

* A Marine officer is murdered when he discovers a contractor is delivering faulty helicopter parts that are causing crashes. His wife (Madigan) and son are tracked by the killers because proof of

the defective parts is hidden in the child's toy. Nothing remotely nears reality in any part of this picture. Its only merit is the beautiful Quebec filming location—but it in no way resembles any USMC base.

\# Madigan's character is assisted by a Vietnam veteran who has withdrawn to a remote, booby-trapped cabin. The evil Marine general who is in cahoots with the parts contractor is also a Vietnam vet. 🖵

Nude Restaurant (1967) **D:** Andy Warhol, 100m. Viva, Taylor Mead, James Davis, Brigid Polk, Julian Burroughs.

* A Greenwich Village waitress bathes and talks with a stoned young man and another girl about friends, hair, and sex. She continues similar conversations at the restaurant where she works and where all the customers are seminude. This Warhol Factory film may have had relevance to some when it was released, but it is doubtful that anyone other than a dedicated voyeur would watch it today.

* One of the restaurant's customers takes center stage to say that he is a draft dodger and to explain why he is against the war in Vietnam. His rationale makes about as much sense as his being dressed only in his underwear.

O.C. & Stiggs (1987) **D:** Robert Altman, 100m. Daniel H. Jenkins, Neill Barry, Paul Dooley, Jane Curtin, Dennis Hopper.

*1/2 Two strange teenagers dedicate their summer vacation to harassing an insurance agent who has canceled the medical coverage of one boy's grandfather. This film has all the weirdness of Altman's other films (including *M*A*S*H* and *Streamers*) but none of the quality or humor.

\# The teens are assisted by two Vietnam veterans who live in a remote desert cabin where they raise marijuana and sell illegal arms and ammunition. One of the vets is played by Hopper, who along with Altman has made a career of exploiting Vietnam and its veterans. 🖵

Odd Angry Shot, The (1979-Australia) **D:** Tom Jeffrey, 90m. John Hargreaves, Graham Kennedy, Bryan Brown, John Jarratt.

*** Elite professional soldiers of the Australian Special Air Service (SAS) find the Vietnam War as difficult, confusing, and frus-

trating as did their American allies. Well made with strong
performances by the entire cast, this is Australia's best effort to
depict the war. It compares extremely favorably with any of the far
more numerous efforts of U.S. filmmakers.

This picture provides a unique insight into Australia's ef-
forts in and feelings toward the Vietnam War. Camp scenes, soldier language (with an Australian twist), and field operations are
expertly portrayed. Patrols by the SAS teams (similar to U.S.
LRRP/Ranger operations) are some of the best on film. Uniforms
and equipment are correct, movement and camouflage are accurate, and noise discipline, including use of arm and hand signals,
is commendable. Also noteworthy is the movie's focus on the soldiers' awareness that they are pawns of the politicians, but they
continue to fight aggressively because it is their job. Poignant references are made to the unconcern of their fellows back home
about the war and the fact that the sons of the rich and influential
are able to avoid the unpleasantness of combat (in the same manner as did their American brothers). [TV]

Officer and a Gentleman, An (1982) D: Taylor Hackford, 126m.
Richard Gere, Debra Winger, David Keith, Louis Gossett, Jr., Lisa
Blount.

*** A misfit (Gere), who grew up in an apartment above a Filipino whorehouse with his enlisted-sailor father, attempts to make
something of himself by going to Naval Officer Candidate School
to become an aviator. Winger plays a local girl who, like her
mother and many of the town's women, aims to make good by
marrying a candidate after he is commissioned. Gossett portrays
the tough Marine drill instructor who attempts to make an officer
out of Gere while warning candidates about the intentions of the
local girls. Although formulistic Hollywood and predictable at
nearly every turn, it works and works extremely well in a gritty,
sentimental, sexy way. Gossett, who wears a uniform as well as any
actor in Hollywood, received an Oscar, as did the theme song "Up
Where We Belong."

This was one of the first post-Vietnam "it's all right to feel
good about the military again" films. Vietnam is in the past, with
references only to the fact that candidate Keith's brother was
killed in the war, as was the brother of his local girlfriend. Gossett
wears several rows of service and valor ribbons from Vietnam and

tells his charges his job is to find out "if you are too peaceful a person to drop napalm on a village where there might be women and children." 📺

Off Limits (1988) **D**: Christopher Crowe, 102m. Willem Dafoe, Gregory Hines, Fred Ward, Amanda Pays, Scott Glenn. .

** Two military policemen patrol the streets of Saigon in search of a serial killer of prostitutes who they suspect is a high-ranking U.S. Army officer. Along the way they manage to curse a lot, to make many comments about gooks, slants, and slopes, and to get into multiple shoot-outs. Dafoe even manages to work in a semiromance with a nun. The only difference between this and the usual television cop-and-robber shows is the "Saigon" setting, which is played by Bangkok.

Attention to detail, or at least to minimal accuracy, was seemingly "off limits" to the director. A radio announcer refers to himself as a specialist first class (no such rank exists), the two MPs use American greenbacks (instead of Military Payment Certificates), an ARVN officer wears U.S. Special Forces insignia on his hat, and the usual mistakes in uniforms and decorations are made. Enlisted men spend a lot of time at the VD clinic, officers have kinky sex habits, and VC prisoners are thrown from helicopters in flight. Only the nun has any redeeming characteristics—and she is sorely suspect. 📺

Omega Syndrome (1987) **D**: Joseph Manduke, 90m. Ken Wahl, George DiCenzo, Doug McClure, Nicole Eggert.

** With the help of a Vietnam War buddy, a boozy, down-and-out journalist (Wahl) tracks down racist, right-wing terrorists who have kidnapped his teenage daughter. This is better than the usual vigilante fare, but not by much.

For such a mediocre movie, there are some good lines. When a woman in a bar notices Wahl's cigarette lighter she asks, "Where did you get this, Vietnam?" "No," he lies, "a pawnshop, but it was in a real dangerous part of town." Wahl's character later gets more serious, saying, "I'm not like one of those guys that wake up in the middle of the night in a cold sweat hearing Hueys. I don't give a damn whether anyone gave me a parade or a monument. I'm getting tired of reliving all this shit." His buddy, a three-tour veteran whose office walls are covered with Vietnam pictures and memen-

tos, responds that he relives the war and has lots of memories because "it's all I got." ⟦TV⟧

Open Season (1974-Spain) **D**: Peter Collinson, 103m. Peter Fonda,
John Phillip Law, William Holden, Cornelia Sharpe, Richard
Lynch.

* Three Vietnam veterans spend their annual summer vacation
kidnapping, molesting, and then releasing, to hunt down again
and kill, a random couple. Fonda, Law, and Lynch play the villains. Holden makes a brief appearance at the end of the film for
what could only have been a much-needed paycheck in his declin-
ing days.

One of the Vietnam vets explains their yearly ritual by saying,
"After you've hunted men, animals just don't rate." Nonetheless,
animals are also the frequent target of the maniacal trio. As they
laugh madly and blast away at anything that moves, the background music is a child singing "All Things Bright and Beautiful,
All Creatures Great and Small." What more could be expected
from a Fonda?

Operation C.I.A. (1965) **D**: Christian Nyby, 90m. Burt Reynolds,
Kieu Chinh, Danielle Aubrey, John Hoyt, Cyril Collack.

** A CIA officer (Reynolds) is sent to Saigon to investigate the
murder of another officer and to stop an assassination plot
directed against the American ambassador. Loads of spies, agents,
double agents, and triple agents offer an interesting look into Vietnamese politics. This is one of Hollywood's early and few efforts
during the war to use Vietnam as a setting for an action film. Its
production in black and white is an indication of the studio's financial support of the project. It is watchable, however, for two
primary reasons. The Vietcong are actually the bad guys as they
kill children in bombing attempts against Americans. Also, this is
Reynolds's first starring role on the big screen.

The most unusual aspect is that neither the CIA nor the
American military is at all criticized. Although action rather than
politics is emphasized, the communists are obviously the bad guys
while the Americans and the South Vietnamese are the good.
Thailand locations reasonably double for Saigon, except for the
right-side-drive automobiles. ⟦TV⟧

Operation 'Nam (1985-Italy) **D**: Larry Ludman, 85m. Oliver Tobias, Christopher Connelly, Manfred Lehman, John Steiner,
Ethan Wayne.

* Four misfit veterans return to Vietnam a decade after the war
to rescue Americans still held captive. The rescuers are opposed
by the Vietnamese as well as by the U.S. military, which has been
secretly providing food and medical supplies to the communists to
give to the POWs while negotiations for their release continue. Totally worthless, this film has only one scene of note: A young Vietnamese provocatively removes her blouse only to reveal horrible
burns and scars. She explains, "American napalm," as she shoots
the man who thinks he is seducing her.

\# Everything in this film is about as accurate about Vietnam as
its Rome shooting location. Uniforms are generally a mixture of
Italian and German, the only authentic American uniform being
the World War II–vintage "pinks and greens" worn by a U.S. officer thirty years after they were retired. As one of the rescuers
leaves home to go on the mission, his girlfriend yells, "You Vietnam vets ain't worth shit; get the hell out of my life." Another of
the rescuers is told by a potential employer, "Three years in Vietnam ain't worth shit at the job site." On their return to Vietnam,
one of the veterans states, "A gook is a gook," and then brags, "It
wouldn't be the first time," as he prepares to destroy a village and
kill its civilian population. ☐ⓉⓋ

Operation War Zone (1989) **D**: David A. Prior, 86m. Joe Spinell,
Fritz Matthews, William Zipp, John Cianetti, Sean Hotton.

* A corrupt Pentagon general schemes to sell arms to the North
Vietnamese for profit and to prolong the war because if the GIs
win, "the money stops." Various groups of American soldiers fight
each other to stop or support the plan—often it is difficult to determine which is which. This may very easily be the worst Vietnam War film made; no, make that the worst war film of any era,
and a strong candidate for worst picture of any kind to ever reach
the screen.

\# The most ridiculous firefights ever recorded on film are in this
movie. Both sides stand in the open and still rarely hit their targets. The NVA, who do not look Oriental, much less Vietnamese,
are dressed in what seems to be loungewear. One enemy soldier
on patrol wears white socks and loafers. The terrain is just as lu-

dicrous, an attempt to pass off southern California as Vietnamese jungle. ☐TV☐

Opposing Force (1986) **D:** Eric Karson, 99m. Tom Skerritt, Lisa Eichhorn, Anthony Zerbe, Richard Roundtree, Robert Wrightman.

** An air force pilot (Eichhorn) volunteers to be the first female to go through a tough joint-service escape-and-evasion course in the Philippines. The camp commandant and his handpicked subordinates don't particularly like women in the military and lose touch with reality as they subject the trainee to rape and torture. Some interesting thoughts on women in combat are included, and the effects of psychological abuse of prisoners are well portrayed. However, a poor conclusion negates much of the positive. The best line is delivered by the female pilot to a male student who is injured in a parachute jump. She says, "You've got a limp and I got tits; these aren't good things to have in the military."

Much of the commandant's madness is apparently a result of his service in Vietnam. At one point he raves about the "clean killing" in Vietnam of women and children and the destruction of villages by airmen dropping bombs and then returning to a nice base. Also, one of the camp's more sadistic guards is a Vietnamese—although no explanation is given as to why he is in the American military. ☐TV☐

Ordinary Heroes (1985) **D:** Peter H. Cooper, 90m. Richard Dean Anderson, Valerie Bertinelli, Richard Baxter, Liz Torres.

* A soldier (Anderson) returns from Vietnam blind and finds it difficult to readjust despite the help of the girl he left behind (Bertinelli). The plot and dialogue are so sweet they threaten to rot your teeth. Anderson and Bertinelli certainly are an attractive couple, but unfortunately they lack the acting range to generate any real emotion on the part of the viewer.

No one in Hollywood seems to be willing simply to check the history books. As a result, we get another movie that shows a unit still in Vietnam years after it was redeployed to the United States. In this case, the Fifth Mechanized Infantry Brigade (incidentally, this is the only film to feature that relatively obscure unit) is shown fighting in Vietnam in 1973—two years after its departure. Despite this inaccuracy, the movie is generally fair to the veteran.

In the hospital, a horribly wounded GI states he has "no regrets." Another adds, "This is still a great country to fight and die for." 📺

Our Winning Season (1979) **D:** Joseph Ruben, 92m. Scott Jacoby, Deborah Benson, Dennis Quaid, Randy Herman, Jan Smithers.

** *American Graffiti* meets *Rocky* in this 1960s coming-of-age film about small-town teenagers. Against a backdrop of dating, drive-ins, and experimentation with drugs and sex, a high school track star (Jacoby) trains to win a race in honor of a friend killed in Vietnam. It's predictable at every turn, but you will find yourself pulling for the runner in the final race. The film was set in California but filmed in Georgia.

\# The friend killed in Vietnam is a college dropout. It is early in the conflict, and few of the teens are concerned about the war until the death notice arrives. Jacoby's character has more than just honoring his friend in mind as he trains for the race. If he wins, he receives a college track scholarship—which will provide him a student deferment from the draft.

Outlaw Force (1987) **D:** David Heavener, 95m. David Heavener, Paul Smith, Frank Stallone, Cecilia Xavier, Stephanie Cicero.

* A hillbilly singer and Vietnam veteran (Heavener) helps a black gas station attendant against a gang of toughs who, in revenge, later rape and kill the vet's wife and sell his daughter into child pornography. Heavener's character gets even with fist and gun—favoring shots from both to the crotch. His singing is about on the same level, with lyrics such as "My neck is red, my socks are white, my jeans are blue." His most endearing characteristic is that he puts peanuts in his cola drink.

\# The only real plus to this routine Vietnam-veteran superhero genre film (beyond the singing, which deserves no further comment) is that Heavener has a happy marriage and family. You can tell he and his wife have a good relationship by the way she tells him not to bring his gun to the supper table. Of course, the wife is killed off early and the daughter makes few appearances (except to whine) after the early scenes. At least the vet's flashbacks are to his wife's murder rather than to combat. 📺

Outside In (1972) **D:** Allen Baron, 90m. Darrel Larson, Heather Menzies, Dennis Olivieri, Peggy Feury, Logan Ramsey.

* A draft dodger (Larson) hiding in Canada returns to California to attend his father's funeral. During the visit, he becomes involved with two old friends, one of whom has recently returned from Vietnam and another who is just out of jail for draft resistance. This was one of the first releases by Harold Robbins International, and it is easy to see why the writer's venture into movie production was short lived.

The film attempts to show the divisiveness caused by the war and the draft but succeeds in accomplishing little except to make a volatile subject extremely boring. A glaring error is that the friend fresh out of jail commits suicide when he finds he is still going to be drafted; with a felony conviction on his record, the army would have had little use for him. One item is true to character for Larson and most draft dodgers—when federal agents get on his trail, the dodger dodges again and votes with his feet.

Package, The (1989) **D:** Andrew Davis, 108m. Gene Hackman, Joanna Cassidy, Tommy Lee Jones, John Heard, Dennis Franz.

**1/2 The United States and the Soviet Union are about to sign a peace treaty that will end the cold war. Neither side's military is happy with the decision, and to sabotage the agreement, they jointly plot to assassinate the Soviet leader during a U.S. visit. Hackman plays an NCO who unwittingly escorts the assassin into the United States from Europe as a military prisoner. Hackman's attempts to foil the plot make for a great adventure with multiple plot twists that occasionally verge on the believable.

With Hackman a veteran of Vietnam as well as of the ill-fated Iran hostage rescue attempt, the film has some balance. Jones as the assassin is also a decorated veteran of the war. He admits to killing for money, the more cash the better, and to not caring who pays or is the target. The American generals and senior officers who plot with the Soviets are also veterans of Vietnam. [tv]

Parades (1972) **D:** Robert J. Siegel, 95m. Russ Thacker, Brad Sullivan, David Doyle, Dorothy Chace, Lewis J. Stadlen.

* This is basically a movie about making a movie. Two film makers go about producing a film about the prisoners in a military stockade while outside the gate protesters chant against the Vietnam War and sing "America the Beautiful." The prisoners, whose crimes are never revealed, are given ample time to state their opinions about the war, love, motherhood, apple pie, and man's general inhumanity to man. More than one-third of the footage was reused in Siegel's *The Line*.

The prison is run by brutal guards, a sadistic sergeant, and an incompetent officer. Vietnam and the military are the villains, as usual, and the media and protesters are the heroes.

Park Is Mine, The (1985) TVM, **D:** Steven Hilliard Stern, 104m. Tommy Lee Jones, Helen Shaver, Yaphet Kotto, Lawrence Dane, Eric Peterson.

* After the suicide of a friend who has spent a year placing explosives and hiding weapons in New York's Central Park, a vet (Jones) decides to implement his buddy's plan to bring attention to the mistreatment of Vietnam veterans. The veteran, who is "sick and tired of hearing what a loser I am," runs everyone out of the park and announces that it belongs to him for the next seventy-two hours. Ultimately he fights police SWAT teams, the National Guard, and city-hired mercenaries while finding friends in the press and the public.

Although there is much talk about Vietnam veterans being normal and deserving of respect, there is no action or deed on the part of Jones's character that supports it. Jones kills the mercenaries, including a former Vietcong, sent into the park to eliminate him and perpetuates the image of the "crazy vet" bent on vengeance. To top it off, the movie was filmed not in New York but in Toronto. [TV]

Patriot, The (1986) **D:** Frank Harris, 90m. Gregg Henry, Simone Griffeth, Michael J. Pollard, Jeff Conaway, Leslie Nielson.

* A former SEAL who was a Vietnam War hero is recruited by the navy, despite his dishonorable discharge, to assist in the recovery of a stolen nuclear warhead. There is nothing good in this film, with the possible exception of the Santa Barbara, California, shooting locations.

No reason is given as to why the navy has to resort to a cashiered officer rather than use its own assets. The former SEAL credits his dishonorable discharge to his refusal to destroy a village of old men and children. He explains, "I didn't quit because I wanted to stop killing people, I quit because I wanted to kill them." He also pontificates, "Patriotism is loving your country, not

blindly following the idiots who run it." And he is prone to pointing out that 30 percent of the American casualties in Vietnam were by accident or friendly fire, and that despite dropping six times the ordnance in Southeast Asia as in World War II, we still failed to win in Vietnam. [TV]

Piranha (1978) **D:** Joe Dante, 90m. Bradford Dillman, Heather Menzies, Kevin McCarthy, Keenan Wynn, Dick Miller.

** An army experiment to breed piranhas to "destroy the river systems of North Vietnam" goes awry, and the fish start eating the citizens of Texas. This *Jaws* spoof is just campy enough, with lines such as "People eat fish, fish don't eat people" and "They're eating the guests, sir" to make it almost watchable.

A Vietnam-veteran army colonel who works on the piranha project is more interested in how the hungry fish will affect his downstream resort than anything else. He remarks, "Sometimes it is necessary to destroy in order to gain." Even his sleazy civilian partners call him a "shmuck." [TV]

Piranha II: The Spawning (1983-Italy) **D:** James Cameron, 88m. Tricia O'Neil, Steve Marachuk, Lance Henriksen, Ted Richert, Richard G. Paul.

* The piranhas are back—and this time they can fly as well as live in the sea *and* on land while they eat vacationers at a Caribbean resort. Despite the low marks it would have had to achieve, as is usual with sequels, it does not live up to the standards of the original. The only reason to watch this movie is that it was the debut of director Cameron, who must have learned much before his later efforts in *Aliens* and *The Terminator*.

As in the first fishy film, the army and the war in Vietnam are acknowledged as the true culprits for the experimentation in "gene splicing" to create killer creatures to fight communism. [TV]

Platoon (1986) **D:** Oliver Stone, 120m. Tom Berenger, Willem Dafoe, Charlie Sheen, Forest Whitaker, Kevin Dillon, Francesco Quinn, Johnny Depp.

**** The Vietnam War is shown through the actions of one infantry platoon along the Cambodian border as seen through the eyes of one soldier—played by Sheen and based on the claimed real-life experiences of director Stone. Every bad, tragic, and rotten incident of the conflict—even though it may have happened only once in the decade-long war—occurs as the men of the platoon fight the enemy and each other. Along the way, the platoon members murder civilians, burn villages, mutilate bodies, smoke dope, and eventually turn their weapons on themselves. One of the platoon members (Dillon) explains that he likes it in Vietnam because he can do what he wants—shooting, killing, whoring, doping—and all he has to worry about is getting himself killed. The direction, acting, costuming, and excellent Philippine locations make this film well deserving of its Academy Awards for best picture and director. What is a shame for the viewer and an insult to every Vietnam veteran is that the vast majority of those who see it believe it is the ultimate true story of what really happened in the war. In reality, it is an excellent picture but poor, extremely biased history.

Beyond the obvious—that everything befalling this platoon could not and did not happen to one platoon over the three or four months covered by the movie—there are other, even more glaring weaknesses and falsehoods. Conflict between the two NCOs, Elias and Barnes, would have been quickly resolved by the platoon leader and/or the company commander with a transfer or judicial action. Platoon members, unless they were at My Lai, which they were not, would not have gotten away with murdering civilians and prisoners. Contrary to what Stone would like the viewer to think, not everyone in Vietnam was a head (doper) or a juicer (drunk). Stone's agenda, as in his other films, goes far beyond simply making a good movie. He strives to rewrite history as he sees it—or as what he would like it to be. Notwithstanding its major flaws and one-sided views, this film has many commendable and watchable portions. Jungle scenes and combat sequences are as good as any on film. GI language, uniforms, equipment, the age of the soldiers, and the living conditions in the field are extremely well done. Unfortunately, a little truth and good film making still result in what may be the unkindest movie yet made about the Vietnam War. ⟨TV⟩

Platoon Leader (1988) **D:** Aaron Norris, 100m. Michael Dudikoff, Robert F. Lyons, Michael De Lorenzo, Rick Fitts, Jesse Dabson.
   ** A West Point graduate discovers he has much to learn as he takes charge of the defense of a small, remote fire base late in the

Vietnam War. Based on the popular (at least within military circles) book by career army officer James McDonough about his personal experiences, the film steers clear of politics and attempts to tell a war story. Acting and content are more than adequate, the film's major drawback being that director Norris has no better understanding of ground combat than does his better-known brother Chuck. Melodrama and clichés, including such lines as "Death is the ultimate alarm clock—it wakes you up," detract. Another minus is that the platoon leader of the title is ultimately not a very sympathetic character.

There are many good and accurate parts of the film; however, there are ample errors and omissions. The relationships between the platoon leader and his platoon sergeant and radio-telephone operator are particularly notable for their accuracy. An American soldier risking and losing his life in an attempt to save a baby in the midst of a firefight is a scene unique to Vietnam movies but not to the war itself. The platoon sergeant's practicing his jump position and parachute-landing falls during breaks and even during conversations, much the way a businessman absentmindedly practices his golf swing in his office or in the conference room, is right on target. Unfortunately, Norris does not understand fields of fire in defensive positions, or that grenades "thump" rather than "crack," and he omits altogether the making of radio reports and the use of air and artillery. Most glaring is the absence of horseplay and humorous interaction among the men of the platoon, which in the real war occupied far more time than any other outlet. Finally, someone should tell Norris and his actors that in the midst of an ambush, it is not necessary to instruct soldiers to take cover—they pretty well get the idea on their own. [TV]

P.O.W. The Escape (1986) **D:** Gideon Amir, 90m (OT: *Behind Enemy Lines*). David Carradine, Charles R. Floyd, Mako, Steve James, Phil Brock.

* A soldier (Carradine) leading a POW rescue finds himself captured, escapes, gets captured again, and eventually escapes along with fellow prisoners and a detachment of troops left behind at a hilltop supply base. Just to be sure you know whose side he is on, in one lengthy scene Carradine is draped in an American flag as he kills a large percentage of the North Vietnamese Army. Along

with the plot, dialogue, and location, Carradine is strictly unbelievable.

Nothing about this film remotely resembles the war in Vietnam—even the Philippine filming locations look, well, like the Philippines. Carradine leads a rescue unit from the 101st Airborne in 1973 despite the division's redeployment to the United States in 1972. This inaccuracy does allow Carradine, in the midst of a desperate run to freedom, to explain to the younger troops that while they remember Jimi Hendrix as the greatest guitar player ever, before his fame he was a paratrooper in the 101st—which is true but seemingly unrelated to the surrounding events. The most interesting point in this uninteresting film occurs when the prison camp commander, played by Mako, asks to go with the escapees because his family is in Miami. In the early minutes of the movie, watch for a cameraman in the corner of the attack on the prison camp. 📺

Presidio, The (1988) **D:** Peter Hyams, 97m. Sean Connery, Mark Harmon, Meg Ryan, Jack Warden, Mark Blum.

**1/2 A San Francisco detective (Harmon) and the provost marshal (Connery) of the Presidio, who don't get along, investigate the murder of a military policewoman. Along the way, the detective falls for the colonel's daughter (Ryan). A great cast, beautiful San Francisco scenery, and exciting chase scenes make up for the mediocre script.

The murderers of the MP, including a lieutenant colonel serving at the Presidio and a group of retired NCOs, are Vietnam veterans who are smuggling diamonds into the country from the Philippines. One of the retired sergeants is a Medal of Honor winner described as "a hero in a war nobody liked." The best line is delivered by an eight-year-old boy who is told about Vietnam at a military museum. He admits he never heard of the war but asks with great enthusiasm, "Did we kick ass?" 📺

Prince of Tides, The (1991) **D:** Barbra Streisand, 132m. Barbra Streisand, Nick Nolte, Blythe Danner, Kate Nelligan, Jeroen Krabbe.

**** A Jewish New York psychiatrist (Streisand) tries to help a southerner (Nolte) deal with his current problems and his family's dark past. Based on the novel by Pat Conroy, the film is outstanding in every aspect.

Nolte's character and his brother and sister were all deeply traumatized by their home life and a single violent incident during their childhood. While Nolte and his sister survived, the brother who "went to Vietnam and came back a hero" was killed after he returned from the war, went crazy, and blew up a construction site on his family's home island. 📺

Prism (1971) **D:** Anitra Pivnick, 80m. Paul Geier, Dale Soules, Nancy Volkman, Ossie Tortora, Robert Root.

* A young, middle-class New York lawyer (Geier) has trouble committing to his job, his wife, or his hippie mistress. He'd prefer to represent more radical clientele and spends much of his time wandering around Greenwich Village and attending parties highlighted by pot smoking, rock music, and antiestablishment conversation. The movie is sufficiently low key to provide a realistic simulation of boredom.

Much conversation is carried on about the evils of the Vietnam War and how the lawyer would like to specialize in assisting draft resisters. One group he does represent are homosexuals who organize demonstrations against the war.

Private War (1990) **D:** Frank De Palma, 95m. Michael Hewitt, Joe Dallesandro, Kimberly Beck.

* A former POW army sergeant, suffering flashbacks of Vietnam, fights to stop gun sales by his corrupt senior U.S. Army officers stationed in Italy. The sergeant's real motivation for his risk-taking is his hope that someone will kill him and put him out of his misery.

The only remotely new idea in this one is the combining of a crazy NCO with a crooked officer. Virtually nothing is correct in regard to uniforms, equipment, and language. Filmed in Yugoslavia, where it should have stayed. 📺

Promise of Love, The (1980) TVM, **D:** Don Taylor, 96m. Valerie Bertinelli, Jameson Parker, Andy Romano, Shelley Long, Craig T. Nelson.

** Bertinelli plays the eighteen-year-old widow of a Marine killed in Vietnam trying to rebuild her life. A bit slow and typically

made-for-television sweet, this movie still makes an impression—
especially on those who were confronted with the same situation
or had the potential to be so. Every veteran's wife will identify
with Bertinelli's next-door neighbor at Camp Pendleton, who says,
"What happened to you could happen to me." No politics are dis-
cussed beyond Bertinelli's old high school friends' reluctantly telling her that they had attended war protests on their college
campuses. As for Bertinelli, she is not concerned about the war,
only with the safety and, ultimately, the death of her husband.

This movie was filmed with the support of the Marine Corps
and Camp Pendleton, and its sights and sounds of a Marine base are
authentic. Of particular note are the accuracy in portraying the
casualty-notification team and the accuracy of the survivor-assistance
officer's efforts to help the widow with gratuity pay, insurance,
burial arrangements, and the move out of government quarters. A
few "old vets" and their wives may remember that officer wives did
not wear short shorts and halter tops on base as shown in the film.
Even though Bertinelli ends up in bed with a long-haired civilian
within four months of her husband's death, this is an excellent, honest representation of a small part of the Vietnam War. 📺

Proud Men (1987) TVM, **D:** William A. Graham, 96m. Charlton
Heston, Peter Strauss, Alan Autry, Belinda Belaski, Nan Martin.

*1/2 A young man (Strauss) who has hidden in France for fifteen
years after his desertion in Vietnam returns home to reunite with
his cattle-rancher father (Heston). A predictable, cliché-ridden plot
is nearly rescued by adequate acting. Interesting in that it marries
two popular movie genres—the western and Vietnam.

Strauss justifies his desertion by saying that he could no
longer kill women and children and to the end claims he has
"done nothing wrong" by deserting. "I took an oath to my country,
not for that [Vietnam]," Strauss claims. Vietnam veterans on the
ranch and in the town are played as red-necked, bigoted bullies
who have not come to the same refined conclusions about the war
as Strauss has.

Purple Haze (1982) **D:** David Burton Morris, 97m. Peter Nelson,
Chuck McQuary, Bernard Baldan, Susanne Lack, Bob Breuler.

*1/2 Two college boys leave school—one is kicked out because of
drugs, and the other quits on his own because he does not like

getting up early—to experience the summer of 1968. Neither of
the dropouts is very appealing or convincing in this effort to re-
create the upheaval of the sixties. The only redeeming feature of
the movie is the excellent use of period music including "Feel Like
I'm Fixin' to Die Rag" by Country Joe McDonald and the title
song by Jimi Hendrix.

The film opens with LBJ's television announcement that he
will not seek a second term. In background news reports, peace
rallies, and antiwar speeches, Vietnam appears directly or indirectly throughout the movie. At one point, Vietnam is compared
to the atomic bombing of Japan: It is implied that dropping the
A-bomb may have been justified but the war in Southeast Asia was
purely due to American aggression. Induction-center scenes include the usual hard-core, mean-talking sergeants. At least they
get the oath of enlistment correct.

Purple Hearts (1984) **D:** Sidney J. Furie, 115m. Cheryl Ladd, Ken
Wahl, Stephen Lee, David Harris, Annie McEnroe, Lee Ermey.

**1/2 A navy surgeon and a nurse fall in love and play doctor in
Vietnam. Wahl's character is not a hospital-based physician but one
who joins the troops in the field at fire bases and on prisoner rescue
missions in the North. He says, "I'm a doctor; I know where to shoot
them." Ladd, as the nurse, has already lost one lover in the war and
is willing to do anything, including buying supplies on the black
market, to help her patients. It's melodramatic and marginally acted,
but Wahl and Ladd make for a beautiful couple in an old-fashioned
love story that works despite the hokey ending.

This is an absolutely unusual movie. The heroes are officers, both believe in what they are doing, and neither burns villages or kills babies. With the exception of the Vietnam setting,
this could easily be confused with a romantic World War II movie.
Filmed in the Philippines with a mixture of military equipment
from several wars and decades, it still ranks—almost by default—as
the best romantic Vietnam film produced thus far. The five technical advisers from the navy and Marine Corps listed in the credits
earned their pay on this one. [TV]

Pursuit of D. B. Cooper, The (1981) **D:** Roger Spottiswoode,
100m. Robert Duvall, Treat Williams, Kathryn Harrold, Ed
Flanders, Paul Gleason.

* In 1971, a hijacker bailed out of an airliner over Washington State with a ransom of $200,000. He was never heard from again—until this film, which, in the guise of fiction, exposes the crook as a Vietnam veteran. As a promotional gimmick, Universal Pictures offered a $1 million reward to anyone who could solve the case. No one has claimed the money. The film is no more successful.

According to this movie, the infamous D. B. Cooper is a Green Beret veteran of the war in Southeast Asia. His pursuer is also a veteran, and so is another character who is after Cooper for a share of the loot. The only prize this film wins is one for carrying the theme of the Vietnam-veteran criminal to a new extreme. 〖TV〗

Quick Change (1990) **Ds:** Howard Franklin and Bill Murray, 110m. Bill Murray, Geena Davis, Randy Quaid, Jason Robards, Philip Bosco.

** Murray (dressed as a clown), Davis, and Quaid rob a New York bank and then have great difficulty in making their escape. "I hate this city" is Murray's frequent comment as they struggle with muggers, cab drivers, the bus system, street signs, the police, and the mob. More tedious than funny, this is really a "one joke, and that joke is New York" film.

While holding hostages in the bank, Murray responds to a police negotiator, "I was in Nam with a jerk like you." The immediate response of the police is that they are dealing with a nut case. No other mention of the war is made, other than a brief remark by the police chief that a former Green Beret is hidden in one of the getaway vehicles to stop Murray. It is unclear whether Murray's character is actually a veteran or if he just claims to be in order to raise the police's level of concern. 〖TV〗

Quiet American, The (1958) **D:** Joseph L. Mankiewicz, 120m. Audie Murphy, Michael Redgrave, Claude Dauphin, Bruce Cabot.

*** In 1952 Saigon, Murphy plays an American with a plan to settle the country's conflicts. This adaptation of Graham Greene's novel strays far from the original, especially the book's anti-American sentiments. Rather than the largely political story of the book, this film version offers a murder mystery and a love story. Murphy seems out of his league in the lead role, but strong performances by the supporting cast make up for his acting weaknesses.

One of the most interesting aspects of this film is the

showing of the multiple political factions in Vietnam and their du-
plicity in pursuit of their goals. Although set in 1952 and filmed
in 1958, the film includes much—such as the difficulties in deter-
mining who is friend and foe and the problems in fighting the
war—that would remain true in the later years of heavier U.S. involvement. This is one of the few movies actually filmed, in part,
in Vietnam, and the Saigon street scenes and the Tay Ninh countryside are intriguing and beautiful even in black and white. Also
unusual is that the majority of the Vietnamese parts are played by
Vietnamese rather than Thais, Filipinos, or other Asians. It is also
worthy of note that Murphy, America's most decorated World War
II hero, is killed in one of the first films to be made about U.S. involvement in Vietnam.

Rambo: First Blood Part II (1985) **D:** George P. Cosmatos, 96m.
Sylvester Stallone, Richard Crenna, Charles Napier, Julia Nickson,
Steven Berkoff.

** Rambo (Stallone) returns to Vietnam to rescue POWs only to
be betrayed by the CIA, captured by the Vietnamese, and tortured
by the Soviets. With the help of a local woman, and armed with
arrows with the explosive power of five-hundred-pound bombs,
Rambo prevails—and manages to kill Vietnamese and Russians at
the rate of one a minute (for a body count of at least ninety-eight,
by conservative measure) for the duration of the comic-strip-like
film. You know where this one is going when Stallone mutters before the opening credits, "Do we get to win this time?" Great adventure, tremendous box office, worthless history.

Mexican shooting locations resemble Vietnam but are more
scenic. Everything else is strictly "man" comic-book stuff—
"Superman," "Batman," and "Spiderman." Within the fantasy are
lines that are either memorable or regrettable, depending on one's
view. Rambo postures, "If I'm alive, Vietnam is alive"; later he says
that "I just want the country to love us [veterans] as much as we
love it." His Green Beret colonel boss (Crenna) says of Rambo,
"What you call hell, he calls home." The colonel advises Rambo,
"The war and everything that happened may have been wrong, but
don't hate your country for it." 📺

Rambo III (1988) **D:** Peter MacDonald, 101m. Sylvester Stallone,
Richard Crenna, Marc de Jonge, Kurtwood Smith, Spiros Focas.

** Rambo (Stallone) is retired to a Thai Buddhist monastery and, except for an occasional stick fight to earn cash for his fellow monks, is searching for inner peace. When his former Special Forces boss (Crenna) is captured by the Soviets in Afghanistan, Rambo rides (literally, on horseback) to the rescue amid what must be the largest explosives budget in film history. This is the usual comic-book Rambo adventure, and it is not all that bad as a burlesque. After all, if Stallone can keep a straight face, the audience should at least try not to laugh. Credits list a total of forty-four stunt men, and they earned their pay. The filming locations in Israel, Thailand, and Arizona are spectacular.

Any similarity among Rambo films, the Vietnam War, and military operations is strictly coincidental. Apparently, in this film, Rambo has to turn to Afghanistan because he killed all the Vietnamese—and many of the Russians—in his preceding film. This time he takes care of the rest of the Soviets, leaving none standing—no wonder the Berlin Wall and the USSR fell a short time later. The most ridiculous scene, among many, is a single Soviet helicopter capturing an Afghan and American Green Beret patrol by use of an aerial machine gun, a searchlight, and a loudspeaker. Little actual reference is made to Vietnam except when Rambo is questioned about his combat record. He admits, "I've fired a few shots." To his Russian captors in Afghanistan, Crenna warns, "We already had our Vietnam. Now you're going to have yours." [TV]

Ravager, The (1970) D: Charles Nizet, 76m. Pierre Gostin, Jo Long, Lynn Hayes, Luanna Wilcox, Diane Thurman.
* An American demolition specialist becomes separated from his unit and witnesses the brutal rape and murder of a Vietnamese civilian by two Vietcong. After returning to the States, the vet develops a compulsion to destroy anyone having sexual intercourse. With his army training and a cache of dynamite, he proceeds to blow up anyone he finds making love. On occasion he also rapes the victims himself before killing them.

Many films have been made about crazy Vietnam veterans. Some add murder to the veterans' skills while others make him into a sex offender. This film's only distinction is that it combines psychotic murder *and* rape as Vietnam-vet characteristics. The only mercy the vet ever shows is to allow two lesbians making love

to live. The movie's one remotely positive feature is that the original crime that motivates the vet is committed by VC rather than Americans.

Red Dust (1932) **D:** Victor Fleming, 83m. Clark Gable, Jean Harlow, Mary Astor, Gene Raymond, Willie Fung.

*** Gable plays the overseer of an Indochina rubber plantation who romances both a prostitute (Harlow), who is on the run from the law, and the wife (Astor) of one of his assistants. Initially he pursues Astor but then feels guilty about their adulterous affair. When he dumps Astor, she shoots him. Harlow nurses him back to health, and he decides that despite her past, she is his true love. This film is funny and extremely frank in subject, dialogue, and action; fifty years after its production, it is still very enjoyable. It was remade as *Congo Maisie* (1940) and as *Mogambo* (1950) with Gable reviving his original role. Neither is as good as *Red Dust*, and neither is set in Vietnam.

As good as the film is as entertainment, it adds nothing to the understanding of Vietnam. Interiors were filmed on MGM's Stage 16, and exteriors on a nearby back lot made up to look like a rubber plantation.

Resting Place (1986) TVM, **D:** John Korty, 100m. John Lithgow, Richard Bradford, Morgan Freeman, G. D. Spradlin, Frances Sternhagen.

** An Army survivor-assistance officer (Lithgow) helps to get a black officer who was killed in Vietnam buried in a previously all-white Georgia cemetery. Along the way he discovers the dead officer's old unit is harboring a mysterious secret. This "Hallmark Hall of Fame" production gained Emmy nominations for Lithgow and Korty.

The difficulty in burying a black soldier in a segregated graveyard was based on an actual incident. The remainder of the story is strictly fiction, and it contains the usual depiction of U.S. soldiers in Vietnam as being inferior warriors. Fort McPherson, Georgia, serves as the picture's army post.

Revenge (1990) **D:** Tony Scott, 123m. Kevin Costner, Anthony Quinn, Madeleine Stowe, Sally Kirkland, Miguel Ferrer.

** Costner plays a Vietnam-veteran navy fighter pilot who

leaves the service after twelve years to "do some other things."
The first "other thing" is to visit a wealthy old friend in Mexico
(Quinn), and the second is to crawl into bed with the friend's
young wife. Quinn's revenge is to have Costner beaten nearly to
death, his cabin burned, and his dog killed. The wife is not so
lucky. Her face is mutilated, she is injected with drugs, and she is
left in a whorehouse with instructions from Quinn to the madam
to let everyone have her. Despite these bursts of action, the film
is boring, a waste of good talent.

Costner's Vietnam service plays a minor role. He admits that
he was married more to jets than to his wife, and that was what
led to divorce. Apparently Vietnam turned him against warfare, at
least until he decides to seek revenge against Quinn. Costner explains his feeling against killing in an insipid story about being ordered to destroy an elephant that was reportedly carrying supplies
for the VC. With misting eyes, Costner relates that to credit the
kill he painted a small elephant on his plane's fuselage. More per-
plexing for the viewer, however, is figuring out how Costner can
afford such a nice cabin on a navy aviator's pay. [TV]

Riders of the Storm (1986-Great Britain) **D:** Maurice Phillips, 92m.
(OT: *The American Way*). Dennis Hopper, Michael J. Pollard, Eugene Lipinski, Nigel Pegram, James Aubrey.

** A group of Vietnam psychological-warfare veterans keeps a
forty-year-old bomber, complete with TV transmitter and jamming
devices, airborne to stop the presidential campaign of a right-wing
woman candidate, to prevent future wars, and, generally, to have
fun. Hopper and crew accent their conversations with a lot of
"mans," smoke much dope, and wear T-shirts with slogans such as
"I wish I was deep instead of macho." Although they are few and
far between, the movie has its moments. It would have been better more deep and less macho.

Vietnam is referred to as a "sick fucking war." Just how the
crew has kept the plane in the air for more than a decade after
the end of the war is neither explained nor explainable. Every
stereotype of crazy, dope-smoking, paranoid Vietnam vet is included in the crew. And, by the way, the fact that the female candidate for president is a man in drag is obvious from the first
scenes, which spoils the "surprise" ending. This throwback to the

protest movies of the sixties is much more a throwback than a keeper. 📺

Rogue's Regiment (1948) **D:** Robert Florey, 86m. Dick Powell, Vincent Price, Marta Toren, Stephen McNally, Edgar Barrier.

** An American intelligence officer (Powell) enlists in the French foreign legion in Indochina in order to track down a Nazi war criminal. McNally plays Martin Bruner, who is obviously based on the highest-ranking German leader to escape justice, Martin Borman. Powell gets his man, and as McNally goes to his death, a narrator says, "The last steps of Martin Bruner upon that scaffold are a warning to the world that such men must not march again. There is no other road to justice and mankind's dream for a lasting peace."

\#\# The most interesting aspect of this otherwise routine action film is what goes on in the background. Frequent skirmishes occur between the legionnaires and the "Indochinese revolutionaries" who would soon become better known as the Vietminh. The film is unclear as to why the "natives" are rebelling, but references are made to food shortages and the desire to vote. No military objectives are directly mentioned, but one French colonel on a train en route to Saigon complains about those who are selling arms to the guerrillas. A fellow passenger responds, "The people of Indochina are fighting only because they are tired of French injustice and misrule." The colonel angrily replies, "No, there are only two marching songs in the world today—the 'Internationale,' which may be theirs, and 'La Marseillaise,' which will always be ours!" Although Universal Pictures certainly had no idea of the future role of Vietnam/Indochina in world affairs, it is interesting to note that their publicity copy for the film carried the banner "Adventure flames in the world's hot-spot of danger and intrigue." Saigon is reproduced with much bamboo furniture and wickerwork against a background of hillsides that are obviously in southern California.

Rolling Thunder (1977) **D:** John Flynn, 123m. William Devane, Tommy Lee Jones, Linda Haynes, Dabney Coleman, Lisa Richards.

** After eight years as a POW, Devane returns to Texas only to very shortly see his wife and son killed and to have his own hand cut off in a garbage disposal by thugs who are after the money presented him as a welcome-home gift. Equipped with a sharpened hook in place of his hand and accompanied by a former POW friend, Devane tracks the gang to Mexico, where he exacts his revenge. If you like bloody shoot-outs in Mexican whorehouses, this one is for you; otherwise skip it.

When Devane returns home from his long captivity to learn his wife has been sleeping with another man, he shrugs and says, "I knew; we [POWs] all knew. It couldn't be any other way." The former POWs are treated as heroes, albeit naive and dumb ones. One of the killer gang is also a Vietnam veteran who admits as he kills Devane's family that he really doesn't like officers. Devane also has the usual flashbacks of torture in Vietnam—especially before and during the killing of his tormentors. From the lack of detail and incorrect uniform decorations, it is obvious without looking at the credits that no military adviser was on the production staff. [TV]

R.P.M. (1970) **D:** Stanley Kramer, 92m. Anthony Quinn, Ann-Margret, Gary Lockwood, Paul Winfield, Graham Jarvis.

* With student approval, a liberal professor (Quinn) is selected to replace an ousted college president. When Quinn fails to meet all of the students' demands and they threaten to destroy a multimillion dollar computer, he calls in the cops. Quinn's graduate-student lover (Ann-Margret) has the film's best line, asking him, "Tell me, what did you do for sex . . . before you were published?" The rest of the movie is about as original as the "revolutions per minute" (R.P.M.) title. It's unlikely that director Kramer would list this one alongside his *Guess Who's Coming to Dinner* and *Judgment at Nuremberg*.

Vietnam and the draft are only two of many targets of the students' protest. According to the film, the school administrators, the police, and just about every other branch of "authority" are totally incorrect and the students are without wrong. The only accomplishment of this film is to make the viewer wonder why students were so coddled in the sixties.

Ruckus (1982) **D:** Max Kleven, 91m. Dirk Benedict, Linda Blair, Ben Johnson, Matt Clark, Richard Farnsworth.

* A Vietnam-veteran escapee from a military psycho ward takes

on a town of red-necks and leads them on a chase by foot, motorcycle, pickup truck, and boat. It's similar to the later *First Blood*,
except *Ruckus* is billed as comedy and is *not* funny while *First
Blood* is billed as drama and *is* funny. Good music by Janie Fricke,
Willie Nelson, and Hank Cochran is featured.

 # Benedict, as the vet, is filthy, wears a field jacket, has not spoken for fourteen months, eats raw hamburger, and sleeps in trees.
He is described as a "weirdo," a "crazy man," and a "damn jungle
freak" by citizens and law-enforcement officials alike. 📺

Rumor of War, A (1980) TVM, **D:** Richard T. Heffron, 200m. Brad
Davis, Keith Carradine, Brian Dennehy, Michael O'Keefe, Richard Bradford.

 *** Philip Caputo (Davis) joins the Marine Corps because of his
love of country, respect for John Kennedy, and desire to win a Silver Star like his hometown-hero bartender. By the end of his tour
in Vietnam, Caputo is disillusioned, embittered, and facing a
court-martial for murdering Vietnamese civilians. In between, this
lengthy film, originally made as a two-part television movie, shows
the brutal Marine Corps training and the complexities of the Vietnam War that changed the young Caputo. Based on Caputo's
best-selling memoir and adapted by John Secret Young ("China
Beach"), this was one of television's first major productions about
the Vietnam War.

 ## Although a much-preferred film would be one about a
gung-ho lieutenant who does *not* murder noncombatants, this
movie does have its positive points. Air assaults by helicopter,
clearing and diagraming fields of fire in defense positions, the dangers of heat stroke, difficulties with terrain and weather, the use of
artillery, and making radio reports are all well done. Dennehy does
a great job playing a Marine NCO—despite his pudginess. Regardless of the good detailing, the portrayal of senior officers as foolish
martinets and the inability of most of the actors to portray believable Marines are obvious failings. More important, apparently
Caputo and the director prefer to place the blame for the war
crimes on the Marine Corps's training methods and its way of
conducting the war rather than on the lack of restraint and leadership displayed by Caputo. Despite themselves, Caputo and the
director counter this argument through the platoon sergeant who
states that he will tell the truth about what occurred. The NCO

tells Caputo that "what went down out there" was the lieutenant's fault and that "you should never have let it happen." USMC technical advisers keep the uniforms and language reasonably accurate, and the Mexico shooting locations resemble Vietnam. 📺

Running on Empty (1988) **D:** Sidney Lumet, 117m. Christine Lahti, River Phoenix, Judd Hirsch, Jonas Abry, Martha Plimpton.
  ** Lahti and Hirsch play sixties radicals who have been on the run for fourteen years after bombing a university military research lab, which resulted in the blinding and crippling of a janitor. Always just a step ahead of the feds, they and their two sons, who are taught to question authority, are constantly on the run from feared fifteen-year prison sentences. The older son, played by Phoenix, is tiring of the fugitive existence and wants to "drop back in" and go to college and study the piano. His girlfriend, played well by Plimpton, asks him, "Why do you have to carry the burden of someone else's life?" The film ends up being more about Phoenix than about his parents. Good acting all around and an Oscar nomination for Phoenix.
  # Hirsch explains the bombing of the lab, which was developing napalm for Vietnam, as "an act of conscience to stop the war." Throughout the film, the couple on the run is treated as the film's heroes and the federal law-enforcement officials as the villains behind dark glasses. Even while dodging the law, Hirsch is able to assist in the organization of a food co-op and a protest against a toxic waste dump. He also tells his son, "Go out there and make a difference. Your mother and I tried." Along with listening to sixties music, Hirsch fondly recalls a "good" LSD trip. Interestingly, the underground is shown as still active, and it provides Hirsch and Lahti with a new car and money on each move—much more, of course, than the feds are providing the real veterans of the Vietnam War. 📺

Russkies (1987) **D:** Rick Rosenthal, 100m. Whip Hubley, Leaf Phoenix, Peter Billingsley, Stefan DeSalle, Susan Walters.
  *1/2 A Soviet sailor washed up on a Florida beach is treated to apple pie, baseball, and video games by three young boys. Before the sailor is rescued by a Russian submarine, he manages to attend a Fourth of July celebration, fall in love with the sister of one of the boys, reunite a divorced couple, and generally bring sun-

shine and happiness everywhere he goes. This one should have a sugar-content warning on its label.

The sailor and one of the kids have an argument about Afghanistan, Vietnam, and Soviet world domination. Another of the boys is the son of a Marine Vietnam veteran who, divorced, sits in his uniform drinking in the dark. [TV]

Saigon (1948) **D:** Leslie Fenton, 94m. Alan Ladd, Veronica Lake, Luther Adler, Wally Cassell, Douglas Dick.

** Two World War II buddies (Ladd and Cassell) take a fellow aviator (Dick), who only has a short time to live due to crash injuries, on one last fling. They inadvertently get involved in the black market, a half-million dollars in war-profiteering spoils, a beautiful woman (Lake), and Indochina when they crash-land into a Vietnamese rice paddy. After much action, intrigue, and pulp-fiction dialogue, Ladd and Lake end up together (as they did in a series of 1940s films). Ladd plays his usual tough guy—often atop a box to make up for his short stature—and snarls such lines to a bartender as, "Bourbon, straight; leave the bottle."

Except for its advertising subtitle, "The Paris of the East," this is a routine action film that reveals little about its namesake. Although at least five pictures set in Indochina preceded it, this movie is often incorrectly credited with being the first film about Vietnam.

Saigon Commandos (1987) **D:** Clark Henderson, 84m. P. J. Soles, John Allen Nelson, Joonee Gamboa, Richard Young.

* Corrupt Saigon officials dispatch assassins to kill monks, nuns, children, and American servicemen. Their aim: to start an anti-U.S. rebellion to cover the drug operations that finance their government. A rogue American military policeman strikes back by killing politicians while other MPs attempt to neutralize both sides. This is a cheap imitation of various cops-and-robbers B flicks.

Little mention is made of the VC and NVA. The message is that the real enemy is the South Vietnamese government and its U.S. supporters. South Vietnamese protesters compete with hordes of drug-dealing American deserters for Saigon street space. The MP officers, identified as West Pointers, are reluctant warriors who are pushed around and/or ignored by their enlisted sub-

ordinates. In early scenes, watch for uniform decorations and badges to change places from shot to shot. Apparently the costume designer knew they were wrong and kept trying to get them right. He didn't. If the locations and actors do not look like Vietnam and the Vietnamese, there is good reason: The film was shot in the Philippines, and all the Vietnamese roles are played by Filipinos. [TV]

Satan's Sadists (1969) **D:** Al Adamson, 86m. Russ Tamblyn, Scott Brady, Kent Taylor, John Cardos, Robert Dix.

* Members of an outlaw motorcycle gang rob, rape, and kill across the Southwest until they meet their match in a hitchhiking Vietnam veteran. Violence for violence's sake is the picture's only apparent purpose. At the time of its 1969 release, its advertising campaign attempted to capitalize on the plot's supposed similarities to the Manson family murders of Sharon Tate and friends. The only item the two really have in common is a needless, bloody body count.

\# The veteran is a proficient killer whose only good trait is that he selects lowlifes for his vengeance. He uses various lethal means including drowning a biker in a toilet bowl, throwing a rattlesnake around the neck of another, and thrusting a knife into the throat of a third. During this film's production in 1969, Vietnam vets were still considered slightly better than outlaw bikers. That would change before long.

Savage Dawn (1985) **D:** Simon Nutchern, 102m. George Kennedy, Richard Lynch, Karen Black, Lance Henricksen, Claudia Udy.

* Two Vietnam veterans defend a desert mining town against a gang of bikers. All three of the leads (Kennedy, Lynch, and Black) are much too old for this type of action role.

\# One of the vets explains that he destroyed a lot of towns in Vietnam during the war and now he wants to help defend one. To add to the Vietnam theme, the town is populated by a large number of Vietnamese, many of whom still dress in typical Southeast Asian fashion. No explanation is given as to why they are living in such a remote site in the United States. [TV]

Search and Destroy (1981) **D:** William Fruet, 93m. Perry King, Tisa Farrow, Don Stroud, Park Jong Soo, George Kennedy.

*1/2 Four survivors of a Vietnam jungle patrol are tracked down ten years later in the United States by a Vietnamese they left behind on one of their missions. The only interesting feature of this "action" film, which has little action, is its Niagara Falls setting, although it does offer meager originality in its twist on the theme of war following veterans home. In this case, the villain is not flashbacks and bad dreams but rather a martial-arts-trained killer known only as "the Assassin."

Vietnam scenes were filmed near Buffalo, New York, and look it. Uniforms are a mixture ranging from World War II to Vietnam and make as much sense as soldiers remaining standing in the midst of an ambush. The local police chief (Kennedy) describes one of the veterans (King) as knowing "eighty-two thousand ways to kill you; his friend knows eighty-thousand more." King's character, who wears the inevitable field jacket, offers this self-analysis: "I've always had a great future. It's just my present that's screwed up." It is the police chief who makes the most pithy statement when he comments on the Assassin's tenacity: "Seems to be a common mistake of underestimating the Vietnamese." [TV]

Shooter (1988) TVM, D: Gary Nelson, 96m. Jeffrey Nordling, Alan Ruck, Noble Willingham, Carol Huston, Rosalind Chao, Steven Ford.

* Two press photographers trade quips, romance nurses, and try to capture the one photo that will depict the Vietnam War. This film, remarkably similar to *Good Morning, Vietnam*, including subplots, follows a macho tack: "It's our job to almost get killed." Humor is black, when included at all, as in a conversation about a soldier who was still receiving American Express bills six months after his death. One of the witty photogs responds, "Yeah, the land mine really screwed up his credit rating." The only remarkable part is the manner in which the pictures they take go to freeze frame and fade to black and white. This was originally made as a pilot for a television series that was not picked up by the networks. To see it is to understand why.

Considering it was created by real-life Pulitzer Prize–winning Vietnam cameraman David Hume Kennedy and the production was assisted by several experts on Southeast Asia, this picture is a real disappointment. Unfortunately, it simply is not very well done—even if the usual correspondent's question at a Vietnam

press conference about the army's cover-up of friendly casualties is not as enthusiastic as the genre's norm. A little better is the effort to re-create Saigon street scenes in Thailand locations. Better yet, even if a bit exploitative, is the dedication at the end which accurately lists the thirty-four photographers killed in the war. Included on the list is the renowned Robert Capa, who did get *the* shot of the Spanish Civil War (one of the few photographs ever made of a man actually being killed in combat) only to die in Vietnam on May 25, 1954.

Siege of Fire Base Gloria, The (1988-Australia) D: Brian Trenchard-Smith, 95m. Wings Hauser, Lee Ermey, Robert Arevala, Mark Neely, Gary Hershberger.

** A Marine patrol assists an army fire base filled with nurses, drunks, and druggies that is surrounded by Vietcong during the Tet Offensive of 1968. The patrol's leader (Ermey) narrates, using lines such as "It really hurt us to see their heads on stakes" when viewing a village destroyed by the VC. With the exception of the depiction of the day-to-day life of the VC in the jungle, the film is just as bad as the dialogue.

The army captain in charge of the fire base hides naked in his bunker reading *Playboy*, smoking dope, and worrying about ice cream. His first sergeant goes outside the wire on one-man patrols. No ones seems to be in charge until Ermey and his five-man patrol arrive. Just why a Marine sergeant major is leading a small recon element is not explained. The portrayal of the VC is much more accurate. Their campaign of terror against civilian and military alike is explicitly shown. Ermey's character observes, "I guess we'd do the same if Charlie occupied South Carolina." Opening the film is excellent actual footage of NVA units infiltrating on the Ho Chi Minh Trail. This authenticity carries over to the film's version of the VC's need to constantly move and dig to protect themselves from Allied air power and ground operations. The VC attack on the fire base is particularly noteworthy. With the division of the VC into three groups—a diversionary attack team, an assault group complete with ladders for breaching barbed wire, and a support group firing mortars—the attack (except for its daytime execution) is extremely close to actual VC offensive doctrine. Also shown is the VC functional chain of command and leaders who are compassionate toward their men. Most interesting is the

VC commander at film's end. As he walks among the hordes of his dead, he remarks to his deputy that Hanoi had said that Tet would be the beginning of the end of the Americans but that it could have also said it would be the end of the VC (accurate in that the Vietcong were never an effective fighting force after their Tet losses, and the NVA took over the bulk of the communist war effort). The VC commander concludes that this may very well have been Hanoi's objective to begin with. The movie was filmed in the Philippines and edited in Australia. TV

'68 (1988) **D:** Steven Kovacks, 99m. Eric Larson, Robert Locke, Neil Young, Sandor Tecsi, Mirlan Kwun, Anna Dukasz.

* A Hungarian refugee family faces the generation gap, the Vietnam War, and the cultural turmoil of 1968 in San Francisco. Through the use of actual radio and television newscasts, the film presents virtually every major news event of the title year as a backdrop to two brothers' confronting the issues and the draft. In addition to the war, scenes of the deaths of Martin Luther King and Bobby Kennedy are included, along with the Soviet invasion of Czechoslovakia, student protests, gay rights demonstrations, draft induction-center procedures, and the prominent role in the era of VW minibuses. The most ludicrous part is a Hungarian gypsy and his daughter joining a country-and-western band. Low budget, low results—the year was much more interesting than its namesake movie.

While 1968 is shown to have had many faults, the greatest evils of the year and of the age were the war in Vietnam and the threat of the draft. U.S. efforts in the war zone are compared to the U.S.S.R.'s actions in Czechoslovakia. One brother is so scared of the draft that he claims to be a homosexual and kisses a major at the induction center to prove it. He justifies his conduct by whining that he fears he will not return if he goes to Vietnam. TV

Slaughter (1972) **D:** Jack Starrett, 92m. Jim Brown, Stella Stevens, Rip Torn, Don Gordon, Cameron Mitchell.

* A former Green Beret captain (Brown) returns from Vietnam to seek revenge on the mobsters who killed his parents. This is typical of the era's blaxploitation flicks. Brown's acting abilities nowhere near match his feats on the gridiron.

Vietnam plays no role except as a brief explanation of Brown's

past. The reason for the war's inclusion in the film is best explained by a line from the movie itself, wherein a reporter remarks to Brown, "You're a Green Beret hero and you're black. That's good copy." Interestingly, the sequel, *Slaughter's Big Rip-Off* (1973), notes Brown's previous adventures against the mob and dwells at length on his sexual and fighting powers. No mention, however, is made of his service in Vietnam. Perhaps this was new director Gordon Douglas's idea, or maybe being a veteran was no longer "good copy." TV

Slaughterhouse Five (1972) **D**: George Roy Hill, 104m. Michael Sacks, Ron Liebman, Eugene Roche, Sharon Gans, Valerie Perrine, Perry King.

*** Billy Pilgrim (Sacks) has become "unstuck" in time; his mind reverts back to his childhood, World War II Dresden, and his marriage, and forward to the future with a sex goddess on a faraway planet. Deeply dramatic at times and funny at others, this film rings true to Kurt Vonnegut's best-selling novel—or at least comes as close as the material allows.

\# In extremely brief scenes, Pilgrim's son Robert appears. Initially, he is long-haired, belligerent, and a vandalizer of graveyards. In his last appearance, he arrives home from Vietnam a Green Beret sergeant first class (a rank that, outside of movies, usually takes eight to twelve years to attain and can't be achieved on one's first enlistment), proud to have done "the right thing" and spouting anticommunist rhetoric. Of course, the transition from worthless son to Vietnam War hero is just another of Vonnegut's ventures into the outrageous. TV

Small Circle of Friends, A (1980) **D**: Rob Cohen, 112m. Brad Davis, Karen Allen, Jameson Parker, John Friedrich, Shelley Long, Gary Springer.

** Two college roommates share a girl as a friend and as a lover at different and the same times during the turmoil of the 1960s and early 1970s. The draft lottery of 1970—"Vietnam bingo"—reduces low-number students who expound "taking a chance" to whiners who will do anything to flunk their induction physicals. This is a formulistic antidraft, antiwar, anti-LBJ, antiauthority, antieverything 1960s film which is unusual only because of the

ménage à trois and its production ten years after the genre had
gone to a well-deserved end.

The three students end up a doctor, a lawyer, and a journalist.
No report is given as to what happened to the unnamed young
man who had to take the place in Vietnam of the draft dodger
who faked a medical condition. Both the male leads are so wimpy
that the audience will agree with a student who says the girlfriend
"has more balls than all the guys at Harvard put together."
Induction-center scenes are off the mark by a wide margin. One
can but wonder as to where the prop man dug out the military police uniforms that appear to be a cross between khakis and
fatigues. 📺

Sneakers (1992) **D:** Phil Alden Robinson, 125m. Robert Redford,
Dan Aykroyd, Ben Kingsley, Mary McDonnell, River Phoenix, Sidney Poitier.

** A team of technowizards work for various organizations "to
break into their places to make sure no one can break into their
places." When they become involved with the NSA, CIA, FBI, and
various other private or foreign agencies over the theft of the ultimate code-breaking machine, they must do their best work
merely to survive. Interesting gadgets, plot twists, and an all-star
cast do not keep this movie from being a half-hour too long.

The film opens in 1969 with Redford's and Kingsley's charac-
ters as pioneer computer hackers breaking into various defense
and political files to protest against and interfere with the Vietnam War. Redford later explains, "We were young; there was a war
on; it was a good way to meet girls." 📺

Soldier's Revenge (1986) **D:** David Worth, 92m. John Savage, Maria Socas, Frank Cane, Paul Lambert, Edgardo Moriera.

* Savage plays the role of a man who returns to his small Texas
hometown branded a traitor for refusing to fly bombing missions
in Vietnam. He quickly becomes involved with Central American
gun runners despite his new pacifism. "No one can convince me
war can be won by anyone," he says. "War is hell on everybody.
Never again." Yet here he is back in combat—this time fighting
because of his love for the daughter of a kidnapped politician.

Contradictions extend far beyond the primary story line. Sav-
age's character is identified as an Army Special Forces team leader

sent on a "difficult mission" by a general whose uniform appears to have been assembled in the dark—practically no decoration or badge is in its proper place. The next scene has Savage parachuting in *pilot's* uniform from a shot-down fighter, witness to the village, women, and children he has, just minutes before, destroyed with bombs. No doubt the Air Force would be quite surprised to learn that a Green Beret was flying one of its planes, but no explanation is offered. Despite Savage's claimed pacifism, he seems more than willing during the remainder of the film to fight the red-necks back home who call him a coward. He shows more zeal in killing hordes of guerrillas in Central America, but a postscript at film's end assures the viewer, "The bravest soldiers are those who seek to understand the enemy." Only a brave viewer would seek to understand this movie and see it to its end. 📺

Some Kind of Hero (1982) **D:** Michael Pressman, 97m. Richard Pryor, Margot Kidder, Ray Sharkey, Lynne Moody, Ronny Cox.
** Pryor's character is captured, literally with his pants down, on his first day in the field in Vietnam. After years as a POW, he returns to the States to find his money spent, his wife with another man, his mother in the hospital with a stroke, and the army harassing him about having signed confessions in prison. None of this comes off very well—especially the parts that are supposed to be funny. Despite Pryor's best efforts, this movie produces little laughter. Of course, the same could be said about the war.
# Typical lines include Pryor's saying, "Neither the army nor my wife gives a fuck about me." A bar patron asks the uniformed Pryor, "Did you lose the war because you smoked too much grass?" Pryor's prison cell and living conditions are fairly accurately depicted, but "Vietnam" exterior shots are strictly southern California. 📺

Some May Live (1967-Great Britain) **D:** Vernon Sewell, 105m (OT: *In Saigon, Some May Live*). Joseph Cotten, Martha Hyer, Peter Cushing, John Ronane, Alec Mango.
* An American intelligence officer stationed in Saigon tries to uncover a communist spy within his organization. The movie's only selling point is a big-name, over-the-hill star (Cotten) in the lead role.
# Except for its setting and reference to communist spies, there

really is little relation between this picture and the war in Vietnam. Any background as to the "whys" or "whats" of the conflict is trivialized or not mentioned at all. The picture's most remarkable attribute is its 1967 production date, which makes it one of the first films about American involvement in the war—even if it was produced by the British.

Somewhere I'll Find You (1942) **D:** Wesley Ruggles, 108m. Clark Gable, Lana Turner, Robert Sterling, Reginald Owen, Lee Patrick.

*** Gable and Sterling play war-correspondent brothers competing for the best news story and the love of fellow correspondent Turner. The trio flirt and fight from New York to Hanoi and from Manila to Bataan. Gable and Turner are at their sexiest and burn up the screen. The film concludes with Gable dictating a flag-waving story to his newspaper by telephone, emphasizing that the only desire of the American heroes on Bataan is to have their names spelled correctly. The final shot is a trailer promising Tokyo "more to come." Filming was delayed when Gable's wife, Carol Lombard, was killed in a plane crash during a bond drive she was supporting. After the film, Gable joined the Army Air Corps and made no more movies until the war's conclusion.

\# Early in the film, all three correspondents travel to Hanoi to report on the Japanese occupation of Vietnam. Turner takes time away from her writing to assist Vietnamese children escaping across the "frontier" into China. Indochina is referred to by the three as "a good opportunity," "a long way off," and "dynamite." Actually, the entire movie was filmed in the studio and back lots of MGM in Hollywood.

Special Delivery (1976) **D:** Paul Wendkos, 99m. Cybill Shepherd, Bo Svenson, Michael Gwynne, Tom Atkins, Jeff Goldblum.

**1/2 Four Marine Vietnam War veterans rob a bank but only one (Svenson) escapes, and he is forced to hide the loot in a mailbox. He is observed by a strange artist running from a divorce (Shepherd) and a junkie bartender with connections to the Chinese Mafia. Svenson, with Shepherd's help, must figure out how to recover the ill-gotten gains before the police, gangsters, or the mailman beats him to the cash. Action and comedy are equally good, and Shepherd is excellent and beautiful as the strange artist.

\# The vets originally claim they are robbing the bank because the bankers and politicians have been glorifying the war, but Svenson eventually admits, "We did it for the money." During the robbery and escape, Svenson has flashbacks to Vietnam. Of the four vets, only one has a job, and it is part-time—other than robbing banks, which is also part-time. Only one of the robbers refers to any family ties—his former wife, who works in a massage parlor where much more than a back rub is provided. [TV]

Splash (1984) **D**: Ron Howard, 109m. Tom Hanks, Daryl Hannah, John Candy, Eugene Levy, Dody Goodman.

*** A vegetable merchant (Hanks) falls in love with a mermaid who is being pursued by a scientist and the military. It is unclear what the latter two want with mermaid Hannah, but there is no doubt why Hanks is interested. The wistful Hannah is beautiful, humorous, and convincing as a half-fish out of water.

\# Although there seems to be absolutely no reason to involve Vietnam in this cute, feel-good film, Howard and the writers still find a need to work in the tired stereotypes of the crazy veteran. When Hanks suddenly runs away after a phone call during a meeting with a "former Green Beret" who is the produce purchaser for a chain of supermarkets, his brother (Candy) explains his behavior as a result of being wounded in Vietnam when a grenade went off *in* his helmet. Hanks is still troubled by ringing telephones, Candy adds. [TV]

Steele Justice (1987) **D**: Robert Boris, 96m. Martin Kove, Sela Ward, Ronny Cox, Bernie Casey, Soon-Teck Oh, Robert Kim.

* Two soldiers on a mission to recover twenty million dollars in CIA gold in Vietnam are double-crossed and left for dead by their ARVN counterpart and American officer commander. After the war, the two soldiers seek revenge against their betrayers, who are now running an Asian Mafia drug ring in San Diego. The quality of action and realism are typified by the rat sent on a suicide mission with a hand grenade tied to its back and by the poisonous snake one of the vets wears like a necklace. Although not intentional, this film is funnier than most comedies.

\# The central character, John Steele, is a divorced hard drinker, usually unemployed, who wears a snake as jewelry. He says about Vietnam, "Nothing seems right since then, nothing at all." His former wife tells him, "The war is not over for you; it just changed locations." Perhaps the firefight (complete with poison darts!) in a luxury hotel lobby full of jungle ferns and plants is supposed to represent a new location. Vietnam scenes include a two-man patrol with no communications, a female soldier wearing the uniform of the U.S. Second Infantry Division (which was in Korea at the time), and operations in "Chu Chi Province" (in reality, Chu Chi is a Vietnamese *city* rather than a province). 📺

Stigma (1972) **D:** David E. Durston, 93m. Philip M. Thomas, Harlan Cary Poe, Josie Johnson, Peter H. Clune, Connie Van Ess.

* A young black doctor fights prejudice and venereal disease on a remote island. The movie is as ugly as the pictures shown of patients with advanced syphilis. This is one of Thomas's earlier roles. He later restored his full middle name of Michael and went on to fame on television's "Miami Vice."

On the way to the island, the doctor meets a newly discharged Vietnam veteran. The vet is met at the ferry landing by a huge, loving family, and he continues to be a "good guy" for the remainder of the film. However, in the vet's first appearance, with his extremely long hair and wearing a uniform with mismatched awards and decorations, he little resembles a soldier. 📺

Stone Killer, The (1973) **D:** Michael Winner, 95m. Charles Bronson, Martin Balsam, Norman Fell, David Sheiner, Ralph Waite.

** A mob boss plans to kill other underworld bosses with an army of Vietnam veterans doing the dirty work. Bronson plays a shoot-first-and-ask-questions-later cop out to stop the killings in his usual violent manner.

No Vietnam footage is included, but this film provides an answer to those who say combat infantrymen have no job skills. They do in this movie—albeit violent ones. According to a police psychologist in the movie, "Vietnam does not make heroes, it makes psychopaths." About vets, he continues, "Aggression and violence are a part of a learning process. They are habit forming." 📺

Stranger on My Land (1988) TVM, **D:** Larry Elikann, 100m. Tommy Lee Jones, Ben Johnson, Dee Wallace Stone, Pat Hingle, Terry O'Quinn.

* A Vietnam veteran (Jones) fights to keep the government from taking away his ranch for use as an air force missile base. This one drips with the sentimentality of "I was born here, my father was born here, and my grandfather was the original homesteader." Listen for such lines as "How many more missiles do they need? How many more ranches are they going to take?" This is an overused plot, and this presentation is below average at best.

The picture opens with Jones and fellow Marines destroying a Vietnamese village and moving its occupants to a new hamlet despite the lamentations of an old man about his family having lived there for a thousand years and about his ancestors being buried there. Jones faces the same situation a decade later; again the villain is the United States government. The oddity for a Vietnam-oriented film is that although Jones is extremely stubborn, he is not crazy. He also has a loving wife, who is a nurse veteran of the war, and well-adjusted children. 🖵

Strawberry Statement, The (1970) **D:** Stuart Hagmann, 103m. Kim Darby, Bob Balaban, Bruce Davison, James Kunen, Bud Cort.

* Students at Columbia University take over the administration building to protest the Vietnam War and the construction of an ROTC building on the site of a former park for poor black children. It is difficult to determine if the film is attempting to deliver social commentary, comedy, or music. As for the students, they seem much more interested in sex and fun than in making a statement of any flavor.

The U.S. government and military are frequently referred to as baby killers and village burners. National Guard troops brought in to clear the protesters are shown assaulting the students as they run over a sidewalk inscription of "Truth, Justice, Tolerance." 🖵

Streamers (1983) **D:** Robert Altman, 118m. Matthew Modine, Michael Wright, David Alan Grier, Mitchell Lichtenstein, Guy Boyd.

*** Two veteran NCOs and four young, rookie privates spend a few days in a barracks pending orders for Vietnam. Waiting for combat proves as dangerous as the war as the group experiences problems with alcohol, manhood, racial strife, and death. Little is changed from David Rabe's play, a barracks interior offering the film's only set. Despite a deeply depressing story, excellent acting by all makes it a quality movie.

The two sergeants are drunk for most of the film; they talk of killing gooks in Korea and Vietnam and tell a lot of stories about parachutes that didn't open (streamers). Neither of the NCOs makes any attempt to demonstrate leadership in the barracks, and, indeed, no chain of command is apparent until blood and death have taken over. The film supposedly takes place at a base near Washington, D.C., and the drill team (which opens and closes the movie and represents the automation of the military) wears helmets with "101" on their sides. Actually the picture was filmed entirely in a Dallas warehouse, with Sam Houston State University in Huntsville, Texas, supplying its ROTC drill team. Altman also directed *M*A*S*H*. 📺

Street Trash (1987) D: Jim Muro, 91m. Bill Chepil, Mike Lackey, Vic Noto, Mark Sferrazza, Jane Arakawa.

* Street bums living in a Brooklyn auto-wrecking yard fight, rape, and kill each other and innocents who cross their path. Adding to the neighborhood's problems is a bad batch of wine that causes bones to dissolve and flesh to melt. Slick technical effects do not make up for a plotless, gruesome, disgusting film.

The leader of the junkyard bums is a Vietnam veteran who carries a knife with a human-bone handle. He laughs uncontrollably when talking about "killing gooks in Nam." When he breaks his knife while killing a policeman, he urinates on the cop's body and then cuts out a leg bone for a new handle. 📺

Strike Commando (1987) D: Vincent Dawn, 92m. Reb Brown, Christopher Connelly, Loes Kamma, Alan Collins, Alex Vitale.

* A soldier (Brown) goes on a one-man mission to gather proof that Russian advisers are assisting the Vietcong. His efforts are hindered by his American colonel commander, who is himself a member of the Soviet KGB and is supplying prisoners to the communists. In addition to the usual POW torture scenes of beatings and electric shock treatments, this film adds burning with a blowtorch. Typical dialogue includes "What are these fly faces doing here?" and "Are you looking for me, Americanski?" Another line informs us, "This goddamn war gets worse and worse." So does the movie. As the credits finally begin to roll, Brown states, "Any similarity between persons living or dead, especially dead, is purely coincidental—like one in a million, maybe."

Most appropriately, Brown and colleagues are reported to be members of "special services" instead of Special Forces. Apparently the writers and director did not know the difference between Green Berets and those special-service personnel who run the clubs and provide entertainment for the troops. The "commandos" do wear berets of various colors, with some sporting MACV patches instead of unit crests or rank. Other uniforms and decorations are equally ridiculous. 🖵

Stripes (1981) **D:** Ivan Reitman, 105m. Bill Murray, Harold Ramis, Warren Oates, P. J. Soles, Sean Young, John Candy, John Larroquette.

** A young man (Murray) who spent his childhood in various institutions loses his job, car, apartment, and girlfriend within a period of two hours. He then convinces a buddy to join the army with him. After a basic-training sequence reminiscent of World War II films, the two misfit soldiers manage to rescue their commander from behind the iron curtain in a highly explosive but bloodless fight. This is one of the all-time worst top-grossing films.

Although set in the all-volunteer post-Vietnam army, all the recruiting and drill sergeants wear combat patches and decorations on their uniforms. Murray, in an attempt to pick up a military policewoman, asks her if she is the one who saved his life in Vietnam. He later brags of being an American soldier in an army with a record of ten and one—the one loss, of course, being Vietnam. The oddest thing about this film—among many oddities—is that it was one of the first after the end of the war in Southeast Asia to receive Department of Defense assistance and support, including authorization to film Fort Knox and the Kentucky National Guard. Surely some DoD public affairs officer's career came to an abrupt halt when this one hit the local post theater. 🖵

Stunt Man, The (1980) **D:** Richard Rush, 100m. Peter O'Toole, Steve Railsback, Barbara Hershey, Chuck Bail, Adam Roarke.

**** A Vietnam veteran (Railsback) on the run from the law stumbles onto a World War I movie set and lands the job of lead stunt man under a weird and dominating director (O'Toole). As for his job qualifications, Railsback explains, "I got out of Nam in one piece. That's a hell of a stunt." His chances of surviving the movie production may not be so positive because nothing is what it

seems to be at first glance or, often, at second. Funny, complicated, and exciting, this outrageous film is best seen on video so
the viewer can rewind again and again to thoroughly understand
and appreciate all the action, hidden gags, and double meanings.
Director Rush worked on this project for nearly a decade and then
took two more years to get it released. It may very well be one of
the best pictures ever seen by a very few people.

Vietnam plays a minor role on the surface but is, in fact, an
essential focus. O'Toole's character is obsessed with making the
ultimate antiwar film, and Railsback's character is "used" as a
stunt man in a manner similar to the way he was "used" as a soldier in Vietnam. The exact symbolism of a dog sitting in the middle of a road licking its genitals is up to each viewer's own
interpretation. With his long hair, beard, and wild eyes, Railsback
resembles mass-murder cult leader Charles Manson. Although he
is confused by flashbacks throughout much of the film, he ultimately survives and copes. TV

Summer Soldiers (1972-Japan) **D:** Hiroshi Teshigahara, 107m.
Keith Sykes, Lee Reisen, Kazuo Kitamura, Toshiko Kobayaski,
Shoichi Ozawa.

* Several American Vietnam War deserters seek sanctuary in Japan with the assistance of Japanese families. With little success,
the film attempts to show the innocence of youth, the horrors of
war, and the conflict between different cultures. Dialogue is a
mixture of English, Japanese, and subtitles.

The Japanese who help the deserters are portrayed as gentle,
kindhearted, peace-loving people. One of the American deserters
claims he abandoned his unit and fellow soldiers because a Vietcong prisoner was being brutalized and killed and "there was nothing I could do" to stop it.

Summertree (1971) **D:** Anthony Newley, 89m. Michael Douglas,
Jack Warden, Barbara Bel Geddes, Brenda Vaccaro, Kirk Callaway.

* Douglas portrays a young man who wants only to play his music, help other people, and romance Vaccaro. His desires are complicated a bit by the looming draft and by the fact that Vaccaro
has a Marine husband in Vietnam. Prevented from fleeing to Canada by his father (Warden), Douglas is drafted, and the movie's final scene is of his parents seeing their dead son in Vietnam flash

across the television evening news. Based on the highly acclaimed off-Broadway play by Ron Cowen, the story does not transfer well to the big screen.

Douglas's mother (Bel Geddes) argues with her husband in support of her son's plan to dodge the draft by going to Canada. She exclaims, "My father came to this country to avoid the draft in Poland." Douglas's only real conviction seems to be a self-centered avoidance of personal hardship or danger, yet the film fully supports him. At least Vaccaro leaves him when her husband returns from the war.

Sundays and Cybele (1962-France) **D:** Serge Bourguignon, 110m. Hardy Kruger, Nicole Courcel, Patricia Gozzi, Daniel Ivernel, Andre Oumansky.

*** A French pilot in the Indochina War returns home to a small town near Paris. He suffers amnesia induced by his having killed a young Vietnamese girl during a bombing raid. At home he wanders aimlessly until he meets a twelve-year-old girl at the local convent school. The nuns mistake the veteran for the child's father and allow the two to begin spending Sunday afternoons together, and they develop a warm friendship. Their relationship is viewed with suspicion by others, and the police are sent to investigate their park meetings. The police believe the vet intends to molest the girl, and they kill him. Although the subtitled film is slow and plods at times, the performances by all are outstanding, and the overall effort is worthy of its Academy Award for Best Foreign Language Film.

This picture may very well be the genesis of the "troubled vet having readjustment problems" genre of Vietnam movie. Many American films about the war would later follow an almost identical track. Also noteworthy is that the prologue is duplicated almost exactly in the introduction to Clint Eastwood's *Firefox* (1982). [TV]

Suppose They Gave a War and Nobody Came (1970) **D:** Hy Averback, 113m. (OT: *War Games*). Tony Curtis, Brian Keith, Ernest Borgnine, Suzanne Pleshette, Don Ameche.

**1/2 Three Vietnam veterans and their fellow soldiers at a remote Stateside missile base have trouble getting along with the police and red-necks in a nearby town. In this poorly titled film, much poignant satire of civilian-military relations, along with a great cast, make for good viewing. By the time the vets flatten the town jail with an armored vehicle, even the most feathered dove will cheer.

This is a strange Vietnam film. It is set during and was produced during the war. Vietnam maps adorn the base commander's wall, and the leading characters all wear uniform decorations documenting war service. Yet, only two direct references to the conflict are made. Keith's character mentions a "kid dying in my arms in Vietnam" and, on another occasion, explains a ribbon on his uniform as being from the French for advising their forces in Indochina in 1956 (an interesting error in itself, because France ceased operations in Southeast Asia after its defeat at Dien Bien Phu in 1954). The director apparently feared that too much mention of Vietnam would hurt the box-office receipts, and so he avoided the central theme of his own movie, leaving the viewer to scratch his head at just what the director was attempting to accomplish in content and title. Even so, all the ingredients are present for an intriguing look at how the military and civilians saw each other during the war. Despite the lack of direct mention of Vietnam, some of the dialogue stands sufficiently accurate without explanation. The post commander summarizes, "People in the community do not like us." A black NCO states, "I'm not embarrassed about being a soldier." His warrant officer friend replies, "You're a little embarrassed; we all are." [TV]

Suspect (1987) **D:** Peter Yates, 121m. Cher, Dennis Quaid, John Mahoney, Philip Bosco, Liam Neeson.

*** A dedicated public defender (Cher) takes the case of a deaf, mute, homeless Vietnam veteran facing murder charges in Washington, D.C. Quaid plays a juror who helps find the real killer while romancing Cher. A bit—perhaps more than a bit—farfetched, it nonetheless works because of outstanding performances by the leads.

The Vietnam vet is violent with the police and hits his own female lawyer. He relates that he does not know why he killed in Vietnam and that he spent six years in a VA psycho ward trying to get over the war. The only twist to this example of the crazy-vet genre is that the drifter is innocent of the crime of which he is accused. [TV]

Swimming to Cambodia (1987) **D:** Jonathan Demme, 85m. Spalding Gray.

** This one-man stage production has Gray talking about his experiences in a minor role in *The Killing Fields* and about life in general. Gray comes across as incredibly wimpish, irritating, and self-serving. Even the unseen audience seems not to know how to react. Only excellent direction keeps this piece from being a total loss. The most interesting aspects are not Gray's opinions but his comments on how films are made in foreign locations—in this case, Thailand.

Although Gray is obviously horrified by the Khmer Rouge killing fields, he manages to place part of the blame on the American bombing of Cambodia and its border with South Vietnam. He also credits the number of prostitutes in Bangkok today to the Vietnam War and the American soldiers who then flocked to Bangkok on R&R. He remarks about the "dark cloud" that hovers over such countries as Cambodia, the USSR, Libya, and the United States. Gray's longest story not directly about *The Killing Fields* concerns a U.S. Navy officer he claims to have met on a train in the States. The alleged officer is said to be a hard-drinking, coke-snorting, womanizing bigot whose job as a nuclear missile launcher gives him, he admits, an erection when he thinks about nuking the Soviet Union. 📺

Targets (1968) **D:** Peter Bogdanovich, 90m. Boris Karloff, Tim O'Kelly, Nancy Hsueh, James Brown, Sandy Baron.

** An aging horror-movie star (Karloff), who is retiring from the screen because he feels that real-life tragedy has surpassed the horror in his films, has his theory verified by a mad sniper at the actor's last public appearance. This is Bogdanovich's first feature film, and although rough in places, the final drive-in-movie shootout gives a good preview of his future brilliance. National Rifle Association members will not care for the brief antigun prologue that was added to most prints after the assassination of Robert Kennedy. The film also contains an excellent line from a writer who states, "All the good movies have been made."

The sniper, in addition to multiple random killings, begins his rampage by murdering his wife and mother. Although he is not specifically identified as being a Vietnam veteran, on the wall of his home are pictures of him in uniform in what appears to be

Southeast Asia, as well as a picture of him and his wife in a typical Hawaii R&R shot. He also carries his weapons in an Army duffle bag and follows military courtesy, using "sir" when talking with others. ☑

Taxi Driver (1976) **D:** Martin Scorsese, 113m. Robert De Niro, Cybill Shepherd, Peter Boyle, Harvey Keitel, Jodie Foster.

** A poorly educated pill-popping Vietnam veteran (De Niro) with an inability to sleep drives a taxi at night. His social skills are such that on a first date he takes a woman (Shepherd) to a porno movie. Finally, fed up with the street vermin of New York, he becomes an urban guerrilla whose idea of improvement is to kill anyone who gets in his way. Vastly overrated at the time of its release and since, *Taxi Driver* is just another gory look at a Vietnam veteran acting out his personal problems in violence. The only difference is that here the film had better-than-usual acting and direction.

No Vietnam footage is included, but De Niro's character claims an honorable discharge and wears a Marine aviator's flight jacket. Little mention is made of the war, but it is critical to understanding De Niro's difficulties. Most viewers will blame the war, but anyone who actually experienced Vietnam will recognize that De Niro's character would have had problems relating to the real world long before his military service. ☑

Tell Me Lies (1968-Great Britain) **D:** Peter Brook, 118m. Glenda Jackson, Kingsley Amis, Stokely Carmichael, Paul Scofield, the Royal Shakespeare Company.

* Songs, skits, and round-table discussions are intermingled with actual news footage to allow members of the British Royal Shakespeare Company to attack and malign United States policy in Vietnam. Several of the actors are obsessed with a photograph of a wounded Vietnamese child. One of them asks, "How long can you look at this before you lose interest?" The correct answer is that the photo will maintain your interest much longer than this hysterical, abysmal, boring movie. It is so bad that even the U.S. antiwar forces panned the result.

The only value of this film is to show that at least a portion of England's movie industry shared Hollywood's emotional anguish about Vietnam.

Tender Mercies (1983) **D:** Bruce Beresford, 90m. Robert Duvall, Tess Harper, Betty Buckley, Ellen Barkin, Allan Hubbard.

**** Duvall plays a former country-and-western music star who is at the bottom of a long slide into boozy oblivion. He declares, "I don't trust happiness; I never did and I never will." However, when he meets a Vietnam widow who manages a rural motel, Duvall begins to put his life back together. Beautifully simple and low-key, this is one of the better films of its decade. It earned a Best Actor Oscar for Duvall and a screenplay Academy Award for Horton Foote.

Although Duvall's recovery is the focus of the story, deeper impressions are made about the impact of Vietnam. A clear message is delivered that second chances are available no matter how low a person has fallen—unless that second chance is denied by death in Vietnam (Harper's husband) or in an automobile accident (Duvall's daughter). Children in a schoolyard tell Harper's son, "Your Daddy got killed in some dumb war." Harper can only respond, "He was just a boy, but a good boy. I think he would have been a fine man." Also worth noting is that director Beresford has sympathy for soldiers who fight for lost causes. His other film credits include *Breaker Morant*. [TV]

Terror in the Sky (1971) TVM, **D:** Bernard Kowalski, 78m. Doug McClure, Leif Erickson, Roddy McDowall, Keenan Wynn, Lois Nettleton.

* Food poisoning hits the flight crew and most of the passengers aboard a charter airliner. The only hope of safely landing the plane rests with a burned-out Vietnam-veteran helicopter pilot. Based on the Arthur Hailey novel *Runway Zero-Eight*, this is, essentially, a poor remake of the 1956 *Flight into Danger* on television's "Alcoa Hour," and of the 1957 theatrical release *Zero Hour*.

McClure plays a tired and despondent man who has been mostly worthless since a tour flying choppers in Vietnam. Neither the flight crew nor the vet's fellow passengers have much faith in him, but he safely lands the plane. Whether he stays a hero or returns to the down-and-out life is left unanswered.

Texas Chainsaw Massacre 2, The (1986) **D:** Tobe Hooper, 95m. Dennis Hopper, Caroline Williams, Bill Johnson, Jim Siedow, Bill Moseley.

* Hopper plays a strange Texas Ranger still on the trail of a cannibal family that killed his brother in Part I. He finds them winning chili cookoffs with a secret-ingredient recipe and terrorizing a female disk jockey who has offended them on her radio show. A long finale takes place amid bones, blood, gore, and buzzing chain saws. This film is gruesome but not scary.

One of the cannibal brothers shouts "Ho Chi Minh" and "incoming" as he beats a man to death with a hammer. He later talks about wanting to establish a theme park called Nam Land. Although the same characters appear in Parts I and III, Vietnam is mentioned only in this segment of the series. Perhaps this is in honor of Hopper's presence; he has made a career out of films featuring crazy Vietnam veterans. [TV]

Thank You, Aunt (1967-Italy) **D:** Salvatore Samperi, 93m. (OT: *Grazie, Zia*). Lou Castel, Lisa Gastoni, Gabriele Ferzetti, Luisa De Santis, Nicoletta Rizzi.

* The seventeen-year-old son (Castel) of wealthy parents is confined to a wheelchair due to paralysis induced by the young man's mental torment. His aunt, who is also a doctor, tries to help him, but she gets caught up in his sexual and mental games and eventually assists in his suicide. Bleak in every aspect, this film is neither fun nor stimulating—just depressing.

Castel's mental anguish is attributed to man's inhumanity to man and his belief in the lack of any real spirituality in humankind. Much of this stems from what is occurring in Vietnam at the time, and one of his few interests is playing miniature war games based on the conflict.

That Was Then, This Is Now (1985) **D:** Christopher Cain, 102m. Emilio Estevez, Craig Sheffer, Kim Delaney, Barbara Babcock, Ramon Sheen, Morgan Freeman.

** Two friends (Estevez and Sheffer) raised as brothers face the challenges of growing up and growing apart. Based on the novel by S. E. Hinton and adapted by Estevez, it has its moments but never totally comes together.

The primary adult friend of the two young men is a black bar owner (Freeman). He is honest, intelligent, and stable—and is killed by two bar patrons who are assaulting the boys for hustling them in pool. No mention of Vietnam is made, but when Shef-

fer's character visits the bar owner's grave in a national cemetery, the headstone notes Vietnam service. [TV]

Thunderheart (1992) **D:** Michael Apted, 110m. Sam Shepard, Val Kilmer, Graham Greene, Fred Ward, Sheila Tousey.

** Two FBI agents (Shephard and Kilmer) investigate a murder in the midst of warring traditional and modern Indians on a South Dakota reservation. "Inspired by incidents of the 1970s," the film offers wonderful scenery but the story falls short. A cheesy ending with the Indians (instead of the cavalry) riding to the rescue does not help.

When the FBI agents arrest an innocent Indian for murder, he resists their manhandling, saying he was "decorated in Nam." Shepard's character jerks him to his feet and mutters, "Me too." No other mention of Vietnam is made. Look closely at the pow-wow scene late in the film for a POW/MIA flag flying above the festivities. [TV]

Tiger by the Tail (1968) **D:** R. G. Springsteen, 99m. Christopher George, Dean Jagger, Tippi Hedren, Charo, Glenda Farrell.

* A soldier (George) returns home from Vietnam to find his brother has been killed in a robbery of the racetrack in which they are both part-owners. George suspects that the robbery is a cover-up for murder by the other shareholders, and with the help of an old girlfriend (Hedren), he begins asking questions and beating out the desired responses. The trail finally leads to the local sheriff, whom George kills. He, Hedren, and the racetrack resume their romance.

The only purpose of the Vietnam tie-in is to offer a reason for George's absence and to provide a rational excuse for his toughness and killing abilities. This is, ultimately, only a "mini-Rambo at the racetrack" film.

To Heal a Nation (1988) TVM, **D:** Michael Pressman, 96m. Eric Roberts, Glynnis O'Connor, Marshall Colt, Brock Peters, Scott Paulin.

*** Roberts plays Vietnam veteran Jan Scruggs, who led the movement to build the Vietnam Veterans Memorial on the Mall in Washington, D.C. The many factions for and against the monument, as well as the controversy over the selected design, are represented. Powerful, dramatic, and sincere, this film is a tribute to Scruggs and all other Vietnam veterans, and a recognition of what a single man can accomplish.

Scruggs, a veteran of the 199th Light Infantry Brigade, is shown becoming motivated to build the memorial while watching *The Deer Hunter* and thinking about the number of men who did not return and the forgotten soldiers who did. The most effective scenes are those at the monument dedication ceremony, where actual and re-created footage is effectively presented. The film's best line comes when Scruggs is approached by a former antiwar activist, who says, "I hated the war, but I should not have hated you."

To Kill a Clown (1972) **D:** George Bloomfield, 82m. Alan Alda, Blythe Danner, Heath Lamberts, Eric Clavering.

** A young couple on an isolated island is terrorized by a disabled Vietnam veteran neighbor and his two Doberman pinschers. Although it is difficult to accept Alda as a deranged veteran, the film does have its suspenseful moments.

Any movie with a "deranged terrorist" as a character needs to present an explanation for the villain's ways, and Vietnam offers a ready excuse. Little is mentioned of Alda's combat service except that he was shot in the kneecaps and left for dead. Alda only adds, "Guns next to bodies look like garbage. Not interesting." What is interesting is the names of Alda's two attack dogs—Rice and Charlie. 🖵

Top Gun (1986) **D:** Tony Scott, 109m. Tom Cruise, Kelly McGillis, Val Kilmer, Anthony Edwards, Meg Ryan.

** The top 1 percent of the navy's aviators train at the Fighter Weapons School and compete for the title of "top gun." Cruise plays an arrogant flier who romances the skies and an astrophysicist (McGillis). The actors, the romance, the flying, and the dialogue are contrived and Boy Scoutish in every aspect. Edwards as "Goose" is the only really interesting character. Despite its many flaws, this film brought great profits to its producers and tremendous positive publicity for naval aviation.

The father of Cruise's character "mysteriously" disappeared over Southeast Asia in an F-4 in 1965. This supposedly has made the son an outcast because, as one character tells him, "Your family name ain't the best in the navy." Apparently, this is what makes

Cruise's character such a "maverick," but the explanation makes no more sense than the rest of the movie. The most informative parts of the movie are the carrier operation scenes filmed aboard the USS *Enterprise.* ⊺⊻

Tornado (1983-Italy) **D:** Anthony M. Dawson, 90m. Timothy Brent, Tony Marsina, Alan Collins.

 * A Special Forces captain and a sergeant fight each other and the Vietcong during the last days of the Vietnam War. The captain cares only about his career, regardless of the number of his men who are killed; the sergeant tells him, "You had your power, and you abused it." The NCO adds that the only people benefiting from the Vietnam War are the arms industry, drug pushers, prostitutes, and black marketeers. With interior scenes shot on a Rome sound stage, this Italian production has it all—a poor script, bad acting, an absolutely unbelievable plot, and a grating sound track.

 # Most of the film's budget was apparently spent on explosives, with no money "wasted" on a technical adviser. Uniforms are of a strange camouflage pattern unknown to any actual U.S. military force. Ribbons and decorations are not of U.S. origin, and the huge "RANGERS" patch worn by the supposed Green Berets is comical. Watch, or better yet don't watch, for American MPs, dressed in World War II white leggings, manning a Vietnamese-Cambodian border crossing. This scene is almost as good as the several knife throws of more than two hundred feet that kill silently. ⊺⊻

To the Shores of Hell (1966) **D:** Will Zens, 82m. Marshall Thompson, Kiva Lawrence, Richard Jordahl, Jeff Pearl, Richard Arlen.

 ** A Marine major, assisted by a priest and a Vietnamese boy, attempts to rescue his doctor brother from the Vietcong. The title, the major's walk along a beach to tell his girl good-bye, and the dialogue make this movie more reminiscent of World War II films than those of Vietnam. Refreshing in its innocence and its support of the American military, it begins and ends with the Marine Corps Hymn playing forcefully. Listen for such lines as those delivered by the American doctor to a wounded VC, "No more attacking defenseless villages for you, you pasty-faced communist fink. You like killing women and you like killing little kids, don't you?"

This film was produced with the full support of the Department of Defense and the Marine Corps, and its first third is primarily footage of actual Marine fleet exercises along the California coast in preparation for deployment to Vietnam (which is amazingly similar to the live televised Somalia landings in late 1992). Included are amphibious operations with infantry, armor, artillery, and helicopters. The chain of command is evident and accurately presented—many of the "actors" are actual Marines. On arrival in Vietnam (southern California continuing to provide the locations), the film sinks into melodrama. It remains, however, positive toward the military and its efforts in Southeast Asia. To a VC officer the doctor remarks, "When are you going to realize that you're not indoctrinating some punk college beatnik, you stupid jerk." Although this is certainly not a great movie—or even a good one—it is one of the very few to show the war and its warriors in a manner similar to the way previous conflicts were shown. 📺

Tough Guys Don't Dance (1987) **D:** Norman Mailer, 110m. Ryan O'Neal, Isabella Rossellini, Wings Hauser, Lawrence Tierney, Frances Fisher.

** O'Neal plays a writer who no longer writes and who may or may not have murdered his wife and his girlfriend. In addition to directing, Mailer adapted the screenplay from his novel, and there are parts of the film that likely only he understands. This movie is strange and at times humorous, but overall it is not as good as its title.

The local police chief (Hauser), self-described as "an enforcer and a maniac," is a Vietnam veteran who is involved in drugs, frame-ups, and murder. He asks O'Neal's character, "Were you in Vietnam?" O'Neal says no, to which Hauser follows up, "Why do I think you were?" O'Neal explains, "I'm an ex-con." 📺

Tracks (1976) **D:** Henry Jaglom, 90m. Dennis Hopper, Taryn Power, Dean Stockwell, Topo Swope, Zack Norman.

* Hopper plays a dope-smoking, Mickey-Mouse-watch-wearing Army first sergeant escorting his buddy's body home from Vietnam by train. En route he encounters a philosophical chess player,

a radical dissident, a traveling salesman, and a sympathetic college girl. Hopper has flashbacks and hallucinations to the point where the viewer can no longer distinguish between reality and nightmare. A great sound track of World War II tunes adds to the surrealism. Although deliberate on the part of the director, the sound of the train on the tracks often makes music and dialogue unintelligible.

Hopper has a wide range as an actor—as long as his roles are limited to the crazed, disturbed, and/or demented. In this film, the demands are well within his range. However, anyone who believes the character he plays could ever achieve the rank of first sergeant has never been in the armed forces of any nation. Listen for songs of the Good War like "We're Going to Slap That Dirty Little Jap" and wonder why, of the two wars, Vietnam is considered the racist conflict. 📺

Trained to Kill (1975) **D:** Daniel J. Vance, 91m (OT: *The No Mercy Man*). Stephen Sandor, Rockne Tarkington, Heidi Vaughn, Richard X. Slattery.

* A tormented Vietnam veteran returns home from the war to find a sadistic gang of teens taking over the town. Their timing is poor because the vet goes berserk and beats, maims, and kills the gang members in a multitude of creative and traditional ways. Made in 1973 and not released until two years later, this film could easily have stayed on the shelf for much longer with no loss to anyone.

The original title, *The No Mercy Man*, is descriptive of the manner in which the veteran is presented. He is not much better than the worthless, moronic gang members he dispatches with no mercy and under the gaze of the locals, who consider him at best the lesser of two evils.

Trial of Billy Jack, The (1974) **D:** Tom Laughlin, 170m. Tom Laughlin, Delores Taylor, William Wellman, Jr., Sacheen Littlefeather, Victor Izay.

* Indian half-breed and Vietnam veteran Billy Jack (Laughlin) continues his defense of the oppressed and downtrodden against red-necks, businessmen, and the National Guard. This sequel to the extremely profitable *Billy Jack* has Laughlin out of jail for his offenses in the first film and again protecting a "freedom school" in northern Arizona. Laughlin continues to prove how peaceful he is by beating hell out of anyone who gets in his way. Its length is only one of this film's great many faults.

\# Little is made of Billy Jack's being a veteran, but the politics of the war take center stage. Billy Jack is angry that all the guilty parties at My Lai are not brought to justice and blames President Nixon "like all the other mealymouthed politicians" for the lack of attention. The final scenes of the National Guard's firing on the "defenseless" children at the school are, of course, an attempted re-creation of the Kent State incident.

Trial of the Catonsville Nine, The (1972) **D:** Gordon Davidson, 85m. Ed Flanders, Gwen Arner, Barton Heyman, Mary Jackson, Richard Jordan.

* On May 17, 1968, nine anti–Vietnam War activists led by Roman Catholic priests Daniel and Patrick Berrigan broke into the Catonsville, Maryland, draft board and burned 378 Selective Service files. Five months later, the nine were convicted in a Baltimore federal court of the crime. Daniel Berrigan wrote a play about the adventure that ran in New York for 159 performances. This is the movie produced from the play. Its purpose is to show that the nine were acting on their individual ideas against the war rather than conforming to the popular antiwar movement. In the film, pictures of maimed Vietnamese refugees are cut into the trial scenes. Dialogue is typified by a poem David Berrigan (Flanders) reads to the court: "We have chosen to say, with the gift of our freedom, that the violence stops here, the death stops here, the suppression of the truth stops here, the war stops here."

\# Although it certainly was not the intent of the producer, director, and cast, this may very well be the most anti-antiwar protester film ever made. The Berrigan brothers and their seven henchmen come across as so piously self-centered, so smugly self-serving, so naively paranoid that it becomes clear that the intent of the nine was solely to act on behalf of the nine rather than for any overall peaceful objectives.

Tribes (1970) TVM, **D:** Joseph Sargent, 90m. (OT: *The Soldier Who Declared Peace*). Darren McGavin, Jan-Michael Vincent, Earl Holliman, John Gruber, Danny Goldman.

** A tough Marine drill sergeant believes in his job and the

Corps. Long-haired, Oriental-robe-wearing Vincent provides a real challenge. The subtitle could have been "Zen and Boot Camp." It was awarded television's Emmy for Best Original Screenplay.

Filmed at the USMC Recruit Depot in San Diego during the Vietnam War, the film offers an excellent look at boot training at its actual location. Because this movie was made for television, profanity is totally absent; drill instructors call trainees ladies, sissies, and even doo-doos. Interestingly, the absence of real examples of the language DIs then used does not detract. Despite being made at the height of the war, the film is neither pro- nor antimilitary; rather, it attempts with some success to show the impact of the times on trainees and trainers. Vincent tells McGavin, "We're from different tribes; you've lost touch with life, your bag is death." McGavin responds, "My bag is patriotism and to defend such rights to talk." 📺

Twilight's Last Gleaming (1977-U.S.-Germany) **D:** Robert Aldrich, 144m. Burt Lancaster, Richard Widmark, Melvyn Douglas, Paul Winfield, Charles Durning.

**1/2 A former POW air force brigadier general (Lancaster) leads a gang of death row escapees to seize a Titan missile silo. Their purpose is to threaten to start World War III if they are not given $9 million and a secret document that contains the "real truth" about the Vietnam War. Good acting from a major-name cast still cannot make up for this too-long, too-preachy effort.

Lancaster states, "The war should have never been fought," and the president of the United States says, "The country still hasn't recovered from Vietnam." A major flaw of the film is that the big secret about the war is anything but. A member of the Joint Chiefs of Staff tells the president that releasing the document will make the military look criminally negligent, but all the secret memo really says is that Vietnam was not fought over land and freedom of a people but for politics and to show the Soviets that we and the president were tough. All of this supposedly ties in with the lack of a U.S. policy on the use of nuclear weapons. Interestingly, although a Cabinet member states the military will kill the president before it lets him read the statement to the public, nothing in it really indicts the armed forces. The statement, like the war, was the product of the executive and legislative

branches of the government. The military does not make policy; it executes that made by Congress and the president. 📺

Twilight Zone—The Movie (1983) **Ds:** John Landis, Steven Spielberg, Joe Dante, George Miller, 101m. Vic Morrow, Scatman Crothers, Kathleen Quinlan, Patricia Barry, Abbe Lane.

** Rod Serling's cult-classic television series is brought to the big screen via four separate episodes (three of which are remakes of TV segments). Each part has its own director, and the four are tied together with an interesting prologue and closing. None of the four tales is nearly as good as the TV series.

The first vignette, written and directed by Landis, is about a bigoted Korean War veteran who brags, "My country paid me to kill gooks," and rails against Jews, blacks, and Orientals in general. Departing a bar, he steps into the Twilight Zone, where he is transformed into a Jew being pursued by the Nazis, then a black being beaten by the KKK, and finally a Vietcong being murdered by dope-smoking American infantrymen in Vietnam. Landis gives no explanation for comparing the U.S. Army in Vietnam to the Nazis in Germany and the KKK in the South. 📺

Two (1975) **D:** Charles Trieschmann, 93m. (OT: *Captive*). Douglas Travis, Sarah Venable, Clifford Villeneuve, Ray Houle, Florence Hadley.

* A Vietnam veteran escapes from a military hospital, kidnaps a girl, and hides her in a mountain cabin. She manages to calm him down and talk him into letting her go safely; in exchange, she promises to spend two days with him. Over the next forty-eight hours the two develop a rapport and an unusual friendship. At the end of the two days, the vet goes to town for food and almost as an aside robs the local bank. When he returns to the cabin, the girl chides him for the theft. He tries to return the money to the bank but is killed in his attempt.

In addition to being a kidnapping, bank-robbing crazy, the veteran also is not very bright. Manipulated by his supposed victim, he is proven a loser at every turn. This movie was entered in the Berlin Film Festival, a Dell book was based on the screenplay, and an excerpt was published in *Redbook* magazine. None of this prevented the film from quickly slipping into a well-deserved oblivion.

Two People (1973) **D:** Robert Wise, 100m. Peter Fonda, Lindsay Wagner, Alan Fudge, Estelle Parsons, Geoffrey Horne.

* A Vietnam War deserter (Fonda) and a high-fashion model (Wagner) travel, love, and talk and talk in North Africa and Paris before returning to New York to face their pasts. The dialogue is full of such memorable lines as "I never knew it could be like this." Music sounds as if it were recorded in a cheap Moroccan restaurant. This film is consistent—consistently bad in every aspect. It is also Wagner's film debut.

Fonda's character has deserted the military in Vietnam because of his principles against war. He confirms his high-mindedness by returning to the United States to face the consequences of his actions—as soon as he's finished wandering from city to city and from bed to bed with Miss Wagner. This is merely another of the "deserter is the hero and everyone else is wrong" genre of Vietnam film.

Ugly American, The (1963) **D:** George H. Englund, 120m. Marlon Brando, Sandra Church, Pat Hingle, Arthur Hill, Eiji Okada.

*** Brando plays the American ambassador to the fictional country of Sarkhan, which is obviously Vietnam in everything but name. The ambassador, his staff, and the American government fail to understand the country, its people, and its problems—with disastrous results. Fine acting by Brando and such appropriate lines as "We have an excellent chance of losing Sarkhan and all Southeast Asia" and "The more we back down, the more they [the communists] will attack" make for an excellent film. Based on the best-selling book by Eugene Burdick and William J. Lederer, the film is notable in its own right. However, beware watching it in hopes of "seeing" the novel—much is left out, and the screen version is much kinder to Americans than is the printed work.

The difficulties, deficiencies, faults, and errors of the United States in dealing with Vietnam, as well as with other countries, are brilliantly brought to the screen. Relationships among the State Department, the media, and Congress are well worth watching. Interestingly, although the book was published in 1958 and the movie made in 1963, little or no heed to the authors' message was paid by anyone in a position to make any difference. Beautiful scenes of Thailand are tempered by an opening credit disclaimer that, while the Thai countryside and cities provide the

film's locations, there is no association between that country and the political situation shown in the movie. 📺

UHF (1989) **D:** Jay Levey, 97m. "Weird Al" Yankovic, Victoria Jackson, Kevin McCarthy, Michael Richards, David Bowie.
** A daydreamer whose overactive imagination keeps him from holding a job finds success in managing a small television station won by his uncle in a poker game. Most of the laughs in this lightweight script come from spoofs of movies, television shows, and commercials. This is music-video parodist Yankovic's film debut, but Richards steals the show and most of the laughs as the station janitor/kids'-show host.
# In one sequence, Yankovic daydreams that he is Rambo fighting Vietcong. One machine-gun burst kills twenty or more at a long distance, while other automatic gunfire from two feet away misses altogether. Yankovic as Rambo blows up bridges and buildings in huge fireball explosions initiated by bursts from his machine gun. Although the Vietnam scenes are played for laughs, they actually are not too much more ridiculous than the real Rambo films. 📺

Uncommon Valor (1983) **D:** Ted Kotcheff, 105m. Gene Hackman, Robert Stack, Fred Ward, Randall "Tex" Cobb, Patrick Swayze.
**1/2 Ten years after the war, a retired Marine (Hackman) leads a mixture of misfit veterans back to Southeast Asia to rescue his son and other POWs. This is better than the usual POW rescue film, but it follows a predictable plot full of clichéd characters including a French arms salesman complete with a parrot on his shoulder, and a vet deranged by Agent Orange (he wears a hand grenade as a necklace). Performances by Hackman et al. make this one watchable.
The basic message of the film is delivered by Hackman's character to the rescue team when he notes that Vietnam veterans are considered criminals by their own countrymen and that the sons of politicians and other powerful families did not serve. He adds that America wants to forget about its Vietnam vets because the war cost too much and did not turn a profit. He concludes by stating that veterans are the only hope of the POWs because only the veterans care. Although much of the action is typical Hollywood, the team training and the detailed rehearsals

are noteworthy. Also, if any POWs have survived, this film is one of the few to portray realistically their probable mental and physical condition. 📺

Under Fire (1983) **D:** Roger Spottiswoode, 128m. Nick Nolte, Gene Hackman, Joanna Cassidy, Ed Harris, Hamilton Camp.

**1/2 A radio correspondent (Cassidy) breaks off her relationship with a magazine reporter (Hackman) and takes up with a photo-journalist (Nolte) in Nicaragua during the 1979 revolution. Although Nolte claims, "I don't take sides, I take pictures," he and his new lover become involved with the revolutionaries and help them overthrow the Somoza government. This is an above-average movie, but the viewer should be careful to separate fact, fiction, and propaganda.

\# While several reporters sit and drink around a hotel pool, they play a news-trivia game. One of the questions has to do with the 1963 assassination of Diem in Vietnam. Nolte's character recalls the date because he took a picture of the event that resulted in his first major magazine cover. In another instance, Hackman's character, with obvious reference to Vietnam, says, "We're backing a fascist government *again*." Still another character, a murderous mercenary played by Harris, never directly mentions his service in Vietnam but alludes to it nonetheless. 📺

Universal Soldier (1992) **D:** Roland Emmerich, 102m. Jean-Claude Van Damme, Dolph Lundgren, Ally Walker, Ed O'Ross, Leon Rippy.

*1/2 U.S. Special Forces regenerates robotlike Universal Soldiers (Unisols), twenty-five years after their deaths in Vietnam, to combat crooks and terrorists. Two of the robosoldiers break away from their controllers to renew a bloody grudge match started in Vietnam and finished in scenic locales in northern Arizona. The most obvious tip-off to this film's type is provided in a trailer that advertises, "Play the Universal Soldier video game from Accolade."

\# The two leading Unisols do not like one another because they killed each other in Vietnam during an argument about the propriety of murdering civilians. Lundgren's character spends much of his time in Vietnam and Arizona fashioning necklaces out of ears. 📺

Unnatural Causes (1986) TVM, **D:** Lamont Johnson, 96m. John Ritter, Alfre Woodard, Patti LaBelle, John Sayles, Sean McCann.

*** Based on a true story, this movie tells of Maude De Victor (Woodard), a Veterans Administration benefits counselor who led efforts (often against the desires of her superiors) to recognize the link between cancer, birth defects, and the spraying of the Agent Orange defoliant in Vietnam. Ritter portrays a cancer victim whose character is based on a composite of several of De Victor's clients. The result is an excellent drama that will have every veteran reviewing the possibility of his exposure to the defoliant and wondering if he is experiencing any of its effects.

In this film, rather than the war and its warriors it is the VA and the Agent Orange manufacturers who are the villains. Before Ritter's character is stricken with cancer, he is a schoolteacher and, apparently, a good one. However, true to Vietnam movie fare, he is divorced. According to his son, Ritter's former wife blames the war for their breakup. As a balance, however, a fellow vet tells Ritter, "You can't blame everything on the war." The film's distributor, New Star Video, contributes $1 per cassette sale to De Victor so she can continue her Agent Orange study and advocacy to have the effects of the chemical classified as service-related, for the purpose of allocating veterans' benefits. 📺

Vanishing Point (1971) **D:** Richard C. Sarafian, 107m. Barry Newman, Cleavon Little, Dean Jagger, Paul Koslo, Gilda Texter.

* A Vietnam vet attempts to drive a Dodge Challenger from Denver to San Francisco in fifteen hours for no apparent reason except to win a small drug bet. Little plays a blind radio disk jockey who lends support. With little dialogue and lots of chase scenes, this is the grandfather to later films such as *Cannonball Run* and *Smokey and the Bandit* (Jerry Reed even sings on the sound track.)

Newman, as the driver, is a Medal of Honor winner described by the police simply as "nuts." In the final scene, the vet makes no attempt to avoid a heavy-equipment roadblock and, with a smile, crashes to his death. 📺

Vestige of Honor (1990) TVM, **D:** Jerry London, 96m. Michael Gross, Gerald McRaney, Cliff Gorman, Season Hubley, Kenny Lao.

** Ten years after the fall of Saigon, a former soldier (Gross) who is a successful building contractor wants to return to Southeast Asia to fulfil a promise to help his Montagnard friends. Confronted by red tape, graft, and bureaucracy at every turn (with, of course, no assistance from the U.S. State Department), Gross enlists the help of an old Green Beret buddy (McRaney) and several of his expatriate friends living in Thailand. Based on the true story of Don Scott, this is one of the better TV movies—even if CBS premiered it on December 30, when it had to compete with the holidays and football bowl games.

McRaney's character, like his expat buddies, lives, drinks, and whores in Thailand because during twelve years in the military before being RIFed after the war, he learned no skills of any use in the civilian world. Gross, even in his usual wimpish manner, is a "good vet," and although McRaney is a "loser vet" in the beginning, he does the right thing in the end. It is also interesting that the film makes a big point of McRaney's being a former soldier while Gross's character appears to be akin to a civilian adviser rather than a soldier. Overall, the most positive aspect of the film is that the veterans are the heroes and it is the government, particularly the State Department, that is the villain.

Vietnam: An American Journey (1981) **D:** Robert Richter, 85m.

* This documentary traces director Richter's seven-week visit to Vietnam in 1978. He tours the major cities and makes such astonishing observations as "the women dress differently" in some places. Richter also visits several of the better-known battle areas and lingers at the site of the My Lai massacre, interviewing people who claim to be survivors. Throughout the picture, Richter is upbeat and positive about how well the Vietnamese are doing under their communist leadership while, at the same time, he is extremely critical of the United States for not helping the rebuilding efforts.

This film is of value only if watched with the volume turned down. Except for the sights of the towns and countryside, it is pure propaganda without accurate analysis. Richter's visit was closely supervised by the communist government, and the control is quite evident. The film is so biased and so poorly produced that the television networks refused to air it, prompting Richter to release it for a limited theater run.

Vietnam, Texas (1990) **D:** Robert Ginty, 92m. Robert Ginty, Haing S. Ngor, Tim Thomerson, Kieu Chinh, Bert Remsen.

*1/2 Fifteen years after the war, a soldier who has become a priest (Ginty) tracks down his old Vietnamese girlfriend, whom he abandoned pregnant. He finds her and his daughter living with a Vietnamese drug dealer (Ngor) in Houston. The priest, in addition to being an expert boxer, is still a fair shot. The religious tie is reinforced when Ginty is crucified with ice picks by Ngor. Another interesting scene takes place in a Vietnamese nightclub where the patrons deal drugs and dance the tango. In spite of its plot twists, or perhaps because of them, the film is barely watchable. Summary: good title, weak movie.

Ginty's character is assisted by a drunken saloonkeeper (Thomerson) who runs a bar "for shitfaced jackasses who can't forget the glory days" and who admits "Saigon followed me home like it did a lot of others." The daughter of the priest adds, "I guess the war messed up a lot of people's lives." Except to repeat the stereotypes of the Vietnamese as gangsters and the American vets as strung-out losers, the film's only contribution to understanding the war is the ninety seconds or so of opening footage of an actual infantry company air-assaulting into a landing zone and moving out on patrol. 📺

Vigilante Force (1976) **D:** George Armitage, 89m. Kris Kristofferson, Jan-Michael Vincent, Victoria Principal, Bernadette Peters, Andrew Stevens.

** A California boomtown hires Vietnam veterans to protect it from hell-raising oil-field workers. The vets, led by Kristofferson, accomplish their mission using "creative police work" but then take over the town for their own fun and profit. Watch for Kristofferson and gang disguised in gaudy high school band uniforms during a robbery. Much action, mediocre movie.

Kristofferson's character is referred to by the town leaders alternately as a "war hero" and "crazy." The apparent message of the film is that regardless of how bad things are, Vietnam vets can make it worse. 📺

Visitors, The (1972) **D:** Elia Kazan, 88m. James Woods, Patrick McVey, Patricia Joyce, Chico Martinez, Steve Railsback.

* Two men, fresh out of prison for sex crimes and murder in

Vietnam, terrorize the soldier (Woods) who testified against them and his family. Director Kazan and his son Chris, who wrote the screenplay, use this low-budget film to make their personal statements against the Vietnam War. It is certainly not worth mention on the same page as Kazan's earlier, 1950s works such as *A Streetcar Named Desire* and *On the Waterfront*. This was the first starring role for Woods.

The two former soldiers were convicted of raping a Vietnamese girl and then bayonetting her to death. They continue this behavior by severely beating Woods and savagely raping his girlfriend. Apparently, Kazan wants to make the point that the brutal, criminal behavior of soldiers in Vietnam carried over to their actions after returning home. By having Woods's character admit that he really cannot explain why he did the right thing and turned in his fellow soldiers for their crimes, Kazan does not even allow him to be sympathetic.

Vixen (1968) **D:** Russ Meyer, 71m. Erica Gavin, Harrison Page, Jon Evans, Michael Donovan O'Donnell, Garth Pillsbury.

* The oversexed wife of a Canadian bush pilot seduces anyone who crosses her path at their British Columbia fishing lodge. Her partners include a Royal Mountie, a fisherman and his wife, her brother, and on occasion her husband. The only person she seems not to want to bed is a black draft dodger from the States. She does enlist his help, however, to prevent a "communist" from hijacking her husband's plane to Cuba. The only excuse for the extremely thin plot is to provide transitions between the sex scenes. For those who care for this type of film, Russ Meyer was the master of the genre at the time.

The draft dodger is not greatly political beyond protecting his own well-being. In the final scenes he does, however, make a stand against the communist's plans to take them all to Cuba. The dodger finally decides to return to the U.S., offering as his rationale that, compared to Cuba, it is "the lesser of two evils."

Volunteers (1985) **D:** Nicholas Meyer, 106m. Tom Hanks, John Candy, Rita Wilson, Tim Thomerson, Gedde Watanabe.

** Hanks portrays a rich, spoiled playboy who joins the Peace Corps in 1962 so he can flee to Thailand rather than face his angry bookie. At a remote river village, Hanks joins Tom Tuttle from

Tacoma (Candy) and a gung-ho girl (Wilson) to build a bridge which is of importance to the Peace Corps, the CIA, communist guerrillas, and a local drug lord. Comedy varies from slapstick to parodies of *Casablanca, Lawrence of Arabia,* and *The Bridge on the River Kwai,* among others.

According to this film, the CIA, Air America, and the Special Forces supported Southeast Asian drug production and trade. Under the guise of comedy, U.S. military personnel are portrayed as corrupt, idiotic warmongers. At their lead is a CIA operative named Mike who talks to his knife. The communist forces, origin unidentified, are not treated much better. Filmed in a part of Mexico that looks reasonably like Thailand. ▣

Walking Tall (1973) **D:** Phil Karlson, 126m. Joe Don Baker, Elizabeth Hartman, Gene Evans, Rosemary Murphy, Noah Beery.

** This film is based (loosely) on the real adventures of Tennessee sheriff Buford Pusser (Baker) in his efforts to rid his county of corruption and crime. Literally wielding a big stick, Baker takes on large numbers and wins—despite being severely beaten and shot and having his dog and wife killed. Pusser served as technical adviser to this violent, bloody, and hugely successful film.

Baker/Pusser is identified as having spent three years in the pre-Vietnam Marine Corps. His informant about the local gangs is a prostitute who helps because she likes big, good-looking former Marines. She adds that she was once married to a Marine "who didn't live through Vietnam." Neither the hooker nor Vietnam reappears in the various big-screen and television sequels that followed. ▣

War Birds (1989) **D:** Ulli Lommel, 89m. Jim Eldert, Cully Holland, Bill Brinsfield, Rick Anthony Monroe, Stephen Quadros.

* Without informing the president, the CIA and the Pentagon recruit F-16 pilots to assist a Mideast ally under attack by rebels. There are not enough negative adjectives in the dictionary to describe this awful movie, and that judgment extends to the plot, acting, dialogue, and technical aspects.

Leading the air attack is a veteran whose wife left him while he was in Vietnam. He is not believable as a vet, and no other part of the film is any more believable. ▣

War Bus (1985) **D:** Ted Kaplan, 90m. Daniel Stephen, Rom Kristoff, Urs Althaus, Don Gordon, Ernie Zarte.

* Three U.S. Marines assist a schoolbus full of missionaries escape the North Vietnamese Army. Despite such pithy dialogue as "Your soul is rotten, like that of every coward" and stirring visuals—such as a snake appearing in a woman's makeup-compact mirror as she applies her lipstick—this is a film to avoid at all costs.

\# Armies around the world should discard their tanks and armored personnel carriers. It is apparent from this movie that bullets cannot penetrate bright yellow schoolbuses, nor can Vietnamese eyes see one as it races down jungle trails. Just as ridiculous is the way the Marines build huge campfires at night and attack the NVA riding a train across the countryside. Not to be outdone, although the setting is supposedly South Vietnam, the elaborate camp of the North Vietnamese is complete with buildings, barbed-wire fences, and guard towers. One even has a sign in *English* that states it is the home of an NVA unit. TV

War Dogs (1986-Sweden) **Ds:** Bjorn Carlstroem and Daniel Hubenbecher, 96m. Tim Earle, Bill Redvers, Sidney Livingston, Catherine Jeppson, David Gillies.

* A Vietnam veteran refuses to believe his brother was killed in the war and uncovers a government program to use MIAs as drug-controlled assassins who "work like machines. It could be a game to them, like follow-the-leader." Swedish interior and exterior shooting locations little resemble United States settings. The acting is so bad the viewer will think the film was dubbed.

\# There is no similarity between this film and Vietnam or any other entity. The only thing that's accurate is half of the title, for this is truly a film of the bow-wow variety. TV

Welcome Home (1989) **D:** Franklin J. Schaffner, 92m. Kris Kristofferson, JoBeth Williams, Sam Waterston, Brian Keith, Trey Wilson.

** After four years as a POW and thirteen more as a fugitive hiding from the Khmer Rouge in the jungle (where he acquired a native wife and two children), an air force pilot (Kristofferson) returns home to his remarried first wife and the son he did not know he had. Only a strong cast saves a thin plot line. This film, as Schaffner's last, is not in the same class as earlier efforts such as *Patton* and *Papillon*.

An integral part of the picture is the claim that the U.S. Air Force and the Defense Intelligence Agency were aware that POWs were alive as early as 1979. They convince Kristofferson not to reveal his return and the presence of other prisoners in Southeast Asia as a matter of "national security." Filming locations in Malaysia, Thailand, Vermont, and Canada are a plus. 📺

Welcome Home, Johnny Bristol (1971) TVM, **D:** George McCowan, 100m. Martin Landau, Jane Alexander, Forrest Tucker, Brock Peters, Martin Sheen.

** Landau plays an army captain who returns to the States after two years as a POW in Vietnam to find that his hometown of Charles, Vermont, has disappeared and that no one will acknowledge that it ever existed. This TV movie plays like a long episode of "The Twilight Zone," but it will keep your attention. Watch for a young Martin Sheen, as a VA hospital patient, in one of his earlier roles.

Landau is plagued by flashbacks to his bamboo prison cage and ultimately ends up in a VA psycho ward because of his belief in a town that does not exist. He rages that the army is responsible for the disappearance of his town "like they were guilty of killing sheep out west in Utah." Despite his accusations, the military and the VA come across as concerned and reasonably fair in their treatment of Landau and other vets. 📺

Welcome Home, Soldier Boys (1972) **D:** Richard Compton, 91m. Joe Don Baker, Alan Vint, Paul Koslo, Elliott Street, Jennifer Billingsley.

* Four Green Beret veterans of Vietnam are discharged from the army in Arkansas and pool their money to buy a used Cadillac to drive to California, where they plan to raise cattle on land owned by one of the soldiers. Along the way they kidnap and gang rape a girl whom they toss from their moving automobile after they are through with her. By the time they reach the ironically named town of Hope, New Mexico, they are nearly broke. After being shot at by a gas station owner whom they are attempting to rob, they unload an arsenal of weapons from their car trunk and proceed to destroy the town and kill its inhabitants. At film's end,

the vets have donned their uniforms to await the police and the army for what they know will be their last fight.

It takes little imagination to see that Hope is but another Vietnam village as far as the Green Berets are concerned. The army and Vietnam have turned the four into such killers that, even after getting home safely, they continue to rob, rape, and murder. As a final insult, they learn that even the California ranch to which they seek to escape is only a picture on a postcard and never really existed.

Whatever It Takes (1986) **D:** Bob Demchuk, 93m. Tom Mason, Martin Balsam, Chris Weatherhead, James Rebhorn.

* A Vietnam veteran does odd jobs while drawing cartoons and dreaming of becoming a syndicated cartoonist. Along with his low-paying employment, he has girlfriend problems and a father dying of heart disease. *Whatever It Takes* was filmed in thirty-two days on twenty-seven New York City locations at a cost of only $750,000, and the low budget is evident.

Director-writer-producer Demchuk served as a photojournalist in Vietnam, but apparently, at least in this film, he knows much more about New York than about Southeast Asia. The best line, in a film with few to choose from, is Vietnam related. About his days in Vietnam, the cartoonist recalls, "There, you made a mistake, you were dead. Here, you make a mistake, you gotta live with it the rest of your life."

When Hell Was in Session (1979) TVM, **D:** Paul Krasny, 104m. Hal Holbrook, Eva Marie Saint, Ronny Cox, Mako, Renne Jarrett.

*** This intense dramatization of the seven and one-half years spent by navy Commander Jeremiah A. Denton, Jr., as a POW in North Vietnam includes his torture and his wife's efforts to cope and to help back home. This is the first movie to tell accurately the story of mistreatment of American prisoners by the Vietnamese and their failure to honor Red Cross and other human-rights protocols.

Scenes of interrogation and torture are explicit and accurate, as is the depiction of the spirit of the POWs. Prison exteriors do not resemble North Vietnam, and many of the interrogators and guards are obviously not Vietnamese. Still, the story rings true in a horrifying manner—especially to anyone who ever ran the risk

of capture and long captivity. The most interesting scene is one that gives a fair explanation of what happened to the more than two thousand Americans still missing. Early in the film, an NVA officer tells Denton to cooperate or he will be turned over to the local civilians. According to the officer, in such circumstances he might easily lose an arm or a leg or his life—any of which would prevent his ever going home, since maimed prisoners would never be released.

When You Comin' Back, Red Ryder? (1979) **D:** Milton Katselas, 116m. Marjoe Gortner, Candy Clark, Lee Grant, Peter Firth, Pat Hingle, Stephanie Faracy.

** A psycho Vietnam veteran (Gortner) terrorizes a group of misfits in a Southwest diner. Mark Medoff's adaptation of his 1973 off-Broadway hit does not work so well on the big screen. Gortner's screaming rages, accompanied by rattlesnake sounds, become tiresome long before the conclusion. Faracy is wonderful as the overweight waitress, deserving of her film name "Angel." Firth is convincing as Red Ryder despite his occasional lapses back into his native English accent. The sound track, which ranges from Hank Snow and B. B. King to a theme duet performed by Tammy Wynette and Freddy Fender, is commendable. In fact, this may be one of the best movies you are not going to like.

Gortner wears a field jacket and refers to Vietnam simply as "the war." In the opening scenes, the vet robs Mexican drug dealers. Later he adds to his character by making fun of a plump girl, mocking a crippled man, and accusing the Red Ryder of being a homosexual. When asked if he is sorry for his loathsome behavior, the veteran replies, "No, but I wish I was." In all fairness, the film does no great favors to the other characters either. The locals and those passing through are nearly as weird as Gortner. The chambers of commerce of Las Cruces, New Mexico, and Fabens, Texas, where the movie was filmed, would not be likely to use it to attract visitors and new residents. 🆃🆅

Where East Is East (1929) **D:** Tod Browning, 70m. Lon Chaney, Lupe Velez, Estelle Taylor, Lloyd Hughes, Louis Stern.

** The daughter (Velez) of a wild-animal trapper (Chaney) in Indochina falls in love with the son of an American circus owner. Her mother, who abandoned her as a child, returns to break up the love affair by romancing the young man herself. In retaliation, Chaney releases a wild gorilla that kills the mother but also mauls Chaney so badly that he dies shortly after seeing his daughter happily married. Chaney, "the man of a thousand faces," is the highlight of the film, in excellent makeup that depicts his present injuries and the scars of past ones. This was one of the last of the totally silent films produced in Hollywood.

Indochina provides the exotic locale for the picture, although neither the country nor any of its inhabitants actually appears in the film. Vietnam is accurately shown as a dangerous place, albeit the film is set thirty-five years before the war. The most notable aspect here is that with a release date of May 4, 1929, it is the first major Hollywood production to be set in Indochina.

Which Way Home (1991-New Zealand) TVM, **D:** Carl Schultz, 101m. Cybill Shepherd, John Waters, Ruben Santiago-Hudson, Marc Gray.

** A Red Cross nurse (Shepherd) tries to escape Cambodia with four orphans as the Khmer Rouge and Vietnamese are overrunning the country. Waters plays an Australian smuggler who reluctantly lends assistance. An abundance of speeches about freedom, melting pots, and brotherly love, combined with much action and great scenery in Thai, Aussie, and Kiwi shooting locations, do not make up for a contrived, predictable story with weak acting.

The strongest point of this film is its showing that the conflict in Southeast Asia did not end when the Americans went home in 1975. Long-term hatred and bigotry between the Vietnamese and Cambodians, which extends to the children, are well portrayed. The Khmer Rouge and the Vietnamese are shown to be brutal killers, rapists, and thieves of every sort. 🔲

White Ghost (1987) **D:** B. J. Davis, 93m. William Katt, Rosalind Chao, Martin Hewitt, Wayne Crawford, Reb Brown.

* An American soldier (Katt), MIA in Vietnam for fifteen years, decides it's time to go home to the States when his girlfriend tells him she is pregnant. His escape from the former war zone is barred by headhunting Vietnamese soldiers and a special assassination team sent by the Pentagon to prevent the vet from returning home and telling of the atrocities he witnessed during the war. Katt's character lives in a luxurious jungle tree house complete

with Rube Goldberg defenses. This ridiculous story is basically Tarzan and Jane meet Vietnam.

\# The leader of the Pentagon hit team is the Katt character's old wartime commander, whom he tried to turn in for killing women and children. According to the film, this was just after My Lai and the army did not want any more bad press, "so nothing happened." Katt's character has spent the past fifteen years gathering dog tags of other MIAs so he can account for them when he gets home. Katt makes Rambo look like a sissy as he wrestles snakes and pulls grenade pins with his teeth. ⬛TV

White Nights (1985) **D:** Taylor Hackford, 135m. Mikhail Baryshnikov, Gregory Hines, Isabella Rossellini, Jerzy Skolimowski, Helen Mirren.

** A Soviet ballet star (Baryshnikov) who defected to the West unwillingly returns to Russia when his air flight makes a forced landing. An American Vietnam War deserter and tap dancer (Hines) and his Russian-born wife are used by the KGB to prevent Baryshnikov from attempting another escape. More dance and less—or better—dialogue would have made this one much better.

\# Hines's character claims to have been a "patriot" but changed his mind when he realized that Uncle Sam forced soldiers to become "murderers, rapists, and robbers." He misses the United States but does not regret giving interviews against the war in Vietnam after his defection. ⬛TV

Who'll Stop the Rain (1978) **D:** Karel Reisz, 126m. Nick Nolte, Tuesday Weld, Michael Moriarty, Ray Sharkey, Charles Haid.

** Nolte and Moriarty play former Marines who return to Vietnam as, respectively, a merchant marine and a news correspondent. They get involved in smuggling heroin back to the States and end up with police and gangsters after them. Weld plays Moriarty's wife and Nolte's girlfriend in only one of the film's many twists and turns—some of which make little sense. Despite a great cast and a script based on the National Book Award–winning novel *Dog Soldiers* by Robert Stone, the result is mediocre.

\# Opening scenes of F-4s dropping napalm and bombs in support of a fire-base defense are worth watching, as are the radio transmissions between the ground and the air. Otherwise, this is the usual fare, with screwed-up Vietnam vets doing weird, unlawful things. The only saving grace is that everyone else in the story seems to be as mixed-up as the vets. Filmed in Mexico. 📺

Wild at Heart (1990) **D:** David Lynch, 125m. Nicolas Cage, Laura Dern, Willem Dafoe, Crispin Glover, Diane Ladd.

*** A paroled convict (Cage) and his girlfriend (Dern) are pursued across the country by the girl's mother and his parole officer. This offbeat, weird film takes a little from *The Wizard of Oz* and a lot from the strange world of Lynch.

\# One of the stranger characters the couple encounters is Bobby Peru (Dafoe), who sports a USMC tattoo on his hand and talks of a village where lots of women and children were killed. Dafoe's character, in addition to being a Vietnam veteran, is a thief, an armed robber, and a murderer, though he is not much weirder than the rest of the cast. 📺

Wild Eye, The (1968-Italy) **D:** Paolo Cavara, 91m. Philippe Leroy, Delia Boccardo, Gabriele Tinti, Giorgio Gargiullo, Lars Bloch.

** A documentary film maker (Leroy) wanders the world to record the bizarre, the provocative, and the repulsive. If a subject is not gruesome enough for his standards, he is not above staging events to meet his needs. Even his own girlfriend (the wife of an acquaintance) puts him down for making money from the shame and suffering of others. In Bombay he films opium addicts undergoing a cure in which they are beaten with large paddles. Deaf-mute prostitutes are his subjects in Bali. In Saigon, he witnesses the execution of a Vietcong suspect. His perceived real chance arrives with the information that the VC will bomb a local bar. Instead of warning anyone, he sets up an automatic camera to record the action. He is elated with the explosive results but is saddened to discover his lover is one of the bomb's victims. He hesitates for only a second before directing an assistant to film the tears as they roll down his cheeks.

\#\#\# This film is basically a satire—some might say an accurate account—of the ethics, or lack thereof, of journalists and film makers. Satire or not, it is extremely revealing of the standards of many photographers who covered the Vietnam War. What is truly amazing about this film is that all the shooting locations, including Vietnam, are real. The Saigon scenes are particularly good in showing how the city appeared in the late 1960s.

Windflowers (1968) **D:** Adolfas Mekas, 75m. John Kramer, Pola Chapelle, Ronnie Gilbert, Maxton Latham, Tina Stoumen.

* The film opens and closes with the killing of a fleeing draft dodger by police who mistake his walking stick for a gun. In between are flashbacks of the draft dodger, friends, and supporters railing against the Establishment and expounding that moral law is higher then man-made law. The dialogue is contrived, the acting is wooden, and the overall effect is terrible, regardless of one's politics.

\# The draft dodger is not a long-haired hippie but a clean-cut, respectful young man who says that he does not want to kill or be killed. Most interesting here is that although the film is set in the 1960s, there is no formal mention of Vietnam, the only war he could be protesting. Apparently the director and writer felt their material to be higher than the war itself.

Wolf Lake (1978) **D:** Burt Kennedy, 105m. Rod Steiger, David Huffman, Jerry Hardin, Robin Mattson, Richard Herd.

*1/2 Four World War II veterans vacation at a remote Canadian hunting lodge managed by a Vietnam War deserter. The older veterans, led by Steiger, who lost a son in Vietnam, vow vengeance against the pacifist. Steiger plays his usual obnoxious, obsessive role in this boring, predictable film.

\# The Vietnam deserter is bearded and long-haired and wears a field jacket. He explains that his fleeing to Canada was a result of the killing of old men, women, and children in Vietnam. Apparently his bias against killing extends only to Vietnamese; he seems to relish shooting Steiger and friends. The most notable part of the film is Steiger's remarking, as he and buddies sing World War I and II songs, that neither Korea or Vietnam produced decent music. [TV]

Woman Inside, The (1981-Canada) **D:** Joseph Van Winkle, 94m. Gloria Manon, Dane Clark, Joan Blondell, Michael Champion, Marlene Tracy.

* A Vietnam veteran named Hollis wants to become a woman named Holly. He saves up his money, has hormone injections and an operation, and becomes beautiful and desirable—and female. Manon plays both parts in this low-budget film fit only for the drive-in circuit or the back shelf of the video store. This was Blondell's last film.

\# Confused vets returning from the war are a Vietnam movie staple. Deciding to have one's sexual organs surgically removed is unique to this film. Vietnam flashbacks are as poorly done and as farfetched as the rest of the picture. 📺

Woodstock (1970) **D:** Michael Wadleigh, 184m. Joan Baez, Jefferson Airplane, Santana, Country Joe and the Fish, Jimi Hendrix.

*** This documentary records the three-day music festival in August 1969 held near Bethel, New York, that would become the identifying event for much of a generation. Included are the mud, drugs, sex, and excesses of the festival-goers and the music they came to hear. Split screens, multiple images, and sound-bite interviews with the crowd make for an accurate, dynamic presentation worthy of its 1970 Best Documentary Oscar. The two words most used in the film also offer a good summary: "peace" and "groovy."

\#\# Without the Vietnam War there would have been no Woodstock as it occurred or as it is remembered today. Woodstock accurately depicts the sentiments of a large portion of America's youth at the time. Watch for Country Joe McDonald and his band performing one of the most famous Vietnam-era songs, "Fixin' to Die Rag," and Jimi Hendrix's show-ending electric-guitar rendition of the national anthem. Woodstock and the Vietnam War are closely related in one other aspect—far more people claim to have participated in either one than really did. 📺

Yank in Indo-China, A (1952) **D:** Wallace Grissell, 67m. John Archer, Douglas Dick, Don Harvey, Jean Willes, Maura Murphy.

*1/2 Two Americans (Archer and Dick) operate an air-freight service in Indochina (the title would actually be more correct if it were "Two Yanks . . ."). When they blow up a planeload of supplies bound for the communist insurgents, they must escape through the jungle on foot, accompanied by two women, one of whom gives birth during the journey. At seemingly the last minute, French and friendly Vietnamese forces rescue the Americans and kill most of the pursuing communists. This is strictly formulistic, low-budget fare.

\# This film fits in much more closely with later Ramboesque treatments of the war than with anything going on at the time or

in the later conflict. The politics of both sides receives little attention beyond the mention of the generic evils of communism. At
least the Americans are the good guys and the Vietminh the bad.

Yank in Viet-Nam, A (1964) **D:** Marshall Thompson, 80m (OT:
Year of the Tiger). Marshall Thompson, Enrique Magalona, Mario
Barri, Urban Drew, Kieu Chinh.

** Thompson plays a U.S. Marine Corps helicopter pilot shot
down in Vietcong territory. He links up with a South Vietnamese
patrol that seeks to rescue a doctor kidnapped by the VC. Along
the way, Thompson falls in love with the doctor's daughter
(Chinh), who is accompanying the patrol. At the finale, the mission is accomplished with help from Marine paratroopers.

This is the only nondocumentary film released in the
United States that was filmed completely in South Vietnam. It
opens with the accurate claim "The motion picture you are about
to see was filmed entirely in South Vietnam, in the actual combat
areas, during the present war against Communist Viet Cong." The
United States role of supporting and advising in the early 1960s is
shown correctly. Although two of the South Vietnamese patrol
leaders are played by Filipinos, the remainder of the cast, including Thompson's romantic interest, are Vietnamese. This film offers a unique look at the real Vietnam and Vietnamese of the
early war period not provided in any other dramatic release. While
the story itself is rather forgettable, the background landscape and
people are remarkable. The best line, or at least the most accurate,
is delivered by one of the South Vietnamese patrol members, who
remarks to Thompson, "First came the Japanese, then came the
French, and now the communists. We've been fighting all our
lives."

Year of the Dragon (1985) **D:** Michael Cimino, 136m. Mickey
Rourke, John Lone, Ariane, Leonard Termo, Ray Barry.

** A hardcore New York cop (Rourke) plays by no rules in his
quest to clean up his new beat, Chinatown. His wife describes
him as an "arrogant, self-centered, condescending son of a bitch"
and his girlfriend agrees, calling him "selfish, callous, and indifferent to suffering." A fellow policeman says of Rourke's character, a
USMC Vietnam vet, that he "has a thing for Chinks." All the de-
scriptions are accurate as Rourke does enough shooting, fighting,

and bloodletting to satisfy even the most sadistic viewer. Rourke typically speaks with his gun or his fists, but when he must utter some dialogue, it is usually something like "I'll last long enough to piss on your grave." New York street scenes were re-created on North Carolina sets.

Rourke wears Marine Corps and American flag pins on his lapel. After a particularly bloody ending to a confrontation, Rourke's police boss tells him to cool it, that he is "not in Vietnam." When his girlfriend learns he was in Vietnam, she says, "I knew it; it ruined you." In another instance, a fellow cop tells Rourke that he is "sick and tired of you guys blaming Vietnam for everything" and continues to brag that he is a Korea vet with no problems. This stereotyping of the Vietnam veteran as crazy and violent makes a lot more sense when the credits roll and it is revealed that Cimino's co-writer was Oliver Stone. TV

Youngblood (1978) **D:** Noel Nosseck, 90m. Lawrence Hilton-Jacobs, Bryan O'Dell, Ren Woods, Tony Allen, Vince Cannon.

** Youngblood (O'Dell), a troubled high school student, tries to fit in by joining a neighborhood gang led by a Vietnam veteran (Hilton-Jacobs). Fighting, beating, and robbing are the bulk of the gang's activities until one of its members dies of a drug overdose and the group sets out to eliminate the local pushers. Despite the thin plot, this is a little better than the usual black exploitation films of the time. Box office was helped by the public's recognition of Hilton-Jacobs from his regular role on the television series "Welcome Back Kotter."

This is really a mixed bag—oppressed black ghetto youth meets Vietnam vet on the set of *West Side Story*. It is also interesting that this type of film is universally known as "black exploitation" while the phrase "Vietnam-vet exploitation" has never been used. Although the veteran in this picture is the gang leader and a skillful killer, he has a surprisingly gentle relationship with his wife.

Zabriskie Point (1970) **D:** Michelangelo Antonioni, 111m. Mark Frechette, Daria Halprin, Rod Taylor, Harrison Ford, Kathleen Cleaver.

* Italian director Antonioni focuses on the alienation of American youth from a materialistic society, parents, and the Vietnam

War. A student who may or may not have killed a policeman during a campus riot is the central character; he compares himself to "old John Brown," who helped bring on the American Civil War. Regardless of its intended deep meanings, this is basically a "smart, sensitive students against dumb, mean cops" movie, so jumbled and difficult to watch that it is hardly worth the effort. Look for Harrison Ford in one of his first appearances, in a minor role—no hint of Indiana Jones here.

\# Actual footage of student demonstrations and police beatings adds authenticity to the campus riots. According to this film, the Vietnam War seems to have been the cause of all problems of youth in the late sixties and early seventies. 🖵

Zebra Force (1977) **D:** Joe Tornatore, 100m. Mike Lane, Richard X. Slattery, Glenn Wilder, Rockne Tarkington, Anthony Caruso.

* A badly scarred and disabled Vietnam veteran uses military tactics to lead his old squad against the mob in southern California. Although the film contains more than the usual number of plot twists for this type of fare, poor production and poorer acting place it far on the minus side. The most creative killing is accomplished by spearing a mobster with a forklift.

\# The vet describes his squad as an "excellent kill team." He claims their purpose is "to rid society of scum" but admits that getting rich in the process is not all that bad. Brief Vietnam flashbacks are shot in southern California and are about as good as the acting. 🖵

ABOUT THE AUTHOR

MICHAEL LEE LANNING retired from the U.S. Army as a lieutenant colonel after more than twenty years of service. In Vietnam he served as an infantry platoon leader, a reconnaissance platoon leader, and a rifle company commander. He later served as public affairs officer for General H. Norman Schwarzkopf. His other books include *Inside the VC and the NVA: The Real Story of North Vietnam's Armed Forces* (with Dan Cragg), *The Battles of Peace, Inside Force Recon: Recon Marines in Vietnam* (with Ray W. Stubbe), *Inside the LRRPs: Rangers in Vietnam, Vietnam 1969–1970: A Company Commander's Journal*, and *The Only War We Had: A Platoon Leader's Journal of Vietnam*. He resides in Phoenix, Arizona, and Eastsound, Washington.